Mahābhārata: Mokṣa-Dharma-Parvan

Volume 1

Nicholas Sutton

Mahābhārata: Mokṣa-Dharma-Parvan

Volume 1

Śānti-parvan, Adhyāya 168–223

HINDU STUDIES PRESS

Hindu Studies Press
An imprint of the Oxford Centre for Hindu Studies Continuing Education Dept
13–15 Magdalen St, Oxford, OX1 3AE
www.ochsonline.org

Published 2024

A CIP Record for this book is available from the British Library.
ISBN: 978-1-9997644-2-5

Contents

Acknowledgements vii
Introduction ix
The Senajit-Piṅgalā-Gīte 1
The Pitā-Putra-Saṁvāda 17
The Śaṁyāka-Gītā 29
The Maṅki-Gītā 37
The Prahrāda-Ājagara-Saṁvāda 55
The Kāśyapa-Sṛgāla-Saṁvāda 69
Instruction from Bhīṣma 83
The Bhṛgu-Bharadvāja-Saṁvāda 91
Bhīṣma's Teachings on Dharma 169
The Adhyātma-Kathanam 179
The Dhyāna-Yoga 197
The Jāpakopākhyānam 207
The Manu-Bṛhaspati-Saṁvāda 257
The Keśava-Māhātmyam 301
The Dik-Pālaka-Kīrtanam 315
The Viṣṇoḥ Varāha-Rūpam 325
The Guru-Śiṣya-Saṁvāda 335
The Pañcaśikha-Janaka-Saṁvāda 395
A Discourse on Proper Conduct 427
The Indra-Prahrāda-Saṁvāda 439
The Bali-Vāsava-Saṁvāda 451
The Śakra-Namuci-Saṁvāda 481
The Bali-Vāsava-Saṁvāda 489
The Śrī-Vāsava-Saṁvāda 515
The Jaigīṣavyāsita-Saṁvāda 537
The Vāsudevograsena-Saṁvāda 545

Acknowledgements

My thanks are due first of all to the Amitabh and Richa Srivastava Family Giving Fund without whose support the publication of this work would not have been possible. On a personal level, I would also like to thank the Oxford Centre for Hindu Studies for providing me with the opportunity to work on this text and particularly to Lal Krishna without whom this work would not have seen the light of day. And finally, my heartfelt thanks to the GoDharmic Charitable Trust for their support of this book. GoDharmic feeds people and provides educational facilities in deprived areas worldwide. Their dedication is an example of dharma in practice.

Introduction

Up until the later decades of the twentieth century, the Sanskrit *Mahābhārata* existed in a number of manuscript versions, which differed from one another to varying degrees both in terms of content and detail. In these earlier years, the version of the text most commonly referred to was that known as the Vulgate, which had the commentary of Nilakantha to accompany it. Between the 1920s and 1960s, however, teams of scholars initially led by V.S. Sukthankar undertook the task of comparing the different manuscripts and thereby creating a single Critical Edition of the Sanskrit text, which included variant readings in the form of footnotes. Despite certain criticisms that have been levelled against this Critical Edition, it is the version of the text that is most widely referred to today, not least because it provides the means by which chapter and verse references can be easily traced and identified. The present translation adheres strictly to the text of the Critical Edition, although there were occasions when I was tempted to adopt one of the variant readings that appeared to convey a clearer meaning.

The Critical Edition divides the *Mahābhārata* into 18 distinct books, or *parvans*, each of which is named roughly in accordance with the main theme or content. These *parvans* vary considerably in length, some containing just a few chapters (known as *adhyāyas*) whilst others have several hundred. This arrangement of the full text means that verse references can be given in a clear form, for example (12.13.14), where 12 indicates the *parvan*, 13 the chapter (*adhyāya*), and 14 the specific verse being cited. The longest of the *Mahābhārata*'s eighteen books is the twelfth, which is named the *Śānti-parvan*,the Book of Peace, and contains a total of 353 chapters. As the name suggests, this *parvan* is placed after the conclusion of the great battle at Kurukṣetra when the surviving warriors surround the fallen Bhīṣma who is questioned by Yudhiṣṭhira on a range of different subjects. The instruction given by the dying Bhīṣma covers almost the whole of the *Śānti-parvan* and most of Book 13, the *Anuśāsana-parvan*, as well, so that this section of the *Mahābhārata* comprises a considerable proportion of the entire Sanskrit text.

The *Śānti-parvan* is itself divided into three sub-*parvans*, named as the *Rāja-dharma-parvan*, the *Āpad-dharma-parvan*, and the *Mokṣa-dharma-parvan*. The first two of these deal primarily, though not exclusively, with the duties of a king, governance, and military endeavours, but from Chapter 168 of the *Śānti-parvan* the focus of the discussion switches dramatically away from this world, as Bhīṣma is questioned by Yudhiṣṭhira about renunciation and liberation from rebirth. These remaining 186 chapters of the *Śānti-parvan* form the *Mokṣa-dharma-parvan*, which is the subject of the present work. Three other English translations of this sub-*parvan* are available, one completed in the nineteenth century by Kisari Mohan Ganguli, and two other more recent contributions, one by Bibek Debroy and another by Alexander Wynne. The present work is, however, the first attempt at a complete translation and detailed study of the *Mokṣa-dharma-parvan* and hence has certain advantages over these previous renditions. The Critical Edition of the text was not available at the time of Ganguli's work and his translation is of the Vulgate manuscript, which differs quite considerably in certain passages. Wynne also used the Vulgate manuscript for his partial translation but Debroy worked mainly from the Critical Edition but does not offer a verse by verse study, preferring instead simply to present a rendition in continuous prose form.

As the name indicates, the principal theme of the *Mokṣa-dharma-parvan* relates to the means by which living entities in this world can gain *mokṣa*, liberation from rebirth. We must be aware, however, that this designation does not impose the strictest limitations on the type of material that the author or editor chose to include in this section of the *Mahābhārata*. That said, there is certainly a continuous emphasis on renunciation of the world, the path of *nivṛtti*, in which the rituals of religious life are largely abandoned and the practitioner becomes indifferent to the changing fortunes that are an inevitable feature of life in this present existence. It is frequently stated that destiny, as shaped by previous acts, holds absolute control over these fortunes and that worldly endeavours will not make one's life successful. Hence, one must turn to spiritual pursuits in order to experience the boundless joy that comes with emancipation from repeated embodiment.

The *Mokṣa-dharma-parvan* is probably most noteworthy for the passages it offers relating to the philosophy of Sāṁkhya and to Yoga practices. The Sāṁkhya system is typically studied with reference to Īśvarakṛṣṇa's classical work, the *Sāṁkhya Kārikā*, but it is almost certain that the treatises on Sāṁkhya contained within the *Mokṣa-dharma-parvan* predate the *Sāṁkhya Kārikā*, and they reveal a great deal more about Sāṁkhya as a whole than does Īśvarakṛṣṇa's single work. We should note that here we find Sāṁkhya teachings in a variety of distinct expressions, some of which are theistic and some not. We must therefore conclude that Sāṁkhya was not a single system, but in its earliest manifestations existed in a variety of different forms. The fundamental ideas are all similar, however, teaching how the elements of matter that comprise this world emerge in succession from a single non-manifest material substance. The true self, *ātman*, *puruṣa*, or *kṣetrajña*, is entirely distinct from these elements even though the embodied entity exists in a state of union with them. We will find differing views on whether this process of manifestation occurs due to the will of the Deity or whether it is a purely natural occurrence, as well as on the precise number of elements and their order of appearance, but the view remains that the aspirant must endeavour to gain knowledge of the distinction between matter and spirit, for it is that realisation which brings liberation from rebirth.

We should also note that the *Mokṣa-dharma-parvan* contains very little that could be referred to as Vedānta and in this sense it stands in marked contrast to the Upaniṣadic revelation. Within the Upaniṣads and the system of Advaita Vedānta that is based on the Upaniṣads, we find a consistent emphasis on the unity of everything that exists. Brahman alone is real and in its true identity the individual *ātman* is also Brahman, whilst, according to Vedāntists at least, the perception of the variegated nature of this world is an illusion. Sāmkhya, by contrast, insists on the absolute reality of the world as it is perceived, and on the eternally individual identity of the *ātman*. Although the mental and physical embodiment is entirely composed of matter, *prakṛti*, which is one substance, the varieties we perceive in the world are real transformations of *prakṛti* and not simply an illusory perception, as is taught by Advaita Vedānta. Moreover, the Sāṁkhya teachings we encounter in the *Mokṣa-dharma-parvan* are assertively dualistic, as they insist on the absolute distinction between the true self, *ātman* or *puruṣa*, and its physical and mental embodiments, which are composed entirely from the elements that have emerged from undifferentiated *prakṛti*. Such ideas are presented repeatedly in this section of the *Mahābhārata*, whilst the Vedāntic insistence on absolute unity is notable only for its absence.

The Yoga teachings located within the *Mokṣa-dharma-parvan* are usually closely associated with passages of Sāṁkhya discourse. Sāṁkhya presents a philosophical understanding of the nature of the world and of ourselves, whilst the Yoga practices offer the means by which the true self can be realised and liberation attained through this realised knowledge. The type of Yoga practice advocated is generally very similar to that taught by Patañjali in his *Yoga Sūtras* and by Chapter 6 of the *Bhagavad-gītā*, with an emphasis on gaining mastery over the mind and senses so that the path of perception can be withdrawn from all external movements and fixed inwardly instead. It is this intense meditation on the innermost core of one's being that is said to bring direct realisation of the spiritual *puruṣa* and the true reality of our existence as is taught by the Sāṁkhya treatises. Significantly, the passages on Yoga practice contained within this section of the *Mahābhārata* are almost certainly the earliest detailed treatises on Yoga that we have access to today. This fact alone gives a clear indication of the significance of the material included within the *Mokṣa-dharma-parvan*.

When we thus consider the importance of the *Mokṣa-dharma-parvan* in the development of Indian religious thought, we might naturally ask why it has received so little attention from commentators and authors, ancient and modern. The Upaniṣads are widely known and read with a number of different English translations readily available, and one might suggest that the *Mokṣa-dharma-parvan* is worthy of equal consideration. I think the answer lies in the fact that Vedānta based on the Upaniṣads has become elevated to a predominant position in Indian religious thought, whilst as philosophical systems Sāṁkhya and Yoga have been largely superseded, although they continue to exert a significant though rarely acknowledged influence. When Sāṁkhya is considered, it is usually with reference to the *Sāṁkhya Kārikā*, whilst the *Yoga Sūtras* holds a similar position in relation to early Yoga. Moreover, the practice of Yoga has been heavily influenced by Tantric ideas relating to the physical body, which has somewhat diminished the significance of the Yoga of the mind as taught in the *Mokṣa-dharma-parvan*. Nonetheless, this neglect of the *Mokṣa-dharma-parvan* is regrettable in terms of our overall understanding of Indian thought and it is hoped that the present work will go some way towards redressing that imbalance.

Despite what has been said above, it is not the case that what we have here is a series of treatises on Sāṁkhya and Yoga, as there is a huge range of material discussed and expounded upon in this section of the *Mahābhārata*. A number of passages deal simply with the renunciation of desire, whilst there are also several chapters of Vaiṣṇava theism, most notably in the lengthy *Nara-nārāyaṇīyam*, which appears almost at the end of the *Mokṣa-dharma-parvan*. There are also teachings given on *dharma*, proper conduct, and how every person should live in this world, with particular emphasis on *ahiṁsā*, never causing harm to any living being with thought, word, or deed, which is an essential part of the path to *mokṣa*. We will also encounter material that appears to have little or nothing to do with gaining liberation from rebirth, straightforward narrative accounts such as those that are found in many of the Purāṇas. Overall, the *parvan* as a whole contains a fascinating range of ideas, stories, and teachings, which I hope the reader will find to be of interest either by dipping in and out of the treatises or by reading it all from first to last. I have included some words of explanation at the beginning of each of the passages and at the beginning of each individual chapter as well. This has meant that a certain amount of repetition was unavoidable, but I would justify this on the grounds that this translation may frequently be referred to for reference purposes relating only to individual chapters rather than it being read from beginning to end.

In presenting this translation, I have adhered quite strictly to the form of the exposition adopted by the Sanskrit text itself. The *Mokṣa-dharma-parvan* is comprised of a series of more or less discrete treatises, which are usually presented in response to a particular question from Yudhiṣṭhira. The general mode of response from Bhīṣma is to cite some earlier conversation, a *saṁvāda*, where a similar question was put to a sagacious individual who responded with a set of teachings that can serve as an answer to Yudhiṣṭhira's inquiry. This pattern is not universal, however, as on some occasions Bhīṣma imparts his own wisdom, and at other points he presents a discourse by a single teacher without any question being put to him. This pattern serves to divide the *Mokṣa-dharma-parvan* into a series of distinct passages most of which are given a particular name within the text only version of Critical Edition, although alternative titles are sometimes given in different manuscripts.

Some of the treatises, chapters, and verses of the *Mokṣa-dharma-parvan* present very real difficulties in terms of grasping the precise meaning that is intended. Some of the verses are extremely obscure, and on these occasions I have tried my best to make sense of what the author is saying, although without absolute certainty of what the intended meaning actually is. In this regard, I am particularly indebted to the late Professor Narasiṁhachary of the

University of Madras who offered frequent advice as to how such difficulties might be resolved. On certain occasions, he suggested that I simply change the Sanskrit text of a verse in order to give greater clarity to the exposition. Tempting as such suggestions were, these were among the few occasions when I did not follow his advice, as I felt that I could not subvert the integrity of the Critical Edition. It is clear, however, from the large number of variants in different manuscripts that earlier transcribers of the ancient text had no such inhibitions.

The Senajit-Piṅgalā-Gīte

Śānti-parvan, Adhyāya 168

THE *MOKṢA-DHARMA-PARVAN* opens with six discrete treatises, all of which are designed to show the futility of material endeavour in achieving success or happiness in life. It is noteworthy that here we find little discussion of the concept of *mokṣa* itself or of the wisdom or techniques, the Sāṁkhya and Yoga, by means of which liberation from rebirth might be attained. In fact, one might say that these passages are barely religious at all and might be better considered as therapeutic guides for dealing with the problems of life. Here, I think, one can detect the hand of the redactor at work for it seems likely that, amongst the works available to him, these first six represented suitable preliminaries for the main enterprise, the task here being to demonstrate that material solutions to the problems of life are untenable. However much one endeavours there is no guarantee of success and ultimately the fundamental problems of death and bereavement will resurface. So in effect the natural conclusion of this opening section is that a new solution is needed. The secondary conclusion would be that in confronting the vicissitudes of fortune one needs to develop a detached, stoical frame of mind through which one can learn to tolerate misfortune and accept that it is an axiomatic feature of life in this world.

The six treatises take the form of three (or perhaps four) *gītās* and three *saṁvādas*. *Gītā* literally means a song but here the word is used to indicate a soliloquy in which the speaker delivers teachings to one who listens, whilst *saṁvāda* means a meeting or conversation in which some form of dialogue occurs between two speakers.This distinction cannot, however, be regarded as absolute, as is evident from the *Bhagavad-gītā*, which might equally be named the *Arjuna-kṛṣṇa-saṁvāda*. The first of these treatises (Chapter 168 of the *Śānti-parvan*) is the *Senajit-piṅgalā-gīte*; as the name suggests, this consists of two distinct *gītās*, one spoken by King Senajit and the other by a courtesan named Piṅgalā. Both have experienced intense misfortune but through this experience come to a superior realisation about the true nature of life in this world and the need for indifference to the fluctuations of fortune. The second is the *Pitā-putra-saṁvāda*, in which a son urges his father to radically reassess his attitude to life and to see that all materially motivated endeavours are simply a distraction from the true path. The third treatise is the short *Śamyāka-gītā* in which Bhīṣma tells Yudhiṣṭhira of the instructions on renunciation and indifference that he once received from a Brahmin named Śamyāka.

The fourth, the *Maṅki-gītā*, gives a similar account to what has gone before. Maṅki is a man whose efforts for prosperity have been thwarted by fate (in the form of a camel); as a result he comes to the established conclusion that endeavour is worthless and that one should instead develop a state of indifference to success or failure, for it is only by this means that a person can free him- or herself from anxiety. The next treatise, the *Prahrāda-ājagara-saṁvāda*, tells of an encounter between the Prahrāda, the *asura* king, and a holy man who followed the dharma of the python (*ajagara*, literally 'goat swallower') by accepting whatever fate bestowed upon him without making any endeavour. The sixth and final treatise of this group, the *Kāśyapa-sṛgāla-saṁvāda*, tells of an encounter between a Brahmin named Kāśyapa and Indra, the king of the gods, who has assumed the form of a jackal (*sṛgāla*). Again the theme is the same. Kāśyapa has been injured in a road accident and is suffering so much that he wishes to die; the jackal then advises him not to be so disturbed by the sufferings of life and to consider how fortunate he is in relationship to others – jackals, for example. As a result, the Brahmin comes to a higher realisation and sees that tolerance of misfortune is a superior mode of being.

This section of the *Mokṣa-dharma-parvan* concludes with a short chapter (174 of the *Śānti-parvan*) in which Bhīṣma himself presents his own views to Yudhiṣṭhira without referring to any previous discourse. This is interesting as it suggests that here we are hearing the voice of the redactor himself (or, if one prefers, of the *Mahābhārata* itself), who clearly feels the need to provide some qualification of, or at least commentary on, the main teachings that have been presented. In summation, the point being made here is a simple one. Life is full of suffering, and suffering cannot be alleviated by material endeavour of any kind. Therefore, one needs to develop a mood of tolerance and indifference to misfortune, for this alone can free one from the constant anxiety that besets us all.

This opening chapter, the *Senajit-Piṅgalā-Gīte* (Chapter 168), consists of a question by Yudhiṣṭhira, a brief response from Bhīṣma, and then recitation of two *gītās*. One of these is presented directly by a Brahmin to King Senajit who is grieving over the death of his son; the second is a short passage spoken by a courtesan named Piṅgalā, which is included by the Brahmin as a part of his instruction to Senajit. A number of kings named Senajit are mentioned in the Purāṇic listings (as, for example, in the *Viṣṇu Purāṇa* 4.19.35) but he does not appear anywhere as a major character in any narrative. We might note, however, that earlier in the *Śānti-parvan*, Bhīṣma had cited teachings given by King Senajit on precisely the same subject as considered here, namely the conquest of grief through philosophical understanding (12.26.13–29). This might explain the slightly anomalous title of our treatise here, which is named as the *Senajit-piṅgalā-gīte* even though the teachings are in fact imparted by an unnamed Brahmin to Senajit. In Chapter 26, Bhīṣma describes the discourse as *gītaṁ rājñā senajitā* 'proclaimed by King Senajit': it appears that what we have are two versions of the same discussion in one of which Senajit is the speaker whilst in our piece, despite the title, he is being instructed.

In the *Bhāgavata Purāṇa* (Book 6, Chapters 14 to 16) we find a similar story narrated wherein a king who has lost a child has his grief assuaged by the teachings of a sage and it may be that this later account represents a further development of the same original narrative. There, however, the king is named as Citraketu and the sage who instructs him as Aṅgiras, whilst the account as a whole is included as a part of the narrative of Indra's conflict with Vṛtra. The *Bhāgavata* also narrates the story of Piṅgalā in greater detail (Book 11, Chapter 8) and again it seems likely that it is using the *Mahābhārata* as its source.

When the Brahmin eventually begins his main instruction, from verse 13 onwards, he urges Senajit to accept that family relationships are always temporary and hence of no ultimate significance. Similarly, happiness and distress are inevitable concomitants of human life and therefore one should neither rejoice nor lament, accepting the inevitable fluctuations of fortune with an equal disposition. Only the intelligent person who views the world from this higher perspective can transcend grief; or perhaps the fool may also escape such suffering as he has no perception at all. It is selfish desire that gives rise to suffering and such desire also leads to the forms of action that produce an unfavourable destiny due to the law of karma.

In verse 46, the Brahmin cites the example of Piṅgalā in order to illustrate the points he has been making. Deserted by her lover, Piṅgalā initially gave way to intense lamentation, but quickly passed through that condition to a state of higher realisation; her suffering was the catalyst that carried her towards perception of the truth. She now renounces all her lovers and accepts the self within as her only true companion. In this state beyond all hope of pleasure she finds true satisfaction, following the path the Brahmin is urging Senajit to adopt.

Although the passage is primarily about mental adjustment and how one should perceive the world and its changing fortunes, there are also hints here of the type of ideas we will encounter later on when the *Mokṣa-dharma-parvan* moves on to pursue its principal lines of discourse. The emphasis on soteriology is introduced here in verses 42 and 44 with the words *brahma saṁpadyate tadā*, a phrase used several times elsewhere to indicate the attainment of liberation from rebirth (see, for example, *Bhagavad-gītā* 13.30, *Mahābhārata* 12.231.21). Another prominent theme we will encounter elsewhere is the emphasis placed on *ahiṁsā*, not harming, as an essential part of the practice of *mokṣa-dharma* – here also (verse 44) we find a passing reference to this principle.

1. *yudhiṣṭhira uvāca*
dharmāḥ pitāmahenoktā rāja-dharmāśritāḥ śubhāḥ
dharmam āśramiṇāṁ śreṣṭhaṁ vaktum arhasi pārthiva

Yudhiṣṭhira said: Grandfather, you have discussed those auspicious forms of dharma that are included in the duties of a king. Now, my lord, please speak about the highest dharma, the way of life to be followed by those who dwell in religious *āśramas*.

2. *bhīṣma uvāca*
sarvatra vihito dharmaḥ svargyaḥ satya-phalaṁ tapaḥ
bahu-dvārasya dharmasya nehāsti viphalā kriyā

Bhīṣma said: Dharma leads to heaven and is ordained for all persons. Acts of austerity certainly yield results. Dharma has many gateways, but nowhere in this world are such actions performed without yielding results.

3. *yasmin yasmiṁs tu vinaye yo yo yāti viniścayam*
sa tam evābhijānāti nānyaṁ bharata-sattama

Whenever a person reaches a firm conclusion in following one of the many disciplines of religious life, he will hold to that particular understanding of the truth and no other, O chief of the Bharatas.

4. *yathā yathā ca paryeti loka-tantram asāravat*
tathā tathā virāgo 'tra jāyate nātra saṁśayaḥ

To the extent that one comes to regard the ways of this world as being without value, so freedom from the ills of this world arises. Of this there is no doubt.

5. *evaṁ vyavasite loke bahu-doṣe yudhiṣṭhira*
ātma-mokṣa-nimittaṁ vai yateta matimān naraḥ

Because this world is afflicted by so many difficulties, Yudhiṣṭhira, the wise man should strive to attain his own liberation.

6. *yudhiṣṭhira uvāca*
naṣṭe dhane vā dāre vā putre pitari vā mṛte
yayā buddhyā nudec chokaṁ tan me brūhi pitāmaha

Yudhiṣṭhira said: Tell me, grandfather, about the state of mind which allows one to transcend grief when one loses one's wealth or one's wife, or experiences the death of one's son or father.

7. *bhīṣma uvāca*
naṣṭe dhane vā dāre vā putre pitari vā mṛte
aho duḥkham iti dhyānañ śokasyāpacitiṁ caret

Bhīṣma said: If he loses his wealth or his wife or experiences the death of his son or father, a person cries out, 'O what misery!' But he must endeavour to assuage that grief through proper reflection.

8. *atrāpy udāharantīmam itihāsaṁ purātanam*
yathā senajitaṁ vipraḥ kaścid ity abravīd vacaḥ

Concerning this subject, they recount this ancient story of how a certain Brahmin gave instructions to Senajit.

9. *putra-śokābhisaṁtaptaṁ rājānaṁ śoka-vihvalam*
viṣaṇṇa-vadanaṁ dṛṣṭvā vipro vacanam abravīt

Seeing the king with a sorrowful countenance, beset with misery, and tormented by grief for his son, the Brahmin spoke these words to him.

10. *kiṁ nu khalv asi mūḍhas tvaṁ śocyaḥ kim anuśocasi*
yadā tvām api śocantaḥ śocyā yāsyanti tāṁ gatim

'How can you be so foolish? How can you mourn like this when you yourself are to be mourned for? And whilst they are mourning for you, the mourners are themselves destined to reach the same condition.

11. *tvaṁ caivāhaṁ ca ye cānye tvāṁ rājan paryupāsate*
sarve tatra gamiṣyāmo yata evāgatā vayam

Both you and I, O king, as well as these others who are gathered around you, will all reach that state from which we have come.'

12. *senajid uvāca*
kā buddhiḥ kiṁ tapo vipra kaḥ samādhis tapo-dhana
kiṁ jñānaṁ kiṁ śrutaṁ vā te yat prāpya na viṣīdasi

Senajit said: O Brahmin, you possess a wealth of austerity. What is the understanding, the austerity, meditation, knowledge, or teaching you have acquired so that you are no longer afflicted by sorrow?

13. *brāhmaṇa uvāca*
paśya bhūtāni duḥkhena vyatiṣaktāni sarvaśaḥ
ātmāpi cāyaṁ na mama sarvā vā pṛthivī mama

The Brahmin said: Behold these living beings with their existence inextricably linked to suffering. Even my own self is not truly mine; or else the entire earth is mine alone.

14. *yathā mama tathānyeṣām iti buddhyā na me vyathā*
etāṁ buddhim ahaṁ prāpya na prahṛṣye na ca vyathe

'Anything that is mine belongs equally to others.' Because of this understanding there is no anguish for me. Having attained such a state of consciousness, I neither rejoice nor lament.

15. *yathā kāṣṭhaṁ ca kāṣṭhaṁ ca sameyātāṁ mahodadhau*
sametya ca vyapeyātāṁ tadvad bhūta-samāgamaḥ

On the vast ocean a small piece of wood may come into contact with another piece of wood and then be separated from it. Of such a nature are the relationships formed by living beings.

16. *evaṁ putrāś ca pautrāś ca jñātayo bāndhavās tathā*
teṣu sneho na kartavyo viprayogo hi tair dhruvam

Hence one should not indulge in affection for sons, grandsons, relatives or friends. Separation from them all is certain.

17. *adarśanād āpatitaḥ punaś cādarśanaṁ gataḥ*
na tvāsau veda na tvaṁ taṁ kaḥ san kam anuśocasi

From a condition of being unknown to you, your son appeared here and now he has returned once more to a state beyond our vision. He does not know you, nor you him. What is it that actually lives? Who are you and who is the one you are grieving for?

18. *tṛṣṇārti-prabhavaṁ duḥkhaṁ duḥkhārti-prabhavaṁ sukham*
sukhāt saṁjāyate duḥkham evam etat punaḥ punaḥ
sukhasyānantaraṁ duḥkhaṁ duḥkhasyānantaraṁ sukham

The origin of misery is the pain of desire and the origin of joy is the pain of misery. Misery arises from happiness and so this cycle repeats itself time and time again. Misery immediately follows joy, and joy immediately follows misery.

19. *sukhāt tvaṁ duḥkham āpannaḥ punar āpatsyase sukham*
na nityaṁ labhate duḥkhaṁ na nityaṁ labhate sukham

You are now afflicted by misery because of the joy you previously experienced, and in the future you will find happiness once again. One never experiences misery that has no end, nor does one attain endless joy.

20. *nālaṁ sukhāya suhṛdo nālaṁ duḥkhāya śatravaḥ*
na ca prajñālam arthānāṁ na sukhānām alaṁ dhanam

No amount of friends can bring complete happiness, nor can one's enemies bring complete distress. Wisdom alone cannot provide one with riches, and wealth alone will not bring the joys of life.

21. *na buddhir dhana-lābhāya na jāḍyam asamṛddhaye*
loka-paryāya-vṛttāntaṁ prājño jānāti netaraḥ

Intelligence may not bring an accumulation of wealth; indolence may not lead to a loss of prosperity. Only the wise person can understand how the course of events will turn out for the people of this world.

22. *buddhimantaṁ ca mūḍhaṁ ca śūraṁ bhīruṁ jaḍaṁ kavim*
durbalaṁ balavantaṁ ca bhāginaṁ bhajate sukham

It is in accordance with their allotted destiny that happiness comes to the wise man and to the fool, to the hero and to the coward, to the imbecile and to the scholar, to the weak and to the strong.

23. *dhenur vatsasya gopasya svāminas taskarasya ca*
payaḥ pibati yas tasyā dhenus tasyeti niścayaḥ

A cow may be regarded as the property of its calf, of its herdsman, of its owner, or of the thief who carries it away. In fact, the cow belongs to the one who drinks her milk; this is certain.

24. *ye ca muḍhatamā loke ye ca buddheḥ paraṁ gatāḥ*
te narāḥ sukham edhante kliśyaty antarito janaḥ

Those who are the greatest fools in the world and those who attain the highest understanding are the people who attain happiness. The person who lies between these two states must suffer misery.

25. *antyeṣu remire dhīrā na te madhyeṣu remire*
antya-prāptiṁ sukhām āhur duḥkham antaram antayoḥ

Those who are steady-minded have found pleasure in these extremes but have never found pleasure anywhere between them. They speak of the joy of attaining these extremes and of the misery of remaining between them.

26. *ye tu buddhi-sukhaṁ prāptā dvaṁdvātītā vimatsarāḥ*
tān naivārthā na cānārthā vyathayanti kadācana

Neither gains nor unwanted occurrences can ever agitate those who have attained the pleasures of the intellect, who are aloof from the fluctuating dualities of the world, and who are free from envy.

27. *atha ye buddhim aprāptā vyatikrāntāś ca mūḍhatām*
te 'tivelaṁ prahṛṣyanti saṁtāpam upayānti ca

Now those who do not attain this state of mind, and take to the wrong path in pursuit of illusion, carry their pleasures to excess and undergo great suffering.

28. *nitya-pramuditā mūḍhā divi deva-gaṇā iva*
avalepena mahatā paridṛbdhā vicetasaḥ

Seeking to live like the celestials in heaven by enjoying constant pleasure, such ignorant fools are held in bondage by their immense pride.

29. *sukhaṁ duḥkhāntam ālasyaṁ duḥkhaṁ dākṣyaṁ sukhodayam*
bhūtiś caiva śriyā sārdhaṁ dakṣe vasati nālase

Happiness must end in suffering; idleness is the cause of suffering; industry is the cause of happiness. Wellbeing combined with prosperity is based upon expert endeavour and never upon idleness.

30. *sukhaṁ vā yadi vā duḥkhaṁ dveṣyaṁ vā yadi vā priyam*
prāptaṁ prāptam upāsīta hṛdayenāparājitaḥ

Whether it be happiness or misery, whether it be loathsome or desirable, one should endure all life's experiences unconquered by the emotions one feels in one's heart.

31. *śoka-sthāna-sahasrāṇi harṣa-sthāna-śatāni ca*
divase divase mūḍham āviśanti na paṇḍitam

Every day thousands of occasions for sorrow and hundreds of occasions for joy beset the foolish person, but these never approach the learned *paṇḍita*.

32. *buddhimantaṁ kṛta-prajñaṁ śuśrūṣum anasūyakam*
dāntaṁ jitendriyaṁ cāpi śoko na spṛśate naram

Grief does not touch a man who is intelligent, wise, obedient to good instruction, free from envy, self-controlled, and the master of his senses.

33. *etāṁ buddhiṁ samāsthāya supta-cittaś cared budhaḥ*
udayāstamaya-jñaṁ hi na śokaḥ spraṣṭum arhati

Maintaining such a mentality, an enlightened person should continue through life with his mind at rest. Grief cannot touch a person who understands that everything must have a beginning and an end.

34. *yan nimittaṁ bhavec chokas trāso vā duḥkham eva vā*
āyāso vā yatomūlas tad ekāṅgam api tyajet

If there is a root cause which is the cause of one's grief, anxiety, misery, and hard labour, one must remove that one factor even if it is a limb of one's body.

35. *yad yat tyajati kāmānāṁ tat sukhasyābhipūryate*
kāmānusārī puruṣaḥ kāmān anu vinaśyati

Whatever object of desire one renounces becomes the cause by which one is filled with joy. The person who indulges his lust in pursuit of various objects of desire is inevitably frustrated in that endeavour.

36. *yac ca kāma-sukhaṁ loke yac ca divyaṁ mahat-sukham*
tṛṣṇākṣaya-sukhasyaite nārhataḥ ṣoḍaśīṁ kalām

Neither the pleasure derived from satisfying one's desires in this world nor the sweetest delights of the heavenly domain can offer one-sixteenth part of the joy that comes with the cessation of hankering.

37. *pūrva-deha-kṛtaṁ karma śubhaṁ vā yadi vāśubham*
prājñaṁ mūḍhaṁ tathā śūraṁ bhajate yādṛśaṁ kṛtam

Whether pure or impure, action performed in a previous bodily form adheres to the wise man, the fool, and the hero, precisely according to the way it was performed.

38. *evam eva kilaitāni priyāṇy evāpriyāṇi ca*
jīveṣu parivartante duḥkhāni ca sukhāni ca

There can be no doubt that it is for this reason alone that delightful and loathsome circumstances continuously occur amongst living beings, as well as happiness and distress.

39 *tad evaṁ buddhim āsthāya sukhaṁ jīved guṇānvitaḥ*
sarvān kāmāñ jugupseta saṅgān kurvīta pṛṣṭhataḥ
vṛtta eṣa hṛdi prauḍho mṛtyur eṣa manomayaḥ

Remaining steady in this state of mind, one endowed with excellent qualities may live happily. One should turn away from all one's desires and leave one's attachments behind, for the materialistic mode of existence grows stronger within the heart and it is a form of mental death.

40. *yadā saṁharate kāmān kūrmo 'ṅgānīva sarvaśaḥ*
tadātma-jyotir ātmā ca ātmany eva prasīdati

When one restrains one's desires, like a tortoise withdrawing all its limbs, then the true self, which is self-illuminated, finds satisfaction within itself.

41. *kiṁcid eva mamatvena yadā bhavati kalpitam*
tad eva paritāpārthaṁ sarvaṁ saṁpadyate tadā

For whenever anything is regarded with a sense of possessiveness, it becomes nothing but a source of sorrow.

42. *na bibheti yadā cāyaṁ yadā cāsmān na bibhyati*
yadā necchati na dveṣṭi brahma saṁpadyate tadā

When a person no longer feels fear and when fear no longer arises because of him, and when he neither desires nor hates, then he has attained Brahman.

43. *ubhe satyānṛte tyaktvā śokānandau bhayābhaye*
priyāpriye parityajya praśāntātmā bhaviṣyati

When he renounces the dualities of truth and falsehood, misery and joy, fear and fearlessness, and becomes indifferent to the things he loves and the things he abhors, a person will then become a soul at peace.

44. *yadā na kurute dhīraḥ sarva-bhūteṣu pāpakam*
karmaṇā manasā vācā brahma saṁpadyate tadā

When the self-controlled aspirant no longer causes harm to any living being with his deeds, his thoughts, or his words, then he has attained Brahman.

45. *yā dustyajā durmatibhir yā na jīryati jīryataḥ*
yo 'sau prāṇāntiko rogas tāṁ tṛṣṇāṁ tyajataḥ sukham

That which is so hard for foolish persons to give up, that which does not decline as one grows older, that which is a life-threatening disease – that is the hankering which must be abandoned in order to find happiness.

46. *atra piṅgalayā gītā gāthāḥ śrūyanti pārthiva*
yathā sā kṛcchra-kāle 'pi lebhe dharmaṁ sanātanam

In this regard, O lord of the Earth, the verses sung by Piṅgalā are referred to, describing how she turned towards the eternal dharma even in a time of great trouble.

47. *saṁkete piṅgalā veśyā kāntenāsīd vinākṛtā*
atha kṛcchra-gatā śāntāṁ buddhim āsthāpayat tadā

The courtesan Piṅgalā was left alone at the place where she had arranged to meet her lover. Being at first distraught, she then brought her mind to a state of tranquillity.

48. *piṅgalovāca*
unmattāham anunmattaṁ kāntam anvavasaṁ ciram
antike ramaṇaṁ santaṁ nainam adhyagamaṁ purā

Piṅgalā said: For so long in this disturbed state of mind I lived alongside my lover who showed no concern. My true beloved is always close to me, but I have never had congress with him.

49. *eka-sthūṇaṁ nava-dvāram apidhāsyāmy agārakam*
kā hi kāntam ihāyāntam ayaṁ kānteti maṁsyate

I will close down this dwelling place, which has one central pillar and nine doors. What young woman ever regards as her beloved the one who comes so close to her??

50. *akāmāḥ kāma-rūpeṇa dhūrtā naraka-rūpiṇaḥ*
na punar vañcayiṣyanti pratibuddhāsmi jāgṛmi

The cunning cheats who have no love for me at all, and are in truth hell in a human form, will never again dishonestly approach me with their feigned affection. I am enlightened. I am awake.

51. *anartho 'pi bhavaty artho daivāt pūrva-kṛtena vā*
saṁbuddhāhaṁ nirākārā nāham adyājitendriyā

The misfortune that arises from destiny or previous actions can sometimes be beneficial. I am now enlightened; I have no goal to pursue. Now I am no longer unable to control my senses.

52. *sukhaṁ nirāśaḥ svapiti nairāśyaṁ paramaṁ sukham*
āśām anāśāṁ kṛtvā hi sukhaṁ svapiti piṅgalā

Lacking any sense of hope, one sleeps easily; to have no expectation is the highest state of happiness. Having made hope into hopelessness, Piṅgalā now sleeps at ease.

53. *bhīṣma uvāca*
etaiś cānyaiś ca viprasya hetumadbhiḥ prabhāṣitaiḥ
paryavasthāpito rājā senajin mumude sukham

Bhīṣma said: Through these and other well-reasoned discourses presented by that Brahmin, King Senajit regained his steadiness of mind and found happiness once more.

The Pitā-Putra-Saṁvāda

Śānti-parvan, Adhyāya 169

As always, the question put into the mouth of Yudhiṣṭhira in order to initiate a new treatise can be regarded as indicative of what the redactor saw as the main point being made by the passage and possibly as revealing why he chose to insert it into the *Mokṣa-dharma-parvan* at this point. Here the question is rather stark. What should one do in life? What form of action has any real value? The passage that Bhīṣma calls to mind in response entails a conversation between a father (*pitā*) and his son (*putra*) in which it is the latter who has the instructing voice. The father appears to be a Brahmin well-versed in the ritual portions of the Veda and devoted to studying the Veda. The question posed by Medhāvin, his son, in verse 5 is not really a question at all, but a criticism of his father's conduct. It is clear that the boy regards the ritualistic religion as futile and tries to get his father to think about liberation from rebirth, which is attained through Yoga. The father's reply is conventional and is based on the notion of there being four *āśramas*, or stages of life; it is in the final stage of life that one turns one's attention to the pursuit of *mokṣa* and hence his current preoccupation with Vedic ritual is quite appropriate.

It is from this point that Medhāvin begins his critique of his father's position, a critique based primarily on the assertion that as death may strike at any time it is foolish to delay one's embracing of the *mokṣa-dharma* until the final stage of life. In any case, any attempt at worldly prosperity is simply futile, for everything will be carried away by death and one thereby risks becoming entangled in the here and now. From verse 25, the pattern of the speech changes slightly as the son moves on from rejecting his father's position to establishing what is in fact the proper conduct of life, the life of the renunciant. One may then pursue the highest goal, which here is designated as *satyam*, truth, and this seems to be an equivalent concept to the gaining of realised knowledge.

In the Sāṁkhya system, knowledge of the self leads one beyond death, which is expressed here by the words, *mṛtyum āpadyate mohāt satyenāpadyate 'mṛtam*, 'one meets with death as a result of illusion, one attains immortality through *satyam*'. Here also we find the view that *ahiṁsā* is an essential element in the pursuit of *mokṣa*, and in verse 31 Medhāvin gives a further insight into his objections to his father's current way of life. The Vedic ritual, the *yajña*, involves the offering of animal sacrifices into the sacred fire, and here we see the advocate of *mokṣa-dharma* criticising such practices as conflicting with the principle of *ahiṁsā*. Such slaughter makes one like a *piśāca*, a type of malevolent spirit that feeds on flesh. We will encounter this rejection of the Vedic ritual later on in the *Mokṣa-dharma-parvan*, but here we may note one of the reasons given for denying its validity as a ritual act. The slaughter of animals is a *kṣatriya* ritual that has been adopted by Brahmins for material gain; *kṣatriyas* are naturally men of violence but when Brahmins perform such acts it is a violation of their true dharma. This is a line of reasoning that is presented by a number of speakers in the *Mokṣa-dharma-parvan* as they seek to undermine the Vedic credentials of ritualised violence. There is reference here to Yoga practice but no details of such techniques are given; the emphasis remains on the lifestyle of renunciation whereby one seeks no pleasure and displays absolute tolerance of life's changing fortunes.

1. *yudhiṣṭhira uvāca*
atikrāmati kāle 'smin sarva-bhūta-kṣayāvahe
kiṁ śreyaḥ pratipadyeta tan me brūhi pitāmaha

Yudhiṣṭhira said: One meanders through the passage of time, which is bringing all living beings to their inevitable end. Tell me, grandfather, what is there of real value that should be accomplished?

2. *bhīṣma uvāca*
atrāpy udāharantīmam itihāsaṁ purātanam
pituḥ putreṇa saṁvādaṁ tan nibodha yudhiṣṭhira

Bhīṣma said: Concerning this subject they cite this ancient account of a discussion between a father and his son. Now learn about this, Yudhiṣṭhira.

3. *dvi-jāteḥ kasyacit pārtha svādhyāya-niratasya vai*
babhūva putro medhāvī medhāvī nāma nāmataḥ

There was once a Brahmin who delighted in the study and recitation of the Veda. He had a very intelligent (*medhāvī*) son, and because of the boy's intelligence he was named Medhāvin.

4. *so 'bravīt pitaraṁ putraḥ svādhyāya-karaṇe ratam*
mokṣa-dharmārtha-kuśalo loka-tattva-vicakṣaṇaḥ

That son was an expert in the *mokṣa-dharma*, and equally well-versed in knowledge of this world. Once he addressed his father who was devoted to the recitation of the Vedas.

5. *dhīraḥ kiṁ svit tāta kuryāt prajānan*
kṣipraṁ hy āyur bhraśyate mānavānām
pitas tadācakṣva yathārtha-yogaṁ
mamānupūrvyā yena dharmaṁ careyam

'My dear father, how should a resolute aspirant act, understanding how quickly the lifespan of human beings slips away? Now teach me about the proper order in which I should perform dharmic duty along with result I will obtain'

6. *pitovāca*
vedān adhītya brahmcaryeṇa putra
putrān icchet pāvanārthaṁ pitṝṇām
agnīnādhāya vidhivac ceṣṭa-yajño
vanaṁ praviśyātha munir bubhūṣet

The father said: My son, after studying the Vedas as a celibate student, one should then aspire to beget sons in order to deliver one's forefathers from blemish. Then after performing sacrifices by making the ordained offerings through the sacred fire, one should enter the forest and become a *muni.*

7. *putra uvāca*
evam abhyāhate loke samantāt parivārite
amoghāsu patantīṣu kiṁ dhīra iva bhāṣase

The son said: When the world is overwhelmed by afflictions from all sides, and when such occurrences cannot be avoided, how can you speak like one who is undisturbed?

8. *pitovāca*
katham abhyāhato lokaḥ kena vā parivāritaḥ
amoghāḥ kāḥ patantīha kiṁ nu bhīṣayasīva mām

His father said: How is the world afflicted? What is it overwhelmed by? What are the unavoidable occurrences that befall one? Why are you making me fearful like this?

9. *putra uvāca*
mṛtyunābhyāhato loko jarayā parivāritaḥ
aho-rātrāḥ patanty ete nanu kasmān na budhyase

The son said: The world is afflicted by death and overwhelmed by old age. Days and nights inevitably pass by. How can you fail to comprehend this?

10. *yadāham etaj jānāmi na mṛtyus tiṣṭhatīti ha*
so 'haṁ kathaṁ pratīkṣiṣye jālenāpihitaś caran

When I understand so clearly that death never remains still, how can I just wait for it to happen, going on through life entangled in this net?

11. *rātryāṁ rātryāṁ vyatītāyām āyur alpataraṁ yadā*
gādhodake matsya iva sukhaṁ vindeta kas tadā
tad eva vandhyaṁ divasam iti vidyād vicakṣaṇaḥ

When with every night that passes one's lifespan becomes shorter, how can one enjoy any form of pleasure, living as one does like a fish in a shallow pond? In truth such pleasure is a worthless paradise and one who is wise must see it as such.

12. *anavāpteṣu kāmeṣu mṛtyur abhyeti mānavam*
śaṣpāṇīva vicinvantam anyatra-gata-mānasam
vṛkīvoraṇam āsādya mṛtyur ādāya gacchati

Whilst his desires are still unsatisfied and his thoughts are roaming elsewhere, death overtakes a man just as blades of grass are cut down. After falling upon him like a she-wolf on a lamb and carrying him off, death then moves on.

13. *adyaiva kuru yac chreyo mā tvā kālo 'tyagād ayam*
akṛteṣv eva kāryeṣu mṛtyur vai saṁprakarṣati

Now you must execute only those actions that are truly beneficial: 'Let not this moment pass thee by.' Even if his duties have not been performed, death drags a person away.

14. *śvaḥ-kāryam adya kurvīta pūrvāhṇe cāparāhṇikam*
na hi pratīkṣate mṛtyuḥ kṛtaṁ vāsya na vā kṛtam
ko hi jānāti kasyādya mṛtyu-senā nivekṣyate

One should perform tomorrow's duty today and the afternoon's duty in the morning. Death does not look to see whether or not one's duty is done. Who can know who it is that the army of death will descend upon today?

15. *yuvaiva dharma-śīlaḥ syād animittaṁ hi jīvitam*
kṛte dharme bhavet kīrtir iha pretya ca vai sukham

A young man should be dedicated to his dharma alone for there is no sign by which one may know the duration of one's life. When one's dharma is properly performed, one gains renown in this world and also enjoys the pleasures of the afterlife.

16. *mohena hi samāviṣṭaḥ putra-dārārtham udyataḥ*
kṛtvā kāryam akāryaṁ vā puṣṭim eṣāṁ prayacchati

Working strenuously on behalf of his sons and wife, performing various prescribed and forbidden activities, one who is in the grip of illusion procures wealth and prosperity for their benefit.

17. *taṁ putra-paśu-saṁmattaṁ vyāsakta-manasaṁ naram*
suptaṁ vyāghraṁ mahaugho vā mṛtyur ādāya gacchati

Just as a raging flood carries away a sleeping tiger, death goes forth carrying away the man who takes delight in his sons and livestock and absorbs his mind in thoughts of them.

18. *saṁcinvānakam evaikaṁ kāmānām avitṛptakam*
vyāghraḥ paśum ivādāya mṛtyur ādāya gacchati

Like a tiger carrying away its prey, death goes forth and carries away a person intent only on accumulating wealth, whilst his desires are still unsatisfied.

19. *idaṁ kṛtam idaṁ kāryam idam anyat kṛtākṛtam*
evam īhāsukhāsaktaṁ kṛtāntaḥ kurute vaśe

'This enterprise is completed, but this must still be undertaken, whilst this matter is only partially concluded.' Whilst a man is absorbed in such thoughts and remains attached to things that bring him no pleasure, death brings him under its control.

20. *kṛtānāṁ phalam aprāptaṁ karmaṇāṁ phala-saṅginam*
kṣetrāpaṇa-gṛhāsaktaṁ mṛtyur ādāya gacchati

Before the fruit of his work is realised, death goes forth carrying away that person who is attached to his land, business, and home, and is desirous of reaping the rewards of his endeavours.

21. *mṛtyur jarā ca vyādhiś ca duḥkhaṁ cāneka-kāraṇam*
anuṣaktaṁ yadā dehe kiṁ sva-stha iva tiṣṭhasi

How can you remain at ease when death, old age, disease, and the misery, arising from various causes, are all abiding within your body?

22. *jātam evāntako 'ntāya jarā cānveti dehinam*
anuṣaktā dvayenaite bhāvāḥ sthāvara-jaṅgamāḥ

From the moment of birth, death and old age pursue an embodied being and bring about its ultimate demise. All forms of life, both moving and stationary, are inextricably linked to these two.

23. *mṛtyor vā gṛham evaitad yā grāme vasato ratiḥ*
devānām eṣa vai goṣṭho yad araṇyam iti śrutiḥ

According to the *śruti*, residence in one's village, which is so pleasing, is in fact the house of death, whilst the forest is the meeting place of the gods.

24. *nibandhanī rajjur eṣā yā grāme vasato ratiḥ*
chittvaināṁ sukṛto yānti naināṁ chindanti duṣkṛtaḥ

The pleasure of living in one's village is a rope that binds a person. Cutting through this rope, those who act properly move on, but wrongdoers will never cut through it.

25. *na hiṁsayati yaḥ prāṇān mano-vāk-kāya-hetubhiḥ*
jīvitārthāpanayanaiḥ karmabhir na sa badhyate

A person who does not harm other living beings with mind, speech, or body is never captured by the actions of others that might take away his life or wealth.

26. *na mṛtyu-senām āyāntīṁ jātu kaścit prabādhate*
ṛte satyam asaṁtyājyaṁ satye hy amṛtam āśritam

With the exception of truth, nothing can repel the approaching army of death even for a moment. Truth must never be abandoned for in truth alone is immortality found.

27. *tasmāt satyavratācāraḥ satya-yoga-parāyaṇaḥ*
satyārāmaḥ samo dāntaḥ satyenaivāntakaṁ jayet

Therefore, adhering to a vow of truthfulness, dedicating oneself to the Yoga of truth, taking pleasure in speaking the truth, being even-minded and restrained, one should overcome death through truth alone.

28. *amṛtaṁ caiva mṛtyuś ca dvayaṁ dehe pratiṣṭhitam*
mṛtyum āpadyate mohāt satyenāpadyate 'mṛtam

Both immortality and death are present within one's body. One attains death because of illusion; one attains immortality through truth.

29. *so 'haṁ hy ahiṁsraḥ satyārthī kāma-krodha-bahiṣkṛtaḥ*
sama-duḥkha-sukhaḥ kṣemī mṛtyuṁ hāsyāmy amartyavat

Never causing harm to other beings, dedicating myself to truthfulness, avoiding anger and desire, being equal-minded in distress and happiness, and remaining fully satisfied, I will free myself from death and become like one of the immortals.

30. *śānti-yajña-rato dānto brahma-yajñe sthito muniḥ*
vāṅ-manaḥ-karma-yajñaś ca bhaviṣyāmy udag-āyane

When the sun begins its progress through the northern sky, I will become a sage devoted to the *yajña* of tranquillity. I will be self-controlled, fixed on the *yajña* of Brahman, employing my words, thoughts, and deeds in that *yajña*.

31. *paśu-yajñaiḥ kathaṁ hiṁsrair mādṛśo yaṣṭum arhati*
antavadbhir uta prājñaḥ kṣatra-yajñaiḥ piśācavat

How can one as wise as myself become like a demonic *piśāca* and perform *yajñas* that involve violence towards animals? These are the *yajñas* of the *kṣatriyas*, which yield only temporary rewards.

32. *yasya vāṅ-manasī syātāṁ samyak praṇihite sadā*
tapas tyāgaś ca yogaś ca sa vai sarvam avāpnuyāt

One whose speech and mind, as well as his austerity, renunciation, and Yoga practice, are always properly directed, may in truth achieve all things.

33. *nāsti vidyā-samaṁ cakṣur nāsti vidyā-samaṁ balam*
nāsti rāga-samaṁ duḥkhaṁ nāsti tyāga-samaṁ sukham

There is no perception equal to wisdom, there is no strength equal to wisdom. There is no misery equal to desire, there is no joy equal to renunciation.

34. *ātmany evātmanā jāta ātma-niṣṭho 'prajo 'pi vā*
ātmany eva bhaviṣyāmi na māṁ tārayati prajā

It was through the self that I was born as this self and now I will depend on myself alone, for I will remain without offspring. I will exist within the self alone and no offspring will deliver me.

35. *naitādṛśaṁ brāhmaṇasyāsti vittaṁ*
yathaikatā samatā satyatā ca
śīle sthitir daṇḍa-nidhānam ārjavaṁ
tatas tataś coparamaḥ kriyābhyaḥ

For a Brahmin there is no wealth like living alone, equanimity, truthfulness, dedication to virtuous conduct, tolerance of the faults of others, honesty, and renunciation of the various types of ritual action.

36. *kiṁ te dhanair bāndhavair vāpi kiṁ te*
kiṁ te dārair brāhmaṇa yo mariṣyasi
ātmānam anviccha guhāṁ praviṣṭaṁ
pitāmahas te kva gataḥ pitā ca

You will die, O Brahmin, so of what use to you are your riches, relatives, or wives? Rather you must seek out the *ātman*, which is concealed within your own being. Where has your grandfather gone? Where is your father now?'

37. *bhīṣma uvāca*
putrasyaitad vacaḥ śrutvā tathākārṣīt pitā nṛpa
tathā tvam api vartasva satya-dharma-parāyaṇaḥ

Bhīṣma said: Now, O king, you should live as that father conducted himself after hearing his son's speech, dedicating yourself to the dharma of truth.

The Śaṁyāka-Gītā

Śānti-parvan, Adhyāya 170

THIS SHORT CHAPTER is again devoted almost entirely to extolling the virtues of renunciation. Here the speaker is a renunciant named Śamyāka, whose teachings were presented to Bhīṣma by a Brahmin he had met many years before in the city of Hastināpura; when Yudhiṣṭhira puts the opening question to Bhīṣma the words spoken by Śamyāka are recalled as providing an apposite response. Yudhiṣṭhira's question represents a certain reservation about the emphasis on renunciation we have been confronted with in the previous treatises. This might well apply to unfortunate persons, but what about those who are rich and powerful?

The Brahmin was one who had himself suffered from various misfortunes, and the main thrust of the discourse he recites is that the only people who find real happiness are the *akiṁcanas*, those who have given up all possessions and live a life of contentment, accepting whatever fate bestows upon them. In other words, Yudhiṣṭhira's implied suggestion that the rich and powerful are somehow a different case is rejected, for they are in the same position as everybody else. The wealthy man must suffer from constant anxiety because he has so much to lose, whilst the renunciant is free of all such concerns. Wealth is to be shunned because it draws out the baser instincts in a man and leads him into an ever greater condition of illusion; the delusion of the intellect leads one to perform wicked acts, which lead in turn to ever greater suffering. So this passage is continuing the principal theme of these opening chapters, namely that the world is a place of suffering and that one should therefore give up all worldly aspirations, embracing the path of renunciation. In verse 22, we see a slight hint of the teachings found later in the *Mokṣa-dharma-parvan* with the words *nātyaktvā vartate param*, without renunciation one cannot achieve the supreme goal, but at this stage it is only the slightest indication of the teachings that are to come.

1. *yudhiṣṭhira uvāca*
dhanino vādhanā ye ca vartayanti sva-tantriṇaḥ
sukha-duḥkhāgamas teṣāṁ kaḥ kathaṁ vā pitāmaha

Yudhiṣṭhira said: Wealthy persons and those who are poor follow their own ways of life and observe different rituals. So what is it, grandfather, that brings happiness and distress to such persons and how does this occur?

2. *bhīṣma uvāca*
atrāpy udāharantīmam itihāsaṁ purātanam
śamyākena vimuktena gītaṁ śānti-gatena ha

Bhīṣma said: Concerning this subject they recite this ancient account of the verses composed by Śamyāka, a man who had attained freedom from mundane existence and had gained complete tranquillity of mind.

3. *abravīn māṁ purā kaścid brāhmaṇas tyāgam āsthitaḥ*
kliśyamānaḥ kudāreṇa kucailena bubhukṣayā

A certain Brahmin who was firm in his vows of renunciation narrated these verses to me some time ago. He was in a state of distress because of his marriage to a bad wife, his ragged clothes, and the constant pangs of hunger.

4. *utpannam iha loke vai janma-prabhṛti mānavam*
vividhāny upavartante duḥkhāni ca sukhāni ca

'From the moment of his birth, various forms of misery and joy come to any person who has appeared in this world.

5. *tayor ekatare mārge yady enam abhisaṁnayet*
na sukhaṁ prāpya saṁhṛṣyen na duḥkhaṁ prāpya saṁjvaret

If something should lead him down either of these two paths, he should not be delighted when he gains happiness and he should not be downcast on encountering misery.

6. *na vai carasi yac chreya ātmano vā yad īhase*
akāmātmāpi hi sadā dhuram udyamya caiva hi

You certainly do not act in a way that is beneficial to you, nor do you make any endeavours in that direction. You have taken up this constant burden, though the *ātman* has no desires at all.

7. *akiṁcanaḥ paripatan sukham āsvādayiṣyasi*
akiṁcanaḥ sukhaṁ śete samuttiṣṭhati caiva hi

Whilst wandering throughout the world without any possessions you will taste real pleasure. Without possessions, one sleeps and then rises again with a contented heart.

8. *ākiṁcanyaṁ sukhaṁ loke pathyaṁ śivam anāmayam*
anamitram atho hy etad durlabhaṁ sulabhaṁ satām

Living without possessions amounts to true happiness in this world. Existing in this way is beneficial, auspicious, and never harmful. Such an existence in which one has no enemies seems hard to achieve, but for righteous persons it is easily realised.

9. *akiṁcanasya śuddhasya upapannasya sarvaśaḥ*
avekṣamāṇas trīḷ lokān na tulyam upalakṣaye

Looking throughout the three worlds I cannot perceive any person who is the equal of one who has arrived at the state of purity by which he can live without possessions.

10. *ākiṁcanyaṁ ca rājyaṁ ca tulayā samatolayam*
atyaricyata dāridryaṁ rājyād api guṇādhikam

Using a balance, I weighed living without possessions and living as a king against each other. Poverty was found to surpass kingship and to be possessed of superior qualities.

11. *ākiṁcanye ca rājye ca viśeṣaḥ sumahān ayam*
nityodvigno hi dhanavān mṛtyor āsya-gato yathā

There is this one great distinction between being without possessions and being the ruler of a kingdom: the wealthy man lives in a state of constant fear, like one entering the jaws of the death.

12. *naivāsyāgnir na cādityo na mṛtyur na dasyavaḥ*
prabhavanti dhana-jyāni-nirmuktasya nirāśiṣaḥ

Neither fire nor the scorching sun, neither death nor robbers can ever overwhelm a person who has no anxiety about gaining or losing wealth and who is untouched by material desires.

13. *taṁ vai sadā kāma-caram anupastīrṇa-śāyinam*
bāhūpadhānaṁ śāmyantaṁ praśaṁsanti divaukasaḥ

The gods in heaven sing the praises of one who always wanders the earth at will, who lies on the ground to sleep without any bedding, who has only his arms for a pillow, and who lives at peace with the world.

14. *dhanavān krodha-lobhābhyām āviṣṭo naṣṭa-cetanaḥ*
tīryag-īkṣaḥ śuṣka-mukhaḥ pāpako bhru-kuṭī-mukhaḥ

One who possesses great wealth is generally beset by anger and greed, having lost his true intelligence. With his eyes glancing sideways suspiciously and his mouth dry with anxiety, such a villain bears a permanent frown on his face.

15. *nirdaśaṁś cādharoṣṭhaṁ ca kruddho dāruṇa-bhāṣitā*
kas tam icchet paridraṣṭuṁ dātum icchati cen mahīm

When he is angry he bites at his lower lip and utters cruel words. Even if he was willing to give away the entire world, who would want to know such a person?

16. *śriyā hy abhīkṣṇaṁ saṁvāso mohayaty avicakṣaṇam*
sā tasya cittaṁ harati śāradābhram ivānilaḥ

Continuous association with wealth deludes one who is devoid of wisdom. Wealth carries away a man's reason just as the wind blows away the autumn clouds.

17. *athainaṁ rūpamānaś ca dhanamānaś ca vindati*
abhijāto 'smi siddho 'smi nāsmi kevala-mānuṣaḥ
ity ebhiḥ kāraṇais tasya tribhiś cittaṁ prasicyate

And so he thinks himself to be blessed with both beauty and wealth. 'I am well-born, I am successful in life, and I am certainly no ordinary man.' In these three ways his reason is swept away.

18. *sa prasikta-manā bhogān visṛjya pitṛ-saṁcitān*
parikṣīṇaḥ parasvānām ādānaṁ sādhu manyate

His mind is addicted to objects of pleasure and after losing the wealth accumulated by his forefathers, he thinks that it is quite acceptable to squander the property of others which he has appropriated.

19. *tam atikrānta-maryādam āda-dānaṁ tatas tataḥ*
pratiṣedhanti rājāno lubdhā mṛgam iveṣubhiḥ

When he has transgressed the laws of the land by appropriating others' property in various ways, the avaricious rulers of the kingdom take action against him, just as they might shoot down a deer with their arrows.

20. *evam etāni duḥkhāni tāni tānīha mānavam*
vividhāny upavartante gātra-saṁsparśajāni ca

So it is that here in this world these and various other miseries fall upon a man, as they afflict the limbs of his body.

21. *teṣāṁ parama-duḥkhānāṁ buddhyā bhaiṣajyam ācaret*
loka-dharmaṁ samājñāya dhruvāṇām adhruvaiḥ saha

One should utilise the intellect to apply the remedy for these terrible miseries by perceiving the true nature of the world in which things that are permanent exist alongside those that are temporary.

22. *nātyaktvā sukham āpnoti nātyaktvā vindate param*
nātyaktvā cābhayaḥ śete tyaktvā sarvaṁ sukhī bhava

Without renouncing the world one cannot achieve happiness, without renouncing the world one cannot attain the highest goal of life, and without renouncing the world one cannot sleep without fear. So become joyful by renouncing everything.'

23. *ity etad dhāstinapure brāhmaṇenopavarṇitam*
śamyākena purā mahyaṁ tasmāt tyāgaḥ paro mataḥ

This teaching of Śamyāka was thus imparted to me by a Brahmin a long time ago in the city of Hastināpura. And so I now regard the way of renunciation to be superior.

The Maṅki-Gītā

Śānti-parvan, Adhyāya 171

THE *MAṄKI-GĪTĀ* IS A FURTHER TREATISE that aims to show that true happiness can never be attained through worldly endeavours and that one should therefore give up all hopes and hankerings, and simply accept unquestioningly the fate one is allotted. Again there is little that is specifically religious here and it might be better to refer to the piece as being wisdom literature that teaches the reader a more appropriate course through life. Despite the position of the chapter at the beginning of the *Mokṣa-dharma-parvan*, there is nothing here that is specifically related to achieving liberation from rebirth; the path of renunciation as advocated here is recommended as one that brings happiness and contentment in this life without any eschatological implication. On the other hand, one senses that treatises of this type are genuinely forming a preface to teachings that are overtly religious and indeed there are indications here of the Sāṁkhya and Yoga teachings that form such a prominent theme of subsequent passages of the *Mokṣa-dharma-parvan*. At this stage we simply get oblique references, as in verses 29 and 30 where Maṅki addresses the elements of his body and then in 31 where he resolves to devote his intellect to the pursuit of Yoga – *yoge buddhiṁ śrute*.

We also find references here to absorption in Brahman, though again the idea is not pursued, and it is clear that these passing references to spiritual attainment are not the main focus of the piece. They do, however, serve to demonstrate that the *Maṅki-gītā* is not Buddhist in orientation despite the fact that most of its teaching is entirely in line with the Buddhist view of the world. The second of the Buddha's noble truths, that of *samudāya*, states that the cause of *duḥkha*, suffering, is our thirst (*tṛṣṇā*) for pleasure and for life. Here the main problem is defined as *kāma*, desire or lust, but the word *tṛṣṇā* is also used on occasion (verses 33, 46), and in the final words of his discourse Maṅki speaks of *tṛṣṇā-kṣaya-sukha*, the joy that comes from the destruction of *tṛṣṇā*. Hence, although we can safely say that this treatise does not come from a Buddhist source, it clearly embodies principles and ideas that are usually identified with Buddhist teachings.

In terms of its structure, the *Maṅki-gītā* is based around a short frame story that tells of an entrepreneur named Maṅki, all of whose business schemes are blighted by misfortune and failure. In one final attempt at success he purchases two young bullocks with the aim of training them and then selling them for a profit as fully fledged farm animals. This scheme also goes awry, however, when the yoked bullocks go either side of a camel sitting in the road and are then dragged to their death by the enraged beast. It is at this point of distress that Maṅki has his realisation of the futility of material endeavour and pronounces the forty-four verses (9–44) that form the *Maṅki-gītā*.

The chapter as a whole also includes three short additional sections; the first of these comes in verses 15 to 17 where Maṅki himself quotes the words spoken by Śuka the son of Vyāsa as he was leaving the palace of King Janaka of Videha. Later in the *Mokṣa-dharma-parvan* we have a treatise named the *Śuka-carita* (*Śānti-parvan*, Chapters 310–320), which narrates incidents from the life of Śuka, including his visit to Janaka. The short speech cited here by

Maṅki is not, however, to be found in that passage.

After the *Maṅki-gītā* is complete, Bhīṣma seeks to confirm his ideas by citing the words of Janaka himself and then the rather cryptic instruction given by a sage named Bodhya to Nahuṣa. Janaka is widely known as the King of Videha and the father of Sītā who marries Rāma, the hero of Vālmīki's *Rāmāyaṇa*. He is also referred to in the *Chāṇḍogya* and *Bṛhad-āraṇyaka Upaniṣads* where he receives spiritual guidance from the famous teacher Yājñavalkya. He is mentioned frequently in the *Mokṣa-dharma-parvan*, sometimes receiving instruction from teachers of religion and sometimes serving to show how a person can pursue the path of renunciation whilst remaining active in the world. It is in this latter role that we encounter him here; this incident of the burning of the city of Mithilā and Janaka's indifference to it is cited on a number of occasions within the *Mokṣa-dharma-parvan*.

The list of six *gurus* given by Bodhya includes the courtesan named Piṅgalā whom we encountered earlier in the *Senajit-piṅgalā-gīte*. Here again it is interesting to note that this seems to be the basis for a passage of the *Uddhava-gītā*, in Book 11 of the *Bhāgavata Purāṇa*, in which Kṛṣṇa refers to a holy man who cites twenty-four *gurus*, a list that includes the six mentioned here as well as eighteen others. It seems likely that the passage from the *Uddhava-gītā* represents an expansion of the speech of Bodhya given here, although it is possible that both are derived from an earlier source that is now lost. It is interesting to note that the *Bhāgavata*'s conversation is between Yadu and a sage designated as an *avadhūta*, although on at least one occasion (11.7.36) Yadu is referred to as *nāhuṣātmaja*, the son of a descendent of Nahuṣa, whilst in some manuscripts of the *Mahābhārata*'s text the inquiring king is designated as Nāhuṣa rather than Nahuṣa, a descendent of Nahuṣa rather than Nahuṣa himself. Moreover, some manuscripts, notably that referred to by the commentator Nīlakaṇṭha, provide twelve additional lines at the end of the chapter in which each of the six *gurus* is explained along with the teachings they can provide.

The forty-four verses of the *Maṅki-gītā* itself begin with an assertion of the primacy of destiny over human endeavour in determining the outcome.

This debate over the tension between fate and endeavour is an ongoing topic within the *Mahābhārata*; this can be seen, for example, in the heated discussion between Draupadī and Yudhiṣṭhira at the start of the *Āraṇyaka-parvan* (Book 3) and the treatise presented by Bhīṣma in the first chapter of the *Anuśāsana-parvan* (Book 13). Different opinions and varying emphases can be detected at different points, depending on the context. Where Dhṛtarāṣṭra blames destiny for the catastrophe at Kurukṣetra, this view is roundly rejected by Saṁjaya who ascribes the outcome solely to Dhṛtarāṣṭra's personal failures. In the *Mokṣa-dharma-parvan*, however, the tendency is to place the emphasis on destiny, as we see here, for this accords with the prevailing view of human existence and the need to renounce all hopes and aspirations for worldly success.

Maṅki himself therefore concludes that he must now abandon all hopes and aspirations and simply accept whatever destiny bestows upon him, accepting it with equanimity and contentment. Success and failure in life are entirely dependent on the karmic reactions to previous acts so it is futile to make endeavours to affect this outcome. Renunciation of all desires is the only way to find satisfaction in life, for desire is insatiable and one will never be content by seeking to fulfil one's desires. From verse 18, Maṅki chastises himself for thinking that he could find happiness through his money-making schemes, and then from verse 23 he starts his address to *kāma*, desire, dismissing it from his person and condemning it for its cold-hearted exploitation of helpless individuals. *Kāma* brings only pain, not joy, for it can never be satisfied, and even when one's desires are met there is no real sense of happiness. Any person seeking to fulfil his desires will inevitably be beset by anxiety and distress, and if he should fail in his endeavours and fall into a state of poverty then he faces humiliation, as all his previous friends and his relatives look upon him with contempt. Therefore, Maṅki announces that he will renounce *kāma* and expel it from his person; in this way he will at last find contentment.

As is the case with the other treatises in this opening section of the *Mokṣa-dharma-parvan*, the *Maṅki-gītā* has little to say about the positive side of the path of renunciation. As we have seen, there are some passing references to spiritual realisation and Yoga practice but no real detail is provided. We also have some description (verses 45–47) of the ideal qualities of the renunciant – tolerance, truthfulness, compassion, satisfaction, peacefulness – and in verse 43 we again encounter the emphasis on non-violence that is such a prominent theme in the teachings of the *Mokṣa-dharma-parvan*. The main focus of the *Maṅki-gītā*, however, is on changing one's view of life so that one no longer aspires for worldly success and adopts a mood of contentment, remaining free of all material desires and simply accepting whatever destiny may bring.

1. *yudhiṣṭhira uvāca*
īhamānaḥ samārambhān yadi nāsādayed dhanam
dhana-tṛṣṇābhibhūtaś ca kiṁ kurvan sukham āpnuyāt

Yudhiṣṭhira said: If a person engaged in various endeavours fails to acquire wealth from them, and if he is overcome by a desire for wealth, how then should he act in order to attain happiness?

2. *bhīṣma uvāca*
sarva-sāmyam anāyāsaḥ satya-vākyaṁ ca bhārata
nirvedaś cāvivitsā ca yasya syāt sa sukhī naraḥ

Bhīṣma said: A man is happy, O Bhārata, when he possesses complete equanimity, an aversion to material endeavours, truthful speech, indifference to the world, and no desire to learn its ways.

3. *etāny eva padāny āhuḥ pañca vṛddhāḥ praśāntaye*
eṣa svargaś ca dharmaś ca sukhaṁ cānuttamaṁ satām

Wise men of the past refer to these as the five steps to tranquillity. For the righteous, this way of life is heaven, it is their dharma, and it is also their ultimate form of happiness.

4. *atrāpy udāharantīmam itihāsaṁ purātanam*
nirvedān maṅkinā gītaṁ tan nibodha yudhiṣṭhira

Concerning this subject they recite this ancient account of the verses composed by Maṅki based on his rejection of the world. Now you should learn about this, Yudhiṣṭhira.

5. *īhamāno dhanaṁ maṅkir bhagnehaś ca punaḥ punaḥ*
kenacid dhana-śeṣeṇa krītavān damya-go-yugam

Maṅki had various schemes to gain wealth, but these endeavours were repeatedly frustrated. So with all that remained of his money he purchased a pair of young oxen to be trained for ploughing.

6. *susaṁbaddhau tu tau damyau damanāyābhiniḥsṛtau*
āsīnam uṣṭraṁ madhyena sahasaivābhyadhāvatām

But while they were yoked tightly together for the purpose of training, those two bullocks broke free and rushed headlong either side of a camel that was sitting down.

7. *tayoḥ saṁprāptayor uṣṭraḥ skandha-deśam amarṣaṇaḥ*
utthāyotkṣipya tau damyau prasasāra mahā-javaḥ

The camel was infuriated by their landing on his shoulders. Leaping up and dragging the two bullocks with it, that swift running animal then raced away.

8. *hriyamāṇau tu tau damyau tenoṣṭreṇa pramāthinā*
mriyamāṇau ca saṁprekṣya maṅkis tatrābravīd idam

Seeing the two bullocks being carried away by that wildly rearing camel so that they were on the point of death, Maṅki then spoke the following words.

9. *na caivāvihitaṁ śakyaṁ dakṣeṇāpīhituṁ dhanam*
yuktena śraddhayā samyag īhāṁ samanutiṣṭhatā

'Even for a talented man who pursues his endeavours in the proper manner and has faith in the outcome, it is not possible to acquire wealth if it is not ordained by destiny.

10. *kṛtasya pūrvaṁ cānarthair yuktasyāpy anutiṣṭhataḥ*
imaṁ paśyata saṁgatyā mama daivam upaplavam

Previously I had made every possible endeavour to gain wealth but without success. Now see what has happened to me by chance, behold my blighted destiny.

11. *udyamyodyamya me damyau viṣameṇeva gacchati*
utkṣipya kāka-tālīyam unmātheneva jambukaḥ

Repeatedly throwing my two bullocks into the air, the camel is going hither and thither, trying to cast aside this crow and Palmyra tree with a shake of the head like that of a jackal.

12. *maṇī voṣṭrasya lambete priyau vatsatarau mama*
śuddhaṁ hi daivam evedam ato naivāsti pauruṣam

But my beloved calves are caught like jewels on the neck of the camel. Without doubt this is destiny alone and human endeavour is playing no part whatsoever.

13. *yadi vāpy upapadyeta pauruṣaṁ nāma karhicit*
anviṣyamāṇaṁ tad api daivam evāvatiṣṭhate

And even if what is recognised as human endeavour does become a factor, it is axiomatic that destiny will also be involved in the outcome.

14. *tasmān nirveda eveha gantavyaḥ sukham īpsatā*
sukhaṁ svapiti nirviṇṇo nirāśaś cārtha-sādhane

Therefore indifference to the world is the only way forward for one who seeks happiness. One who has neither hope nor desire for the acquisition of wealth sleeps easily.

15. *aho samyak śukenoktaṁ sarvataḥ parimucyatā*
pratiṣṭhatā mahāraṇyaṁ janakasya niveśanāt

O how true is the declaration made by Śuka, who was completely free of worldly ties, when departing for the great forest from the abode of King Janaka.

16. *yaḥ kāmān prāpnuyāt sarvān yaś cainān kevalāṁs tyajet*
prāpaṇāt sarva-kāmānāṁ parityāgo viśiṣyate

"There may be one person who fulfils all his desires and another who renounces them completely. The renunciation of all desires is superior to their achievement.

17. *nāntaṁ sarva-vivitsānāṁ gata-pūrvo 'sti kaścana*
śarīre jīvite caiva tṛṣṇā mandasya vardhate

No one in the past ever reached the end of all the things he wished to discover. And indeed the hankering of a fool continually increases as long as life remains in his body."

18. *nivartasva vivitsābhyaḥ śāmya nirvidya māmaka*
asakṛc cāsi nikṛto na ca nirvidyase tano

So turn away from the things you long to find. Be at peace by abandoning them, O greedy one. To my own body I say: You are let down time and time again but still you will not give up your endeavours.

19. *yadi nāhaṁ vināśyas te yady evaṁ ramase mayā*
mā māṁ yojaya lobhena vṛthā tvaṁ vitta-kāmuka

If I am to avoid being destroyed by you and if, moreover, you would find happiness with me, then although you lust after riches you must not force me to act on the basis of your greed.

20. *saṁcitaṁ saṁcitaṁ dravyaṁ naṣṭaṁ tava punaḥ punaḥ*
kadā vimokṣyase mūḍha dhanehāṁ dhana-kāmuka

Again and again the wealth you accumulated has been lost. You fool, always hankering after money! When will you be free from these money-making schemes?

21. *aho nu mama bāliśyaṁ yo 'haṁ krīḍanakas tava*
kiṁ naiva jātu puruṣaḥ pareṣāṁ preṣyatāmiyāt

Well now this is my folly. I am just your plaything. Has there ever been a person who was not forced to act by the will of others?

22. *na pūrve nāpare jātu kāmānām antam āpnuvan*
tyaktvā sarva-samārambhān pratibuddho 'smi jāgṛmi

No one in the past has ever reached the end of his desires and no one will ever do so in the future. So I have now abandoned all my endeavours to gain wealth. I am enlightened. I am awake.

23. *nūnaṁ te hṛdayaṁ kāma vajra-sāra-mayaṁ dṛḍham*
yad anartha-śatāviṣṭaṁ śatadhā na vidīryate

O desire, your heart is as hard as rock and cannot be moved. Even when afflicted by a hundred misfortunes it does not shatter into a hundred parts.

24. *tyajāmi kāma tvāṁ caiva yac ca kiṁcit priyaṁ tava*
tavāhaṁ sukham anvicchann ātmany upalabhe sukham

I am renouncing you, desire, and whatever is dear to you. Now when seeking out happiness for you, I shall obtain the pleasure that exists within my own self.

25. *kāma jānāmi te mūlaṁ saṁkalpāt kila jāyase*
na tvāṁ saṁkalpayiṣyāmi samūlo na bhaviṣyasi

Desire, I know your source. You certainly arise from an individual's inclination. I will no longer incline my will towards you and so neither you nor your source will exist within me.

26. *īhā dhanasya na sukhā labdhvā cintā ca bhūyasī*
labdha-nāśo yathā mṛtyur labdhaṁ bhavati vā na vā

Endeavours to attain wealth are never pleasurable, and after one has gained some prosperity the anxiety only increases. The loss of what one has earned is just like death, and for all one's efforts success may or may not occur.

27. *paretya yo na labhate tato duḥkhataraṁ nu kim*
na ca tuṣyati labdhena bhūya eva ca mārgati

What could be more miserable than losing something that one has first obtained? Nobody is satisfied with the profit he acquires and so inevitably one takes up one's endeavours once more.

28. *anutarṣula evārthaḥ svādu gāṅgam ivodakam*
mad-vilāpanam etat tu pratibuddho 'smi saṁtyaja

Like the sweet-tasting water of the Ganges River, wealth is nothing but a cause of desire. This has been the cause of my lamentation. But now I am enlightened. Leave it all behind!

29. *ya imaṁ māmakaṁ dehaṁ bhūta-grāmaḥ samāśritaḥ*
sa yātv ito yathā-kāmaṁ vasatāṁ vā yathā-sukham

It has come to reside in the combination of elements that together form this body of mine. It may go wherever it wishes, or if it pleases it may continue to reside here.

30. *na yuṣmāsv iha me prītiḥ kāma-lobhānusāriṣu*
tasmād utsṛjya sarvān vaḥ satyam evāśrayāmy aham

But my pleasure in this world will no longer be found amongst you all, for desire and greed are essential to your nature. Having thus cast you all aside, I will now absorb myself in truth alone.

31. *sarva-bhūtāny ahaṁ dehe paśyan manasi cātmanaḥ*
yoge buddhiṁ śrute sattvaṁ mano brahmaṇi dhārayan

Perceiving the presence of all the elements of matter within my own body and mind, dedicating my intellect to Yoga practice, my existence to the wisdom of the Vedas, and my mind to Brahman,

32. *vihariṣyāmy anāsaktaḥ sukhī lokān nirāmayaḥ*
yathā mā tvaṁ punar naivaṁ duḥkheṣu praṇidhāsyasi

I shall wander across the worlds without attachment, feeling joyful and being free of all these causes of distress so that you will never again submerge me in such miseries.

33. *tvayā hi me praṇunnasya gatir anyā na vidyate*
tṛṣṇā-śoka-śramāṇāṁ hi tvaṁ kāma prabhavaḥ sadā

Whilst I am still agitated by you, no alternative course of action is open to me, for you, desire, are just a constant source of hankering, sorrow, and extreme exertion.

34. *dhana-nāśo 'dhikaṁ duḥkhaṁ manye sarva-mahattaram*
jñātayo hy avamanyante mitrāṇi ca dhana-cyutam

I consider the terrible grief caused by loss of wealth to be the greatest of all sorrows, for both relatives and friends despise a person who is deprived of wealth.

35. *avajñāna-sahasrais tu doṣāḥ kaṣṭatarādhane*
dhane sukha-kalā yā ca sāpi duḥkhair vidhīyate

Along with the thousands of humiliations one has to endure due to poverty come even more terrible afflictions. Yet the small amount of pleasure one enjoys during a period of prosperity is also blighted by various types of suffering.

36. *dhanam asyeti puruṣaṁ purā nighnanti dasyavaḥ*
kliśyanti vividhair daṇḍair nityam udvejayanti ca

Tribes of robbers first take away a person's riches and then strike him dead. They torture people with various cruel afflictions and are a constant source of terror.

37. *manda-lolupatā duḥkham iti buddhaṁ cirān mayā*
yad yad ālambase kāma tat tad evānurudhyase

"The delusion caused by greed is true sorrow", this is the realisation that has come to me after such a long time. Whenever you attach yourself to an object, desire, you then cleave tenaciously to it.

38. *atattva-jño 'si bālaś ca dustoṣo 'pūraṇo 'nalaḥ*
naiva tvaṁ vettha sulabhaṁ naiva tvaṁ vettha durlabham

Like a foolish child, you do not comprehend the truth and you are so hard to please. You are a blazing fire that is never satisfied. You do not acknowledge that an object may be easy or difficult to obtain.

39. *pātālam iva duṣpūro māṁ duḥkhair yoktum icchasi*
nāham adya samāveṣṭuṁ śakyaḥ kāma punas tvayā

Like the lower part of this creation, you can never be filled up and so you wish to embroil me in further miseries. But from this day forth, desire, I will no longer be able to keep your company.

40. *nirvedam aham āsādya dravya-nāśād yad-ṛcchayā*
nirvṛttiṁ paramāṁ prāpya nādya kāmān vicintaye

Having experienced disappointment due to the loss of my property, which occurred by chance, and having thereby reached a state of complete renunciation, I now no longer contemplate the objects of desire.

41. *atikleśān sahāmīha nāhaṁ budhyāmy abuddhimān*
nikṛto dhana-nāśena śaye sarvāṅga-vijvaraḥ

I can now withstand the terrible afflictions of this world, for my understanding is no longer that of an unenlightened person. Made destitute by loss of wealth, I now sleep easily, free of all anxiety.

42. *parityajāmi kāma tvāṁ hitvā sarva-mano-gatīḥ*
na tvaṁ mayā punaḥ kāma nasyoteneva raṁsyase

Having given up all the longings that were in my heart, I am renouncing you, desire. Never again will you enjoy pleasure through me, desire, leading me on as if bound by a rope through the nose.

43. *kṣamiṣye 'kṣamamāṇānāṁ na hiṁsiṣye ca hiṁsitaḥ*
dveṣyam uktaḥ priyaṁ vakṣyāmy anādṛtya ca tad apriyam

I will be tolerant of persons who are by nature intolerant and I will not seek to harm others, even when injured by them. When spoken to harshly I will reply with sweet words, remaining indifferent to such abuse.

44. *tṛptaḥ svasthendriyo nityaṁ yathā-labdhena vartayan*
na sakāmaṁ kariṣyāmi tvām ahaṁ śatrum ātmanaḥ

Fully satisfied, with my senses always at ease, living on what comes my way of its own accord, I will no longer act under the impulse of desire, for you are my real enemy.

45. *nirvedaṁ nirvṛttiṁ tṛptiṁ śāntiṁ satyaṁ damaṁ kṣamām*
sarva-bhūta-dayāṁ caiva viddhi māṁ śaraṇāgatam

Now you must know me as a place of residence for indifference, freedom from endeavour, contentment, peacefulness, truthfulness, self-control, tolerance, and compassion for all beings.

46. *tasmāt kāmaś ca lobhaś ca tṛṣṇā kārpaṇyam eva ca*
tyajan tu māṁ pratiṣṭhantaṁ sattva-stho hy asmi sāṁpratam

And therefore desire, greed, hankering, and pettiness are all abandoning me as their abode. I am now constant in my adherence to the quality of *sattva*.

47. *prahāya kāmaṁ lobhaṁ ca krodhaṁ pāruṣyam eva ca*
nādya lobha-vaśaṁ prāpto duḥkhaṁ prāpsyāmy anātmavān

Having renounced desire, greed, anger, and hostility, I will no longer be a fool who falls under the control of his own greed and suffers misery as a result.

48. *yad yat tyajati kāmānāṁ tat sukhasyābhipūryate*
kāmasya vaśa-go nityaṁ duḥkham eva prapadyate

The number of desires one gives up marks the extent of the joy that fills one's heart. One who is always controlled by desire attains only suffering.

49. *kāmān vyudasya dhunute yat kiṁcit puruṣo rajaḥ*
kāma-krodhodbhavaṁ duḥkham ahrīr aratir eva ca

After giving up the objects of desire, a person then frees himself from whatever trace of *rajas* remains. Misery, immodesty, and anxiety are born from desire and anger.

50. *eṣa brahma-praviṣṭo 'haṁ grīṣme śītam iva hradam*
śāmyāmi parinirvāmi sukham āse ca kevalam

I have now entered this state of Brahman, which is just like a cool lake in the summer heat. I am contented, I am liberated from this world, and I exist in a realm of unadulterated joy.

51. *yac ca kāma-sukhaṁ loke yac ca divyaṁ mahat-sukham*
tṛṣṇā-kṣaya-sukhasyaite nārhataḥ ṣoḍaśīṁ kalām

Neither the pleasures derived from satisfying one's desires in this world nor the sweetest delights of the heavenly domain can offer one-sixteenth part of the joy that comes with the cessation of hankering.

52. *ātmanā saptamaṁ kāmaṁ hatvā śatrum ivottamam*
prāpyāvadhyaṁ brahma-puraṁ rājeva syām ahaṁ sukhī

After vanquishing desire, the seventh element, through realisation of the *ātman*, I am like a person who has defeated his greatest foe. Having gained the indestructible city of Brahman, I can now be joyful like the king who rules it.'

53. *etāṁ buddhiṁ samāsthāya maṅkir nirvedam āgataḥ*
sarvān kāmān parityajya prāpya brahma mahat sukham

Having attained this realisation, Maṅki thus came to a state of indifference to the world. Abandoning all his desires, he attained the great joy that is Brahman.

54. *damya-nāśa-kṛte maṅkir amaratvaṁ kilāgamat*
acchinat kāma-mūlaṁ sa tena prāpa mahat sukham

From the loss of his bullocks Maṅki undoubtedly achieved immortality. He cut out the very root of desire, thereby attaining happiness beyond measure.

55. *atrāpy udāharantīmam itihāsaṁ purātanam*
gītaṁ videha-rājena janakena praśāmyatā

Concerning this subject, they also recite this ancient account of the words spoken by Janaka, the King of Videha, whose mind was always at peace.

56. *anantaṁ bata me vittaṁ yasya me nāsti kiṁcana*
mithilāyāṁ pradīptāyāṁ na me dahyati kiṁcana

'My wealth is without limit and yet nothing at all is mine. When the city of Mithilā was consumed by flames, nothing was burnt that truly belonged to me.'

57. *atraivodāharantīmaṁ bodhyasya pada-saṁcayam*
nirvedaṁ prati vinyastaṁ pratibodha yudhiṣṭhira

Concerning this subject they also recite this collection of verses composed by Bodhya, urging one towards indifference to the world. Now you should learn them, Yudhiṣṭhira.

58. *bodhyaṁ dāntam ṛṣiṁ rājā nahuṣaḥ paryapṛcchata*
nirvedāc chāntim āpannaṁ śāntaṁ prajñāna-tarpitam

King Nahuṣa once questioned Bodhya, a self-controlled *rishi* who had gained peace of mind due to his indifference to the world, and who was calm and satisfied by wisdom alone.

59. *upadeśaṁ mahā-prājña śamasyopadiśasva me*
kāṁ buddhiṁ samanudhyāya śāntaś carasi nirvṛttaḥ

'Your wisdom is vast, so please instruct me on the subject of inner tranquillity. What is the understanding of life you meditate upon which leads you to roam the world as a renunciant without making any endeavour?'

60. *bodhya uvāca*
upadeśena vartāmi nānuśāsmīha kaṁcana
lakṣaṇaṁ tasya vakṣye 'haṁ tat svayaṁ pravimṛśyatām

Bodhya said: I live in accordance with the teachings I have received, but I never pass this understanding on to others. I will, however, reveal some indication of it and people may reflect on it for themselves.

61. *piṅgalā kuraraḥ sarpaḥ sāraṅgānveṣaṇaṁ vane*
iṣukāraḥ kumārī ca ṣaḍ ete guravo mama

Piṅgalā, the osprey, the snake, the antelope roaming in the forest, the arrow maker, and the young girl; these are my six *gurus*.

The Prahrāda-Ājagara-Saṁvāda

Śānti-parvan, Adhyāya 172

IN THIS CHAPTER we read of an encounter between Prahrāda, the king of the *asuras*, and an *ājagara muni*, a sage who lives after the manner of an *ajagara*. The word *aja-gara* literally means 'one who swallows a goat' and is usually taken to mean the Indian python, which can still grow to a length of around four metres and has a taste for large mammals as its food. It is also said that the python can go for a year or more without eating after it has consumed a large meal. The *ājagara* is one who lives like an *ajagara*; the point here is that it is believed that the python does not make an effort to hunt for prey but simply lies in wait until such time as something edible happens to come its way.

Whether or not this is true, the idea is used here as a guide for living whereby one makes no endeavour to acquire wealth, food, or happiness, but simply accepts what destiny bestows; this is the way of the *ājagara*. Prahrāda (also Prahlāda) is well known from Purāṇic sources as the saintly *asura*, the son of the demonic Hiraṇyakaśipu, who becomes a devotee of Viṣṇu and plays a leading role in the descent of the Narasiṁha *avatāra*. The *Mahābhārata* is aware of Viṣṇu's appearance as Narasiṁha but the story is not narrated in full and Prahrāda's role as a devotee of Viṣṇu is not mentioned. It seems likely that for the *Mahābhārata* Prahrāda is like Bali, a king of the *asuras* who is virtuous by nature.

The story of Prahrāda and the descent of the Narasiṁha *avatāra* dominates the seventh book of the *Bhāgavata Purāṇa*, and after that narrative is complete we find the story of his encounter with the *ājagara* also inserted into that book as its thirteenth chapter. It is impossible to say whether the *Bhāgavata*'s version of the encounter is derived directly from the *Mokṣa-dharma-parvan*, as the conversation is presented in a very different form and the sage is not referred as an *ājagara* but as one who follows the lifestyle of a *mahā-sarpa*, a great serpent. There does seem, however, to be a tendency for the *Bhāgavata* to use passages taken from this section of the *Mahābhārata*, introducing them with the same phrase used here, *atrāpy udāharantīmam itihāsaṁ purātaṇam.*

In considering what the passage is about, it is as always instructive to look at the question from Yudhiṣṭhira that instigates its recital, and here there are two elements to the inquiry: how can one live free from sorrow and what is the conduct required in order to achieve the *paramāṁ gatim*, the highest end? This latter phrase may indicate that here Yudhiṣṭhira is inquiring about a *mokṣa-dharma*, a path to liberation from rebirth, but it is imprecise and at no stage in his discourse does the *ājagara* make any reference to escaping from this world; his entire presentation focuses on how a person can live in this world free from distress and anxiety, and perhaps it is this alone that is to be taken as the *paramāṁ gatim*. The only possible indication that his speech is related to *mokṣa* is to be found in verses 6 and 7 where he announces that he has abandoned all interest in dharma, *artha*, and *kāma*, which implies *mokṣa* as the fourth of the usual *puruṣārthas*, the four goals of life that human beings should pursue.

Within the structure of the *ājagara*'s speech we can recognise a pattern that is frequently encountered throughout the course of the *Mokṣa-dharma-parvan* whereby philosophical instruction is first given that explains the nature of the world and our existence within it, and then teachings are presented regarding the practices that are a natural concomitant to the philosophical exposition. In several passages, this twofold division is designated as Sāṁkhya, the philosophy, and Yoga, the practice. These terms are not employed by our speaker here, but still we can recognise that in verses 10 to 18 he presents Prahrāda with his realisations about the nature of our existence and then from verse 19 onwards outlines the lifestyle he adheres to as a result of this realisation, the Sāṁkhya and then the Yoga.

The *ājagara*'s philosophical realisation is certainly not a complex one and displays a certain tendency towards unorthodoxy or even atheism. In verse 10, he states that the progression of life takes place *animittataḥ*, without cause, and that living beings are bound to act as they do because of their inherent nature, their *sva-bhāva*. This intensely determinist view leads him to conclude that all aspirations for worldly success, all hankering, and all endeavours are useless. Like Maṅki, he observes that the result of action is determined by destiny alone and that human endeavour is powerless to alter the course of destiny. Moreover, whatever we might achieve in life is temporary, for death is an ever present reality that is certain to take everything away.

With this understanding of the nature of human existence established, the *ājagara* then explains the consequent lifestyle, or *dharma*, he has adopted. As an *ājagara* he accepts the way of the python. He does not strive to achieve anything but neither does he refuse anything that comes to him by chance. Thus he sometimes lives in luxury and eats the finest foods, presumably due to the largesse of a wealthy patron, but at other times he is dressed in rags and consumes only a few scraps of food. There are no rules that govern his conduct, for the point of this *dharma* is that the practitioner should be entirely indifferent to the world. Thus it is apparent from verse 21 that he may eat meat, although some restriction on his conduct is suggested by the phrase *dharmyam upabhogam* in verse 24. Here he states that he will indulge in any form of pleasure that comes to him by chance but lest one suspect that he is therefore prone to bouts of licentious conduct the word *dharmyam* is again inserted to qualify the type of pleasure he permits himself; in other words, it must be pleasure that is in accordance with the accepted standards of *dharma*.

The final section of the chapter, running from verses 24 to 36, contains longer verses in the *triṣṭubh* metre, all but the last two of which conclude with the refrain, *vratam idam ājagaraṁ śuciś carāmi*, 'being pure I follow this *ājagara-vrata*'. Here the principal points about the *ājagara* lifestyle are restated. There are no regulations he must adhere to other than cultivating a mood of absolute indifference towards the world. He renounces the conventional pattern of life and exists without endeavour, hankering, rejoicing, or lamentation. Worldly success can only be achieved through great sacrifices and it is always temporary; everything comes to pass as a result of destiny and hence endeavour is worthless. Scholars and *pandits* argue back and forth about this or that philosophical concept, but this also is a worthless endeavour. The *ājagara* has no hopes, plans, or expectations, and by developing this renounced state of consciousness he finds absolute contentment. It seems that this mood of contentment, achieved whilst living in this world, is the *paramāṁ gatim*, the highest goal that Yudhiṣṭhira asked about, and in the concluding verse of the chapter Bhīṣma asserts that anyone who accepts the way of life indicated here will certainly become happy and live his life without a care.

1. *yudhiṣṭhira uvāca*
kena vṛttena vṛtta-jña vīta-śokaś caren mahīm
kiṁ ca kurvan naro loke prāpnoti paramāṁ gatim

Yudhiṣṭhira said: You are an expert in the different ways of living. What is that way of life in which one wanders across the earth free from sorrow? And how does a man conduct himself in this world in order to attain the highest goal?

2. *bhīṣma uvāca*
atrāpy udāharantīmam itihāsaṁ purātanam
prahrādasya ca saṁvādaṁ muner ājagarasya ca

Bhīṣma said: Concerning this subject they recite this ancient account of a conversation between Prahrāda and a sage who lived after the manner of a python.

3. *carantaṁ brāhmaṇaṁ kiṁcit kalya-cittam anāmayam*
papraccha rājan prahrādo buddhimān prājña-saṁmataḥ

Prahrāda, my lord, was an intelligent man, highly regarded by men of wisdom. He once put questions to an itinerant Brahmin who displayed a sharp intellect and was free from any ailment.

4. *svasthaḥ śakto mṛdur dānto nirvivitso 'nasūyakaḥ*
suvāg bahu-mato loke prājñaś carasi bālavat

'You are in perfect health, full of energy and of a gentle disposition. You are self-controlled, devoid of interest in worldly affairs, and free from envy. Your speech is excellent, you are widely respected in the world, and possess great wisdom, yet you roam the earth like a child.

5. *naiva prārthayase lābhaṁ nālābheṣv anuśocasi*
nitya-tṛpta iva brahman na kiṁcid avamanyase

You never seek to acquire anything, nor do you lament when nothing is obtained. And although you always appear content with your lot, O Brahmin, you never refuse anything that is offered.

6. *srotasā hriyamāṇāsu prajāsv avimanā iva*
dharma-kāmārtha-kāryeṣu kūṭa-stha iva lakṣyase

Whilst other creatures appear quite happy to be carried away by the stream of life, you seem to be aloof from activities dedicated to dharma, acquisition of wealth, and the satisfaction of desire.

7. *nānutiṣṭhasi dharmārthau na kāme cāpi vartase*
indriyārthān anādṛtya muktaś carasi sākṣivat

You show no interest in dharma or the acquisition of wealth and you do not pursue sensual pleasure. Without concern for the objects of the senses, you roam freely, observing everything as a witness.

8. *kā nu prajñā śrutaṁ vā kiṁ vṛttir vā kā nu te mune*
kṣipram ācakṣva me brahmañ śreyo yad iha manyase

What is the wisdom you possess? What is the teaching you follow? And what is the way of life you adhere to, O sage? Instruct me at once, O Brahmin. Tell me what you consider to be beneficial for a person living in this world.'

9. *anuyuktaḥ sa medhāvī loka-dharma-vidhāna-vit*
uvāca ślakṣṇayā vācā prahrādam anapārthayā

Questioned in this way, that man of wisdom who understood the principles by which the world is governed replied to Prahrāda with gentle words that were not devoid of significance.

10. *paśyan prahrāda bhūtānām utpattim animittataḥ*
hrāsaṁ vṛddhiṁ vināśaṁ ca na prahṛṣye na ca vyathe

'I feel neither pleasure nor grief, Prahrāda, in observing the birth, growth, decline, and destruction of these living beings, which takes place without any apparent cause.

11. *sva-bhāvād eva saṁdṛśya vartamānāḥ pravṛttayaḥ*
sva-bhāva-niratāḥ sarvāḥ paritapye na kenacit

Understanding that actions are performed only because of a person's inherent nature (*svabhāva*), and that all beings find satisfaction according to their inherent nature, I do not feel pain from any cause whatsoever.

12. *paśyan prahrāda saṁyogān viprayoga-parāyaṇān*
saṁcayāṁś ca vināśān tān na kvacid vidadhe manaḥ

Seeing people coming together, Prahrāda, and then separating and drifting apart, and noting how their possessions are accumulated and then lost, I never set my mind on anything at all.

13. *antavanti ca bhūtāni guṇa-yuktāni paśyataḥ*
utpatti-nidhana-jñasya kiṁ kāryam avaśiṣyate

If a person sees that all beings imbued with the *guṇas* must meet with destruction, and if he understands the beginning and end of living beings, what action is he bound to perform?

14. *jala-jānām api hy antaṁ paryāyeṇopalakṣaye*
mahatām api kāyānāṁ sūkṣmāṇāṁ ca mahodadhau

Even though some creatures in the great ocean are huge and some have tiny bodies, I observe that in course of time death comes to all those creatures born in the water.

15. *jaṅgama-sthāvarāṇāṁ ca bhūtānām asurādhipa*
pārthivānām api vyaktaṁ mṛtyuṁ paśyāmi sarvaśaḥ

Furthermore, O lord of the *asuras*, I see death appearing everywhere amongst the living beings that inhabit the land, both those that move and those that remain still.

16. *antarikṣa-carāṇāṁ ca dānavottama pakṣiṇām*
utiṣṭhati yathā-kālaṁ mṛtyur balavatām api

And at the ordained time, O best of the Dānava race, death also arises amongst the mightiest of the birds that course through the sky.

17. *divi saṁcaramāṇāni hrasvāni ca mahānti ca*
jyotīṁṣi ca yathā-kālaṁ patamānāni lakṣaye

I note also that whether they be great or small, the stars above that journey across the heavens fall down from the sky at the time ordained for them.

18. *iti bhūtāni saṁpaśyann anuṣaktāni mṛtyunā*
sarva-sāmāny ato vidvān kṛta-kṛtyaḥ sukhaṁ svape

Thus observing that all living beings exist in the company of death and so share the same fate, I have become wise and sleep easily, knowing that I have done all I need to do.

19. *sumahāntam api grāsaṁ grase labdhaṁ yad-ṛcchayā*
śaye punar abhuñjāno divasāni bahūny api

Sometimes I consume a huge amount of food that comes to me by chance, but at other times I lie down for many days without eating anything.

20. *āsravaty api mām annaṁ punar bahu-guṇaṁ bahu*
punar alpa-guṇaṁ stokaṁ punar naivopapadyate

At times great quantities of excellent food come my way. But sometimes it is just a morsel of poor quality food, and at other times nothing at all.

21. *kaṇān kadācit khādāmi piṇyākam api ca grase*
bhakṣaye śāli-māṁsāni bhakṣāṁś coccāvacān punaḥ

Sometimes I chew some grains of wheat or a dry cake baked with oil. But at other times I eat rice cooked with different meats and various other delicacies.

22. *śaye kadācit paryaṅke bhūmāv api punaḥ śaye*
prāsāde 'pi ca me śayyā kadācid upapadyate

Sometimes I sleep on a soft bed, but at other times I lie down on the bare earth. And sometimes I may even take my repose in the palace of a king.

23. *dhārayāmi ca cīrāṇi śāṇīṁ kṣaumā-jināni ca*
mahārhāṇi ca vāsāṁsi dhārayāmy aham ekadā

I may be dressed in rags, in hemp, in linen, or in animal skins, but at other times I wear costly garments of great value.

24. *na saṁnipatitaṁ dharmyam upabhogaṁ yad-ṛcchayā*
pratyācakṣe na cāpy enam anurudhye sudurlabham

Provided its enjoyment is in accordance with dharma, I never refuse any pleasure that comes to me by chance. But then I never hanker after anything that is difficult to obtain.

25. *acalam anidhanaṁ śivaṁ viśokaṁ*
śucim atulaṁ viduṣāṁ mate niviṣṭam
anabhimatam asevitaṁ ca mūḍhair
vratam idam ājagaraṁ śuciś carāmi

This vow must be performed without wavering and without ceasing. It is beneficial and frees one from grief, it is pure and unequalled, and it is undertaken on the advice of men of wisdom, though it is neither respected nor followed by fools. Thus remaining pure, I follow this vow of the python.

26. *acalita-matir acyutaḥ sva-dharmāt*
parimita-saṁsaraṇaḥ parāvara-jñaḥ
vigata-bhaya-kaṣāya-lobha-moho
vratam idam ājagaraṁ śuciś carāmi

With unflinching resolve, never deviating from the dharma I have adopted, with my progress through life strictly regulated, understanding past and present, free from fear, contamination, greed, and illusion, I remain pure as I follow this vow of the python.

27. *aniyata-phala-bhakṣya-bhojya-peyaṁ*
vidhi-pariṇāma-vibhakta-deśa-kālam
hṛdaya-sukham asevitaṁ kadaryair
vratam idam ājagaraṁ śuciś carāmi

There is no restriction on the objects I acquire, the foods I eat, the pleasures I enjoy, or the drinks I consume. Everything is dictated by destiny and so there are no restrictions to be observed in terms of place and time. This dharma brings joy to the heart but sinful men can never adhere to it; thus remaining pure I follow this vow of the python.

28. *idam idam iti tṛṣṇayābhibhūtaṁ*
janam anavāpta-dhanaṁ viṣīdamānam
nipuṇam anuniśāmya tattva-buddhyā
vratam idam ājagaraṁ śuciś carāmi

"I must have this, I must have that" is the cry of the dejected person who is devoid of wealth and yet overwhelmed by desires. After contemplating the nature of the world in depth, employing my true intellectual abilities, I remain pure as I follow this vow of the python.

29. *bahu-vidham anudṛśya cārtha-hetoḥ*
kṛpaṇam ihāryam anāryam āśrayantam
upaśama-rucir ātmavān praśānto
vratam idam ājagaraṁ śuciś carāmi

Having watched such individuals begging for money from anyone and everyone, be it from a miser, a righteous man, or a sinner, I take my pleasure in inner tranquillity, always in control of myself and at peace with the world. Thus remaining pure I follow this vow of the python.

30. *sukham asukham anartham artha-lābhaṁ*
ratim aratiṁ maraṇaṁ ca jīvitaṁ ca
vidhi-niyatam avekṣya tattvato 'haṁ
vratam idam ājagaraṁ śuciś carāmi

Having observed how true it is that joy and misery, poverty and affluence, delight and despondency, death and life all come about by the dictate of destiny, I remain pure as I follow this vow of the python.

31. *apagata-bhaya-rāga-moha-darpo*
dhṛti-mati-buddhi-samanvitaḥ praśāntaḥ
upagata-phala-bhogino niśāmya
vratam idam ājagaraṁ śuciś carāmi

With my fear, passion, illusion, and pride now dispelled, being endowed with fortitude, resolution, and intelligence, whilst remaining at peace with the world, enjoying those things that come to me without effort, I am now completely content. Thus remaining pure I follow this vow of the python.

32. *aniyata-śayanāsanaḥ prakṛtyā*
dama-niyama-vrata-satya-śauca-yuktaḥ
apagata-phala-saṁcayaḥ prahṛṣṭo
vratam idam ājagaraṁ śuciś carāmi

With no restriction on the type of bed or seat I accept, but naturally adhering to the principles of self-control, strict regulation, religious vows, truthfulness and cleanliness, and having cast aside everything I accumulated in life, I am now filled with joy, remaining pure as I follow this vow of the python.

33. *abhigatam asukhārtham īhanārthair*
upagata-buddhir avekṣya cātma-saṁsthaḥ
tṛṣitam aniyataṁ mano niyantuṁ
vratam idam ājagaraṁ śuciś carāmi

I am self-sufficient, for I have achieved the realisation by which I see that nothing pleasurable comes from people's endeavours to obtain wealth. In order to control the unregulated mind that is full of longing, I remain pure and follow this vow of the python.

34. *na hṛdayam anurudhyate mano vā*
priya-sukha-durlabhatām anityatāṁ ca
tad ubhayam upalakṣayann ivāhaṁ
vratam idam ājagaraṁ śuciś carāmi

Neither my heart nor my mind feels any attachment for the happiness people long for, which is so hard to attain and is always temporary. Aware of these two drawbacks, I remain pure and follow this vow of the python.

35. *bahu kathitam idaṁ hi buddhimadbhiḥ*
kavibhir abhiprathayadbhir ātma-kīrtim
idam idam iti tatra tatra tat tat
sva-paramatair gahanaṁ pratarkayadbhiḥ

This subject has been widely discussed by learned scholars wishing to establish their own reputation. "This is my understanding, this is my view", such are the proclamations heard here and there on different subjects from those who seek to challenge the ideas of others, but this profound matter cannot be resolved by such debates.

36. *tad aham anuniśāmya viprayātaṁ*
pṛthag abhipannam ihābuddhair manuṣyaiḥ
anavasitam ananta-doṣa-pāraṁ
nṛṣu viharāmi vinīta-roṣa-tṛṣṇaḥ

I know that men of limited intelligence have been led here and there in different directions by these arguments. But this vow I follow is an effective means of transcending unlimited bad qualities and so I wander amongst human beings with anger and desire removed from my heart.'

37. *bhīṣma uvāca*
ajagara-caritaṁ vrataṁ mahātmā
ya iha naro 'nucared vinīta-rāgaḥ
apagata-bhaya-manyu-lobha-mohaḥ
sa khalu sukhī vihared imaṁ vihāram

Bhīṣma said: That superior man who, without attachment, follows the vow based on the behaviour of the python, with his fear, anger, greed, and illusion left behind, truly finds happiness as he follows this way of life.

The Kāśyapa-Sṛgāla-Saṁvāda

Śānti-parvan, Adhyāya 173

The last of this first group of six passages is the *Kāśyapa-sṛgāla-saṁvāda*, a slightly whimsical treatise that has the flavour of the *Pañcatantra* about it, with talking beasts and little jokes about the delights of possessing hands. The frame story here tells of a Brahmin referred to as Kāśyapa, which one presumes merely means that he was born as a descendant of the Vedic *rishi* named Kaśyapa. He is scrupulous in his observance of the Vedic ritual and practice of austerity, but one day he is run down by the chariot of an arrogant *vaiśya*; because of the agony he suffers he decides that he will die there and then. At that time Indra, the Lord of the Gods, takes the form of a jackal and gives him instruction on the value of birth in a human form and on the ideal attitude of renunciation and indifference to the world. It may well be that this passage was added at a slightly later date to those we have previously considered, and one has a suspicion that the emphasis on Vedic orthodoxy may be a reaction against the potential heterodoxy of the words of the *ājagara* in the previous chapter. Here we encounter a rather different perspective, with the Brahmins praised as supreme amongst human beings, the Vedic ritual presented as the path to the highest happiness, and the anti-Vedic teachings of *nāstikas* shown as leading to birth in a lower species. So if there was any tendency towards non-Vedic ideals in the previous passages, here we have a thoroughly orthodox counterbalance that vigorously reasserts the *varṇa dharma* and the efficacy of Vedic practice.

The suspicion that this is a later addition is reinforced by Bhīṣma's words in verse 3, which refer to Bali, Prahrāda, and Namuci, as well Maṅki who appeared a few chapters earlier as a failed entrepreneur. Although Prahrāda, of course, figured in the previous chapter one suspects that the reference here is derived from later passages of the *Mokṣa-dharma-parvan* in which Bali, Prahrāda, and Namuci, along with Vṛtra, are shown as powerful enemies of Indra who were eventually vanquished by the Lord of the Gods yet display a mood of wholesale world-indifference when questioned by him about their plight (*Śānti-parvan*, Chapters 215–220). Hence it seems reasonable to conclude that this chapter was added to the opening phase of the *Mokṣa-dharma-parvan* at a time when these other treatises, along with the *Maṅki-gītā*, were already present, and my suspicion would be that this was done in order to counteract any possible anti-Vedic sentiment that the reader might have detected within the *Prahrāda-ājagara-saṁvāda*. The response here is that the Brahmin is supreme amongst living beings (verse 18), and that study of the Veda and performance of the Vedic ritual is to be regarded as the path to the greatest happiness (verse 43). The jackal attributes his abominable birth to the actions performed in his previous life when he was a *nāstika* (non-believer), a *haituka* (relying on reason alone), a proponent of *tarka-vidyā* (wisdom based purely on logic), and a *veda-nindaka* (a critic of the Veda) who mocked the priests when they performed the Vedic *yajñas*.

The teachings delivered to Kāśyapa by the jackal (*sṛgāla*) are not particularly profound or philosophical. Yudhiṣṭhira's preliminary inquiry asks Bhīṣma for a decision as to the proper basis (*pratiṣṭhā*) on which a person should build his life; is it higher wisdom (*prajñā*) or is it the conventional accoutrements of worldly existence such as family, wealth, and work? As might be expected, Bhīṣma responds with the judgement that *prajñā* should be the *pratiṣṭhā*, for such wisdom brings true happiness and is the ultimate achievement in life. The story of the conversation between Kāśyapa and the jackal is then presented to illustrate this point, although the connection is somewhat tenuous. On finding the Brahmin about to give up his life because of the terrible pain he is suffering, Indra assumes the form of a jackal and reminds him of the good fortune of his auspicious birth. Human beings are in a far superior position to the beasts who must suffer because of their inability to counter the miseries inflicted by natural circumstances. The tone here is light, as the jackal praises the hands of a human being that enable a person to scratch itches all over the body and remove the lice that bite and irritate.

This discussion of the desirability of human life runs through verses 8 to 21, but from verse 22 the jackal changes his subject and returns to the familiar theme of these opening chapters as he insists that no one in this world can ever find complete contentment. It is perhaps here that we find the connection between this *itihāsa* and Bhīṣma's opening assertion, as the point seems to be that however successfully one arranges one's worldly circumstances there will never be complete satisfaction. Humans seek to become wealthy, a wealthy man wishes to be a king, a king wishes to become one of the gods, and each of the gods desires the position of Indra. Therefore a wise person should remain aloof and restrain the mind from dwelling on the objects of desire. And in any case, both one's disposition and conduct are already preordained by destiny shaped by previous acts, so all the endeavours humans make for success are virtually worthless. The highest goals of life can therefore be attained by renunciation and adherence to the religious practices ordained by the Vedas, and as Kāśyapa was already advanced along that path his decision to give up his life was sheer folly.

Hence this final chapter of the six presents us with a view that typifies the perspective of the *Mokṣa-dharma-parvan*. Renunciation is essential for spiritual progress, but this is not the renunciation of those who rely on their own reasoning and who reject the revelation of the Vedas. Such persons are not named here but one suspects the author might have in mind Cārvākas, Buddhists, Jains, Ājīvikas, and other similar groups who seem to have proliferated in India around 2,000 years ago. Their teachings included a rejection of the Vedas and a denial of their authoritative status; such persons were therefore classified as *nāstikas*, faithless persons. Here renunciation is central to the teachings, but it is renunciation within the purview of the Vedic tradition, and the point is clearly made that *nāstikas* who deny the Vedas will suffer degradation in the world to come whilst the Vedic renunciant will go on to attain the ultimate spiritual goal.

1. *yudhiṣṭhira uvāca*
bāndhavāḥ karma vittaṁ vā prajñā veha pitāmaha
narasya kā pratiṣṭhā syād etat pṛṣṭo vadasva me

Yudhiṣṭhira said: What is the real basis for a man's life, grandfather? Is it his relatives, work, and wealth, or is it his wisdom? Please answer this question.

2. *bhīṣma uvāca*
prajñā pratiṣṭhā bhūtānāṁ prajñā lābhaḥ paro mataḥ
prajñā naiḥśreyasī loke prajñā svargo mataḥ satām

Bhīṣma said: It is wisdom that is the basis of life for living beings; in my opinion wisdom is the supreme wealth. In this world, wisdom is happiness, and according to the righteous wisdom is heaven as well.

3. *prajñayā prāpitārtho hi balir aiśvarya-saṁkṣaye*
prahrādo namucir maṅkis tasyāḥ kiṁ vidyate param

It was by his wisdom alone that Bali was led to the real goal of life when his sovereignty over the world was destroyed, and the same is true of Prahrāda, Namuci, and Maṅki. What could ever be superior to wisdom?

4. *atrāpy udāharantīmam itihāsaṁ purātanam*
indra-kāśyapa-saṁvādaṁ tan nibodha yudhiṣṭhira

And in this connection they recite this ancient account of the conversation between Indra and Kāśyapa. You should now learn about this, Yudhiṣṭhira.

5. *vaiśyaḥ kaścid ṛṣiṁ tāta kāśyapaṁ saṁcita-vratam*
rathena pātayāmāsa śrīmān dṛptas tapasvinam

My son, a wealthy *vaiśya* with an arrogant nature once knocked down a *rishi* with his chariot. This was Kāśyapa who was following vows of renunciation and practising religious austerities.

6. *ārtaḥ sa patitaḥ kruddhas tyaktvātmānam athābravīt*
mariṣyāmy adhanasyeha jīvitārtho na vidyate

Whilst lying on the ground, giving up his life, he cried out in his agony and rage, 'Now I shall die. For one who is bereft of property there is no reason to go on living in this world.'

7. *tathā mumūrṣum āsīnam akūjantam acetasam*
indraḥ sṛgāla-rūpeṇa babhāṣe kruddha-mānasam

He then lay slumped unconscious and on the point of death without making a sound. At that time Indra assumed the form of a jackal and addressed that man whose mind was filled with rage.

8. *manuṣya-yonim icchanti sarva-bhūtāni sarvaśaḥ*
manuṣyatve ca vipratvaṁ sarva evābhinandati

'All living entities in all places wish to take birth from the womb of a human being. And amongst human births they especially long to be born as a Brahmin.

9. *manuṣyo brāhmaṇaś cāsi śrotriyaś cāsi kāśyapa*
sudurlabham avāpyaitad adoṣān martum icchasi

You, O Kāśyapa, are both a human being and a Brahmin, and, moreover, one who is learned in the Vedas. Yet having gained this state of existence which is so hard to attain, you now wish to give up your life, thinking there is no fault in doing so.

10. *sarve lābhāḥ sābhimānā iti satyā bata śrutiḥ*
saṁtoṣaṇīya-rūpo 'si lobhād yad abhimanyase

"Along with everything one achieves comes a feeling of contempt." Alas, how true the Vedas are in this assertion! Your attitude seems one of contentment, but your ideas now are based on greed.

11. *aho siddhārthatā teṣāṁ yeṣāṁ santīha pāṇayaḥ*
pāṇimadbhyaḥ spṛhāsmākaṁ yathā tava dhanasya vai

O how perfect is the achievement of those who are endowed with hands! An agitated longing to possess hands affects us in the same way that despair over riches affects you humans.

12. *na pāṇi-lābhād adhiko lābhaḥ kaścana vidyate*
apāṇitvād vayaṁ brahman kaṇṭakān noddharāmahe

There is no greater gain than the possession of hands. Because we beasts lack hands, O Brahmin, we cannot even pull thorns from out of our flesh.

13. *atha yeṣāṁ punaḥ pāṇī deva-dattau daśāṅgulī*
uddharanti krimīn aṅgād daśamānān kaṣanti ca

Moreover, those who possess the blessing of the gods in the form of two hands and ten fingers can remove lice from their body and scratch the itches they cause.

14. *hima-varṣā-tapānāṁ ca paritrāṇāni kurvate*
celam annaṁ sukhaṁ śayyāṁ nivātaṁ copabhuñjate

They can construct shelters to protect themselves from the cold, the rain, and the heat, and then enjoy clothing, food, happiness, a comfortable bed, and a secure home.

15. *adhiṣṭhāya ca gāṁ loke bhuñjate vāhayanti ca*
upāyair bahubhiś caiva vaśyān ātmani kurvate

They can also enjoy life in this world by looking after a cow and making it carry burdens, using various techniques to keep it under their control.

16. *ye khalv ajihvāḥ kṛpaṇā alpa-prāṇā apāṇayaḥ*
sahante tāni duḥkhāni diṣṭyā tvaṁ na tathā mune

Those wretched creatures that cannot speak, have little strength, and are devoid of hands, must endure so many miseries. O sage, it is your great good fortune that you will never have to suffer like that.

17. *diṣṭyā tvaṁ na sṛgālo vai na kṛmir na ca mūṣakaḥ*
na sarpo na ca maṇḍūko na cānyaḥ pāpa-yoni-jaḥ

It is your great good fortune that you are not a jackal, a louse, a rat, a snake, or a frog; or indeed any other abominable form of existence.

18. *etāvatāpi lābhena toṣṭum arhasi kāśyapa*
kiṁ punar yo 'si sattvānāṁ sarveṣāṁ brāhmaṇottamaḥ

O Kāśyapa, you should be satisfied with what you have attained. How much more so when you are a Brahmin, the highest amongst all forms of life?

19. *ime māṁ kṛmayo 'danti teṣām uddharaṇāya me*
nāsti śaktir apāṇitvāt paśyāvasthām imāṁ mama

These lice gnaw away at me and because of my having no hands I lack the power to remove them from my body. Just look at the state I am in!

20. *akāryam iti caivemaṁ nātmānaṁ saṁtyajāmy aham*
netaḥ pāpīyasīṁ yoniṁ pateyam aparām iti

I do not give up this body because to do so would certainly be improper. So at least in the future I will not fall down into an even more wretched state of being as a result of that sinful action.

21. *madhye vai pāpa-yonīnāṁ sārgālī yām ahaṁ gataḥ*
pāpīyasyo bahutarā ito 'nyāḥ pāpa-yonayaḥ

This jackal existence that I have come to stands about in the middle of the abominable forms of life. In this world there are many other births one can take more wretched even than this.

22. *jātyaivaike sukhatarāḥ santy anye bhṛśa-duḥkhitāḥ*
naikānta-sukham eveha kvacit paśyāmi kasyacit

Because of the state of existence they are born into, some living beings may find life easier than others who must endure terrible suffering. But I do not see any living being anywhere in the world whose life consists only of happiness.

23. *manuṣyā hy āḍhyatāṁ prāpya rājyam icchanty anantaram*
rājyād devatvam icchanti devatvād indratām api

After acquiring wealth, human beings then desire dominion over a kingdom that has no end. If they attain kingship they then desire to live amongst the gods, and having entered the host of divine beings, still they long to take the position of Indra, the Lord of the Gods.

24. *bhaves tvaṁ yady api tv āḍhyo na rājā na ca daivatam*
devatvaṁ prāpya cendratvaṁ naiva tuṣyes tathā sati

Even if you were to become wealthy you would not become a king, nor as a king would you become one of the gods. And even after becoming a god you would not be satisfied because of longing for the status of Indra.

25. *na tṛptiḥ priya-lābhe 'sti tṛṣṇā nādbhiḥ praśāmyati*
saṁprajvalati sā bhūyaḥ samidbhir iva pāvakaḥ

Even after attaining what one has longed for there is never complete contentment; thirst is not permanently extinguished by water. One's desire will burst into flame once more, just like a fire that has been covered with fuel.

26. *asty eva tvayi śoko vai harṣaś cāsti tathā tvayi*
sukha-duḥkhe tathā cobhe tatra kā paridevanā

As there has been joy in your life, so there is also grief. So what cause is there for lamentation over this inevitable cycle of delight and misery?

27. *paricchidyaiva kāmānāṁ sarveṣāṁ caiva karmaṇām*
mūlaṁ rundhīndriya-grāmaṁ śakuntān iva pañjare

You must cut down the root of all your desires and activities. Keep your senses in a state of captivity, like birds locked in a cage.

28. *na khalv apy arasa-jñasya kāmaḥ kvacana jāyate*
saṁsparśād darśanād vāpi śravaṇād vāpi jāyate

Desire for an object will never arise in one who has no comprehension of the pleasure it offers. It is from touching, seeing, or hearing about such things, that desire for them comes into being.

29. *na tvaṁ smarasi vāruṇyā laṭvākānāṁ ca pakṣiṇām*
tābhāṁ cābhyadhiko bhakṣyo na kaścid vidyate kvacit

You cannot call to mind the pleasure that comes from drinking *vāruṇī* and eating the birds known as *laṭvākas*, and nowhere in this world is there any food superior to this.

30. *yāni cānyāni dūreṣu bhakṣya-bhojyāni kāśyapa*
yeṣām abhukta-pūrvaṁ te teṣām asmṛtir eva ca

O Kāśyapa, because you have not enjoyed other types of delightful food that are found in distant lands they can never prey upon your mind.

31. *aprāśanam asaṁsparśam asaṁdarśanam eva ca*
puruṣasyaiṣa niyamo manye śreyo na saṁśayaḥ

I consider the vow of renunciation that entails not relishing good food, not touching any objects of pleasure, and not looking at them either, to be the best a human being can undertake. I have no doubt about this.

32. *pāṇimanto dhanair yuktā balavanto na saṁśayaḥ*
manuṣyā mānuṣair eva dāsatvam upapāditāḥ

Undoubtedly, those powerful living beings that possess hands are blessed with prosperity. But human beings can be brought to a state of servitude by other human beings.

33. *vadha-bandha-parikleśaiḥ kliśyante ca punaḥ punaḥ*
te khalv api ramante ca modante ca hasanti ca

Time and again they are made to suffer the affliction of beatings and captivity, but still they can also enjoy pleasure in life, and they rejoice and laugh.

34. *apare bāhu-balinaḥ kṛta-vidyā manasvinaḥ*
jugupsitāṁ sukṛpaṇāṁ pāpāṁ vṛttim upāsate

And then there are others who have mighty arms, who are well educated and highly intelligent, but adhere to a way of life that is despicable, miserly, and full of wickedness.

35. *utsahante ca te vṛttim anyām apy upasevitum*
sva-karmaṇā tu niyataṁ bhavitavyaṁ tu tat tathā

Although such persons certainly possess the ability to follow a different way of life, the fact is that one's future is preordained according to one's previous actions.

36. *na pulkaso na caṇḍāla ātmānaṁ tyaktum icchati*
asaṁtuṣṭaḥ svayā yonyā māyāṁ paśyasva yādṛśīm

Neither the *pulkasa* nor the *caṇḍāla* wishes to give up his body. But you are dissatisfied with the form of life you have been born into. Just see the extent of your delusion!

37. *dṛṣṭvā kuṇīn pakṣa-hatān manuṣyān āmayāvinaḥ*
susaṁpūrṇaḥ svayā yonyā labdha-lābho 'si kāśyapa

Having seen people who lack the use of an arm, suffer from paralysis, or are afflicted by disease, O Kāśyapa, it is clear that you are in an advantageous position, having been endowed with all the blessings of the body you have been born into.

38. *yadi brāhmaṇa dehas te nirātaṅko nirāmayaḥ*
aṅgāni ca samagrāṇi na ca lokeṣu dhik-kṛtaḥ

If, O Brahmin, your body does not cause you pain and is free from affliction, and if your limbs are undamaged, then nowhere in the world will you ever be condemned.

39. *na kenacit pravādena satyenaivāpahāriṇā*
dharmāyottiṣṭha viprarṣe nātmānaṁ tyaktum arhasi

Even if criticised by a factual account of misconduct on your part, you should still arise for the sake of dharma. O Brahmin *rishi*, you should not give up your life.

40. *yadi brahmañ śṛṇoṣy etac chraddadhāsi ca me vacaḥ*
vedoktasya ca dharmasya phalaṁ mukhyam avāpsyasi

If, O Brahmin, you listen with faith to this instruction of mine you will reap the highest reward that can be gained by following the path of dharma expounded by the Vedas.

41. *svādhyāyam agni-saṁskāram apramatto 'nupālaya*
satyaṁ damaṁ ca dānaṁ ca spardhiṣṭhā mā ca kenacit

You should diligently maintain your recitation of the Vedas and the ritual offerings you make into the sacred fire, as well as your vows of truthfulness, self-control, and charity. Do not see others as your rivals and compete against them.

42. *ye kecana svadhyayanāḥ prāptā yajana-yājanam*
kathaṁ te jātu śoceyur dhyāyeyur vāpy aśobhanam

How can those who have completed their studies of the Vedas and performed ritual offerings for themselves and as priests for others lament in any way or brood over life's misfortunes?

43. *icchantas te vihārāya sukhaṁ mahad avāpnuyuḥ*
uta jātāḥ sunakṣatre sutīrthāḥ sumuhūrta-jāḥ

There is no doubt that if they are born under an auspicious constellation, in a place of sanctity, at an auspicious hour of the day, those Brahmins who seek pleasure can experience great happiness in life.

44. *nakṣatreṣv āsureṣv anye dustīrthā durmuhūrta-jāḥ*
saṁpatanty āsurīṁ yoniṁ yajña-prasava-varjitām

But others born under malevolent constellations, in a place of sin, at an inauspicious hour, assume an asuric form of existence and are bereft of *yajñas* and offspring.

45. *aham āsaṁ paṇḍitako haituko veda-nindakaḥ*
ānvīkṣikīṁ tarka-vidyām anurakto nirarthikām

In my previous life I was a rationalist scholar who rejected the authority of the Vedas, devoting myself to that useless form of philosophical reasoning that is based solely on logic and deduction.

46. *hetu-vādān pravaditā vaktā saṁsatsu hetumat*
ākroṣṭā cābhivaktā ca brahma-yajñeṣu vai dvijān

As a speaker in learned assemblies, I would use reason and argument to present logical conclusions. And at ceremonies where the Vedic rituals were executed I would direct critical words at the Brahmins.

47. *nāstikaḥ sarva-śaṅkī ca mūrkhaḥ paṇḍita-mānikaḥ*
tasyeyaṁ phala-nirvṛttiḥ sṛgālatvaṁ mama dvija

I was a *nāstika* without faith in anything at all, a fool who thought himself a learned scholar. O Brahmin, this jackal form I now find myself in is a direct result of my previous conduct.

48. *api jātu tathā tat syād aho-rātra-śatair api*
yad ahaṁ mānuṣīṁ yoniṁ sṛgālaḥ prāpnuyāṁ punaḥ

And indeed, even after hundreds of days and nights have passed like this, if I who am presently a jackal should ever again obtain a human birth,

49. *saṁtuṣṭaś cāpramattaś ca yajña-dāna-tapo-ratiḥ*
jñeya-jñātā bhaveyaṁ vai varjya-varjayitā tathā

Then I would be completely satisfied and always careful of my conduct. I would devote myself to performing *yajñas*, giving gifts in charity and executing religious austerity. I would understand things as they truly are and would strictly avoid those things that are forbidden.'

50. *tataḥ sa munir utthāya kāśyapas tam uvāca ha*
aho batāsi kuśalo buddhimān iti vismitaḥ

Getting to his feet, the sage Kāśyapa then said to him, 'O how right you are, how intelligent you are! So much so that I am filled with wonder!'

51. *samavaikṣata taṁ vipro jñāna-dīrgheṇa cakṣusā*
dadarśa cainaṁ devānām indraṁ devaṁ śacī-patim

The Brahmin now looked upon that jackal with his vision broadened by wisdom, and saw instead the Lord of the Gods, that deity who is the husband of Śacī.

52. *tataḥ saṁpūjayāmāsa kāśyapo hari-vāhanam*
anujñātaś ca tenātha praviveśa svam āśramam

Kāśyapa then worshipped Indra who rides upon tawny horses, and with his permission he returned to his own *āśrama*.

Instruction from Bhīṣma

Śānti-parvan, Adhyāya 174

BETWEEN THE OPENING SIX PASSAGES and the longer *Bhṛgu-bharadvāja-saṁvāda* that follows we have a short chapter in which Bhīṣma responds directly to a further question from Yudhiṣṭhira without citing any previous discussion on the subject This chapter, therefore, may have been composed by the redactor himself who wished to add further elucidation to the themes previously pursued; one should probably be cautious in reaching this conclusion, however, particularly as Bhīṣma's words are wholly devoid of vocatives addressed to Yudhiṣṭhira, which might suggest the use of an existing text from another context. Either way, the point of the chapter seems quite clear as the previous debate over adherence to the Vedic path is continued. Here one cannot but be aware of the historical context, in particular of the manner in which certain religious groups in India around 2,000 years ago came to regard the rejection of Vedic orthodoxy as a part of the path of renunciation and the pursuit of liberation from rebirth. And one must presume that the *Mahābhārata*'s discourse here forms a part of those debates and can be identified as a riposte from the side of orthodoxy, arguing that *mokṣa-dharma* must not be anti-Vedic and need not involve any rejection of the ritual life followed by the Brahmin class. It seems certain that it is the teachings of the previous two chapters, from the *ājagara* and the *sṛgāla*, that have brought this discussion to the fore, with the former being uninterested in Vedic practice but the latter emphasising its necessity and indeed the dreadful punishments that await those who rely on logic alone and become critical of the Vedas.

The chapter opens with Yudhiṣṭhira posing a follow-on question as to whether acts of *yajña*, *dāna*, and *tapas* (sacrifice, charity, and austerity) should still be performed, and whether service should be rendered to one's *gurus*. This debate is one that has long currency within the Indian religious traditions; it is interesting to note how it plays a significant role in the ideology of the *Bhagavad-gītā* and reoccurs centuries later as a central theme in the writings and commentaries of Śaṅkarācārya. In its wider context, the issue centres on the notion that liberation depends upon realised knowledge alone and that ritual action cannot be effective in leading to this highest state of consciousness, except perhaps as a preliminary form of purification. Śaṅkarācārya is quite adamant on this point and indeed it is one of the principal arguments he employs to refute the ideas of the *pūrva-mīmāṁsā* school. The very same question is raised in almost identical terms within the final chapter of the *Bhagavad-gītā*, reflecting the fact that the reassertion of Vedic orthodoxy is one of the central themes of the *Mahābhārata*'s discussion of renunciation and *mokṣa-dharma*. Buddhists, Jains, and others may have their ideas on the validity of Vedic ritual acts, but for the *Mahābhārata*, including the *Bhagavad-gītā*, such actions are not to be given up. According to Kṛṣṇa, *yajña-dāna-tapaḥ karma na tyājyaṁ kāryam eva tat*, 'acts of sacrifice, charity and religious austerity must not be abandoned but must be performed' (*Bhagavad-gītā*, 18.5), and here we find Bhīṣma making exactly the same point.

The ideas emphasised by the chapter are relatively simple. Bhīṣma starts by insisting that righteous actions bring happiness in future lives and therefore should be performed. The *nāstikas* give up the ritualised lifestyle of Vedic orthodoxy and, as we saw with the jackal in the previous chapter, they must therefore undergo terrible sufferings in the world to come. The remainder of the chapter, from verses 8 to 20, consists of a reassertion of the doctrine of karma as Bhīṣma emphasises the fact that all our success and failure, our joy and our misery, arise from the destiny we have created for ourselves through previous acts. Just as a cloth can be scrubbed clean, acts of a ritual nature, such as charity, *yajña*, and austerity, have the power to remove the effect of any sinful activities we may have performed. Therefore, in answer to Yudhiṣṭhira's question, such acts should never be given up; it is the *nāstikas* who abandon the Vedic injunctions and as result they will suffer terribly in future lives.

There is of course a slight anomaly in this line of teaching. Here the emphasis is on the enjoyment of positive karma in future lives, whilst the main theme of this part of the *Mahābhārata* is *mokṣa*, which is the absolute liberation from all forms of karma. Hence the question arises as to the relevance of what Bhīṣma says here within the present context; enjoyment of pleasure in a future life is not *mokṣa*, for axiomatically it involves future rebirth. The explanation must lie in what the *Mahābhārata* is attempting to achieve here, which is to advocate a form of *mokṣa-dharma* that can be reconciled with Vedic orthodoxy, and we must be aware that the *Bhagavad-gītā* devotes itself to precisely the same task. The *Gītā*, however, deals with the problem far more thoroughly than Bhīṣma does here through its advocacy of a *karma-yoga* whereby ritual acts are performed without any desire in order to promote the required mood of detachment from the world. The Vedic rituals are thus to be performed not to gain any reward in a future life but simply as a duty in a mood of utter detachment. In this way the *Bhagavad-gītā* is able to offer some reconciliation between the Vedic lifestyle and the quest for liberation; here the *Mahābhārata* seems to be confronting the same dilemma but without being able to propose the same kind of sophisticated solution.

1. *'yudhiṣṭhira uvāca*
yady asti dattam iṣṭaṁ vā tapas taptaṁ tathaiva ca
gurūṇāṁ cāpi śuśrūṣā tan me brūhi pitāmaha

Yudhiṣṭhira said: Tell me, grandfather, whether charity should be given, *yajñas* performed, acts of religious austerity undertaken, and service rendered to one's teachers.

2. *bhīṣma uvāca*
ātmanānartha-yuktena pāpe niviśate manaḥ
sa karma kaluṣaṁ kṛtvā kleśe mahati dhīyate

Bhīṣma said: Through its natural inclination towards what is improper, the mind enters a state of sinful degradation. And after indulging in impure activities, a person is destined for great degradation.

3. *durbhikṣād eva durbhikṣaṁ kleśāt kleśaṁ bhayād bhayam*
mṛtebhyaḥ pramṛtaṁ yānti daridrāḥ pāpa-kāriṇaḥ

The unfortunate purveyors of wickedness thus move from one state of starvation to another, from one torment to another, and from one state of fear to another, as they go forward from their previous deaths to taste death once again.

4. *utsavād utsavaṁ yānti svargāt svargaṁ sukhāt sukham*
śraddadhānāś ca dāntāś ca dhanāḍhyāḥ śubha-kāriṇaḥ

But those who are blessed with faith, who possess self-mastery, who are prosperous, and whose activities are righteous, move from one celebration to another, from one heaven to another, and from one state of joy to another.

5. *vyāla-kuñjara-durgeṣu sarpa-cora-bhayeṣu ca*
hastāvāpena gacchanti nāstikāḥ kim ataḥ param

With their hands fettered, the *nāstikas* go into exile in remote regions where ferocious elephants roam and there is constant fear from snakes and robbers. What fate awaits them apart from this?

6. *priya-devātitheyāś ca vadānyāḥ priya-sādhavaḥ*
kṣemyam ātmavatāṁ mārgam āsthitā hasta-dakṣiṇam

But generous persons who take delight in serving the gods and their guests, and are affectionate towards *sādhus*, are following the correct path that leads to prosperity, the path that is followed by those who are self-possessed.

7. *pulākā iva dhānyeṣu puttikā iva pakṣiṣu*
tad-vidhās te manuṣyeṣu yeṣāṁ dharmo na kāraṇam

Those men who do not act in accordance with dharma are like empty husks amongst grains of wheat or like gnats amongst birds.

8. *suśīghram api dhāvantaṁ vidhānam anudhāvati*
śete saha śayānena yena yena yathā kṛtam

Even if a man runs away at great speed his destiny will follow him. It sleeps according to his sleep and is active in whatever action he performs.

9. *upatiṣṭhati tiṣṭhantaṁ gacchantam anugacchati*
karoti kurvataḥ karma chāyevānuvidhīyate

It stands still when he is standing still, and sets off again when he goes forth. It acts whenever he is performing an action, following his every movement like a shadow.

10. *yena yena yathā yad yat purā karma samācitam*
tat tad eva naro bhuṅkte nityaṁ vihitam ātmanā

The fortune a man experiences moment by moment as it is allotted to him throughout his life is due only to the aggregate of his previous actions.

11. *sva-karma-phala-vikṣiptaṁ vidhāna-parirakṣitam*
bhūta-grāmam imaṁ kālaḥ samantāt parikarṣati

Time has absolute dominion over this host of living beings, for they are controlled by the dictates of destiny and placed in various positions according to the previous actions each has performed.

12. *acodyamānāni yathā puṣpāṇi ca phalāni ca*
sva-kālaṁ nātivartante tathā karma purā-kṛtam

As flowers and fruits ripen without any external impulse, so living beings cannot escape the ripening of their previous actions at the time that is ordained.

13. *saṁmānaś cāvamānaś ca lābhālābhau kṣayodayau*
pravṛttā vinivartante vidhānānte punaḥ punaḥ

Over and over again, praise and censure, gain and loss, decline and growth, are manifest in a living being's existence, only to disappear when one's allotted destiny is concluded.

14. *ātmanā vihitaṁ duḥkham ātmanā vihitaṁ sukham*
garbha-śayyām upādāya bhujyate paurva-dehikam

One's suffering is created by oneself alone; one's joy is created by oneself alone. After accepting another womb for rebirth, the living being experiences the results of the deeds performed in its previous life.

15. *bālo yuvā ca vṛddhaś ca yat karoti śubhāśubham*
tasyāṁ tasyām avasthāyāṁ bhuṅkte janmani janmani

As one performs righteous and wicked deeds as a child, as a youth, and as an old man, so, lifetime after lifetime, one experiences the results of these actions in exactly the same stage of life – in childhood, in youth, and in old age.

16. *yathā dhenu-sahasreṣu vatso vindati mātaram*
tathā pūrva-kṛtaṁ karma kartāram anugacchati

As a calf finds its mother amongst thousands of cows, so actions previously performed seek out the one who performed them.

17. *samunnam agrato vastraṁ paścāc chuddhyati karmaṇā*
upavāsaiḥ prataptānāṁ dīrghaṁ sukham anantakam

A garment is first moistened and then cleansed by vigorous action; through their acts of renunciation, eons of unbroken happiness come to those who follow the path of asceticism.

18. *dīrgha-kālena tapasā sevitena tapo-vane*
dharma-nirdhūta-pāpānāṁ saṁsidhyante mano-rathāḥ

By undertaking a long period of religious austerity in the forest where austerity is performed, all the goals sought by those whose dharma frees them from sin are finally achieved.

19. *śakunīnām ivākāśe matsyānām iva codake*
padaṁ yathā na dṛśyeta tathā jñāna-vidāṁ gatiḥ

Just as the course followed by birds through the sky or by fish through water cannot be seen, so the path of those who comprehend true wisdom cannot be perceived.

20. *alam anyair upālambhaiḥ kīrtitaiś ca vyatikramaiḥ*
peśalaṁ cānurūpaṁ ca kartavyaṁ hitam ātmanaḥ

There is no need to speak any more words of condemnation or praise, or about the wrongs that people do. It is enough to say that whatever is good and proper should be undertaken to bring benefit to oneself.

The Bhṛgu-Bharadvāja-Saṁvāda

Śānti-parvan, Adhyāya 175–185

THE FIRST SUBSTANTIAL TREATISE of the *Mokṣa-dharma-parvan* is the *Bhṛgu-bharadvāja-saṁvāda*, the conversation between Bhṛgu and Bharadvāja, which includes a total of eleven chapters, 175 to 185 of the *Śānti-parvan*. Bhṛgu is well known in ancient Sanskrit literature as one of the seven great *rishis* who were born from the mind of Brahmā and became progenitors of living beings. He is known as the ancestor and founder of the Bhārgava dynasty of Brahmin sages who are referred to repeatedly throughout the *Mahābhārata*. Even within the *Bhagavad-gītā*, we find the statement, *maharṣīṇāṁ bhṛgur aham*, 'amongst the great *rishis* I am Bhṛgu' (10.25), indicating his preeminent status. In the *saṁvāda* it is therefore natural that Bhṛgu should take on the role of being the main speaker, although the passage is notable for the speeches made by Bharadvāja who is not content merely to pose questions but does himself make significant contributions. This is perhaps to be expected for Bharadvāja is also known as a *maharṣi*, a great *rishi*, who appears in both the *Mahābhārata* and the *Rāmāyaṇa*. In the *Mahābhārata* he is said to be the father of Droṇācārya, the teacher of both the Pāṇḍavas and Kauravas, whilst in the *Rāmāyaṇa* the exiled Rāma spends some time as a guest in his *āśrama* before being advised by him to make his residence at Chitrakuta.

The eleven chapters of the *Bhṛgu-Bharadvāja-Saṁvāda* can be divided into two distinctive sections loosely connected by the common theme of the creation of the world. In the first of these sections (Chapters 1–6), Bhṛgu responds to questions from Bharadvāja first by presenting a brief exposition on the process of creation and then moving on to discuss the presence of the material elements and perceptual senses in every life form. This passage does not quite amount to a Sāṁkhya treatise although it makes extensive use of the understanding of the world that has come to be associated with the Sāṁkhya system. It seems that the primary intention of the author here is not to provide any form of systematic exposition of Sāṁkhya, as is found elsewhere in the *Mokṣa-dharma-parvan*, but rather to make use of Sāṁkhya doctrines in order to pursue his own line of discourse. It might also be suggested that within this treatise we can detect signs of the interest in the natural sciences characteristic of the Vaiśeṣika system: the passage as a whole certainly makes more use of observation and rational inference than it does of recourse to revealed scripture. The fifth and sixth chapters follow the typical pattern of Sāṁkhya analysis in proclaiming that there must also be a spiritual dimension to the living being, a soul or *ātman* that transcends the material elements and survives the death of the body. It is to be noted, however, that within this discussion there is little or no interest shown in the liberation of *ātman* from the cycle of rebirth, which is always the ultimate goal and purpose of Sāṁkhya wisdom. This factor would again seem to suggest that the primary purpose of this first section of our treatise is to explain the origin and nature of this world rather than to prescribe a process of 'knowing' for soteriological purposes; it uses Sāṁkhya concepts to achieve this purpose but it is not therefore an exposition of Sāṁkhya.

In the second of the two sections (Chapters 7–11), the focus of the discussion switches quite dramatically towards a consideration of the division of society into four *varṇas,* or social classes, and four *āśramas,* or stages of life. Continuing his discourse on the creation of the world, Bhṛgu reveals that the division of society into four *varṇas* was inaugurated by Brahmā himself when the world began. He then outlines the characteristics of each of the four classes before presenting an ardent advocacy of a lifestyle based on *dharma*, asserting that this is the only way for human beings to find happiness. Within the *Mokṣa-dharma-parvan* this view might be regarded as slightly aberrant, for worldly pleasure is not usually given high regard in these passages, and Bharadvāja is quick to express his doubts about this line of teaching. Bhṛgu, however, does not back down and points out that existence in the higher forms of life in this world is wholly dependent on acting in accordance with *dharma*. Again perhaps we might note that despite his extensive use of ideas usually associated with Sāṁkhya teachings, Bhṛgu is not particularly concerned with the idea of gaining liberation from rebirth, although there are a few occasions when the discussion does move in that direction.

Chapters 10 and 11 deal with the *āśramas,* the stages of an individual's life. These are designated as *brahmacārya*, the celibate student, *gṛhastha*, the householder who begets offspring, *vānaprastha* where one retires to the forest for spiritual pursuits, and *parivrājaka*, the wandering mendicant who has renounced all connection with society. When taken together with the four *varṇas* this concept of human life is known as the *varṇāśrama* system and is of great significance in the construction of the Hindu worldview. Within this system we can recognise the enormous scope for diversity that is characteristic of Hindu teachings, for the different *varṇas* and *āśramas* have very different codes of conduct attached to them and seek different goals from the paths they pursue. And it is within the *Bhṛgu-bharadvāja-saṁvāda* that we encounter the clearest exposition of this notion to be found anywhere within the *Mahābhārata*. Taken as a whole, the passage probably just about merits inclusion under the heading of *mokṣa-dharma*, first of all because of its close association with Sāṁkhya discourse and then because the *varṇāśrama* divisions do ultimately allow for an individual to pursue the highest goal of liberation from rebirth. It does, however, have its own unique perspectives and certainly stands as a passage in its own right with nothing fully equivalent appearing elsewhere in the *Mahābhārata*.

Śānti-parvan, Adhyāya 175

The first chapter begins predictably with questions from Yudhiṣṭhira to Bhīṣma; the wording of these questions does not allow us any insight into the editor's understanding of what the treatise as a whole is about, as these initial questions are word for word identical to those posed by Bharadvāja when Bhīṣma begins to recite the treatise he selects. A remarkable coincidence, or perhaps the editor saw no need to modify the text by inventing questions of his own to put into the mouth of Yudhiṣṭhira. In both cases, the questions pertain primarily to the creation of the world and of the living beings who inhabit it, although the final question looks for a conclusion on the question of life after death.

The discourse proper gets underway from verse 11 where Bhṛgu begins his teachings. The first phase covers eleven verses before Bharadvāja poses a further question in verse 22; in these opening verses Bhṛgu describes how the Deity he names as Mānasa first manifests the five great elements beginning with space (also designated as *mahat*, the great element) and only then brings Brahmā into being from a lotus that sprouts from his navel. The account is notable for the way it seeks to integrate the Sāṁkhya idea of the evolution of elements with the Vaiṣṇava creation story. The name of Mānasa given here to the primal creator is unusual but is known as an epithet of Viṣṇu and the reference to the creation of Brahmā from the lotus confirms this identification. Viṣṇu himself is transcendent to this world. It is he who produces the five elements through the evolutionary process as taught by Sāṁkhya philosophy and it is these which form the fabric of the created world. Verse 16 describes Brahmā as the creator and identifies him with the *ahaṁkāra*, the self-awareness that in Sāṁkhya analysis combines with mind and intellect (*manas* and *buddhi*) to form the mental elements of the material embodiment. In verses 17 to 21, however, the text switches its focus abruptly back to Viṣṇu, the original transcendent Deity who manifests himself as Brahmā and who pervades the entire created world. The account of the all-pervasive nature of the Deity is reminiscent of the *Bhagavad-gītā*'s revelation of the *viśva-rūpa* and relates to the notion of the identity between the Deity and the true self within every being, an idea that is also prominent in the *Gītā*'s theistic exposition.

When this initial account of the creation is complete, Bharadvāja moves the focus of the discussion on by inquiring about the dimensions of the world that is brought into existence in this way. This inquiry gives rise to a brief discourse on cosmology as Bhṛgu describes the different features of the creation and its higher and lower regions. In keeping with the somewhat rationalistic tenor of the entire passage he admits, however, that the exact dimensions of the world cannot be known. This knowledge may be derived from texts written by learned scholars but as no one has actually seen or measured these dimensions there must be some doubts about their accuracy. Moreover, as the created world is an expansion from the Deity and is subsequently withdrawn back into him, its dimensions are not fixed.

Within this chapter it is at times quite difficult to draw a clear distinction between Viṣṇu (also designated as Mānasa and Ananta) and Brahmā who is the actual creator. In verse 34 we are given further information about the relationship between them, where it is indicated that Viṣṇu is the original formless Deity but when he begins the process of creation he manifests himself with a form and becomes Brahmā. Hence the indication here is that although Viṣṇu is the supreme transcendent Deity, Brahmā is not an alternative Deity but rather the form in which Viṣṇu appears in the world in order to fulfil the function of creation. This point is fully clarified by means of Bharadvāja's question in verse 35: how is it that Brahmā is designated as the origin of the world when in fact he appeared from out of a lotus flower, which must therefore have preceded his coming into being? The answer is that Brahmā is a manifestation of Mānasa, the original Supreme Deity, and it is for this reason that he is to be understood as the original source of the entire world. Clearly we have here an exposition of an essentially Vaiṣṇava theology in relation to the creation of the world; at no point is there any reference to Śiva as a manifestation of God. The text, however, is less concerned with giving an account of the well known Vaiṣṇava creation story than with integrating that account into the Sāṁkhya doctrine of the evolution of elements. In other passages, this evolutionary process of creation is described in a manner that appears non-theistic, but here Bhṛgu is demonstrating that Sāṁkhya discourse and Vaiṣṇava theology are recognised by some authorities as being wholly compatible.

1. *yudhiṣṭhira uvāca*
kutaḥ sṛṣṭam idaṁ viśvaṁ jagat sthāvara-jaṅgamam
pralaye ca kam abhyeti tan me brūhi pitāmaha

Yudhiṣṭhira asked: Where did this world come from when it was created with its host of moving and stationary beings? And at the time of dissolution what state will it go to? Tell me this, grandfather.

2. *sasāgaraḥ sagaganaḥ saśailaḥ sabalāhakaḥ*
sabhūmiḥ sāgni-pavano loko 'yaṁ kena nirmitaḥ

This world consists of oceans, vast heavens, mountains, clouds, the earth, fire, and wind. By whom was it originally brought into being?

3. *kathaṁ sṛṣṭāni bhūtāni kathaṁ varṇa-vibhaktayaḥ*
śaucāśaucaṁ kathaṁ teṣāṁ dharmādharmāv atho katham

How were the living beings of this world created and how were they divided into different *varṇas*? How were purity and impurity generated amongst them as well as dharma and *adharma*?

4. *kīdṛśo jīvatāṁ jīvaḥ kva vā gacchanti ye mṛtāḥ*
asmāl lokād amuṁ lokaṁ sarvaṁ śaṁsatu no bhavān

What constitutes the life of living beings? Where do they go to when they die and depart from this world? Please tell us everything about this other world as well.

5. *bhīṣma uvāca*
atrāpy udāharantīmam itihāsaṁ purātanam
bhṛguṇābhihitaṁ śreṣṭhaṁ bharadvājāya pṛcchate

Bhīṣma replied: In this connection they recite this ancient account of the wonderful discourse delivered by Bhṛgu when he was questioned by Bharadvāja

6. *kailāsa-śikhare dṛṣṭvā dīpyamānam ivaujasā*
bhṛguṁ maharṣim āsīnaṁ bharadvājo 'nvapṛcchata

Seeing the mighty *rishi* Bhṛgu seated on the summit of Mount Kailāsa, radiant with his inner potency, Bharadvāja inquired from him.

7. *sasāgaraḥ sagaganaḥ saśailaḥ sabalāhakaḥ*
sabhūmiḥ sāgni-pavano loko 'yaṁ kena nirmitaḥ

'This world consists of oceans, vast heavens, mountains, clouds, the earth, fire, and wind. By whom was it originally brought into being?

8. *kathaṁ sṛṣṭāni bhūtāni kathaṁ varṇa-vibhaktayaḥ*
śaucāśaucaṁ kathaṁ teṣāṁ dharmādharmāv atho katham

How were the living beings of this world created and how were they divided into different *varṇas*? How were purity and impurity generated amongst them as well as dharma and *adharma*?

9. *kīdṛśo jīvitāṁ jīvaḥ kva vā gacchanti ye mṛtāḥ*
para-lokam imaṁ cāpi sarvaṁ śaṁsatu no bhavān

What constitutes the life of living beings? Where do they go to when they die? Please tell us everything about the other world and about this world as well.'

10. *evaṁ sa bhagavān pṛṣṭo bharadvājena saṁśayam*
maharṣir brahma-saṁkāśaḥ sarvaṁ tasmai tato 'bravīt

When questioned in this way by Bharadvāja concerning his doubts, that exalted person, the mighty *rishi* whose appearance was like that of Brahman, taught him everything he had inquired about.

11. *mānaso nāma vikhyātaḥ śruta-pūrvo maharṣibhiḥ*
anādi-nidhano devas tathābhedyo 'jarāmaraḥ

'The Deity is known by the name Mānasa for in ancient times he was perceived by the great *rishis* within their minds. He has neither beginning nor end and he is indivisible; he never ages or meets with death.

12. *avyakta iti vikhyātaḥ śāśvato 'thākṣaro 'vyayaḥ*
yataḥ sṛṣṭāni bhūtāni jāyante ca mriyanti ca

He is also described as invisible, eternal, without decay, and changeless. It is due to him that the created beings take birth and then experience death.

13. *so 'sṛjat prathamaṁ devo mahāntaṁ nāma nāmataḥ*
ākāśam iti vikhyātaṁ sarva-bhūta-dharaḥ prabhuḥ

That Deity, the lord who sustains all living beings, first created that which is referred to by the name *mahat*, the Great Element. This is more commonly identified as space.

14. *ākāśād abhavad vāri salilād agni-mārutau*
agni-māruta-saṁyogāt tataḥ samabhavan mahī

From space, water came into being, and from water came fire and wind. From the combination of fire and wind, earth then came into existence.

15. *tatas tejomayaṁ divyaṁ padmaṁ sṛṣṭaṁ svayaṁbhuvā*
tasmāt padmāt samabhavad brahmā vedamayo nidhiḥ

The self-born Deity then created an effulgent celestial lotus flower. Out of that lotus flower Brahmā took his birth; he is the receptacle in which the Vedas are contained.

16. *ahaṁkāra iti khyātaḥ sarva-bhūtātma-bhūta-kṛt*
brahmā vai sumahā-tejā ya ete pañca dhātavaḥ

This Brahmā is filled with tremendous potency; he is understood to be *ahaṁkāra*, self-awareness. He is the creator of living beings who is the very self of all beings, and he is those five basic elements of matter.

17. *śailās tasyāsthi-saṁjñās tu medo māṁsaṁ ca medinī*
samudrās tasya rudhiram ākāśam udaraṁ tathā

The mountains are considered to be his bones, the fat and flesh of his body is the level ground. The oceans are his blood and space is his abdomen.

18. *pavanaś caiva niḥśvāsas tejo 'gnir nimnagāḥ sirāḥ*
agnīṣomau tu candrārkau nayane tasya viśrute

The wind is his breathing, fire is the heat of his body, the rivers are his veins. Agni and Soma, the sun and the moon, are referred to as his eyes.

19. *nabhaś cordhvaṁ śiras tasya kṣitiḥ pādau diśo bhujau*
durvijñeyo hy anantatvāt siddhair api na saṁśayaḥ

The sky above is his head, the earth is his feet, the directions are his arms. Because his form is without limit, this is certainly difficult to comprehend even for the Siddhas, the perfect beings.

20. *sa eva bhagavān viṣṇur ananta iti viśrutaḥ*
sarva-bhūtātma-bhūta-stho durvijñeyo 'kṛtātmabhiḥ

He is none other than the worshipful Viṣṇu who is known as Ananta, the Unlimited. He is the inner self of all beings, situated within every living entity, but for those devoid of self-mastery he is difficult to comprehend.

21. *ahaṁkārasya yaḥ sraṣṭā sarva-bhūta-bhavāya vai*
yataḥ samabhavad viśvaṁ pṛṣṭo 'haṁ yad iha tvayā

He is the creator of the *ahaṁkāra* principle to make possible the existence of all living beings, and it is from him that this world came into being. This is the answer to the questions I was asked by you.'

22. *bharadvāja uvāca*
gaganasya diśāṁ caiva bhūtalasyānilasya ca
kāny atra parimāṇāni saṁśayaṁ chindi me 'rthataḥ

Bharadvāja said: What are the dimensions of the sky and the directions, of the surface of the earth and the blowing of the wind? Please fully remove my uncertainty about this.

23. *bhṛgur uvāca*
anantam etad ākāśaṁ siddha-cāraṇa-sevitam
ramyaṁ nānāśrayākīrṇaṁ yasyānto nādhigamyate

Bhṛgu said: The sky above us is the dwelling place of perfect beings and celestial singers; it is without limit. Beautiful to behold, it is made up of various constituent parts, the extent of which has never been reached.

24. *ūrdhvaṁ gater adhastāt tu candrādityau na dṛśyataḥ*
tatra devāḥ svayaṁ dīptā bhāsvarāś cāgni-varcasaḥ

The sun and moon do not look upon those parts of the sky that are above and below the path they follow. In those regions the divine beings are themselves luminous, blazing with a fiery radiance.

25. *te cāpy antaṁ na paśyanti nabhasaḥ prathitaujasaḥ*
durgamatvād anantatvād iti me viddhi mānada

And despite their widespread potencies, O respectful one, you must understand that even those entities cannot perceive the end of the sky, for it is unlimited and impossible to traverse.

26. *upariṣṭopariṣṭāt tu prajvaladbhiḥ svayaṁ-prabhaiḥ*
niruddham etad ākāśam aprameyaṁ surair api

The sky is filled with blazing luminaries situated one above the other in the heavens, each endowed with its own effulgence. It is thus immeasurable even for the gods.

27. *pṛthivyante samudrās tu samudrānte tamaḥ smṛtam*
tamaso 'nte jalaṁ prāhur jalasyānte 'gnir eva ca

At the end of the earth are the oceans and beyond the oceans there is known to be darkness. They say that beyond the darkness there is water again and at the end of this water there is fire.

28. *rasātalānte salilaṁ jalānte pannagādhipaḥ*
tad ante punar ākāśam ākāśānte punar jalam

Beyond the Rasātala, the world below the earth, there is water, and beyond this water resides the lord of the celestial serpents. Beyond this region there is space once again, and at the end of this space there is another body of water.

29. *evam antaṁ bhagavataḥ pramāṇaṁ salilasya ca*
agni-māruta-toyebhyo durjñeyaṁ daivatair api

I have thus described the extent of that exalted Deity and also the calculation for the extent of the ocean. The fire, the air, and the water are difficult even for the gods to comprehend.

30. *agni-māruta-toyānāṁ varṇāḥ kṣiti-talasya ca*
ākāśa-sadṛśā hy ete bhidyante tattva-darśanāt

The nature of fire, wind, and water as well as of the surface of the earth is identical to that of space. They are distinguished through proper understanding of the elements.

31. *paṭhanti caiva munayaḥ śāstreṣu vividheṣu ca*
trai-lokye sāgare caiva pramāṇaṁ vihitaṁ yathā
adṛśyāya tv agamyāya kaḥ pramāṇam udāharet

Learned men read in various sacred texts about the precise dimensions of the three worlds and of the great ocean. But as these cannot be seen or visited, who is there who can properly describe these dimensions?

32. *siddhānāṁ devatānāṁ ca yadā parimitā gatiḥ*
tadā gauṇam anantasya nāmānanteti viśrutam
nāmadheyānurūpasya mānasasya mahātmanaḥ

When the path through the heavens of the perfect beings and the gods is measured, then the nature of the name and form of the infinite one might possibly be known. He is the Supreme Soul, Mānasa, who is known by the name of Ananta.

33. *yadā tu divyaṁ tad rūpaṁ hrasate vardhate punaḥ*
ko 'nyas tad vedituṁ śakto yo 'pi syāt tad vidho 'paraḥ

But as his divine form grows smaller and then expands once again, how then can another being whose existence is inferior truly comprehend it?

34. *tataḥ puṣkarataḥ sṛṣṭaḥ sarva-jño mūrtimān prabhuḥ*
brahmā dharma-mayaḥ pūrvaḥ prajāpatir anuttamaḥ

Endowed with a recognisable form, the omniscient lord was first created from that lotus. He is Brahmā, Prajāpati, in whom dharma resides and who is without equal in the world.

35. *bharadvāja uvāca*
puṣkarād yadi saṁbhūto jyeṣṭhaṁ bhavati puṣkaram
brahmāṇaṁ pūrva-jaṁ cāha bhavān saṁdeha eva me

Bharadvāja said: If Brahmā took birth from the lotus, then the lotus must be the primal object as it was born before him. Please address this doubt of mine.

36. *bhṛgur uvāca*
mānasasyeha yā mūrtir brahmatvaṁ samupāgatā
tasyāsana-vidhānārthaṁ pṛthivī padmam ucyate

Bhṛgu replied: The being identified as Brahmā is the form assumed by Mānasa in this world. The earth, which is described as the lotus flower, exists in order to provide a sitting place for him.

37. *karṇikā tasya padmasya merur gaganam ucchritaḥ*
tasya madhye sthito lokān sṛjate jagataḥ prabhuḥ

As the central stem of that lotus, the mountain known as Meru towers above everything else. From his position on this mountain the lord of the universe creates all its worlds.

Śānti-parvan, Adhyāya 176

The second chapter of the *Bhṛgu-bharadvāja-saṁvāda* continues the previous discussion by focusing on the sequential appearance of the five great elements delineated within the Sāṁkhya system: space, water, air, fire, and earth. It is again noteworthy that the chapter opens with a question from Bharadvāja about how Brahmā creates the living beings who inhabit this world, which receives a reply that relates the creative action of the Deity designated as Mānasa, the primeval Viṣṇu. Hence the indication of the previous chapter is confirmed once more and we are shown that Brahmā is not a Deity distinct from Viṣṇu but is rather a form of Viṣṇu manifest for the purpose of creation.

In response to Bharadvāja's question about the creation of living beings, Bhṛgu says that the Deity first created water, for all living beings depend on water for life, and this water in turn was transformed into earth, the substance of the created world. This initial assertion gives rise to a second question from Bharadvāja about the generation of the great elements, and it is this second inquiry that shapes the content of the remainder of the chapter. Bhṛgu responds by citing a previous occasion on which this subject was considered and how the answer was delivered to ancient *rishis* by a celestial voice. This answer is cited verbatim in the final nine verses of the chapter (9–17) in which we can find no trace of the theism that characterised the first chapter of the *Bhṛgu-bharadvāja-saṁvāda* or the opening verses of the second. In this passage of our text, it is Sāṁkhya that provides the basis for the analysis, though again one would be reluctant to describe the passage as a Sāṁkhya discourse, for it is by no means a systematic exposition.

We are first reminded of the primeval chaos noted in the Vedic account of creation; in this state space alone exists, as was noted in the previous chapter when space was designated as *mahat*, the great element. Within that space water appears, although here there is no indication of any deity who brings about that manifestation – or indeed any sort of cause that sets the process in motion. The movement of water generates a secondary movement in space which forms into the element of air, possessing the quality of sound and filling the space with its movement. When the movements of wind and water come into contact with one another, the friction generates heat and this heat is the element of fire. Then when wind and fire come into contact with water, the cooling process gives rise to earth, perhaps in the manner of lava cooling, and earth forms the basis of the bodies of all living beings. In this way the treatise explains the primal generation of the five great elements, the *mahā-bhūtas* that comprise five of the twenty-four principles in the classical

Sāṁkhya analysis of evolved matter.

At first glance, the account seems to be a statement of the Sāṁkya idea of the elements evolving one from the other, but in fact this is not the case. It is not said that water comes into being by evolving from out of space but rather that water simply appeared within space; similarly, wind does not become manifest from an unevolved existence within water but rather it is produced as a result of the movement of water within space. The same can be said about the appearance of the other two elements: there is little here to indicate an evolutionary theory and in fact the appearance of each of the *mahā-bhūtas* is explained in terms of causality rather than evolution. Hence although it is clear that this account is drawing on principles found within the Sāṁkhya system, we should be a little cautious in concluding that it can properly be described as a Sāṁkhya treatise.

1. *bharadvāja uvāca*
prajā-visargaṁ vividhaṁ kathaṁ sa sṛjate prabhuḥ
meru-madhye sthito brahmā tad brūhi dvija-sattama

Bharadvāja said: O best of Brahmins, please tell me how the mighty Brahmā executed the creation of the diverse kinds of creatures whilst remaining situated in the centre of Mount Meru.

2. *bhṛgur uvāca*
prajā-visargaṁ vividhaṁ mānaso manasāsṛjat
saṁdhukṣaṇārthaṁ bhūtānāṁ sṛṣṭaṁ prathamato jalam

Bhṛgu said: It was with his mind alone that the great Deity known as Mānasa executed the creation of the diverse kinds of creatures. In order for these living beings to live, water was created first of all.

3. *yat prāṇāḥ sarva-bhūtānāṁ vardhante yena ca prajāḥ*
parityaktāś ca naśyanti tenedaṁ sarvam āvṛtam

Water represents life for all living beings, for it is through water that creatures thrive.Those deprived of water meet with destruction and so this whole world is filled with water.

4. *pṛthivī parvatā meghā mūrtimantaś ca ye pare*
sarvaṁ tad vāruṇaṁ jñeyam āpas tastambhire punaḥ

The earth, the mountains, the clouds, and other objects that have recognisable forms are all known to possess liquidity, for water transformed itself into solid forms.

5. *bharadvāja uvāca*
kathaṁ salilam utpannaṁ kathaṁ caivāgni-mārutau
kathaṁ ca medinī sṛṣṭet yatra me saṁśayo mahān

Bharadvāja said: How was this water produced and how were fire and wind brought into being? How was the earth created? Therein lies my great uncertainty.

6. *bhṛgur uvāca*
brahma-kalpe purā brahman brahmarṣīṇāṁ samāgame
loka-saṁbhava-saṁdehaḥ samutpanno mahātmanām

Bhṛgu said: Long ago, O Brahmin, in the era known as the *brahma kalpa*, doubts arose amongst the great persons in an assembly of Brahmin *rishis* concerning the origin of the world.

7. *te 'tiṣṭhan dhyānam ālambya maunam āsthāya niścalāḥ*
tyaktāhārāḥ pavana-pā divyaṁ varṣa-śataṁ dvijāḥ

Remaining in their places, those Brahmins pursued their meditation for one hundred years of the gods, unwavering in their vow of silence, eating nothing at all and consuming air alone.

8. *teṣāṁ dharma-mayī vāṇī sarveṣāṁ śrotram āgamat*
divyā sarasvatī tatra saṁbabhūva nabhas-talāt

Words imbued with dharma then entered the hearing of all of them.
This divine speech appeared there from out of the sky.

9. *purā stimita-niḥśabdam ākāśam acalopamam*
naṣṭa-candrārka-pavanaṁ prasuptam iva saṁbabhau

'In the beginning space existed, still and silent, appearing to be entirely motionless.
At that time there was no sun, no moon, and no wind. It was as if they were all asleep.

10. *tataḥ salilam utpannaṁ tamasīvāparaṁ tamaḥ*
tasmāc ca salilotpīḍād udatiṣṭhata mārutaḥ

Water then came into being as another dark element appearing within the darkness. And from the pressure of the water as it burst forth the wind came into existence.

11. *yathā bhājanam acchidraṁ niḥśabdam iva lakṣyate*
tac cāmbhasā pūryamāṇaṁ saśabdaṁ kurute 'nilaḥ

An unbroken pot appears completely silent. As the wind endows such a pot with sound when it is filled with water,

12. *tathā salila-saṁruddhe nabhaso 'nte nirantare*
bhittvārṇava-talaṁ vāyuḥ samutpatati ghoṣavān

So when the unbounded limits of space are filled with water, the wind arises with a roaring sound bursting through the surface of the ocean.

13. *sa eṣa carate vāyur arṇavotpīḍa-saṁbhavaḥ*
ākāśa-sthānam āsādya praśāntiṁ nādhigacchati

The wind that comes into being due to the compression of the water never remains still as it reaches across the extent of space.

14. *tasmin vāyv-ambu-saṁgharṣe dīpta-tejā mahā-balaḥ*
prādurbhavaty ūrdhva-śikhaḥ kṛtvā vitimiraṁ nabhaḥ

When there is friction between the wind and water, a powerful, blazing light appears that casts its rays upwards and dispels the darkness from the sky.

15. *agniḥ pavana-saṁyuktaḥ khāt samutpatate jalam*
so 'gnir māruta-saṁyogād ghanatvam upapadyate

Combining with the wind, this fire brought space into contact with the water. Because of its combination with the wind, the fire is transformed into a solid state.

16. *tasyākāśe nipatitaḥ snehas tiṣṭhati yo 'paraḥ*
sa saṁghātatvam āpanno bhūmitvam upagacchati

Whilst descending through space that part of fire which remains viscous becomes compressed and in this way fire develops into earth.

17. *rasānāṁ sarva-gandhānāṁ snehānāṁ prāṇināṁ tathā*
bhūmir yonir iha jñeyā yasyāṁ sarvaṁ prasūyate

Earth is recognised as being the origin of all the tastes, aromas, liquids, and living beings that exist in this world. All things arise from the element of earth.'

Śānti-parvan, Adhyāya 177

The third chapter of the *Bhṛgu-bharadvāja-saṁvāda* continues the discussion of the five *mahā-bhūtas* that was begun Chapter 2, expanding upon the previous discussion by showing how each of the elements is related to a particular sense and the object perceived by that sense. Bhṛgu first explains that the designation 'great element' (*mahā-bhūta*) is appropriate because every one of the five is present in the bodily form of every type of living being, both plants and animals. Bharadvāja expresses doubts about this assertion especially with regard to trees, which he regards as being comprised of earth alone and being devoid of the five senses employed by animal and human life. As a result of this expression of doubt, Bhṛgu takes the time to demonstrate that all the *mahā-bhūtas* are present within trees which, moreover, in their own way are able to perceive sounds, forms, tastes, aromas, and touch sensations. Hence the first part of the chapter is given over to demonstrating that the previous assertion of the presence of all elements and all senses in all types of living being can be sustained.

From verse 20, Bhṛgu turns to an analysis of the human body, essentially making the same point that all five of the *mahā-bhūtas* are present in the human form and pointing out where each of them can be identified. Here we see a clear recognition of the Sāṁkhya idea of the relationship between each of the five elements with one of the *tanmātras* (although this term is not used), that is, its specific quality, and the sense faculty that perceives that object. So earth possesses as its quality the *tanmātra* known as aroma, which is perceived by the sense of smell; water possesses as its quality the *tanmātra* of flavour, which is perceived by the sense of taste; fire possesses as its quality the *tanmātra* known as form or colour, which is perceived by the sense of sight; air possesses as its quality the *tanmātra* known as the sensation of touch, which is perceived by the sense of touch; and space possesses as its quality the *tanmātra* known as sound, which is perceived by the sense of hearing. The final section of this third chapter is given over to an analysis of each of the *tanmātras*, breaking them down into the different component parts which may be identified through sensory perception. Again it must be said that this is not at all a straightforward exposition of any Sāṁkhya system, but rather a discussion of the nature of the created world that starts off from a Vaiṣṇava perspective but makes primary use of Sāṁkhya principles in its analysis.

1. *bharadvāja uvāca*
ete te dhātavaḥ pañca brahmā yān asṛjat purā
āvṛtā yair ime lokā mahā-bhūtābhisaṁjñitaiḥ

Bharadvāja said: These worlds consist of those five substances that Brahmā created in the beginning. They are referred to as the *mahā-bhūtas,* the great elements of matter.

2. *yadāsṛjat sahasrāṇi bhūtānāṁ sa mahā-matiḥ*
pañcānām eva bhūtatvaṁ kathaṁ samupapadyate

But as that Deity of vast intellect has created thousands of entities, how is it that only these five possess the status of being the primal elements?

3. *bhṛgur uvāca*
amitānāṁ mahā-śabdo yānti bhūtāni saṁbhavam
tatas teṣāṁ mahā-bhūta-śabdo 'yam upapadyate

Bhṛgu replied: Entities whose existence is without limits attain the title of 'Great'. Hence the title 'Great Elements' applies to these five.

4. *ceṣṭā vāyuḥ kham ākāśam ūṣmāgniḥ salilaṁ dravaḥ*
pṛthivī cātra saṁghātaḥ śarīraṁ pāñca-bhautikam

Internal motions are the wind, space within the body is sky, bodily heat is fire, water is the body fluids, and earth is the solid parts of the body. Hence the body consists of these five elements.

5. *ity etaiḥ pañcabhir bhūtair yuktaṁ sthāvara-jaṅgamam*
śrotraṁ ghrāṇaṁ rasaḥ sparśo dṛṣṭiś cendriya-saṁjñitāḥ

Thus all moving and stationary beings consist of these five elements. Hearing, scent, taste, touch, and sight are known as the senses.

6. *bharadvāja uvāca*
pañcabhir yadi bhūtais tu yuktāḥ sthāvara-jaṅgamāḥ
sthāvarāṇāṁ na dṛśyante śarīre pañca dhātavaḥ

Bharadvāja asked: If both moving and stationary beings consist of the five elements, why are these five constituent parts not visible in the bodies of stationary beings?

7. *anūṣmaṇām aceṣṭānāṁ ghanānāṁ caiva tattvataḥ*
vṛkṣāṇāṁ nopalabhyante śarīre pañca dhātavaḥ

Trees do not possess heat, they have no internal movements, and they are completely solid in form, so five constituent parts are certainly not found in trees.

8. *na śṛṇvanti na paśyanti na gandha-rasa-vedinaḥ*
na ca sparśaṁ vijānanti te kathaṁ pāñca-bhautikāḥ

They cannot hear, they cannot see, they have no perception of aroma or taste, and they have no awareness of touch. How then can they consist of five elements?

9. *adravatvād anagnitvād abhaumatvād avāyutaḥ*
ākāśasyāprameyatvād vṛkṣāṇāṁ nāsti bhautikam

Because they contain no liquid, no fire, no earth, and no air, and because no space can be identified within them, trees cannot be comprised of these elements.

10. *bhṛgur uvāca*
ghanānām api vṛkṣāṇām ākāśo 'sti na saṁśayaḥ
teṣāṁ puṣpa-phale vyaktir nityaṁ samupalabhyate

Bhṛgu replied: Even in the solid forms of trees space is undoubtedly present. Some manifestation of flowers and fruit is always found on trees.

11. *ūṣmato glāna-parṇānāṁ tvak phalaṁ puṣpam eva ca*
mlāyate caiva śītena sparśas tenātra vidyate

The withering of a tree's leaves, as well as the bark, fruit, and flowers, takes place due to intense heat, and the same deterioration occurs because of the cold. From this the presence of the sense of touch can be recognised.

12. *vāyv-agny-aśani-niṣpeṣaiḥ phala-puṣpaṁ viśīryate*
śrotreṇa gṛhyate śabdas tasmāc chṛṇvanti pāda-pāḥ

Fruits and flowers are shed due to the roaring sound of wind, fire, and thunder. Sound is grasped by the sense of hearing. Therefore those living beings that drink through their roots can also hear.

13. *vallī veṣṭayate vṛkṣaṁ sarvataś caiva gacchati*
na hy adṛṣṭeś ca mārgo 'sti tasmāt paśyanti pāda-pāḥ

The creeper wraps itself around the tree, moving here and there in all directions. No such path can be taken by a being that lacks sight. Therefore those living beings that drink through their roots can also see.

14. *puṇyāpuṇyais tathā gandhair dhūpaiś ca vividhair api*
arogāḥ puṣpitāḥ santi tasmāj jighnanti pāda-pāḥ

Trees become free from disease and bear flowers as a result of pleasant and unpleasant aromas and by means of various forms of aromatic incense. Therefore those living beings that drink through their roots can also smell.

15. *pādaiḥ salila-pānaṁ ca vyādhīnām api darśanam*
vyādhi-pratikriyatvāc ca vidyate rasanaṁ drume

It is seen that trees drink water through their roots even from places where the water is contaminated with disease. Because of their ability to resist such diseases it is recognised that the sense of taste exists in a tree.

16. *vaktreṇotpala-nālena yathordhvaṁ jalam ādadet*
tathā pavana-saṁyuktaḥ pādaiḥ pibati pāda-paḥ

A plant uses air to drink water through its roots in the same way as one might suck water into one's mouth with the hollow stem of a lotus.

17. *grahaṇāt sukha-duḥkhasya chinnasya ca virohaṇāt*
jīvaṁ paśyāmi vṛkṣāṇām acaitanyaṁ na vidyate

Because of their experiencing joy and distress and because a severed limb will sprout again, I perceive that there is life in trees. They are not considered to be devoid of consciousness.

18. *tena taj jalam ādattaṁ jarayaty agni-mārutau*
āhāra-parināmāc ca sneho vṛddhaś ca jāyate

A tree digests the water it draws up by means of fire and air. Moistness inside a tree and its continuing growth both take place because of this digestion of food.

19. *jaṅgamānāṁ ca sarveṣāṁ śarīre pañca dhātavaḥ*
pratyekaśaḥ prabhidyante yaiḥ śarīraṁ viceṣṭate

The same five elements occur in the bodies of all moving entities. Each of them is dispersed throughout the body in differing degrees and it is through them that the body performs its actions.

20. *tvak ca māṁsaṁ tathāsthīni majjā snāyu ca pañcamam*
ity etad iha saṁkhyātaṁ śarīre pṛthivī-mayam

The manifestation of earth within the body is analysed as being in five forms, as skin, flesh, bones, marrow, and sinew.

21. *tejo 'gniś ca tathā krodhaś cakṣur ūṣmā tathaiva ca*
agnir jarayate cāpi pañcāgneyāḥ śarīriṇaḥ

Fiery energy, rage, sight, bodily heat, and the fire that digests food constitute the five forms of fire within the body.

22. *śrotraṁ ghrāṇam athāsyaṁ ca hṛdayaṁ koṣṭham eva ca*
ākāśāt prāṇinām ete śarīre pañca dhātavaḥ

The ears, the nostrils, the organ of speech, the heart, and the stomach are five parts of the living being's body that arise from space.

23. *śleṣmā pittam atha svedo vasā śoṇitam eva ca*
ity āpaḥ pañcadhā dehe bhavanti prāṇināṁ sadā

Mucus, bile, sweat, fat, and blood are the five forms of water that always exist in the living being's body.

24. *prāṇāt praṇīyate prāṇī vyānād vyāyacchate tathā*
gacchaty apāno 'vāk caiva samāno hṛdy avasthitaḥ

It is due to the presence of the internal breath known as *prāṇa* that a living being can progress through life and it is due to the *vyāna* breath that it becomes active. The *apāna* moves downwards and the *samāna* is situated in the region of the heart.

25. *udānād ucchvasiti ca pratibhedāc ca bhāṣate*
ity ete vāyavaḥ pañca ceṣṭayantīha dehinam

Due to the *udāna* breath a living being breathes heavily and when the *udāna* is divided a living being makes sounds. These five forms of air enable the living being to become active.

26. *bhūmer gandha-guṇān vetti rasaṁ cādbhyaḥ śarīravān*
jyotiḥ paśyati cakṣurbhyāṁ sparśaṁ vetti ca vāyunā

It is due to earth that an embodied being perceives various types of aroma and because of water it identifies taste. It sees light by means of the eyes and identifies touch through air.

27. *tasya gandhasya vakṣyāmi vistarābhihitān guṇān*
iṣṭaś cāniṣṭa-gandhaś ca madhuraḥ kaṭur eva ca

I shall now present a detailed explanation of the qualities of aroma. An aroma can be pleasant or unpleasant, it can be sweet or it can reek of decay.

28. *nirhārī saṁhataḥ snigdho rūkṣo viśada eva ca*
evaṁ nava-vidho jñeyaḥ pārthivo gandha-vistaraḥ

It can have a fragrance that spreads far and wide, it can be a combination of scents, and it can be mild, pungent, or enticing. In this way nine separate types of aroma are identified, all arising out of the element earth.

29. *śabdaḥ sparśaś ca rūpaṁ ca rasaś cāpāṁ guṇāḥ smṛtāḥ*
rasa-jñānaṁ tu vakṣyāmi tan me nigadataḥ śṛṇu

Sound, touch, form, and flavour are recognised as the qualities inherent in water. I will next impart to you an understanding of flavour, so listen to my words of instruction.

30. *raso bahu-vidhaḥ proktaḥ sūribhiḥ prathitātmabhiḥ*
madhuro lavaṇas tiktaḥ kaṣāyo 'mlaḥ kaṭus tathā
eṣa ṣaḍ-vidha-vistāro raso vārimayaḥ smṛtaḥ

It is said by the foremost amongst learned men that flavour is of many different types. It can be sweet, savoury, bitter, acidic, sour, or rotten. This represents a six-fold analysis of flavour, which is based on the element of water.

31. *śabdaḥ sparśaś ca rūpaṁ ca tri-guṇaṁ jyotir ucyate*
jyotiḥ paśyati rūpāṇi rūpaṁ ca bahudhā smṛtam

Light is described as possessing three qualities, identified as sound, touch, and form. It is light that sees forms and form is recognised as being of many different types.

32. *hrasvo dīrghas tathā sthūlaś catur-asro 'ṇu vṛttavān*
śuklaḥ kṛṣṇas tathā rakto nīlaḥ pīto 'ruṇas tathā
evaṁ dvādaśa-vistāro jyotī-rūpa-guṇaḥ smṛtaḥ

It can be short or long, large, rectangular, minute, or round. It can be light or dark, red, blue, yellow, or pink. This represents a twelve-fold analysis; light is known to have form as its inherent quality.

33. *śabda-sparśau tu vijñeyau dvi-guṇo vāyur ucyate*
vāyavyas tu guṇaḥ sparśaḥ sparśaś ca bahudhā smṛtaḥ

Now it is said that sound and touch should be recognised as the two qualities possessed by air. Touch, however, is the specific quality related to air and touch is known to be of many different types.

34. *kaṭhinaś cikkaṇaḥ ślakṣṇaḥ picchalo mṛdu-dāruṇaḥ*
uṣṇaḥ śītaḥ sukho duḥkhaḥ snigdho viśada eva ca
evaṁ dvādaśa-vistāro vāyavyo guṇa ucyate

It can be rough, smooth, soft, slippery, gentle, or hard. It can be hot, cold, pleasing, painful, moist, or tender. This represents a twelve-fold analysis of the quality that is referred to as having air as its basis.

35. *tatraika-guṇaṁ ākāśaṁ śabda ity eva tat smṛtam*
tasya śabdasya vakṣyāmi vistaraṁ vividhātmakam

In the same way, space possesses just one quality and that is known to be sound. I shall now present an analysis of the various types of sound.

36. *ṣaḍja ṛṣabha-gāndhārau madhyamaḥ pañcamas tathā*
dhaivataś cāpi vijñeyas tathā cāpi niṣādakaḥ

These are known as *ṣaḍja*, *ṛṣabha*, *gāndhāra*, *madhyama*, *pañcama*, *dhaivata*, and *niṣādaka* – the notes of the musical scale.

37. *eṣa sapta-vidhaḥ prokto guṇa ākāśa-lakṣaṇaḥ*
traisvaryeṇa tu sarvatra sthito 'pi paṭahādiṣu

This is referred to as the seven-fold division of sound, which is the quality that distinguishes space. By means of the three accents these are present everywhere but especially in drums and other musical instruments.

38. *ākāśa-jaṁ śabdam āhur ebhir vāyu-guṇaiḥ saha*
avyāhataiś cetayate na vetti viṣam āgataiḥ

They say that sound is produced from space. One can perceive sound when it exists in a state of equilibrium with the qualities of air. When these qualities of touch are not active one cannot perceive the sound.

39. *āpyāyante ca te nityaṁ dhātavas tais tu dhātubhiḥ*
āpo 'gnir mārutaś caiva nityaṁ jāgrati dehiṣu

Each of these elements will always become more pronounced when combining with the other elements. Water, fire, and air are always active within the embodied living beings.

Śānti-parvan, Adhyāya 178

At the beginning of the fourth chapter of the *Bhṛgu-bharadvāja-saṁvāda*, Bharadvāja asks for further elaboration of some of the information imparted in the previous chapter. There we were informed about the presence of the five *mahā-bhūtas* within all bodies and specifically within the body of a tree and within the human body. Here in the opening verse, Bharadvāja asks for more information about the presence of air and fire in the human body as was briefly mentioned in verse 21 and verses 24 and 25 of Chapter 3. As a result, the whole of this chapter is devoted to a short discourse relating to the presence and activity of these two elements in the body. The first part of the chapter discusses the function of the five airs within the body, the *prāṇa*, *samāna*, *apāna*, *udāna*, and *vyāna*. *Prāṇa* is proclaimed to be the life of the living being, in line with the teachings of Chapter 3 of the *Praśna Upaniṣad*. The *ātman* is the life of the body and because life is dependent upon breathing, the *prāṇa* breath is equated with life and with the eternal *ātman*.

From verse 9, Bhṛgu moves on to consider the presence of fire within the body. Fire exists in conjunction with the bodily airs by means of which its heat is transported to the various limbs and organs. It is even suggested in verse 12 that it is friction created by contact between the different airs that generates the bodily heat, which then remains present within the airs. The primary function of the fiery element within the body is the digestion of food; this is an important element in the *āyurveda* teachings on maintaining the health of the body. Here the discussion moves into the realm of Indian anatomy and indeed the Haṭha Yoga system described in some of the tantric works. The relationship with Yoga is made explicit in verse 16 – an interesting reference to note. As a general rule, the Yoga discourses found in the *Mahābhārata* and the *Bhagavad-gītā* are closely related to the ideas of Patañjali in the *Yoga-sūtras* with the emphasis on internal meditation and the realisation of the *ātman*. The tantric ideas of the Haṭha Yoga system are more concerned with a transformation of the body than the realisation that the true self is distinct from the body, and it is often thought that these are from a later date as they are almost entirely ignored by Patañjali.

1. *bharadvāja uvāca*
pārthivaṁ dhātum āśritya śārīro 'gniḥ kathaṁ bhavet
avakāśa-viśeṣeṇa kathaṁ vartayate 'nilaḥ

Bharadvāja said: How does fire exist within the body, attaching itself to the solid substance comprised of earth? How does air cause the body to become active by means of the specific location it finds?

2. *bhṛgur uvāca*
vāyor gatim ahaṁ brahman kīrtayiṣyāmi te 'nagha
prāṇinām anilo dehān yathā ceṣṭayate balī

Bhṛgu said: O pure-hearted Brahmin, I shall now instruct you about the movement of the wind and the way in which this powerful element of air causes the bodies of living beings to become active.

3. *śrito mūrdhānam agnis tu śarīraṁ paripālayan*
prāṇo mūrdhani cāgnau ca vartamāno viceṣṭate

Now the form of fire that exists in the head has the function of sustaining the body. The *prāṇa* air in the head exists within this fire and makes the body move.

4. *sa jantuḥ sarva-bhūtātmā puruṣaḥ sa sanātanaḥ*
mano buddhir ahaṁkāro bhūtāni viṣayāś ca saḥ

That *prāṇa* is the actual living entity, the true *ātman* of all beings, the eternal *puruṣa*. It is the mind, the intellect, self-awareness, the material elements, and the objects of sensory perception connected to each of them.

5. *evaṁ tv iha sa sarvatra prāṇena paripālyate*
pṛṣṭhataś ca samānena svāṁ svāṁ gatim upāśritaḥ

In this way, as each living being pursues its own movement it is sustained by the *prāṇa*, and from behind by the *samāna* air as well, as each (sense) attaches itself to its own object.

6. *vasti-mūlaṁ gudaṁ caiva pāvakaṁ ca samāśritaḥ*
vahan mūtraṁ purīṣaṁ cāpy apānaḥ parivartate

Operating in conjunction with fire, the *apāna* has the function of carrying urine and stool to the aperture of the bladder and to the anus respectively.

7. *prayatne karmaṇi bale ya ekas triṣu vartate*
udāna iti taṁ prāhur adhyātma-viduṣo janāḥ

One of the internal airs is present in three distinct functions, in physical exertion, in performing action, and in bodily strength. Persons who comprehend the science of *adhyātma* refer to this air as the *udāna*.

8. *saṁdhiṣv api ca sarveṣu saṁniviṣṭas tathānilaḥ*
śarīreṣu manuṣyāṇāṁ vyāna ity upadiśyate

The air present in all the joints of the bodies of human beings is identified as the *vyāna*.

9. *dhātuṣv agnis tu vitataḥ samānena samīritaḥ*
rasān dhātūṁś ca doṣāṁś ca vartayann avatiṣṭhati

Fire is spread throughout the other elements in the body by the *samāna* air. Thus pervading the body, this heat operates on the liquid and solid substances and on the bodily humours as well.

10. *apāna-prāṇayor madhye prāṇāpāna-samāhitaḥ*
samanvitaḥ svadhiṣṭhānaḥ samyak pacati pāvakaḥ

Fire exists in the midst of the *prāṇa* and the *apāna* and combines itself with them. When it is properly situated, it acts in conjunction with these airs to digest the food a person consumes.

11. *āsyaṁ hi pāyu-saṁyuktam ante syād guda-saṁjñitam*
srotas tasmāt prajāyante sarva-srotāṁsi dehinām

There is a passage connecting the mouth to the anus, the end of which is called the rectum. All the other channels within the body originate from this passage.

12. *prāṇānāṁ saṁnipātāc ca saṁnipātaḥ prajāyate*
ūṣmā cāgnir iti jñeyo yo 'nnaṁ pacati dehinām

When there is contact between them, a mingling of the bodily airs takes place. This merging together is known as the *ūṣman*, the fire within the body that digests the food consumed by embodied beings.

13. *agni-vega-vahaḥ prāṇo gudānte pratihanyate*
sa ūrdhvam āgamya punaḥ samutkṣipati pāvakam

The *prāṇa* air that bears the movement of fire within the body turns back at the end of the rectum. Returning upwards again, it carries that fire up with it.

14. *pakvāśayas tv adho nābher ūrdhvam āmāśayaḥ sthitaḥ*
nābhi-madhye śarīrasya sarve prāṇāḥ samāhitāḥ

The area of the body that contains digested food lies below the navel whilst the place for undigested food is above it. All the airs found in the body gather together within the navel.

15. *prasṛtā hṛdayāt sarve tiryag ūrdhvam adhas tathā*
vahanty anna-rasān nāḍyo daśa prāṇa-pracoditāḥ

Impelled by these ten airs, the veins carry the liquids derived from food to all parts of the body, spreading out from the heart crossways, upwards and downwards.

16. *eṣa mārgo 'tha yogānāṁ yena gacchanti tat padam*
jita-klamāsanā dhīrā mūrdhany ātmānam ādadhuḥ

This is the path utilised in the Yoga systems through which practitioners attain the position they seek. By mastering very difficult sitting postures, steadfast sages transfer the *ātman* along this path to the region of the head.

17. *evaṁ sarveṣu vihitaḥ prāṇāpāneṣu dehinām*
tasmin sthito nityam agniḥ sthālyām iva samāhitaḥ

It is in this way that fire is distributed within all the *prāṇa* and *apāna* airs in the body of an embodied being. Fire is always present within the body, just as fire is contained in an earthen vessel

Śānti-parvan, Adhyāya 179

The fifth chapter of the *Bhṛgu-bharadvāja-saṁvāda* is unusual in that Bharadvāja is the sole speaker as he expresses to Bhṛgu the doubts that have arisen as a result of the previous exposition. Up until this point, Bhṛgu has focused on the Sāṁkhya analysis of the nature of matter as it is found in the bodies of living beings, pointing out how the five *mahā-bhūtas* and the five senses are universally present. Now Bharadvāja seeks to take the discussion on to the next stage by asking about the presence of a transcendent element within the body, which he refers to here as the *jīva*. Classical Sāṁkhya presents an analysis of matter in twenty-four distinct categories and then attempts to show that the true self that brings life to matter is of a wholly different substance that is non-material. We might refer to this as the soul of a living being, which is usually designated as *puruṣa* or *ātman*.

In the last chapter Bhṛgu explained that the life of a living being is located within the *prāṇa* breath and that the body functions and retains its living nature through the interaction of the material elements it contains. Here Bharadvāja observes that this explanation appears to rule out the presence of any higher entity within the body, for its functioning and living existence has been explained entirely in terms of material elements. If the *jīva* soul were present within the *prāṇa* then it could not transmigrate into another body, for when death occurs the air within the body is merged back into the totality of air, and so the *jīva* existing within it would cease to have any specific location. It has been explained that life and death are entirely contingent on the interaction of the five *mahā-bhūtas* and this being so then the idea of a soul becomes unnecessary and irrelevant, for life can be explained entirely in material terms. This assertion in turn undermines fundamental principles of religious ideology, such as the transmigration of the soul, the doctrine of karma, and the efficacy of ritual acts. It is understood that the gift of a cow in charity is a righteous act that will bring good fortune to the giver in a future existence, but if life is understood purely as an interaction of material elements then there can be no possibility of any such future rewards, for death brings about the wholesale dissolution of those elements.

Here Bharadvāja is referring to the rationalist perspective, pointing out that if life can be defined in purely material terms then the very notion of a transcendent soul is redundant; I think we may be sure that this type of scepticism was widely current at the time of the composition of our text. It is interesting to note that Bharadvāja does not seek to include the Vedic revelation within the discourse by citing scripture as evidence to be included in the debate. Bhṛgu has structured his presentation entirely on the basis of rational insights and Bharadvāja here uses the same perspective in expressing doubts about the existence of the soul. Furthermore, it may be that Bharadvāja's point about the doctrine of karma and rebirth is something of a critique of Buddhist ideas, for Buddhism teaches a doctrine of karma but denies the existence of the transcendent *ātman*. Bharadvāja seems to have detected in Bhṛgu's previous presentation a statement of the Buddhist doctrine of *anātman* and his words represent a standard critique of that idea. The final five verses of this chapter could hence be taken as a rejection of the doctrine of *anātman* by suggesting that if there is no transmigration of the *ātman* to another bodily form then the whole notion of experiencing the results of previous acts is meaningless.

1. *bharadvāja uvāca*
yadi prāṇāyate vāyur vāyur eva viceṣṭate
śvasity ābhāṣate caiva tasmāj jīvo nirarthakaḥ

Bharadvāja said: If it is air that animates a living being, if it is air alone that is the source of its movement, and if it is air that respires and air that produces speech, then the notion of the *jīva* is meaningless.

2. *yady ūṣma-bhāva āgneyo vahninā pacyate yadi*
agnir jarayate caiva tasmāj jīvo nirarthakaḥ

If the existence of heat within the body is derived from the fire element, if food is broken down by fire, and if it is fire that causes the food to be digested, then the notion of the *jīva* is meaningless.

3. *jantoḥ pramīyamāṇasya jīvo naivopalabhyate*
vāyur eva jahāty enam ūṣma-bhāvaś ca naśyati

No *jīva* is ever perceived when the life of a living being comes to an end. Rather it is air alone that comes out from the corpse, and the existence of fire is extinguished.

4. *yadi vātopamo jīvaḥ saṁśleṣo yadi vāyunā*
vāyu-maṇḍalavad dṛśyo gacchet saha marud-gaṇaiḥ

If the *jīva* is nothing but air or if it exists in conjunction with air, then it would be visible like a swirling wind and would move across the earth in the company of the various winds that blow here.

5. *śleṣo yadi ca vātena yadi tasmāt praṇaśyati*
mahārṇava-vimuktatvād anyat-salila-bhājanam

Furthermore, if life existed in a state of union with air and then became separated from it, the *jīva* would be like a drop of water becoming separated from the ocean and then becoming a part of another body of water.

6. *kūpe vā salilaṁ dadyāt pradīpaṁ vā hutāśane*
prakṣiptaṁ naśyati kṣipraṁ yathā naśyaty asau tathā

In such circumstances the *jīva* would disappear, just as a drop of water that is put into a well or a flame put on a larger fire cease to exist as soon as they are cast there.

7. *pañca-sādhāraṇe hy asmiñ śarīre jīvitaṁ kutaḥ*
yeṣām anyatara-tyāgāc caturṇāṁ nāsti saṁgrahaḥ

How can there truly be a life element within a body that is five-fold in substance? When any one of them becomes separated from the whole, then the other four can no longer sustain their combined existence.

8. *naśyanty āpo hy anāhārād vāyur ucchvāsa-nigrahāt*
naśyate koṣṭha-bhedāt kham agnir naśyaty abhojanāt

Water disappears when it is no longer replenished and air is destroyed when breathing is restricted. Space is destroyed when the bowels cannot be evacuated and the fire in the body dwindles as a result of starvation.

9. *vyādhi-vraṇa-parikleśair medinī caiva śīryate*
pīḍite 'nyatare hy eṣāṁ saṁghāto yāti pañcadhā

Earth is destroyed by the afflictions of disease and injury. When one of these bodily substances is reduced in this way, their combination is dissolved and they become five separate entities once more.

10. *tasmin pañcatvam āpanne jīvaḥ kim anudhāvati*
kiṁ vedayati vā jīvaḥ kiṁ śṛṇoti bravīti vā

When the body dissolves into its five constituent parts, what course does the *jīva* then pursue? What does the *jīva* understand then, what does it hear and what does it say?

11. *eṣā gauḥ para-loka-sthaṁ tārayiṣyati mām iti*
yo dattvā mriyate jantuḥ sā gauḥ kaṁ tārayiṣyati

It is said that when I reach the other world this cow will be the cause of my deliverance. But after making the gift the living being then dies, so what will the cow grant deliverance to?

12. *gauś ca pratigrahītā ca dātā caiva samaṁ yadā*
ihaiva vilayaṁ yānti kutas teṣāṁ samāgamaḥ

When the receiver of the cow and the giver are equal in this world in that they must both meet with annihilation, how can there be any possibility of their subsequent reunion?

13. *vihagair upayuktasya śailāgrāt patitasya vā*
agninā copayuktasya kutaḥ saṁjīvanaṁ punaḥ

How can life ever return when one's body has been devoured by birds or fallen from the top of a mountain or been consumed by fire?

14. *chinnasya yadi vṛkṣasya na mūlaṁ pratirohati*
bījāny asya pravartante mṛtaḥ kva punar eṣyati

When the root of a tree is severed, its root will not grow back again. The new growth comes from the seeds alone, so where has the entity that has died gone?

15. *bīja-mātraṁ purā sṛṣṭaṁ yad etat parivartate*
mṛtā mṛtāḥ praṇaśyanti bījād bījaṁ pravartate

In the beginning, only the original seed of life was created and this developed into the world we see around us. All things that die meet with complete destruction and each seed of life emerges from a previous seed.

Śānti-parvan, Adhyāya 180

The sixth chapter provides a conclusion to the first section of the *Bhṛgu-bharadvāja-saṁvāda* and it is here finally that the discussion moves away from its focus on the material workings of the body and considers the existence of a transcendent soul. This, of course, is in line with the Sāṁkhya revelation that the *puruṣa* is the source of life and is entirely distinct from the elements into which *prakṛti* evolves. However, it takes a little while and some persistent prompting from Bharadvāja before Bhṛgu is finally persuaded to move on to this topic. In Chapter 5, Bharadvāja expressed a series of doubts as to how the concept of a transcendent soul could be reconciled with Bhṛgu's previous discourse on the manner in which the great elements sustain life within the body. Chapter 6 opens with Bhṛgu giving the briefest of responses to these doubts, an answer that is nothing more than an assertion that there is a soul that survives the death of the body.

Apparently not satisfied with this response, Bharadvāja continues to pursue his theme, first questioning the validity of the metaphor Bhṛgu has employed to demonstrate the continued existence of the soul after death. Bhṛgu again asserts the point that the soul transcends the death of the body but quickly moves back to his previous line of discussion, which focused primarily on the elements within the body and the way in which they sustain the life of the living being. It almost seems that Bhṛgu is reluctant to embrace Bharadvāja's interest in a more spiritual line of discussion and it is only after the latter reasserts his doubts that Bhṛgu finally delivers a meaningful consideration of the element of life that is distinct from the material faculties.

Bhṛgu then confirms the Sāṁkhya perspective on the transcendence of the soul, which is here designated by the terms *ātman*, *jīva*, and *kṣetrajña*. Is there any distinction between what is designated as *ātman* and *jīva* respectively? One might suggest that the term *jīva* refers to the *ātman* in association with the subtle body of mind, intellect, and ego, but there is no overt statement to confirm this and in the final verses the terms *ātman* and *jīva* appear to be used interchangeably. This *ātman* is the life of the living being. It is entirely distinct from the five *mahā-bhūtas*; when the body dies it moves on to another birth. Even here the discourse on the nature of the self is notably brief and is concluded by verse 26. The remainder of the chapter gives us an interesting suggestion that although the *ātman* is by nature beyond the range of sensory perception it can be perceived through the techniques of Yoga practice. No detail of this practice is given here and this is certainly not one of the *Mokṣa-dharma-parvan*'s Yoga discourses, but from the information that is included it is possible to infer that the techniques indicated here are approximate to the meditational practices suggested in the sixth chapter of the *Bhagavad-gītā*, whereby the external perception is stilled and a path of internal perception pursued until one gains direct awareness of the true self within. In the final verse we are returned to the idea that the original Deity, Mānasa or Viṣṇu, is identical with this innermost *ātman*. The theistic tendency of this passage stands in contrast to the teachings of classical Sāṁkhya but is again congruent with the ideas found within the *Bhagavad-gītā* and some other passages of the *Mokṣa-dharma-parvan* (for example, Chapters 290 and 306).

These final twelve verses of this sixth chapter conclude the first section of the *Bhṛgu-bharadvāja-saṁvāda*. It is noteworthy that although the treatise as a whole has formed something approximating to a Sāṁkhya discourse there is no soteriological conclusion; Bhṛgu refrains from drawing any link between an understanding of the knowledge of the *jīva* he has now revealed and the attainment of liberation from the cycle of rebirth. Certainly within the *Mokṣa-dharma-parvan* this omission must be regarded as unusual, and it does serve to reinforce our impression that the main interest of the composer of this work is anatomical rather than spiritual and is primarily concerned with providing an explanation of the functioning of the material body in relation to the presence of the five *mahā-bhūtas*. From this point onwards, the discussion changes direction entirely and becomes focused on the lifestyle of human beings. Hence it might seem reasonable to regard these first six chapters as a work in their own right, a work that employs Sāṁkhya concepts in order to provide the reader with some explanation of the functioning of the material body whilst simultaneously acknowledging that the ultimate source of life is the transcendent *ātman*.

1. *bhṛgur uvāca*
na praṇāśo 'sti jīvānāṁ dattasya ca kṛtasya ca
yāti dehāntaraṁ prāṇī śarīraṁ tu viśīryate

Bhṛgu said: Living entities are never destroyed and neither are their acts of charity or the deeds they perform. The living being proceeds to a different body whilst the body it inhabited meets with destruction.

2. *na śarīrāśrito jīvas tasmin naṣṭe praṇaśyati*
yathā samitsu dagdhāsu na praṇaśyati pāvakaḥ

The *jīva* existing within the body is not destroyed when the body is destroyed, just as the fire present in wood is not destroyed when the wood is burnt.

3. *bharadvāja uvāca*
agner yathā tathā tasya yadi nāśo na vidyate
indhanasyopayogānte na cāgnir nopalabhyate

Bharadvāja said: If the premise that no destruction of the *jīva* can occur is based on equivalence to the indestructible quality of fire, it is to be noted that when its consumption of fuel is complete fire is no longer present.

4. *naśyatīty eva jānāmi śāntam agnim anindhanam*
gatir yasya pramāṇaṁ vā saṁsthānaṁ vā na dṛśyate

I define fire that is extinguished and devoid of fuel as 'ceased to exist', for its movements, its dimensions, and its location can no longer be observed.

5. *bhṛgur uvāca*
samidhām upayogānte sann evāgnir na dṛśyate
ākāśānugatatvād dhi durgrahaḥ sa nirāśrayaḥ

Bhṛgu said: It is indeed the case that fire is no longer visible after its consumption of the fuel. It then has no permanent station and because of its being absorbed into space, it is impossible to detect.

6. *tathā śarīra-saṁtyāge jīvo hy ākāśavat sthitaḥ*
na gṛhyate susūkṣmatvād yathā jyotir na saṁśayaḥ

In the same way, the *jīva* exists as space when it leaves the body. Just as fire cannot be perceived because of its extremely subtle nature, so the departed soul cannot be perceived. Of this there is no doubt.

7. *prāṇān dhārayate hy agniḥ sa jīva upadhāryatām*
vāyu-saṁdhāraṇo hy agnir naśyaty ucchvāsa-nigrahāt

It is heat that sustains life in living beings and this heat should be understood as the *jīva*. The fire that sustains the bodily air perishes when the breathing process is constrained.

8. *tasmin naṣṭe śarīrāgnau śarīraṁ tad acetanam*
patitaṁ yāti bhūmitvaṁ ayanaṁ tasya hi kṣitiḥ

When the heat of the body is thus extinguished the body itself becomes lifeless. It falls down and becomes earth in quality, with the soil of the earth its resting place.

9. *jaṅgamānāṁ hi sarveṣāṁ sthāvarāṇāṁ tathaiva ca*
ākāśaṁ pavano 'bhyeti jyotis tam anugacchati
tatra trayāṇām ekatvaṁ dvayaṁ bhūmau pratiṣṭhitam

The air present in the bodies of all moving and stationary beings then enters space and the body's fire enters the air. Hence the three elements exist in a state of unity as the other two are absorbed into earth.

10. *yatra khaṁ tatra pavanas tatrāgnir yatra mārutaḥ*
amūrtayas te vijñeyā āpo mūrtās tathā kṣitiḥ

Wherever there is space there is also air and wherever air is found there is also fire.These elements are known to be formless whilst water is endowed with form and so is earth.

11. *bharadvāja uvāca*
yady agni-mārutau bhūmiḥ kham āpaś ca śarīriṣu
jīvaḥ kiṁ lakṣaṇas tatrety etad ācakṣva me 'nagha

Bharadvāja said: If fire, air, earth, space, and water are the substances present in all bodies, what indication is there of the existence of the *jīva*? Explain this to me, O sinless one.

12. *pañcātmake pañca-ratau pañca-vijñāna-saṁyute*
śarīre prāṇināṁ jīvaṁ jñātum icchāmi yādṛśam

The body of a living being consists of five primary elements, offers five forms of pleasure, and has a combination of five modes of perception, but I wish to understand the nature of the *jīva* that exists within such a body.

13. *māṁsa-śoṇita-saṁghāte medaḥ-snāyv-asthi-saṁcaye*
bhidyamāne śarīre tu jīvo naivopalabhyate

The body also consists of a combination of flesh and blood, as well as fat, sinews, and bone. But when such a body is dissected no trace of the *jīva* is ever found.

14. *yady ajīvaṁ śarīraṁ tu pañca-bhūta-samanvitam*
śārīre mānase duḥkhe kas tāṁ vedayate rujam

However, if the body, which is made up of five primary substances, does not also possess a *jīva*, what is it that actually experiences the affliction when one undergoes physical or mental pain?

15. *śṛṇoti kathitaṁ jīvaḥ karṇābhyāṁ na śṛṇoti tat*
maharṣe manasi vyagre tasmāj jīvo nirarthakaḥ

The *jīva* hears what someone is saying by means of the ears, but if the mind is distracted, O mighty *rishi*, no hearing takes place. Therefore the notion of a *jīva* is meaningless.

16. *sarvaṁ paśyati yad dṛśyaṁ mano-yuktena cakṣuṣā*
manasi vyākule tad dhi paśyann api na paśyati

When the eyes act in conjunction with the mind, the *jīva* sees everything that is visible. But again, if the mind is preoccupied then even though it is looking at something it does not see it.

17. *na paśyati na ca brūte na śṛṇoti na jighrati*
na ca sparśa-rasau vetti nidrā-vaśa-gataḥ punaḥ

And when it has fallen under the power of sleep the *jīva* cannot see, speak, hear, smell, or perceive sensations of touch or taste.

18. *hṛṣyati krudhyati ca kaḥ śocaty udvijate ca kaḥ*
icchati dhyāyati dveṣṭi vācam īrayate ca kaḥ

So what is it that actually experiences the sensations of joy and anger? What is it that feels grief and fear? What is it that has desires, thinks, hates, and enunciates words?

19. *bhṛgur uvāca*
na pañca-sādhāraṇam atra kiṁcic
charīram eko vahate 'ntarātmā
sa vetti gandhāṁś ca rasāñ śrutiṁ ca
sparśaṁ ca rūpaṁ ca guṇāś ca ye 'nye

Bhṛgu said: What you are inquiring about does not share the same five elements for it is the *ātman* within, standing alone, that sustains the body. It is that *ātman* which perceives aromas, tastes, sound, touch, and form in their various manifestations.

20. *pañcātmake pañca-guṇa-pradarśī*
sa sarva-gātrānugato 'ntarātmā
sa vetti duḥkhāni sukhāni cātra
tad viprayogāt tu na vetti dehaḥ

The innermost *ātman* is present in all the different parts of this body of five substances as the seer of their five qualities. It is the *ātman* that is conscious of the pains and pleasures of this world, for the body no longer perceives these sensations when it is separated from the *ātman*.

21. *yadā na rūpaṁ na sparśo noṣma-bhāvaś ca pāvake*
tadā śānte śarīrāgnau dehaṁ tyaktvā sa naśyati

When its colour fades, the sense of touch disappears, and no heat remains in its fire, a living being meets with destruction and its fire is extinguished, for the *ātman* has abandoned that body.

22. *ammayaṁ sarvam evedaṁ āpo mūrtiḥ śarīriṇām*
tatrātmā mānaso brahmā sarva-bhūteṣu loka-kṛt

This entire world is formed from water alone, for water gives form to the embodied being. Within such forms is the *ātman*, which is the Deity named Mānasa who becomes Brahmā, the creator of the world, and is present in all beings.

23. *ātmānaṁ taṁ vijānīhi sarva-loka-hitātmakam*
tasmin yaḥ saṁśrito dehe hy ab-bindur iva puṣkare

You should know this as the *ātman*, as that which maintains the wellbeing of the entire world. It is situated within this body like a drop of water resting on a lotus flower.

24. *kṣetra-jñaṁ taṁ vijānīhi nityaṁ loka-hitātmakam*
tamo rajaś ca sattvaṁ ca viddhi jīva-guṇān imān

You should understand it as the *kṣetrajña*, as that which constantly maintains the wellbeing of the world. You should also know *tamas*, *rajas*, and *sattva* as the qualities that attach themselves to the *jīva*.

25. *sacetanaṁ jīva-guṇaṁ vadanti*
sa ceṣṭate ceṣṭayate ca sarvam
tataḥ paraṁ kṣetra-vidaṁ vadanti
prāvartayad yo bhuvanāni sapta

They say that possession of consciousness is the quality that characterises the *jīva* and that the *jīva* is itself active and activates all things. They also assert that beyond the *jīva* is that which knows the *kṣetras* (bodies), that which originally set the seven worlds of this creation in motion.

26. *na jīva-nāśo 'sti hi deha-bhede*
mithyaitad āhur mṛta ity abuddhāḥ
jīvas tu dehāntaritaḥ prayāti
daśārdhataivāsya śarīra-bhedaḥ

The *jīva* is not destroyed when the body disintegrates, but persons lacking in intelligence present a false conclusion by arguing, 'It is indeed dead.' In fact, the *jīva* within the body moves on whilst the body itself disintegrates and dissolves back into the five primary elements.

27. *evaṁ sarveṣu bhūteṣu gūḍhaś carati saṁvṛtaḥ*
dṛśyate tv agryayā buddhyā sūkṣmayā tattva-darśibhiḥ

The *jīva* exists in this way within all living beings, concealed and covered over. When, however, those who understand the truth attain a more subtle and elevated state of awareness, they can then perceive the *jīva*.

28. *taṁ pūrvāpara-rātreṣu yuñjānaḥ satataṁ budhaḥ*
laghvāhāro viśuddhātmā paśyaty ātmānam ātmani

The man of wisdom who applies himself to this endeavour every day at dusk and daybreak, eating only a small amount and maintaining inner purity, perceives the *ātman* within his own being.

29. *cittasya ca prasādena hitvā karma śubhāśubham*
prasannātmātmani sthitvā sukham akṣayam aśnute

Removing the reactions to one's righteous and wicked deeds by purifying the mind and then fixing that pacified mind on the *ātman*, one attains a joy that never fades.

30. *mānaso 'gniḥ śarīreṣu jīva ity abhidhīyate*
sṛṣṭiḥ prajāpater eṣā bhūtādhyātma-viniścaye

The Deity named Mānasa who is the heat within all bodies is referred to as the *jīva*. When one reaches a true understanding of the spiritual identity of living beings then one understands that the creation of the world arises from that same Prajāpati.

Śānti-parvan, Adhyāya 181

The radical change in the subject of debate that we can observe from this point onwards might suggest that the *Bhṛgu-bharadvāja-saṁvāda* is in fact a conflation and re-editing of two previous works, one on the presence of the elements in the body and the other on the *varṇāśrama* system of social organisation. Of course, any such idea can only be a conjecture, but the change in style we see here, with the introduction of lengthy prose passages, might serve to strengthen that view. In this second phase of our work, Bhṛgu provides Bharadvāja with an explanation, firstly, of the four *varṇas* or social classes and, secondly, of the four *āśramas* or stages of life through which an individual should ideally pass. Some link with the previous discussion is provided at the start of Chapter 7 through the theme of creation. The first discourse began with Viṣṇu's manifestation of the *mahā-bhūtas* (earth, water, air, fire, and space); our second section begins with reference to the secondary creation in which the living beings are created on the basis of these *mahā-bhūtas*. Inherent within the creation of human beings is the primeval division into *varṇa* and *āśrama* and from this introduction the discussion pursues this idea in depth. Chapters 7 and 8 consider the *varṇas*, Chapter 9 describes the importance of adhering to this *dharma*, and Chapters 10 and 11 discuss the four *āśramas*. There are some minor distractions from this central theme, but it is this topic of *varṇa* and *āśrama* that dominates this second phase of our text.

As noted above, Chapter 7 opens with a return to the subject of creation. Here we notice that Viṣṇu (Mānasa) is not mentioned, for after manifesting the primal elements and bringing Brahmā into being, the Supreme Deity withdraws and allows his Brahmā expansion to execute the secondary creation. It is now that the different types of living entity are generated; in terms of human society this includes the four *varṇas*: the Brahmins, *kṣatriyas*, *vaiśyas*, and *śūdras*. It is well known that the word *varṇa* literally means colours or shades and it has sometimes been suggested that this is due to a connection between social class and race in early Indian society. Here, however, it seems clear that the idea of colour has nothing to do with race, as the colour in question seems to be a metaphorical representation of the inner qualities of the individuals in each of the groups. The question that arises from the *varṇa* designations is over the extent of the differences between them. Are they wholly distinct orders of humanity or does the commonality of that humanity transcend the inherent class divisions? This is the point that Bharadvāja raises in verses 6 to 9 and it is clear that he is dubious about the implications of the idea that the *varṇa* divisions exist as an integral feature of the created world. Hence his point is that the members of these different groups cannot be so different from one another because their common humanity far outweighs any apparent differences we might perceive between the groupings.

In effect Bhṛgu accepts the point Bharadvāja has made and in the process he seems to backtrack somewhat on his previous statement that it was Brahmā who created the *varṇas* when the world began. We now read that in fact all humans were originally created as Brahmins but, because of different types of deviation from brahminical conduct, the three other classes came into being at a subsequent stage. Hence Bharadvāja's assertion concerning the commonality of human existence is broadly accepted; the *varṇas* are different from one another but the differences are more superficial than integral. It may well be that the statement that the first human beings were all Brahmins relates to the creation of the seven *rishis* who were born from the mind of Brahmā as his first creative act. These seven were all Brahmins but were the progenitors of different types of human being, including those whose deviations from the required standard led to them being classified amongst the three lower *varṇas*. All four of the social classes originally had access to the Veda and lived their lives according to Vedic regulation. However, the conclusion of the chapter informs us that there are others who live outside any such injunction and are wholly independent of the Vedic rule; it is made quite clear that all such living beings are of a degraded and sinful nature in a manner that possibly suggests the notion of outcasting that emerges in later Hindu thought.

1. *bhṛgur uvāca*
asṛjad brāhmaṇān eva pūrvaṁ brahmā prajāpatiḥ
ātma-tejobhir nirvṛttān bhāskarāgni-samaprabhān

Bhṛgu said: Using his own energies, Brahmā Prajāpati first created Brahmins. They were produced from his own energy and radiated an effulgence equal to that of the sun or fire.

2. *tataḥ satyaṁ ca dharmaṁ ca tapo brahma ca śāśvatam*
ācāraṁ caiva śaucaṁ ca svargāya vidadhe prabhuḥ

The Lord then created truth, dharma, austerity, and the eternal Veda, as well as proper conduct and purity, so that people might gain entrance to the realm of the gods.

3. *deva-dānava-gandharva-daityāsura-mahoragāḥ*
yakṣa-rākṣasa-nāgāś ca piśācā manujās tathā

4. *brāhmaṇāḥ kṣatriyā vaiśyāḥ śūdrāś ca dvija-sattama*
ye cānye bhūta-saṁghānāṁ saṁghās tāṁś cāpi nirmame

He then created the gods, *dānavas*, *gandharvas*, *daityas*, *asuras*, mighty serpents, *yakṣas*, *rākṣasas*, *nāga* serpents, *piśācas*, and human beings, including the Brahmins, *kṣatriyas*, *vaiśyas*, and *śūdras*, O best of Brahmins, as well as the various other types of living beings.

5. *brāhmaṇānāṁ sito varṇaḥ kṣatriyāṇāṁ tu lohitaḥ*
vaiśyānāṁ pītako varṇaḥ śūdrāṇām asitas tathā

White is the colour of the Brahmins and red of the *kṣatriyas*. The colour of the *vaiśyas* is yellow and black is the colour of the *śūdras*.

6. *bharadvāja uvāca*
cātur-varṇyasya varṇena yadi varṇo vibhajyate
sarveṣāṁ khalu varṇānāṁ dṛśyate varṇa-saṁkaraḥ

Bharadvāja said: If each social class is demarcated by these colours in a fourfold division, it is apparent that there must have been a mixing together of all four classes.

7. *kāmaḥ krodho bhayaṁ lobhaḥ śokaś cintā kṣudhā śramaḥ*
sarveṣāṁ naḥ prabhavati kasmād varṇo vibhajyate

Desire, anger, fear, greed, grief, anxiety, hunger, and exhaustion arise in all of us, so on what basis is social class to be determined?

8. *sveda-mūtra-purīṣāṇi śleṣmā pittaṁ saśoṇitam*
tanuḥ kṣarati sarveṣāṁ kasmād varṇo vibhajyate

In all people the body carries sweat, urine, stool, mucus, bile, and blood, so on what basis is social class to be determined?

9. *jaṅgamānām asaṁkhyeyāḥ sthāvarāṇāṁ ca jātayaḥ*
teṣāṁ vividha-varṇānāṁ kuto varṇa-viniścayaḥ

There are innumerable species of moving and stationary beings, so how can the categories of these different types of living entity ever be identified?

10. *bhṛgur uvāca*
na viśeṣo 'sti varṇānāṁ sarvaṁ brāhmam imaṁ jagat
brahmaṇā pūrva-sṛṣṭaṁ hi karmabhir varṇatāṁ gatam

Bhṛgu said: There is no absolute distinction between the social classes, for Brahmā originally created all people as Brahmins. Human society became divided into different classes by the activities each group performed.

11. *kāma-bhoga-priyās tīkṣṇāḥ krodhanāḥ priyasāhasāḥ*
tyakta-svadharmā raktāṅgās te dvijāḥ kṣatratāṁ gatāḥ

Those Brahmins who took delight in pleasure and the objects of desire, who were aggressive, inclined to become angry and were impulsive in their actions, gave up their original duties, gained a reddish bodily hue and attained the status of *kṣatriyas.*

12. *goṣu vṛttiṁ samādhāya pītāḥ kṛṣy upajīvinaḥ*
svadharmaṁ nānutiṣṭhanti te dvijā vaiśyatāṁ gatāḥ

Those Brahmins who did not follow the duties of their class, but instead made their living from cows and depended on agriculture for their livelihood became yellow in colour and attained the status of *vaiśyas.*

13. *hiṁsānṛta-priyā lubdhāḥ sarva-karmopajīvinaḥ*
kṛṣṇāḥ śauca-paribhraṣṭās te dvijāḥ śūdratāṁ gatāḥ

And those Brahmins who took delight in harming others and in falsehood, who were greedy and made their livelihood from any type of work, who were black in colour and devoid of purity, attained the status of *śūdras.*

14. *ity etaiḥ karmabhir vyastā dvijā varṇāntaraṁ gatāḥ*
dharmo yajña-kriyā caiṣāṁ nityaṁ na pratiṣidhyate

By acting in this way, these Brahmins became separated from their own class and attained a different social position, but their previous dharma, including the sacrificial rituals, is not forbidden for them.

15. *varṇāś catvāra ete hi yeṣāṁ brāhmī sarasvatī*
vihitā brahmaṇā pūrvaṁ lobhāt tv ajñānatāṁ gatāḥ

These then are the four social classes that religious teachings prescribe. At first they followed the duties ordained for them by Brahmā, but because of their greed they were afflicted by ignorance.

16. *brāhmaṇā dharma-tantra-sthās tapas teṣāṁ na naśyati*
brahma dhārayatāṁ nityaṁ vratāni niyamāṁs tathā

The austerity of those Brahmins who remain true to the principles of their dharma has never been lost. They remain well versed in the wisdom of the Veda and adhere to proper vows and observances.

17. *brahma caitat purā sṛṣṭaṁ ye na jānanty atad-vidaḥ*
teṣāṁ bahu-vidhās tv anyās tatra tatra hi jātayaḥ

But there are others who have no knowledge of the Veda, which was originally manifested by Brahmā, and are incapable of comprehending its teachings. Such persons appear in many other types of birth throughout the creation.

18. *piśācā rākṣasāḥ pretā bahudhā mleccha-jātayaḥ*
pranaṣṭa-jñāna-vijñānāḥ svacchandācāra-ceṣṭitāḥ

They are born as evil spirits known as *piśācas*, *rākṣasas*, and *pretas*, or amongst the many types of *mlecchas*. Such people are devoid of knowledge and understanding, and conduct their lives as they please with no order or regulation.

19. *prajā brāhmaṇa-saṁskārāḥ svadharma-kṛta-niścayāḥ*
ṛṣibhiḥ svena tapasā sṛjyante cāpare paraiḥ

By the power of their austerity, the *rishis* first created by Brahmā later produced offspring who strictly observed the ritual dharma of the Brahmins and resolutely adhered to the duties of their social class.

20. *ādi-deva-samudbhūtā brahma-mūlākṣayāvyayā*
sā sṛṣṭir mānasī nāma dharma-tantra-parāyaṇā

The primary creation that arose from the original divine being had the Veda as its basis and was imperishable and unfading. This creation was known as Mānasī, that which is manifest through the mind, and its existence was based entirely on dharma.

Śānti-parvan, Adhyāya 182

In the short eighth chapter, Bhṛgu builds on his previous introduction to the four *varṇas* by describing the qualities and duties that pertain to each of them. Naturally enough, primary attention is focused upon the Brahmins but each is dealt with in turn and we might note here the very negative view that is taken of the *śūdras* as a social class. Verse 8 is interesting and highly significant for it gives a clear indication that *varṇa* designation is not based on birth alone, a factor that is particularly relevant in light of contemporary debates over caste. Here Bhṛgu makes it clear that if one who is a *śūdra* by birth displays the qualities associated with a Brahmin then he is to be accepted as a Brahmin, birth notwithstanding. And we might note that this same verse is cited by Yudhiṣṭhira earlier in the *Mahābhārata* during his conversation with King Nahuṣa, who has been cursed to live as a serpent (3.177.20). The second section of this chapter (verses 9–17) seems to equate the *dharma* of a Brahmin with the path of renunciation and in fact the tendency towards *mokṣa-dharma*. Here the Brahmin is neither a ritualist nor a teacher but rather one who has renounced the world and pursues his goals by developing a mood of detachment. This is a slightly unusual interpretation of the *varṇa dharma* of the Brahmin class but it does correspond with the discussion of the *āśramas*, which we will encounter in the final two chapters of the *Bhṛgu-bharadvāja-saṁvāda*.

1. *bharadvāja uvāca*
brāhmaṇaḥ kena bhavati kṣatriyo vā dvijottama
vaiśyaḥ śūdraś ca viprarṣe tad brūhi vadatāṁ vara

Bharadvāja said: O best of Brahmins, O Brahmin *rishi*, what is it that determines whether one is a Brahmin or a *kṣatriya*, a *vaiśya* or a *śūdra*? Tell me about this, O best of teachers.

2. *bhṛgur uvāca*
jāta-karmādibhir yas tu saṁskāraiḥ saṁskṛtaḥ śuciḥ
vedādhyayana-saṁpannaḥ ṣaṭsu karmasv avasthitaḥ

3. *śaucācāra-sthitaḥ samyag vighasāśī guru-priyaḥ*
nitya-vratī satya-paraḥ sa vai brāhmaṇa ucyate

Bhṛgu said: One who is consecrated by the birth ceremony and other Vedic *saṁskāras*, who is pure in body and mind, who engages in the study of the Veda, who resolutely adheres to the six duties incumbent on a Brahmin, who observes the rites of purification, who eats only the consecrated food from religious ceremonies, who is dear to his teacher, who is constant in his religious vows, and who is honest in all ways, is said to be a Brahmin.

4. *satyaṁ dānaṁ damo 'droha ānṛśaṁsyaṁ kṣamā ghṛṇā*
tapaś ca dṛśyate yatra sa brāhmaṇa iti smṛtaḥ

Where the qualities of truthfulness, charity, self-control, freedom from malice, not harming others, tolerance, compassion, and austerity are observed, then that person is to be recognised as a Brahmin.

5. *kṣatra-jaṁ sevate karma vedādhyayana-saṁmataḥ*
dānādāna-ratir yaś ca sa vai kṣatriya ucyate

One who executes the duties of sovereignty, who has a high regard for the study of the Vedas, and who takes pleasure both in giving charity and in acquiring wealth is said to be a *kṣatriya*.

6. *kṛṣi-go-rakṣya-vāṇijyaṁ yo viśaty aniśaṁ śuciḥ*
vedādhyayana-saṁpannaḥ sa vaiśya iti saṁjñitaḥ

One who always maintains his purity, takes up agriculture, tending cows, or trade, and is engaged in the study of the Vedas is said to be a *vaiśya*.

7. *sarva-bhakṣa-ratir nityaṁ sarva-karma-karo 'śuciḥ*
tyakta-vedas tv anācāraḥ sa vai śūdra iti smṛtaḥ

An impure person who enjoys any type of food and accepts any kind work whatever the circumstances, who disregards the Vedas and is devoid of good conduct is known as a *śūdra*.

8. *śūdre caitad bhavel lakṣyaṁ dvije caitan na vidyate*
na vai śūdro bhavec chūdro brāhmaṇo na ca brāhmaṇaḥ

If the marks of a Brahmin described above are found in a *śūdra* or are not found in a Brahmin, then the person born as a *śūdra* is certainly not a *śūdra* and the person born as a Brahmin is not a Brahmin.

9. *sarvopāyais tu lobhasya krodhasya ca vinigrahaḥ*
etat pavitraṁ jñātavyaṁ tathā caivātma-saṁyamaḥ

The eradication of greed and anger by all possible means, combined with the practice of self restraint, should be understood as the way to reach a state of purity.

10. *nityaṁ krodhāt tapo rakṣec chriyaṁ rakṣeta matsarāt*
vidyāṁ mānāvamānābhyām ātmānaṁ tu pramādataḥ

One should constantly guard one's austerity against anger and one should guard one's good fortune against selfishness. One should guard one's wisdom against arrogance and contempt for others, but one must guard one's very self against idleness.

11. *yasya sarve samārambhā nirāśīr bandhanās tv iha*
tyāge yasya hutaṁ sarvaṁ sa tyāgī sa ca buddhimān

One who executes all the undertakings that bind one to this world without desire for personal gain, and who makes all his offerings into the sacred fire in a spirit of renunciation, has indeed renounced the world and is a man endowed with intelligence.

12. *ahiṁsraḥ sarva-bhūtānāṁ maitrāyaṇa-gataś caret*
avisrambhe na gantavyaṁ visrambhe dhārayen manaḥ

One should avoid harming any living being and adhere to the path of universal benevolence. Never being suspicious of others, one should maintain a trusting state of mind.

13. *parigrahān parityajya bhaved buddhyā jitendriyaḥ*
aśokaṁ sthānam ātiṣṭhed iha cāmutra cābhayam

Renouncing one's property and possessions, one should master the senses by means of the intellect. One may then exist in a state beyond sorrow and be free from fear both here and in the world to come.

14. *tapo-nityena dāntena muninā saṁyatātmanā*
ajitaṁ jetu-kāmena bhāvyaṁ saṅgeṣv asaṅginā

This is the result achieved by one who practises unceasing austerity, who restrains his desires, who lives as a holy sage, who attains self-mastery, and who longs to conquer that which appears unconquerable, whilst remaining indifferent in the midst of his own attachments.

15. *indriyair gṛhyate yad yat tat tad vyaktam iti sthitiḥ*
avyaktam iti vijñeyaṁ liṅga-grāhyam atīndriyam

Whatever is perceived by the senses is the state of existence designated as the *vyakta*, the manifest. That which lies beyond the perception of the senses, and can therefore be ascertained only by an indication of its existence, should be known as the *avyakta*, the non-manifest.

16. *manaḥ prāṇe nigṛhṇīyāt prāṇaṁ brahmaṇi dhārayet*
nirvāṇād eva nirvāṇo na ca kiṁcid vicintayet
sukhaṁ vai brāhmaṇo brahma sa vai tenādhigacchati

One should hold the mind within the *prāṇa* breath and then locate the *prāṇa* within Brahman. The state of liberation (*nirvāṇa*) is attained only by the cessation of material existence (*nirvāṇāt*) and so one should not allow the mind to contemplate any other object. In this way a Brahmin readily attains the state of Brahman.

17. *śaucena satataṁ yuktas tathācāra-samanvitaḥ*
sānukrośaś ca bhūteṣu tad dvijātiṣu lakṣaṇam

Always performing one's duty with purity, displaying the proper mode of conduct, and having compassion for other beings are the defining characteristics of the Brahmins.

Śānti-parvan, Adhyāya 183

The consideration of the four *varṇas* is now concluded, but before Bhṛgu moves on to discuss the *āśramas* there is something of a hiatus here in Chapter 9, which at first seems to be a distraction from the main themes of the current discussion. In verses 1 to 8, Bhṛgu explains that there are two paths that human beings may pursue in life, the way of *dharma*, which is also the way of light and truth, and the way of *adharma*, which is also the way of darkness and falsehood. This assertion must relate to the teachings on *varṇa* we have just encountered, for the way of *dharma* means to accept the religious duties related to *varṇa* and in particular to the ideal conduct of a Brahmin, discussed in the second half of Chapter 8. Adherence to truth, light, and *dharma* is recommended because it leads to happiness, whilst *adharma* produces suffering as the course of karma unfolds. In the prose passage that forms verse 10, Bharadvāja responds to this idea by questioning whether worldly pleasure is an acceptable goal to aspire to. Bhṛgu seems to be suggesting that sensual enjoyment should be sought through dharmic conduct, but in fact it is the renunciation of pleasure that represents the highest mode of conduct.

In the final section of the chapter (verses 11–16), Bhṛgu responds to this objection by reasserting his opinion that *dharma* yields rewards in the form of future happiness, even amongst the gods in heaven. In other words, Bhṛgu is saying that one should act in accordance with dharma because such action brings worldly pleasure and the avoidance of suffering. Verses 15 and 16 take us back to the theme of creation with which this part of the discussion commenced as we are told that Brahmā created the world, which has within it this eternal principle of *dharma*.

1. *bhṛgur uvāca*
satyaṁ brahma tapaḥ satyaṁ satyaṁ sṛjati ca prajāḥ
satyena dhāryate lokaḥ svargaṁ satyena gacchati

Bhṛgu said: Truth is Brahman. Austerity is truth. Truth creates the living beings. The world is sustained by truth. Through truth one reaches the realm of the gods.

2. *anṛtaṁ tamaso rūpaṁ tamasā nīyate hy adhaḥ*
tamo-grastā na paśyanti prakāśaṁ tamasāvṛtam

Falsehood is the external form of darkness (*tamas*). One is carried downwards by that *tamas*. Those possessed by *tamas* cannot see the light, for it is covered by that darkness.

3. *svargaḥ prakāśa ity āhur narakaṁ tama eva ca*
satyānṛtāt tad ubhayaṁ prāpyate jagatī-caraiḥ

They say that the heaven of the gods is illumination whilst hell is the darkness of *tamas*. In this world, human beings attain these two regions through truth and falsehood respectively.

4. *tatra tv evaṁ-vidhā vṛttir loke satyānṛtā bhavet*
dharmādharmau prakāśaś ca tamo duḥkhaṁ sukhaṁ tathā

For in the world there are alternative ways of life based either on truth or on falsehood. These are manifest in terms of dharma and *adharma*, illumination and darkness, sorrow and joy.

5. *(i) tatra yat satyaṁ sa dharmo yo dharmaḥ sa prakāśo yaḥ prakāśas tat sukham iti (ii) tatra yad anṛtaṁ so 'dharmo yo 'dharmas tat tamo yat tamas tad duḥkham iti*

(i) This is to be understood as follows: that which is truth is also dharma, that which is dharma is also illumination, and that which is illumination is also joy. (ii) And in the same way, that which is falsehood is also *adharma*, that which is *adharma* is also *tamas*, and that which is *tamas* is also sorrow.

6. *atrocyate*
śārīrair mānasair duḥkhaiḥ sukhaiś cāpy asukhodayaiḥ
loka-sṛṣṭiṁ prapaśyanto na muhyanti vicakṣaṇāḥ

Concerning this subject it is said: The wise who understand the origin of the world are not confused by the sorrows of body and mind, or by the pleasures of the world which inevitably end in misery.

7. *tatra duḥkha-vimokṣārthaṁ prayateta vicakṣaṇaḥ*
sukhaṁ hy anityaṁ bhūtānām iha-loke paratra ca

Therefore the wise man should endeavour to free himself from suffering. The pleasure enjoyed by living beings is impermanent, both here in this world and in the world to come.

8. *rāhu-grastasya somasya yathā jyotsnā na bhāsate*
tathā tamobhibhūtānāṁ bhūtānāṁ bhraśyate sukham

When the moon is seized by the planet Rāhu, its light no longer shines. In the same way, the joy of these living beings is dissipated by the darkness (*tamas*) that afflicts them.

9. *(i) tat khalu dvi-vidhaṁ sukham ucyate śārīraṁ mānasaṁ ca (ii) iha khalv amuṣmiṁś ca loke sarvārambha-pravṛttayaḥ sukhārthā abhidhīyante (iii) na hy atas tri-varga-phalaṁ viśiṣṭataram asti (iv) sa eṣa kāmyo guṇa-viśeṣo dharmārthayor ārambhas tad dhetur asyotpattiḥ sukha-prayojanā*

(i) It is said that happiness is of two types, the physical and the mental. (ii) All the rituals that are undertaken are described as having happiness as their goal, either here or in the world to come. (iii) The threefold results of action never offer anything superior to that happiness. (iv) Happiness is always to be sought after for it is the most excellent quality of life. It is the reason for adhering to dharma and for seeking prosperity (*artha*). The origin of both dharma and *artha* is the human impulse towards happiness.

10. *bharadvāja uvāca*
(i) yad etad bhavatābhihitaṁ sukhānāṁ paramāḥ striya iti tan na gṛhṇīmaḥ (ii) na hy eṣām ṛṣīnāṁ mahati sthitānām aprāpya eṣa guṇa-viśeṣo na cainam abhilaṣanti (iii) śrūyate ca bhagavāṁs tri-loka-kṛd brahmā prabhur ekākī tiṣṭhati (iv) brahmacārī na kāma-sukheṣv ātmānam avadadhāti (v) api ca bhagavān viśveśvara umāpatiḥ kāmam abhivartamānam anaṅgatvena śamam anayat (vi) tasmād brūmo na mahātmabhir ayaṁ

pratigṛhīto na tv eṣa tāvad viśiṣṭo guṇa iti naitad bhagavataḥ pratyemi (vii) bhagavatā tūktaṁ sukhānāṁ paramāḥ striya iti (viii) loka-pravādo 'pi ca bhavati dvi-vidhaḥ phalodayaḥ sukṛtāt sukham avāpyate duṣkṛtād duḥkham iti (ix) atrocyatām

Bharadvāja said: (i) What you are now asserting is that women represent the best of all forms of happiness. We cannot accept this argument. (ii) The most excellent quality of life is never unobtainable for those *rishis* who are situated in the highest position, and yet they do not crave this type of happiness. (iii) We have learned that Brahmā, the exalted Lord who creates the three worlds, always remains alone. (iv) Remaining celibate, he never engages himself in the pleasures of carnal desire. (v) Similarly, when Lord Śiva Umāpati, the master of all existence, was approached by Kāma, the God of Desire, he rendered him powerless by depriving him of his bodily form. (vi) So we would argue that such happiness is never indulged in by persons who are truly wise, nor is it to be taken as the highest quality of life; hence although it has been taught by such an exalted person, I cannot follow the idea you have presented. (vii) For it has actually been asserted by one as exalted as yourself that women represent the highest point of happiness. (viii) The idea of two types of results arising from one's actions, in the sense that happiness is due to virtue and misery is due to wickedness, is one that finds currency only in the understanding of the common people. (ix) This is what is said.

11. *bhṛgur uvāca*
(i) anṛtāt khalu tamaḥ prādurbhūtaṁ tamo-grastā adharmam evānuvartante na dharmam (ii) krodha-lobha-moha-mānānṛtādibhir avacchannā na khalv asmiḷ loke na cāmutra sukham āpnuvanti (iii) vividha-vyādhi-gaṇopatāpair avakīryante (iv) vadha-bandha-roga-parikleśādibhiś ca

kṣut-pipāsā-śrama-kṛtair upatāpair upatapyante (v) caṇḍa-vātātyuṣṇātiśīta-kṛtaiś ca pratibhayaiḥ śārīrair duḥkhair upatapyante (vi) bandhu-dhana-vināśa-viprayoga-kṛtaiś ca mānasaiḥ śokair abhibhūyante jarā-mṛtyu-kṛtaiś cānyair iti

Bhṛgu replied: (i) *Tamas* certainly comes into being because of falsehood and those who are in the grip of *tamas* pursue *adharma* and never dharma. (ii) Persons overwhelmed by anger, greed, folly, pride, falsehood, and other bad qualities attain happiness neither in this world nor in the world to come. (iii) They are tormented by the miseries caused by a host of different kinds of disease and affliction. (iv) They must endure beatings, captivity, illness, pain, and other afflictions as well as the suffering caused by hunger, thirst, and exhaustion. (v) They must also suffer the terrifying bodily afflictions caused by raging winds and the extremes of heat and cold. (vi) They are further overwhelmed by the mental torment caused by separation from family members and loss of wealth as well as the suffering that arises from old age and imminent death.

12. *(i) yas tv etaiḥ śārīrair mānasair duḥkhair na spṛśyate sa sukhaṁ veda (ii) na caite doṣāḥ svarge prādurbhavanti (iii) tatra bhavati khalu*

(i) But one who remains unaffected by these bodily and mental torments certainly comprehends the nature of happiness. (ii) The afflictions I have described do not arise in the realm of the gods. (iii) There it is like this:

13. *susukhaḥ pavanaḥ svarge gandhaś ca surabhis tathā*
kṣut-pipāsā-śramo nāsti na jarā na ca pāpakam

In that heaven there are pleasant winds blowing and there are sweet aromas. Hunger, thirst, and exhaustion are not found there, and neither are old age or wickedness.

14. *nityam eva sukhaṁ svarge sukhaṁ duḥkham ihobhayam*
narake duḥkham evāhuḥ samaṁ tu paramaṁ padam

In heaven there is constant joy, in this world there is both pleasure and pain, and they say that in hell there is only misery. So that domain of heaven equates to the supreme position.

15. *pṛthivī sarva-bhūtānāṁ janitrī tad-vidhāḥ striyaḥ*
pumān prajāpatis tatra śukraṁ tejo-mayaṁ viduḥ

The earth is the mother of all living beings and women are of the nature of the earth. In the same way, man is Prajāpati, the Lord of all Beings, and his seed is understood as brimming with potent energy.

16. *ity etal loka-nirmāṇaṁ brahmaṇā vihitaṁ purā*
prajā viparivartante svaiḥ svaiḥ karmabhir āvṛtāḥ

It was in this way that the creation of this world was accomplished by Brahmā in the very beginning. Carrying with them the results of their previous actions, the living beings proceed through life, each one pursuing its individual course.

Śānti-parvan, Adhyāya 184

It is in the tenth chapter that the discourse moves on to consider the first two of the four *āśramas*. These are the stages of an individual's life that allow him to pursue all four of the *puruṣārthas,* the desirable goals of life, without conflict or tension emerging between them. Thus whilst a man ives with his wife as the proprietor of a household he can accumulate wealth (*artha*) and satisfy sensual desires (*kāma*) whilst still adhering to the rules of proper conduct within human society (*dharma*). When he reaches a certain age, he then renounces the household with its pleasures and attachments and seeks instead the highest spiritual goal of *mokṣa.* This discussion does not commence, however, until verse 7 of Chapter 10 when Bharadvāja poses a specific question about the *āśramas.* Prior to that he asks two questions about *dharma* in general and, specifically, the results gained through *dāna*, *tapa*, *huta*, and *svādhyāya*, i.e. charity, acts of austerity, Vedic ritual, and recitation of the Veda. In verse 5, he asks a series of questions relating to the proper execution of *dharma*, to which Bhṛgu responds in a rather perfunctory manner that seems barely adequate given the complexity of Bharadvāja's inquiry.

In response to the direct question about the four *āśramas* that comes in verse 7, Bhṛgu begins by explaining that the first stage of life is that of the celibate student. Here a young person should render service to his *guru* whilst living a simple lifestyle in his home and acquiring knowledge of the Vedas from him. From verse 10, Bhṛgu moves on to describe the second *āśrama*, which is that of the *gṛha-stha*, the person who remains in his own home, his *gṛha*. In this stage of life an individual should marry and beget offspring, engaging in various activities to secure the wealth and prosperity that allow him to enjoy the pleasures of life. He must not, however, transgress the ordinances of *dharma* and he must ensure that a portion of his wealth is used to perform Vedic rituals and to provide support for persons in the other stages of life. Verse 11 makes reference to the third *āśrama*, that of the forest-dweller, the *vānaprastha*, but this is just in relation to the *gṛhastha*'s duty to provide sustenance for such persons and a full account of this stage of life is presented in the opening section of Chapter 11.

1. *bharadvāja uvāca*
dānasya kiṁ phalaṁ prāhur dharmasya caritasya ca
tapasaś ca sutaptasya svādhyāyasya hutasya ca

Bharadvāja said: What do they say is the result obtained from giving charity, and what does one gain by adhering to one's dharma and following proper modes of conduct? What result is gained from austerity when it is strictly followed, from study of the Veda, and making offerings into the fire?

2. *bhṛgur uvāca*
hutena śāmyate pāpaṁ svādhyāye śāntir uttamā
dānena bhoga ity āhus tapasā sarvam āpnuyāt

Bhṛgu said: By making offerings into the fire one neutralises the effect of previous sins and by reciting the Veda one finds profound tranquillity. They say that one gains pleasure as a result of giving charity, but one may obtain all things through austerity.

3. *dānaṁ tu dvi-vidhaṁ prāhuḥ paratrārtham ihaiva ca*
sadbhyo yad dīyate kiṁcit tat paratropatiṣṭhati

They say, however, that charity is by nature twofold. One type of charity yields its result in the next world and the other bestows benefits here. That which is given to righteous persons comes to fruition in the world to come.

4. *asatsu dīyate yat tu tad dānam iha bhujyate*
yādṛśaṁ dīyate dānaṁ tādṛśaṁ phalam āpyate

But the result of charity given to wicked persons is enjoyed in this world. According to the amount given in charity, an appropriate result is gained.

5. *bharadvāja uvāca*
kiṁ kasya dharma-caraṇaṁ kiṁ vā dharmasya lakṣaṇam
dharmaḥ kati-vidho vāpi tad bhavān vaktum arhati

Bharadvāja said: What constitutes the proper observance of dharma and for which persons? What is the defining feature of dharma? How many different forms of dharma are there? You should kindly discuss this topic.

6. *bhṛgur uvāca*
sva-dharma-caraṇe yuktā ye bhavanti manīṣiṇaḥ
teṣāṁ dharma-phalāvāptir yo 'nyathā sa vimuhyati

Bhṛgu said: Those who properly observe the duties of their personal dharma are indeed the wise ones. They will gain the welcome fruits of dharma, but one who follows the opposite course is deluded.

7. *bharadvāja uvāca*
yad etac cātur-āśramyaṁ brahmarṣi-vihitaṁ purā
teṣāṁ sve sve ya ācārās tān me vaktum ihārhasi

Bharadvāja said: In ancient times, the *rishi* Brahmā ordained the division of life into four separate *āśramas*. You must now explain to me the rules of conduct incumbent on those in each of these stages of life.

8. *bhṛgur uvāca*
(i) pūrvam eva bhagavatā loka-hitam anutiṣṭhatā dharma-saṁrakṣaṇārtham āśramāś catvāro 'bhinirdiṣṭāḥ (ii) tatra gurukula-vāsam eva tāvat prathamam āśramam udāharanti (iii) samyag atra śauca-saṁskāra-vinaya-niyama-praṇīto vinītātmā ubhe saṁdhye bhāskarāgni-daivatāny upasthāya vihāya tandrālasye guror abhivādana-vedābhyāsa-śravaṇa-pavitrī-kṛtāntarātmā tri-ṣavaṇam upaspṛśya brahmcaryāgni-paricaraṇa-guru-śuśrūṣā-nityo bhaikṣādi-sarva-niveditāntarātmā guru-vacana-nirdeśānuṣṭhānāpratikūlo guru-prasāda-labdha-svādhyāya-tat-paraḥ syāt

Bhṛgu said: (i) In the very beginning, these four *āśramas* were ordained by the Lord, dedicated as he was to the welfare of the world, in order that the path of dharma might be protected. (ii) They assert that the first *āśrama* extends as long as one remains in residence at the house of one's teacher. (iii) Here one should live with a controlled mind, observing ritual purity, the rules of conduct, and the restrictions of religious life, attending to the worship of the dawn and the twilight, the sun, the sacred fire and the gods, casting off sloth and indolence, showing respect to one's teacher, listening to the recitation of the Veda, keeping one's heart and mind pure, bathing with water three times daily, practising celibacy, tending the sacred fire, serving one's teacher, regularly following the routine of begging alms and other prescribed practices, and then, with a contented heart, presenting everything that is obtained to the teacher, willingly obeying the words of instruction spoken by the teacher, and devoting oneself to the Vedic teachings received by the grace of the teacher.

9. *bhavati cātra ślokaḥ*
guruṁ yas tu samārādhya dvijo vedam avāpnuyāt
tasya svarga-phalāvāptiḥ sidhyate cāsya mānasam

And concerning this subject there is a verse: For a Brahmin who satisfies his teacher and acquires knowledge of the Veda, the attainment of a heavenly reward is certain, along with anything else he sets his mind on.

10. *(i) gārhastyaṁ khalu dvitīyam āśramaṁ vadanti (ii) tasya samudācāra-lakṣaṇaṁ sarvam anuvyākhyāsyāmaḥ (iii) samāvṛttānāṁ sadārāṇāṁ saha-dharmacaryā-phalārthināṁ gṛhāśramo vidhīyate (iv) dharmārtha-kāmāvāptir hy atra tri-varga-sādhanam avekṣāgarhitena karmaṇā dhanāny ādāya svādhyāya-prakarṣopalabdhena brahmarṣi-nirmitena vā adri-sāra-gatena vā havya-niyamābhyāsa-daivata-prasādopalabdhena vā dhanena gṛhastho gārhasthyaṁ pravartayet (v) tad dhi sarvāśramāṇāṁ mūlam udāharanti (vi) gurukula-vāsinaḥ parivrājakā ye cānye saṁkalpita-vrata-niyama-dharmānuṣṭhāyinas teṣām apy ata eva bhikṣā-bali-saṁvibhāgāḥ pravartante*

(i) They say that the second stage of life is that in which one maintains a household. (ii) I will now explain in full the characteristic modes of conduct appropriate for that stage of life. (iii) The householder *āśrama* is ordained for those who have returned from the place of their teacher and taken a wife, but still seek the reward obtained by strict adherence to dharma. (iv) In this *āśrama*, success may be attained in three separate forms in terms of dharma, prosperity (*artha*), and the satisfaction of sensual desires (*kāma*). Making money by work to which no blame can be attached, or else living in the manner of the Brahmin *rishis* on the choice gifts received for recitation of the Vedas, or by journeying to the mountains which are full of riches, or else on what is obtained from sacrifices, religious vows, and the daily offerings to the gods, the householder can then maintain his household. (v) They declare that the householder *āśrama* is the basis for all the other *āśramas*. (vi) For it is those in the householder *āśrama* who provide for the distribution of alms and gifts to those residing at the place of their teacher, to the wandering ascetics, and to others who follow the religious path based on resolute vows and restraints.

11. *vānaprasthānāṁ dravyopaskāra iti prāyaśaḥ khalv ete sādhavaḥ sādhu-pathya-darśanāḥ svādhyāya-prasaṅginas tīrthābhigamana-deśa-darśanārthaṁ pṛthivīṁparyaṭanti (ii) teṣāṁ pratyutthānābhivādanānasūyā-vāk pradāna-saumukhya-śakty-āsana-śayanābhyavahāra-satkriyāś ceti*

(i) For those who are forest dwellers (*vānaprasthas*), wealth is superfluous. There is no doubt that such persons are generally righteous souls who comprehend the ways of virtuous men. Devoted to the recitation of the Vedas, they travel across the earth journeying to pilgrimage sites in order to see each holy place. (ii) The householder should welcome them with the proper marks of hospitality, and, according to his ability to do so, offer a respectful greeting, a show of reverence, gentle words, gifts, a pleasant demeanour, enthusiasm, a seat, a bed, and the provision of food.

12. *bhavati cātra ślokaḥ*
atithir yasya bhagnāśo gṛhāt pratinivartate
sa dattvā duṣkṛtaṁ tasmai puṇyaṁ ādāya gacchati

In this connection there is the following verse: When a guest goes away from a person's house disappointed, he passes on to the householder the results of his wicked deeds, whilst the accumulated merit of the householder's piety passes to the dissatisfied guest.

13. *(i) api cātra yajña-kriyābhir devatāḥ prīyante nivāpena pitaro vedābhyāsa-śravaṇa-dhāraṇena ṛṣayaḥ (ii) apatyotpādanena prajāpatir iti*

(i) In the householder *āśrama*, the gods are satisfied by the performance of sacrificial ceremonies, the forefathers are satisfied by the *śrāddha* offerings, and the *rishis* are satisfied by one's observance of the daily hearing of the recitation of the Vedas. (ii) Prajāpati, the Lord of all Beings, is satisfied by the generation of offspring.

14. *ślokau cātra bhavataḥ*
vatsalāḥ sarva-bhūtānāṁ vācyāḥ śrotra-sukhā giraḥ
parivādopaghātau ca pāruṣyaṁ cātra garhitam

And in this connection there are the following two verses: For all living beings the sound of kind words is that which is most pleasing to the ear. Criticism, abuse, and harsh speech are to be condemned.

15. *avajñānam ahaṁkāro dambhaś caiva vigarhitaḥ*
ahiṁsā satyam akrodhaḥ sarvāśrama-gataṁ tapaḥ

Contempt for others, egotism, and dishonesty represent that which should be rejected, whilst never harming others, truthfulness, and the avoidance of anger represent the austerity that should be pursued by persons in all the *āśramas*.

16. *api cātra mālyābharaṇa-vastrābhyaṅga-gandhopabhoga-nṛtta-gīta-vāditra-śruti-sukha-nayanābhirāma-saṁdarśanānāṁ prāptir bhakṣya-bhojya-peya-lehya-coṣyāṇām abhyavahāryāṇāṁ vividhānām upabhogaḥ sva-dāra-vihāra-saṁtoṣaḥ kāma-sukhāvāptir iti*

In the householder *āśrama* one obtains sensual pleasure from flower garlands, ornaments, and fine clothes, smearing the body with perfumes, dancing, singing, music that is a delight to the ear and beholding sights that are pleasing to the eye; from the enjoyment of various types of food that can be chewed, swallowed, drunk, licked, or sucked; and from amusing distractions and sensual pleasures in the company of one's wife.

17. *tri-varga-guṇa-nirvṛttir yasya nityaṁ gṛhāśrame*
sa sukhāny anubhūyeha śiṣṭānāṁ gatim āpnuyāt

Three types of objective in life are thus always cultivated by a person in the householder *āśrama*. Having enjoyed various pleasures in this world he then attains the destination achieved by those who have left this world.

18. *uñcha-vṛttir gṛhastho yaḥ sva-dharma-caraṇe rataḥ*
tyakta-kāma-sukhārambhas tasya svargo na durlabhaḥ

The heaven of the gods is not hard to obtain for a householder who lives by gathering leftover grains from the fields (*uñcha-vṛtti*), is resolute in adhering to his own dharma, and has given up endeavouring for the pleasures of sensual enjoyment.

Śānti-parvan, Adhyāya 185

The eleventh and final chapter of the *Bhṛgu-bharadvāja-saṁvāda* concludes the discussion of *varṇa* and *āśrama* by moving on to consider the third and fourth stages of life in which a person wholly renounces the world and seeks the highest spiritual goal, liberation from the cycle of rebirth. Here at last then we find the treatise, albeit briefly, turning its attention directly to the pursuit of *mokṣa-dharma*. This line of discussion is, however, completed in the first six verses of the chapter, which include two lengthy prose passages that form verses 1 and 3. Here we first have an outline of the lifestyle of one living in the *vānaprastha āśrama*. In this third stage of life a man gives up his home and family and takes up residence in the forest. He has no permanent shelter, eats little, endures the harshness of the elements, and leaves his hair and nails uncut. He also undertakes unspecified forms of Yoga practice, which seem to be performed primarily to maintain the health of the body so that it can endure the deprivations of forest living. Hence one might presume that it is some form of *haṭha-yoga* that is being referred to here although no details are given. Despite the emphasis on renunciation in this *āśrama*, it is doubtful whether the lifestyle and practices referred to should be categorised as *mokṣa-dharma*. Whilst living in the forest, a man should continue to enact the Vedic ritual by making offerings into the sacred fire and, moreover, the result of living in this way is referred to as *lokān durjayān*, worlds that are very difficult to attain, a phrase that one feels must refer to the heavenly regions attained through strict adherence to worldly *dharma*.

It is only when Bhṛgu moves on to consider the fourth *āśrama* that he speaks directly about the quest for liberation from rebirth, and he designates this stage of life as the *mokṣa āśrama*. Here a person lives as a wandering mendicant who has renounced all facets of worldly life, including even the Vedic ritual which is no longer performed. He is utterly indifferent to the changing fortunes of the world and will stay for only a few days in the proximity of human habitation. He dwells in the forest and deserted places, or else in the houses of the gods, *devatāyatana*, an interesting early reference, which probably indicates the worship of sacred images alongside the Vedic ritual. Now the goal sought is nothing to do with good karma or any form of higher rebirth. He goes beyond the heavenly worlds gained by those who perform the Vedic ritual and reaches what is referred to as the *brahma-loka*, the world of Brahman. It is not clear exactly what *brahma-loka* means, but as this stage of life is the *mokṣa āśrama* one must presume that it is equivalent to the Buddhist *nirvāṇa*, a state from which one is never again reborn.

This discussion of the *varṇas* and *āśramas* reveals how the idea of *dharma* and higher rebirth can be reconciled with ideas of world renunciation and the quest for liberation from rebirth, the solution being that different religious goals are pursued at different times of life. Moreover, it is accepted that *mokṣa* is the highest form of spiritual attainment, though Bhṛgu is quite clear in asserting that this priority does not render the lesser goal of superior rebirth invalid. Both are advocated herein.

The discussion of the four *āśramas* is concluded by verse 6 and the final passage of the *Bhṛgu-bharadvāja-saṁvāda* consists of a revelation of the existence of a quasi-heavenly world to the north of the Himalaya range. This is a rather curious passage that has no obvious connection with the two main lines of discourse that have gone before. The belief that there is a higher world beyond the Himalaya range is one that is encountered occasionally within the *Mahābhārata*, notably in the *Nara-nārāyaṇīya-parvan* towards the end of the *Śānti-parvan* where it is referred to as Śvetadvīpa, the abode of Nārāyaṇa. We might speculate as to whether there is any historical basis for the idea, but perhaps it is better to keep these accounts firmly within the domain of textual revelation. That northern land is where people are born as a result of the righteous deeds they perform here in this world. In this world there is suffering and pleasure intermixed, as well as virtue and wickedness, but in that land there is no suffering and the people are all inherently righteous. This is in fact a heavenly domain, akin to the worlds of the gods, for in that region no karma is generated as it is in this world; it is a place where those who act properly in this world can enjoy the fruits of their virtue in a land free of vice and misery. And on that slightly anomalous note, the *Bhṛgu-bharadvāja-saṁvāda* draws to a close.

1. *bhṛgur uvāca*
(i) vānaprasthāḥ khalu ṛṣi-dharmam anusarantaḥ puṇyāni tīrthāni nadī-prasravaṇāni suviviktesv araṇyeṣu mṛga-mahiṣa-varāha-sṛmara-gajākīrṇeṣu tapasyanto 'nusaṁcaranti (ii) tyakta-grāmya-vastrāhāropabhogā vanyauṣadhi-mūla-phala-parṇa-parimita-vicitra-niyatāhārāḥ sthānāsanino bhūmi-pāṣāṇa-sikatā-śarkarā-vālukā-bhasma-śāyinaḥ kāśa-kuśa-carma-valkala-saṁvṛtāṅgāḥ keśa-śmaśru-nakha-roma-dhāriṇo niyata-kālopasparśanā askanna-homa-bali-kālānuṣṭhāyinaḥ samit-kuśa-kusumopahāra-homārjana-labdha-viśrāmāḥ śītoṣṇa-pavana-niṣṭapta-vibhinna-sarva-tvaco vividha-niyama-yoga-caryā-vihita-dharmānuṣṭhāna-hṛta-māṁsa-śonitās-tvag-asthi-bhūtā dhṛti-parāḥ sattva-yogāc charīrāṇy udvahanti

Bhṛgu said: (i) Those in the forest-dweller (*vānaprastha*) stage of life adhere to the dharma of the *rishis*. They execute austerities in deserted forests full of deer, buffaloes, boars, fawns, and elephants, and journey to the pilgrimage sites along the flowing rivers where religious merit is acquired. (ii) Giving up the fine clothes and good food they enjoyed in their village life, they consume a modest amount of the plants, roots, fruits, and leaves found in the forest, regulating their diet with various restraints. The ground is their seat and they make their bed on the earth, on rocks, rough soil, gravel, sand, and ashes. They wrap their bodies in *kāśa* and *kuśa* grass, in animal hides and the bark of trees, and leave their hair, beard, nails, and bodily hair uncut. They bathe at regular times, pour flowing oblations of clarified butter into the sacred fire, and make ritual offerings to the gods at the appropriate times. They take their repose only after collecting fuel, *kuśa* grass, *kusuma* flowers, and substances suitable for the daily offerings and oblations. Afflicted by cold, heat, and blasting winds their skin becomes cracked and pitted all over. Performing various austerities and Yoga practices, and strictly adhering to their prescribed dharma, they experience a wasting away of their flesh, blood, skin, and bones, but remain firm in their resolve and are able to sustain their bodies because of the physical Yoga techniques they undertake.

2. *yas tv etāṁ niyataścaryāṁ brahmarṣi-vihitāṁ caret*
sa dahed agni-vad doṣāñ jayel lokāṁś ca durjayān

One who follows the way of life ordained for the Brahmin *rishis* by accepting such restraints burns away his impurities like a fire and gains worlds that are difficult to attain.

3. *(i) parivrājakānāṁ punar ācāras tad yathā (ii) vimucyāgni-dhana-kalatra-paribarha-saṅgān ātmanaḥ sneha-pāśān avadhūya parivrajanti sama-loṣṭāśma-kāñcanās tri-varga-pravṛtteṣv ārambheṣv asakta-buddhayo 'ri-mitrodāsīneṣu tulya-vṛttayaḥ sthāvara-jarā-yujāṇḍa-ja-sveda-jodbhijjānāṁ bhūtānāṁ vāṅ-manaḥ-karmabhir anabhidrohiṇo 'niketāḥ parvata-pulina-vṛkṣa-mūla-devatāyatanāny anucaranto vāsārtham upeyur nagaraṁ grāmaṁ vā nagare pañca-rātrikā grāmaika-rātrikāḥ (iii) praviśya ca prāṇa-dhāraṇa-mātrārthaṁ dvijātīnāṁ bhavanāny asaṁkīrṇa-karmaṇām upatiṣṭheyuḥ pātra-patitāyācita-bhaikṣāḥ kāma-krodha-darpa-moha-lobha-kārpaṇya-dambha-parivādābhimāna-hiṁsā-nivṛttā iti*

(i) Now the behaviour of the wandering mendicants. This is how they live: (ii) Giving up all contact with the sacred fire, wealth, wife, and property and casting aside the ropes of affection, they wander across the earth regarding clay, stones, and gold with equal vision. Within their minds there is no attraction for any endeavour in the three fields of activity pursued by the householders. Their behaviour towards others is always the same; it makes no difference whether one is a friend, an enemy, or neither. They never cause harm through words, thoughts, or deeds to any living being, be they stationary, born from within the body, born from an egg, born from perspiration, or sprouted from a seed. Devoid of any permanent abode, they betake themselves to the mountains, the sandy banks of rivers, the roots of trees, and the temples of the gods in order to find a dwelling place. Sometimes they may enter a town or village and remain in a town for five nights and a village for one night only. (iii) When they enter towns or villages they should go to the houses of Brahmins of pure conduct in order to receive a morsel of food that will sustain their life. They never beg for food and live on whatever alms are placed in their bowls. They remain ever free from desire, anger, pride, folly, greed, pettiness, dishonesty, harsh speech, arrogance, and aggression.

4. *bhavati cātra ślokaḥ*
abhayaṁ sarva-bhūtebhyo dattvā carati yo muniḥ
na tasya sarva-bhūtebhyo bhayam utpadyate kvacit

And in this connection there is the following verse: No fear of any other creature arises in the heart of a sage who wanders the earth bestowing fearlessness on all other beings.

5. *kṛtvāgni-hotraṁ sva-śarīra-saṁsthaṁ*
śārīram agniṁ sva-mukhe juhoti
yo bhaikṣa-caryopagatair havibhiś
citāgnināṁ sa vyatiyāti lokān

One who makes offerings through his mouth into the bodily fire, using whatever he obtains from begging as the oblations, goes beyond the worlds attained by those who make offerings into fires made from piles of wood by thus performing the *agnihotra* ritual within his own body.

6. *mokṣāśramaṁ yaḥ kurute yathoktaṁ*
śuciḥ susaṁkalpita-buddhi-yuktaḥ
anindhanaṁ jyotir iva praśāntaṁ
sa brahma-lokaṁ śrayate dvi-jātiḥ

When a pure-hearted Brahmin who has the proper resolve and is blessed with intelligence performs the duties I have described for those in the *mokṣa āśrama*, he then exists like a fire when its fuel is spent, abiding in the world of Brahman.

7. *bharadvāja uvāca*
asmāl lokāt paro lokaḥ śrūyate nopalabhyate
tam ahaṁ jñātum icchāmi tad bhavān vaktum arhati

Bharadvāja said: We have heard that beyond this world there is another realm that cannot be reached. I wish to know about that world. You should now kindly discuss this topic.

8. *bhṛgur uvāca*
uttare himavat-pārśve puṇye sarva-guṇānvite
puṇyaḥ kṣemyaś ca kāmyaś ca sa varo loka ucyate

Bhṛgu said: To the north of here in that auspicious region endowed with good qualities on the side of the Himavat range is a land that is sacred, hospitable, and much sought after. It is this region that is spoken of as the most excellent country.

9. *tatra hy apāpa-karmāṇaḥ śucayo 'tyanta-nirmalāḥ*
lobha-moha-parityaktā mānavā nirupadravāḥ

The people of that land are sinless in their deeds, pure in heart, and completely free from wickedness. They are untouched by greed and folly and are not afflicted by misfortunes.

10. *sa svarga-sadṛśo deśas tatra hy uktāḥ śubhā guṇāḥ*
kāle mṛtyuḥ prabhavati spṛśanti vyādhayo na ca

That land is just like the heaven of the gods for it is said to be delightful in all its features. Death comes to the inhabitants at the appointed time but diseases never touch them.

11. *na lobhaḥ para-dāreṣu sva-dāra-nirato janaḥ*
na cānyonya-vadhas tatra dravyeṣu na ca vismayaḥ
parokṣa-dharmo naivāsti saṁdeho nāpi jāyate

A man there remains attached to his own wife and does not hanker after the wives of others. People never commit acts of violence nor do they feel any longing for each other's possessions. There is no form of dharma that is unknown there and so doubts cannot arise.

12. *kṛtasya tu phalaṁ tatra pratyakṣam upalabhyate*
śayyāyānāsanopetāḥ prāsāda-bhavanāśrayāḥ
sarva-kāmair vṛtāḥ kecid dhemā-bharaṇa-bhūṣitāḥ

The fruit of righteous action is clearly visible there for the inhabitants of that land possess beds, carriages, and seats and live in palatial residences. They are well provided with everything one could desire and some are adorned with jewellery made of gold.

13. *prāṇa-dhāraṇa-mātraṁ tu keṣāṁcid upapadyate*
śrameṇa mahatā kecit kurvanti prāṇa-dhāraṇam

But for some merely to maintain their life is sufficient, whilst some make strenuous endeavours in practising the restraint of the *prāṇa* breath.

14. *iha dharma-parāḥ kecit kecin naikṛtikā narāḥ*
sukhitā duḥkhitāḥ kecin nirdhanā dhanino 'pare

In this land here, however, some men dedicate themselves to the way of dharma but others are wicked and vile. Some live happily but others must endure misery, some are poor whilst others are rich.

15. *iha śramo bhayaṁ mohaḥ kṣudhā tīvrā ca jāyate*
lobhaś cārtha-kṛto nṝṇāṁ yena muhyanti paṇḍitāḥ

Here exhaustion, fear, delusion, and biting hunger all arise, as well as the greed caused by desire for wealth. Even those amongst men who are learned scholars are deluded in this way.

16. *iha cintā bahu-vidhā dharmādharmasya karmaṇaḥ*
yas tad vedobhayaṁ prājñaḥ pāpmanā na sa lipyate

Here there are various shades of opinion concerning which actions constitute dharma and which actions are *adharma*. The wise man who knows the answer to both these questions is never tainted by sin.

17. *sopadhaṁ nikṛtiḥ steyaṁ parivādo 'bhyasūyatā*
paropaghāto hiṁsā ca paiśunyam anṛtaṁ tathā

18. *etān āsevate yas tu tapas tasya prahīyate*
yas tv etān nācared vidvāṁs tapas tasyābhivardhate

The austerity of one who indulges in fraud, dishonesty, theft, harsh speech, envy, brutality, violence, slander, and falsehood is soon abandoned. But the austerity of the wise man who avoids these vices grows ever stronger.

19. *karma-bhūmir īyaṁ loka iha kṛtvā śubhāśubham*
śubaiḥ śubham avāpnoti kṛtvāśubham ato 'nyathā

This is the land where one's actions produce future results. After performing various righteous and unrighteous actions in this world, one attains an agreeable outcome from the righteous actions but the opposite result from performing unrighteous deeds.

20. *iha prajāpatiḥ pūrvaṁ devāḥ sarṣi-gaṇās tathā*
iṣṭveṣṭa-tapasaḥ pūtā brahma-lokam upāśritāḥ

It was here that in ancient times Prajāpati along with the gods and *rishis* all purified themselves by performing sacrifices and acts of austerity, and thereby became inhabitants of the world known as Brahmaloka.

21. *uttaraḥ pṛthivī-bhāgaḥ sarva-puṇyatamaḥ śubhaḥ*
ihatyās tatra jāyante ye vai puṇya-kṛto janāḥ

The northern part of the earth is a pure land that is the most auspicious of all the regions of the world. Persons living here in this domain who perform virtuous activities take their next birth in that land.

22. *asat-karmāṇi kurvantas tiryag-yoniṣu cāpare*
kṣīṇāyuṣas tathaivānye naśyanti pṛthivī-tale

23. *anyonya-bhakṣaṇe saktā lobha-moha-samanvitāḥ*
ihaiva parivartante na te yānty uttarāṁ diśam

Some who perform wicked actions then take birth from the wombs of animals. Others who meet with death on earth when their duration of life is exhausted delight in devouring one another and are overwhelmed by greed and illusion. Such persons return once more to this world and never move on to the land in the north.

24. *ye gurūn upasevante niyatā brahma-cāriṇaḥ*
panthānaṁ sarva-lokānāṁ te jānanti manīṣiṇaḥ

Wise men who render devoted service to their teachers, who practise self-restraint, and who adhere to the lifestyle of the celibate students, comprehend the path that must be trodden by all types of person.

25. *ity ukto 'yaṁ mayā dharmaḥ saṁkṣepād brahma-nirmitaḥ*
dharmādharmau hi lokasya yo vai vetti sa buddhimān

I have now concisely explained the way of dharma that was originally ordained by Brahmā himself. In this world, one who understands both dharma and *adharma* is truly learned.

26. *bhīṣma uvāca*
ity ukto bhṛguṇā rājan bharadvājaḥ pratāpavān
bhṛguṁ parama-dharmātmā vismitaḥ pratyapūjayat

Bhīṣma said: In this way, O king, the mighty sage Bharadvāja was instructed by Bhṛgu. Having dharma in his heart and amazed by his wisdom, he then worshipped Bhṛgu.

27. *eṣa te prabhavo rājañ jagataḥ saṁprakīrtitaḥ*
nikhilena mahāprājña kiṁ bhūyaḥ śrotum icchasi

This topic of the creation of the world has been narrated to you in full, O king. What subject do you wish to hear about now, O man of wisdom?

Bhīṣma's Teachings on Dharma

Śānti-parvan, Adhyāya 186

Following on from the *Bhṛgu-bharadvāja-saṁvāda*, we get three relatively short passages dealing with three distinct topics, *dharma*, Sāṁkhya, and Yoga, each of which is presented directly by Bhīṣma himself without reference to any previous dialogue. This in itself is interesting as it might suggest that these are original compositions from the redactor himself. I am not, however, convinced that this is the case; it seems more likely that in these chapters the redactor was making use of earlier sources that for some reason did not lend themselves to verbatim inclusion. It is noteworthy that all three of the passages are remarkably free of vocatives addressed to Yudhiṣṭhira, except in the opening verses of each. This is unusual and does suggest that the passages were not originally composed with the present setting in mind and have been extracted from an unnamed external source.

The first of these treatises, Chapter 186 of the *Śānti-parvan*, is also unusual in that it is left untitled and hence apears to stand as no more than an introduction to the next two, the *Adhyātma-kathanam* and the *Dhyāna-yoga*. We must note, however, that it does not function in that way at all: the teachings it provides consist primarily of a list of rules of ritual and moral conduct that have nothing at all to do with the Sāṁkhya and Yoga discourses that follow. The *Adhyātma-kathanam*, literally the discourse on *adhyātma*, is the first substantive treatise on Sāṁkhya in the *Mokṣa-dharma-parvan*, although the term Sāṁkhya is never used in this passage. The natural linkage between Sāṁkhya and Yoga, insisted upon throughout the *Mokṣa-dharma-parvan*, is then confirmed by the inclusion of the *Dhyāna-yoga* immediately following the *Adhyātma-kathanam*. This is a very short passage that in truth contains but scant details on the practice of meditational (*dhyāna*) Yoga – although enough to reveal that the techniques referred to are quite closely related to the classical Yoga *darśana* of Patañjali and the teachings on *dhyāna-yoga* found in the sixth chapter of the *Bhagavad-gītā*.

Here then we see the *Mokṣa-dharma-parvan* starting to include passages that can be more clearly identified as having a location within the schools of Sāṁkhya and Yoga, predating the formulation of the classical *darśanas* of Īśvarakṛṣṇa's *Sāṁkhya-kārikā* and Patañjali's *Yoga-sūtras*. Whilst it is virtually impossible to make any form of suggestion as to the date of these treatises, one must presume that they are amongst the earliest works still extant that give direct teachings on Sāṁkhya and Yoga: their significance for understanding the development of the Indian religious traditions cannot be overstated.

Why then did our redactor choose to include a passage of teachings on ritualised conduct at the point he does? This is a difficult question to answer, particularly as the text itself gives no indication whatsoever of the reasoning behind it. The only suggestion I can make is that a need is felt to show that the religious doctrines and practices presented here are not to be seen as an alternative to the heavily ritualised lifestyle of Vedic orthodoxy, as Buddhists or Jains might suggest, but rather as the logical outcome of the orthodox path.

And if this suggestion is accepted it may be that here again we are witnessing the *Mahābhārata*'s desire to show that the way of renunciation and the quest for liberation from rebirth does not come at the expense of the orthodox traditions, but is entirely compatible with them.

This short passage seems somewhat out of place within a *mokṣa-dharma-parvan* as it has little if anything to do with *mokṣa*, stating overtly that the practices it advocates lead to good fortune in the here and now and higher rebirth in the world to come. It begins with a question from Yudhiṣṭhira concerning *ācāra* (proper conduct), to which Bhīṣma responds by pointing out that good and bad conduct (*durācāra*) are the marks by which the righteous and the wicked (*santa* and *asanta*) are identified. He then proceeds to outline the type of practices he regards as falling under the heading of *ācāra*. Although there is a moral component to the ideas presented, the analysis of good conduct places a substantial emphasis on action of a ritual nature in relation to eating, evacuating, sleeping, fasting, and showing respect to Brahmins, guests, cows, elders, and teachers. It is notable that here Bhīṣma makes no mention of moral precepts such charity, *ahiṁsā*, or showing compassion for all beings, which he expounds upon at length both here in the *Śānti-parvan* and in the *Anuśāsana-parvan* (Book 13).

From verse 25, we can detect a change in the direction of the discourse; it seems likely that after verse 24 the redactor abandons his original source and concludes with his own commentary on the verses previously recited. No more rules of conduct are given but rather the observation that no one can escape the karmic effects of his own actions even though they may be performed in secret. The results of action inevitably catch up with the performer at some time in the future. And in verse 30 we find a statement about *dharma* that repeats assertions found elsewhere in the *Mahābhārata* to the effect that *dharma* cannot be reduced simply to a set of rules and regulations. According to learned authorities, *dharma* and *adharma* are in fact states of consciousness (*mānasam ... dharmam āhur manīṣiṇaḥ*) that impel a person towards virtue, wickedness, or a combination of both; and virtue is defined as being a benign state of mind in relation to other beings (*manasā sarveṣu bhūteṣu śivam ācaret*). This might seem a little contradictory in light of the teachings on proper conduct given earlier in the chapter but should probably be regarded as a caveat rather than an outright contradiction, in line with the understanding of *dharma* given by Kṛṣṇa to Arjuna in the *Mahābhārata*'s *Karṇa-parvan* (Book 8, Chapter 49).

1. *yudhiṣṭhira uvāca*
ācārasya vidhiṁ tāta procyamānaṁ tvayānagha
śrotum icchāmi dharma-jña sarva-jño hy asi me mataḥ

Yudhiṣṭhira said: My dear grandfather, O sinless one, you truly comprehend dharma. I now wish to hear from you about the rules that govern an individual's conduct, for in my opinion everything is known to you.

2. *bhīṣma uvāca*
durācārā durviceṣṭā duṣprajñāḥ priya-sāhasāḥ
asanto hy abhivikhyātāḥ santaś cācāra-lakṣaṇāḥ

Bhīṣma said: Wicked persons are identified by their bad conduct, evil deeds, lack of wisdom, and ill-conceived behaviour. The righteous are identified by the marks of good conduct.

3. *purīṣaṁ yadi vā mūtraṁ ye na kurvanti mānavāḥ*
rāja-mārge gavāṁ madhye dhānya-madhye ca te śubhāḥ

There are human beings who will never pass stool or urine on the king's highway, in the midst of cows, or in fields where grain is growing. They are the righteous persons.

4. *śaucam āvaśyakaṁ kṛtvā devatānāṁ ca tarpaṇam*
dharmam āhur manuṣyāṇām upaśpṛśya nadīṁ taret

After evacuating one's bowels in an appropriate place and making the ritual offering of water to the gods, one should bathe in a river and perform ritual ablutions. They say that this is dharma for human beings.

5. *sūryaṁ sadopatiṣṭheta na svapyād bhāskarodaye*
sāyaṁ prātarjapan saṁdhyāṁ tiṣṭhet pūrvāṁ tathāparām

One should always perform the act of worship to the sun and never sleep through the dawn. For the prayers recited at dawn and at dusk, one should face the east for the former and the west for the latter.

6. *pañcārdro bhojanaṁ kuryāt prāṅ-mukho maunam āsthitaḥ*
na ninded anna-bhakṣyāṁś ca svādv-asvādu ca bhakṣayet

After washing five parts of the body, one should take food in silence facing towards the east. One should never find fault with he food one is eating and be willing to partake of palatable or unpalatable dishes.

7. *nārdra-pāṇiḥ samuttiṣṭhen nārdra-pādaḥ svapen niśi*
devarṣi-nārada-proktam etad ācāra-lakṣaṇam

One should never begin one's daily duties whilst one's hands are still wet and one should never go to sleep at night whilst one's feet are wet. The divine *rishi* Nārada has instructed that the patterns of behaviour presented above are the true marks of good conduct.

8. *śuci-kāmam anaḍvāhaṁ deva-goṣṭhaṁ catuṣ-patham*
brāhmaṇaṁ dhārmikaṁ caiva nityaṁ kuryāt pradakṣiṇam

Every day one should circumambulate a person whose desires are pure, a bull, a temple of the gods, a crossroads, and a Brahmin who is dedicated to his dharma.

9. *atithīnāṁ ca sarveṣāṁ preṣyāṇāṁ sva-janasya ca*
sāmānyaṁ bhojanaṁ bhṛtyaiḥ puruṣasya praśasyate

With regard to all guests, attendants, and relatives, food equal in kind and quality should be provided. A man is highly praised for treating his servants in this way.

10. *sāyaṁ prātar manuṣyāṇāṁ aśanaṁ deva-nirmitam*
nāntarā bhojanaṁ dṛṣṭam upavāsī tathā bhavet

It has been ordained by the gods that if a man takes food at dawn and dusk but does not even look at food between these times, then he has properly observed a fast.

11. *homa-kāle tathā juhvann ṛtu-kāle tathā vrajan*
ananya-strī-janaḥ prājño brahmacārī tathā bhavet

A wise man who pours libations when it is time for the sacrificial rites, engages in sexual congress with his wife only at the appropriate time of the month, and who avoids contact with any other woman is then a *brahmacārin* (one who follows the vow of celibacy).

12. *amṛtaṁ brāhmaṇocchiṣṭaṁ jananyā hṛdayaṁ kṛtam*
upāsīta janaḥ satyaṁ satyaṁ santa upāsate

The remnant of a Brahmin's meal is the nectar of immortality formed within the heart of a mother. A person must venerate truth, for a righteous man certainly venerates truth.

13. *yajuṣā saṁskṛtaṁ māṁsaṁ nivṛtto māṁsa-bhakṣaṇāt*
na bhakṣayed vṛthā-māṁsaṁ pṛṣṭa-māṁsaṁ ca varjayet

One who has given up the eating of meat must not even consume flesh made pure by being offered in sacrifice. Otherwise, one should avoid meat from animals slaughtered just for food, as well as meat from the back of an animal.

14. *sva-deśe para-deśe vā atithiṁ nopavāsayet*
kāmyaṁ karma-phalaṁ labdhvā gurūṇām upapādayet

Whether one is at home or abroad one should never allow a guest to go without food. If something desirable is obtained as a result of one's endeavours, one should present it to one's teachers.

15. *gurubhya āsanaṁ deyaṁ kartavyaṁ cābhivādanam*
gurūn abhyarcya yujyante āyuṣā yaśasā śriyā

One should offer one's teachers a seat and show them due reverence. One who shows proper respect to his teachers is blessed with long life, renown, and prosperity.

16. *nekṣet ādityam udyantaṁ na ca nagnāṁ para-striyam*
maithunaṁ samaye dharmyaṁ guhyaṁ caiva samācaret

One should never look upon the sun when it is high in the sky, nor upon another man's wife when she is naked. One should undertake sexual activities in a private place in accordance with the rules of dharma.

17. *tīrthānāṁ hṛdayaṁ tīrthaṁ śucīnāṁ hṛdayaṁ śuciḥ*
sarvam ārya-kṛtaṁ śaucaṁ vāla-saṁsparśanāni ca

The true place of pilgrimage is the heart of all pilgrimage sites; purity itself is the heart of all things that are pure. All actions performed by a righteous man are pure and so are all things touched by the hair on a cow's tail.

18. *darśane darśane nityaṁ sukha-praśnam udāharet*
sāyaṁ prātaś ca viprāṇāṁ pradiṣṭam abhivādanam

Whenever one meets another person one should make inquiries about his welfare. At dawn and again at dusk it is ordained that one should respectfully salute the Brahmins.

19. *deva-goṣṭhe gavāṁ madhye brāhmaṇānāṁ kriyā-pathe*
svādhyāye bhojane caiva dakṣiṇaṁpāṇim uddharet

In the temple of the gods, in the midst of cows, when executing the rituals ordained for Brahmins, when reciting the Vedas, and before eating, one should raise the right hand as a mark of respect.

20. *paṇyānāṁ śobhanaṁ paṇyaṁ kṛṣīṇāṁ bādyate kṛṣiḥ*
bahu-kāraṁ ca sasyānāṁ vāhye vāhyaṁ tathā gavām

In business activities, trade then flourishes and in agricultural endeavours the harvest is certain; there is a great abundance of grain to be carried on the cart and an abundance of cows as well.

21. *saṁpannaṁ bhojane nityaṁ pānīye tarpaṇaṁ tathā*
suśṛtaṁ pāyase brūyād yavāgvāṁ kṛsare tathā

One should always say, 'This has a good flavour' when taking food, 'This is refreshing' when drinking, and 'This is well prepared' when taking milk products, rice soup, or *krisara* made with rice and dahl.

22. *śmaśru-karmaṇi saṁprāpte kṣute snāne 'tha bhojane*
vyādhitānāṁ ca sarveṣām āyuṣyam abhinandanam

After shaving, sneezing, bathing, or eating one should wish for a long life for all persons suffering from disease.

23. *pratyādityaṁ na meheta na paśyed ātmanaḥ śakṛt*
suta-striyā ca śayanaṁ saha-bhojyaṁ ca varjayet

One should never urinate whilst facing the sun and one should never look upon one's own stool. One should avoid reclining on a bed with one's daughter-in-law or even eating in her company.

24. *tvaṁkāraṁ nāmadheyaṁ ca jyeṣṭhānāṁ parivarjayet*
avarāṇāṁ samānānām ubhayeṣāṁ na duṣyati

One should avoid speaking disrespectfully to one's elders by addressing them s 'You' or by their name. This mode of address is not offensive when directed towards those junior to oneself or equal in years.

25. *hṛdayaṁ pāpa-vṛttānāṁ pāpam ākhyāti vaikṛtam*
jñāna-pūrvaṁ vinaśyanti gūhamānā mahā-jane

The heart of those who live by unrighteous means proclaims the sins they have wickedly performed. O mighty king, those who try to cover over the wicked deeds they planned still meet with destruction.

26. *jñāna-pūrvaṁ kṛtaṁ pāpaṁ chādayanty abahu-śrutāḥ*
nainaṁ manuṣyāḥ paśyanti paśyanti tri-divaukasaḥ

Persons who have little understanding of the scriptures conceal the sinful deeds they have planned. Men may not see their wickedness but the gods in heaven see it all.

27. *pāpena hi kṛtaṁ pāpaṁ pāpam evānuvartate*
dhārmikeṇa kṛto dharmaḥ kartāram anuvartate

When sin is performed by a wrongdoer, further sin inevitably follows. When acts of dharma are performed by an adherent of dharma, then further dharma inevitably follows.

28. *pāpaṁ kṛtaṁ na smaratīha mūḍho*
vivartamānasya tad eti kartuḥ
rāhur yathā candram upaiti cāpi
tathābudhaṁ pāpam upaiti karma

A foolish person never recalls the wickedness he has done, but still the sin descends upon the deluded wrongdoer, for wicked deeds certainly return to the fool who performed them just as Rāhu, the dark planet, moves across the moon.

29. *āśayā saṁcitaṁ dravyaṁ yat kāle neha bhujyate*
tad budhā na praśaṁsanti maraṇaṁ na pratīkṣate

In this world, wealth that is never enjoyed is accumulated with hope and anticipation. Wise men never praise this practice for death waits for no one.

30. *mānasaṁ sarva-bhūtānāṁ dharmam āhur manīṣiṇaḥ*
tasmāt sarveṣu bhūteṣu manasā śivam ācaret

These wise ones insist that for all living beings dharma is a state of mind. Therefore one should direct one's mind towards working for the welfare of all living beings.

31. *eka eva cared dharmaṁ nāsti dharme sahāyatā*
kevalaṁ vidhim āsādya sahāyaḥ kiṁ kariṣyati

One must pursue one's dharma alone for there is no other person who can perform dharma on one's behalf. When one adheres strictly to the proper rules, what assistance can a companion render?

32. *devā yonir manuṣyāṇāṁ devānām amṛtaṁ divi*
pretya-bhāve sukhaṁ dharmāc chaṣvattair upabhujyate

The gods are the origin of human beings. In heaven there is immortality for the gods. The eternal joy experienced in the afterlife is the result of living in accordance with dharma.

The Adhyātma-Kathanam

Śānti-parvan, Adhyāya 187

In the *Adhyātma-kathanam* we have the first passage of the *Mokṣa-dharma-parvan* that we can properly identify as a treatise on Sāṁkhya. Moreover, the natural progression into the *Dhyāna-yoga* establishes the link between Sāṁkhya and Yoga, which is a significant feature of the teachings we will encounter throughout the *Mokṣa-dharma-parvan*. Despite that assertion, however, we must be aware that the passage here still falls short of being a systematic presentation of the classical system and in fact does not use the word 'Sāṁkhya' at any point in its discourse. There is no clear enumeration of elements and the distinction between body and soul, which is such a salient feature of classical Sāṁkhya, is blurred somewhat by the inclusion of the *kṣetrajña* within the primary analysis of the personality.

Nonetheless, this passage is of immense significance for our understanding of development of the Sāṁkhya system, as it probably represents one of the earliest renditions of Sāṁkhya thought to which we have access today. Although this is still some distance from the developed system of Īśvarakṛṣṇa's *Sāṁkhya-kārikā*, it can be readily identified as representing a particular stage in the development of Sāṁkhya ideas. Many points of interest can be noted here – indeed the passage as a whole is certainly worthy of detailed study in establishing the history of Sāṁkhya – but for the purposes of this translation we must confine ourselves to a few observations on the most salient points of interest.

The topic introduced by Yudhiṣṭhira's initial question is designated as *adhyātma*, which might literally be translated as 'in relation to the self'; here it seems to mean something like 'the nature of a person'. In the *Bhagavad-gītā* (8.3), Kṛṣṇa offers the definition of *sva-bhāva*, meaning 'one's inherent nature', for *adhyātma* but here I think we can take it in a rather less specific way. It seems that Yudhiṣṭhira is asking Bhīṣma to explain what a person consists of in terms of his material, psychical, and spiritual components, and the interpretation offered in reply is one that is clearly based on early Sāṁkhya. We may note that the *Adhyātma-kathanam* appears to have been used as a source by one of the later treatises of the *Mokṣa-dharma-parvan*, the *Śukānupraśna*, which runs for twenty-four chapters, from Chapter 224 to Chapter 247 of the *Śānti-parvan*. In Chapter 16 of the *Śukānupraśna* (*Śānti-parvan*, Chapter 239), Śuka asks his father Vyāsa about the subject of *adhyātma*; although the discourse that follows is considerably shorter than the *Adhyātma-kathanam* it is apparent that a considerable number of the verses are common or partially common to both passages. Although one can never be certain in such matters, it seems likely that the *Śukānupraśna* has used the *Adhyātma-kathanam* as a source text for its presentation at this point, and this in turn might suggest that the *Adhyātma-kathanam* is one of the earlier Sāṁhya treatises available to us.

I think, therefore, that we must accept that in his opening question Yudhiṣṭhira is asking Bhīṣma to explain to him the true nature of a person's identity. What is it that a person consists of and what constitutes one's ultimate identity? This is the knowledge he seeks, here designated as the *adhyātma*. After briefly acknowledging the importance of this subject, Bhīṣma begins by referring to the five *mahā-bhūtas*, the great elements of earth, air, space, water, and fire that jointly comprise the physical forms of all living beings. These elements are typically recorded in any Sāṁkhya analysis, but it is interesting to note that here Bhīṣma adds a theistic component to the discussion by suggesting that it is the *bhūta-kṛt*, the creator of living beings, who establishes these five great elements within them. We should further note that this 'creator' is also referred to as the *bhūtātman*, the soul of living beings, suggesting that the theism here is of a specific type that postulates the identity of the Deity with the individual self, a doctrine also encountered in the *Bhagavad-gītā*.

From verse 8 onwards, the analysis of the person is carried forward to the next stage as each of the *mahā-bhūtas* is connected to one of the sense organs and the object it perceives, in the manner typical of Sāṁkya teachings. The discussion, however, adds a further component by pointing out the features of the physical body in which each particular element appears. From verse 11, the analysis moves on to consider the psychological features of the person, designated as the five senses of hearing, sight, taste, smell, and touch, and then the *manas* (mind), the *buddhi* (intellect), and the *kṣetrajña* (literally 'knower of the field', usually used as a synonym for *ātman* or *puruṣa*, indicating the eternal spiritual part of a person's identity). It is clear from verses 36 to 40, later in the chapter, that *kṣetrajña* is indeed used here as an equivalent term for the *ātman*, although it is unusual for Sāṁkhya teachings to include the spiritual identity as a part of its analysis or enumeration of the component elements of the person in this way (though it is interesting to note that the *Śukānupraśna* follows the *Adhyātma-kathanam* in doing so). Also noteworthy is the absence of any mention of *ahaṁkāra* (ego or self-awareness) from the analysis of the psyche of a living being. In most Sāṁkhya treatises, including Chapter 13 of the *Bhagavad-gītā*, it is *buddhi*, *manas*, and *ahaṁkāra* that jointly comprise the *antaḥ-karaṇa*, the inner mental organ of a living being, but here *ahaṁkāra* is omitted and replaced rather anomalously by *kṣetrajña*.

After this listing of the mental and spiritual elements of a living being, the focus switches to the *buddhi*. The word *buddhi* is usually translated as 'intellect' or 'intelligence' but in truth it is very difficult to find a satisfactory English equivalent, and it is therefore best left untranslated so that the context can reveal its meaning. Here the indication seems to be that *buddhi* is comparable to what we might refer to as our personality, making decisions on the basis of the information received through the senses via the *manas*. Verses 14 to 24 reveal that the *buddhi* acts in different ways through the different senses, experiencing the world it inhabits and undergoing joy, misery, or a mixture of both due to the fluctuating fortunes of life. The discussion of the *buddhi* then moves forward with the introduction of the notion of there being three qualities (*guṇas*) that exert an influence over it, another idea that represents one of the fundamental tenets of Sāṁkhya teachings. Now we are told that the joy felt by the *buddhi* is due to the influence of the *guṇa* designated as *sattva*, distress is due to *rajas*, and folly or delusion is the result of *tamas*.

From verse 36, we encounter the usual transition found in Sāṁkhya discourses from the analysis of matter to the assertion of the existence of a non-material element that is wholly distinct and wholly transcendent. We have, of course, already had some mention of this *kṣetrajña* in verses 11 to 13 where it was included in a listing along with the senses, *manas*, and *buddhi*, but the discussion here adheres to the usual Sāṁkhya insistence on the absolute distinction between matter and spirit, with the relationship between them compared to that of a fly living within a fruit or a fish existing in water. There is some sense of co-existence between the two, but in terms of their actual identity they remain utterly distinct. We have therefore a statement here of the absolute duality between the body and the soul that enlivens it. The terminology used to designate the soul is interesting. The main term employed is *kṣetrajña*, which is less commonly encountered than the equivalents of *ātman* or *puruṣa*. In verse 40, the word *ātman* is used in a manner that shows that it is synonymous with *kṣetrajña*, then in verse 41 we encounter *paramātman* (the supreme or higher soul) as a further equivalent term indicating the individual soul. The point I would note here is that the context makes it clear that for the *Adhyātma-kathanam* the three terms *kṣetrajña*, *ātman*, and *paramātman* are absolutely synonymous and do not indicate different phenomena. It might also be pointed out that the absence of the terms *puruṣa* and *prakṛti* is unusual for a treatise on Sāṁkhya and does serve to distance our text a little further from the classical Sāṁkhya of the *Sāṁkihya-kārikā*.

We also have indications here of the inherent connection between Sāṁkhya and Yoga, such a significant feature of the *Mokṣa-dharma-parvan*'s exposition. Verses 36, 44, 55, and 56 all refer to the stilling of the mind and senses so that the reality of the existence of the *ātman* can be perceived, in line with the techniques advocated in Chapter 6 of the *Bhagavad-gītā* and in Patañjali's *Yoga-sūtras*. Like the *Gītā*, the *Adhyātma-kathanam* also addresses the question of whether the person who is pursuing the path of *adhyātma* should continue to perform ritual acts, but whereas the *Gītā* makes a clear statement to the effect that ritual activities must be continued for the sake of purification (18.1–5), the *Adhyātma-kathanam* leaves the matter open, accepting that there are two equally valid opinions on this subject.

The final ten verses of the treatise deal with the results that can be gained through the knowledge designated as *adhyātma*. Here one would expect to find reference to soteriological gains in the form of release from the cycle of rebirth, but there is little here that indicates directly that this is the goal to be achieved, although the removal of the effects of action, mentioned in verse 58, might be placed in that category. Rather, the result gained through mastering an understanding of *adhyātma* is a state of joy, relief, and tranquillity, as if the doubts and fears that naturally beset a person in the human condition are overcome when one has a complete grasp of the actual nature of that condition. Hence again doubts are raised as to whether or not the *Adhyātma-kathanam* can be properly regarded as a treatise on Sāṁkhya. Overall, I would say that there is enough here to justify such a classification and the fact that the redactor has placed it in close juxtaposition with the *Dhyāna-yoga* would suggest that he also regarded it in this light. However, it cannot be taken as a complete or systematic exposition of Sāṁkhya; it would be equally reasonable to regard the *Adhyātma-kathanam* as a treatise that explains the nature of a human being by drawing on Sāṁkhya concepts, or perhaps a form of proto-Sāṁkhya composed at a time when the system was still not fully developed.

1. *yudhiṣṭhira uvāca*
adhyātmaṁ nāma yad idaṁ puruṣasyeha cintyate
yad adhyātmaṁ yataś caitat tan me brūhi pitāmaha

Yudhiṣṭhira said: That which is named *adhyātma* is a fitting subject for a person in this world to consider. Please instruct me, grandfather, about this science of *adhyātma* and from whence it is derived.

2. *bhīṣma uvāca*
adhyātmam iti māṁ pārtha yad etad anupṛcchasi
tad vyākhyāsyāmi te tāta śreyas-karataraṁ sukham

Bhīṣma said: My dear boy, O Pārtha, I will now explain to you the topic known as *adhyātma*, which you have asked me about, for it is most pleasing to discuss and brings great joy to the hearer.

3. *yaj jñātvā puruṣo loke prītiṁ saukhyaṁ ca vindati*
phala-lābhaś ca sadyaḥ syāt sarva-bhūta-hitaṁ ca tat

After acquiring knowledge of *adhyātma*, a person feels both joy and contentment even whilst still in this world. Everything he seeks is immediately attained for this knowledge bestows benefit on all living beings.

4. *pṛthivī vāyur ākāśam āpo jyotiś ca pañcamam*
mahā-bhūtāni bhūtānāṁ sarveṣāṁ prabhavāpyayau

Earth, air, space, water, and fire are the five great elements; these are the beginning and the end of all living beings.

5. *tataḥ sṛṣṭāni tatraiva tāni yānti punaḥ punaḥ*
mahā-bhūtāni bhūteṣu sāgarasyormayo yathā

Over and over again the living beings are created from this source and then return to it once more. As the ocean pervades each individual wave so the great elements pervade these living beings.

6. *prasārya ca yathāṅgāni kūrmaḥ saṁharate punaḥ*
tadvad bhūtāni bhūtātmā sṛṣṭvā saṁharate punaḥ

Just as a tortoise extends its limbs and then withdraws them once more, so the self of all beings first brings these living entities into existence and then withdraws them again.

7. *mahā-bhūtāni pañcaiva sarva-bhūteṣu bhūta-kṛt*
akarot teṣu vaiṣamyaṁ tat tu jīvo 'nu paśyati

The creator of living beings distributed the same five great elements within each creature, but the individual *jīva* perceives distinctions between them.

8. *śabdaḥ śrotraṁ tathā khāni trayam ākāśa-yoni-jam*
vāyos tvak sparśa-ceṣṭāś ca vāg ity etac catuṣṭayam

Sound, the sense of hearing, and open spaces comprise a threefold manifestation born from the great element sky. Skin, the sense of touch, motion, and speech comprise the four-fold manifestation from the element air.

9. *rūpaṁ cakṣus tathā paktis tri-vidhaṁ teja ucyate*
rasaḥ kledaś ca jihvā ca trayo jala-guṇāḥ smṛtāḥ

Form, the sense of sight, and the digestive system are referred to as the three manifestations of fire, whilst flavour, the quality of viscosity, and the tongue are known as the three qualities of water.

10. *ghreyaṁ ghrāṇaṁ śarīraṁ ca te tu bhūmi-guṇās trayaḥ*
mahā-bhūtāni pañcaiva ṣaṣṭhaṁ tu mana ucyate

And then the three qualities related to the element earth are aroma, the sense of smell, and the physical body. There are thus five great elements whilst the mind (*manas*) is referred to as the sixth.

11. *indriyāṇi manaś caiva vijñānāny asya bhārata*
saptamī buddhir ity āhuḥ kṣetrajñaḥ punar aṣṭamaḥ

The senses and the *manas*, O Bhārata, represent the means by which a living being acquires knowledge. They refer to *buddhi* as the seventh element and then the *kṣetrajña* as the eighth.

12. *cakṣur ālokanāyaiva saṁśayaṁ kurute manaḥ*
buddhir adhyavasāyāya kṣetrajñaḥ sākṣi-vat sthitaḥ

Perception is the function of the sense of sight and then the *manas* foments doubt. Reaching conclusions is the function of the *buddhi*, but the *kṣetrajña* remains like a witness.

13. *ūrdhvaṁ pāda-talābhyāṁ yad arvāg ūrdhvaṁ ca paśyati*
etena sarvam evedaṁ viddhy abhivyāptam antaram

From the soles of the feet upwards, it is this knower that perceives all things higher and lower. You should understand that all this existence and everything within it is pervaded by the *kṣetrajña*.

14. *puruṣe cendriyāṇīha veditavyāni kṛtsnaśaḥ*
tamo rajaś ca sattvaṁ ca viddhi bhāvāṁs tad āśrayān

The senses present in each person should be fully understood. You should also know that *tamas*, *rajas*, and *sattva* take their position in the senses.

15. *etāṁ buddhvā naro buddhyā bhūtānām āgatiṁ gatim*
samavekṣya śanaiś caiva labhate śamam uttamam

When he has grasped this teaching and, by using the *buddhi*, has gradually come to understand the emergence and departure of living beings, a man then attains to the highest state of tranquillity.

16. *guṇān nenīyate buddhir buddhir evendriyāṇy api*
manaḥ-ṣaṣṭhāni sarvāṇi buddhy-abhāve kuto guṇāḥ

The *buddhi* is the master of the three *guṇas*, for the five senses and the mind (which is the sixth) are nothing but the *buddhi*. So how could these qualities exist without the presence of *buddhi*?

17. *iti tan-mayam evaitat sarvaṁ sthāvara-jaṅgamam*
pralīyate codbhavati tasmān nirdiśyate tathā

So we see that as it is withdrawn and comes into existence once more, this entire host of moving and stationary beings is based on *buddhi* alone. Therefore this is the doctrine that is widely proclaimed.

18. *yena paśyati tac cakṣuḥ śṛṇoti śrotram ucyate*
jighrāti ghrāṇam ity āhū rasaṁ jānāti jihvayā

The sense by which one sees is known as the eye and that by which one hears is called the ear. They say that the nose perceives aromas and one identifies taste with the tongue.

19. *tvacā spṛśati ca sparśān buddhir vikriyate 'sakṛt*
yena saṁkalpayaty arthaṁ kiṁcid bhavati tan manaḥ

One perceives sensations of touch with the skin; hence the *buddhi* is subject to constant transformations. That by which one determines the precise nature of an object is the *manas*.

20. *adhiṣṭhānāni buddher hi pṛthag arthāni pañcadhā*
pañcendriyāṇi yāny āhus tāny adṛśyo 'dhitiṣṭhati

There are five positions for the *buddhi*, each with a distinct object. They call these the five senses. The *buddhi* occupies these five senses but is itself beyond their range of perception.

21. *puruṣādhiṣṭhitā buddhis triṣu bhāveṣu vartate*
kadācil labhate prītiṁ kadācid anuśocati

It is the *buddhi* that is the governing principle within each person and in this capacity it exists in three different states. Sometimes it experiences delight but at other times it laments.

22. *na sukhena na duḥkhena kadācid api vartate*
evaṁ narāṇāṁ manasi triṣu bhāveṣv avasthitā

And at other times it exists in a condition of neither happiness nor distress. In this way the *buddhi* is situated in three states within the mind (*manasi*) of human beings.

23. *seyaṁ bhāvātmikā bhāvāṁs trīn etān nātivartate*
saritāṁ sāgaro bhartā mahā-velām ivormimān

The *buddhi* thus consists of different states of being and hence cannot move beyond these three states, just like the ocean which is the master of the rivers but cannot carry its waves beyond its shores.

24. *atibhāva-gatā buddhir bhāve manasi vartate*
pravartamānaṁ hi rajas tad bhāvam anuvartate

Moving beyond the senses, the *buddhi* assumes an existence within the *manas*. The quality of *rajas* then impels it towards action as it gravitates towards that mental state.

25. *indriyāṇi hi sarvāṇi pradarśayati sā sadā*
prītiḥ sattvaṁ rajaḥ śokas tamo mohaś ca te trayaḥ

The *buddhi* constantly reveals the perceptions of all the senses. The three *guṇas* are present in this process of perception, *sattva* as joy, *rajas* as grief, and *tamas* as illusion.

26. *ye ye ca bhāvā loke 'smin sarveṣv eteṣu te triṣu*
iti buddhi-gatiḥsarvā vyākhyātā tava bhārata

All states of existence in this world are located within the purview of these three qualities. Now everything about the action of the *buddhi* has been explained to you, Bhārata.

27. *indriyāṇi ca sarvāṇi vijetavyāni dhīmatā*
sattvaṁ rajas tamaś caiva prāṇināṁ saṁśritāḥ sadā

A wise man must keep all his senses under control. *Sattva*, *rajas*, and *tamas* are constant associates of all living beings.

28. *tri-vidhā vedanā caiva sarva-sattveṣu dṛśyate*
sāttvikī rājasī caiva tāmasī ceti bhārata

In all circumstances of life, it is recognised that there are three types of emotional response. These are based on the qualities of *sattva*, *rajas*, and *tamas*, Bhārata.

29. *sukha-sparśaḥ sattva-guṇo duḥkha-sparśo rajo-guṇaḥ*
tamo-guṇena saṁyuktau bhavato 'vyāvahārikau

Feelings of joy represent the *sattva-guṇa* whilst feelings of distress represent the *rajo-guṇa*, but when they combine with the *tamo-guṇa* they no longer display these usual manifestations.

30. *tatra yat prīti-saṁyuktaṁ kāye manasi vā bhavet*
vartate sāttviko bhāva ity avekṣeta tat tadā

So whenever there are feelings of pleasure in either the body or mind, then it should be understood that the *sāttvika* state of being is predominant.

31. *atha yad duḥkha-saṁyuktam atuṣṭi-karam ātmanaḥ*
pravṛttaṁ raja ity eva tann asaṁrabhya cintayet

And whenever one encounters some distress, which brings dissatisfaction to the mind, one should dispassionately observe it as an expansion of the quality of *rajas*.

32. *atha yan moha-saṁyuktam avyaktam iva yad bhavet*
apratarkyam avijñeyaṁ tamas tad upadhārayet

The state of being in which illusion arises is imperceptible for by definition it is not detected by reason and thus remains unrecognised. When illusion predominates one should regard it as the representation of *tamas*.

33. *praharṣaḥ prītir ānandaḥ sukhaṁ saṁśānta-cittatā*
kathaṁcid abhivartanta ity ete sāttvikā guṇāḥ

Delight, joy, bliss, happiness, and complete peace of mind, however they arise, are the qualities associated with *sattva*.

34. *atuṣṭiḥ paritāpaś ca śoko lobhas tathākṣamā*
liṅgāni rajasas tāni dṛśyante hetv-ahetubhiḥ

Dissatisfaction, pain, and grief, as well as greed and intolerance, arising with or without cause, are identified as the marks of *rajas*.

35. *abhimānas tathā mohaḥ pramādaḥ svapna-tandritā*
kathaṁcid abhivartante vividhās tāmasā guṇāḥ

Conceit, illusion, negligence, sleep, and drowsiness, however they arise, are the different qualities associated with *tamas*.

36. *dūra-gaṁ bahudhā-gāmi prārthanā-saṁśayātmakam*
manaḥ suniyataṁ yasya sa sukhī pretya ceha ca

By nature the mind wanders far away in many different directions and is full of hankerings and doubts. But one who keeps his mind under firm control is happy both in this world and in the world to come.

37. *sattva-kṣetrajñayor etad antaraṁ paśya sūkṣmayoḥ*
sṛjate tu guṇān eka eko na sṛjate guṇān

Now note the distinction between the material existence and the *kṣetrajña*, both of which may be subtle by nature. It is this: one manifests qualities and the other does not manifest qualities.

38. *maśakodumbarau cāpi samprayuktau yathā sadā*
anyonyam anyau ca yathā samprayogas tathā tayoḥ

The co-existence of these two is like that of the *udumbara* fruit and the fly living within it, which always exist in a state of union and yet retain distinctive identities.

39. *pṛthag bhūtau prakṛtyā tau samprayuktau ca sarvadā*
yathā matsyo jalaṁ caiva samprayuktau tathaiva tau

In terms of their inherent nature, the character of the two is entirely distinct though they remain in a constant state of union. They are like a fish and the water it swims through, which always remain united.

40. *na guṇā vidur ātmānaṁ sa guṇān vetti sarvaśaḥ*
paridraṣṭā guṇānāṁ ca saṁsraṣṭā manyate sadā

The qualities present in the world do not perceive the *ātman* but the *ātman* perceives all the qualities of existence. The *ātman* is the perceiver of the qualities and always regards itself as the one that has generated them.

41. *indriyais tu pradīpārthaṁ kurute buddhi-saptamaiḥ*
nirviceṣṭair ajānadbhiḥ paramātmā pradīpa-vat

The senses, including the *buddhi* as the seventh amongst them, are by themselves inactive and devoid of knowledge. The *paramātman* is like a glowing lamp that acts through these senses to gain illumination of the world.

42. *sṛjate hi guṇān sattvaṁ kṣetrajñaḥ paripaśyati*
saṁprayogas tayor eṣa sattva-kṣetrajñayor dhruvaḥ

It is material nature that manifests the qualities of the world, whilst the *kṣetrajña* merely observes them. This is the only true point of contact between matter and the *kṣetrajña*.

43. *āśrayo nāsti sattvasya kṣetrajñasya ca kaścana*
sattvaṁ manaḥ saṁsṛjati na guṇān vai kadācana

There is no basis on which the existence of material nature and the *kṣetrajña* depends. This primal matter generates the *manas* but not the *guṇas*.

44. *raśmīṁs teṣāṁ sa manasā yadā samyaṅ niyacchati*
tadā prakāśate 'syātmā ghaṭe dīpo jvalann iva

When a person uses the *manas* to restrain the binding ropes of these *guṇas*, then the *ātman* is revealed, like a lamp that has been shining in an earthen pot.

45. *tyaktvā yaḥ prākṛtaṁ karma nityam ātma-ratir muniḥ*
sarva-bhūtātma-bhūtaḥ syāt sa gacchet paramāṁ gatim

A sage who renounces conventional duties and finds unceasing joy within his own self then exists as the self that is within all beings. Such a person will attain the highest goal.

46. *yathā vāri-caraḥ pakṣī lipyamāno na lipyate*
evam eva kṛta-prajño bhūteṣu parivartate

The wise man exists amongst the people of the world in the same way that a bird swims through water, coming into contact and yet remaining untouched.

47. *evaṁ sva-bhāvam evaitat sva-buddhyā viharen naraḥ*
aśocann aprahṛṣyaṁś ca cared vigata-matsaraḥ

It is in this way that a man should proceed in accordance with his inherent nature, guided by proper use of the *buddhi*. Without lamenting or rejoicing he should live his life free from malice towards any living being.

48. *sva-bhāva-siddhyā saṁsiddhān sa nityaṁ sṛjate guṇān*
ūrṇa-nābhir yathā sraṣṭā vijñeyās tantu-vad guṇāḥ

By perfectly harmonising his inherent nature (*sva-bhāva*) in this way, a person constantly creates ideal qualities around himself, just as the spider is the creator of visible qualities in the form of threads.

49. *pradhvastā na nivartante nivṛttir nopalabhyate*
pratyakṣeṇa parokṣaṁ tad anumānena sidhyati

When they are removed, these qualities do not return but one who follows the path of renunciation never acquires them. This matter is beyond one's direct perception and must be resolved through inference.

50. *evam eke vyavasyanti nivṛttir iti cāpare*
ubhayaṁ saṁpradhāryaitad adhyavasyed yathā mati

Hence some aspirants perform religious duties whilst others stress the renunciation of action. Having carefully considered both opinions one should follow the path one considers most suitable.

51. *itīmaṁ hṛdaya-granthiṁ buddhi-bheda-mayaṁ dṛḍham*
vimucya sukham āsīta na śocec chinna-saṁśayaḥ

In this way, after casting off this hard knot in the heart caused by differing intellectual perspectives, one who has dispelled his doubts finds happiness and laments no more.

52. *malināḥ prāpnuyuḥ śuddhiṁ yathā pūrṇāṁ nadīṁ narāḥ*
avagāhya suvidvāṁso viddhi jñānam idaṁ tathā

You should know that just as dirty men may become clean by bathing in a flowing stream, so wise men can use this wisdom to cleanse their minds.

53. *mahā-nadīṁ hi pāra-jñas tapyate na taran yathā*
evaṁ ye vidur adhyātmaṁ kaivalyaṁ jñānam uttamam

As a person familiar with the opposite bank is distressed when he is unable to cross a mighty river, so those who know that *adhyātma* alone is the highest form of knowledge are dissatisfied until they reach its conclusion.

54. *etāṁ buddhvā naraḥ sarvāṁ bhūtānām āgatiṁ gatim*
avekṣya ca śanair buddhyā labhate śaṁ paraṁ tataḥ

When a man has completely understood this subject and observed the constant arrival and departure of living beings, then by means of the *buddhi* he gradually attains the highest form of happiness.

55. *tri-vargo yasya viditaḥ prāg jyotiḥ sa vimucyate*
anviṣya manasā yuktas tattva-darśī nirutsukaḥ

One who thus understands the three states of existence through the light of his intelligence and then puts them aside, and who applies his mind to Yoga practice, is one who sees the truth and finds perfect tranquillity.

56. *na cātmā śakyate draṣṭum indriyeṣu vibhāgaśaḥ*
tatra tatra visṛṣṭeṣu durjayeṣv akṛtātmabhiḥ

As long as the senses roam in all directions and remain unrestrained, it is impossible for one who has no self-control to perceive the *ātman* as a distinct entity.

57. *etad buddhvā bhaved buddhaḥ kim anyad buddha-lakṣaṇam*
vijñāya tad dhi manyante kṛta-kṛtyā manīṣiṇaḥ

One who has understood this becomes an enlightened soul. Apart from such wisdom, what true mark of enlightenment is there? Upon acquiring this knowledge, men of wisdom consider that they have thereby reached their goal.

58. *na bhavati viduṣāṁ tato bhayaṁ*
yad aviduṣāṁ sumahad bhayaṁ bhavet
na hi gatir adhikāsti kasyacit
sati hi guṇe pravadanty atulyatām

At that point those things that are such terrible sources of dread for the ignorant no longer hold any fear for such men of wisdom. There is no higher achievement for anyone in this world for they say that nothing can equal such a quality of existence.

59. *yat karoty anabhisaṁdhi-pūrvakaṁ*
tac ca nirṇudati yat purā kṛtam
nāpriyaṁ tad ubhayaṁ kutaḥ priyaṁ
tasya taj janayatīha kurvataḥ

Whatever actions he now performs are done without prior planning or expectation and this mode of conduct destroys the effect of the actions he performed previously. Hence neither the past actions he has performed nor his present actions generate unwanted results for him in this world, and how would anything be desirable here?

60. *loka ātura-janān virāviṇas*
tat tad eva bahu paśya śocataḥ
tatra paśya kuśalān aśocato
ye vidus tad ubhayaṁ padaṁ sadā

Behold all these afflicted persons suffering in the world and how much they lament over the various sorrows they face. Look also at those who prosper. Persons who understand that both these conditions always exist in this world do not lament.

The Dhyāna-Yoga

Śānti-parvan, Adhyāya 188

It is interesting to note that the transition from the *Adhyātma-kathanam* to the *Dhyāna-yoga* takes place without any question from Yudhiṣṭhira to prompt the change in subject, suggesting again that the topics of the two chapters are closely related. In the first verse, Bhīṣma announces that he will now speak about the subject of *dhyāna-yoga*, which is *catur-vidham*, of four categories or types. This fourfold division is never fully explained, although it might refer to the subjugation of the mind and senses, discussed in the opening part of the chapter, and then the three processes of *vitarka*, *vicāra*, and *viveka* mentioned in verse 15. The term *dhyāna* is widely translated as meaning meditation and is the original form of the Buddhist Zen; it is also included as one of the eight limbs of Patañjali's *aṣṭāṅga-yoga* and is probably best understood as the process by which the consciousness is directed inwards rather than outwards, with the purpose of gaining realised knowledge of the true self and thereby achieving liberation from rebirth. The process is described here only very briefly and the focus seems to be confined to the beginning stages of Yoga practice rather than the higher realisations that follow. Indeed, one has some sense that the discourse is incomplete and concludes after the introductory section's warning that the process is difficult and must be applied repeatedly, without discouragement, in order to gain success.

Passages of this type within the *Mokṣa-dharma-parvan* are of immense significance for an understanding of the Indian religious traditions, as they may well represent the earliest known treatises on the practice of the Yoga system. The Yoga *darśana* is usually regarded as being derived from Patañjali's *Yoga-sūtras*. The dating of this work is uncertain but it was probably composed some time between 200 and 500 CE, and hence almost certainly post-dates the material found in *Mahābhārata*. We can only speculate as to the relationship between our passages and the *Yoga-sūtras* but it does not seem unreasonable to suspect that what we have here, and in the *Bhagavad-gītā*, was used by Patañjali in formulating his composition. Given the rather scanty nature of the teachings in this passage, however, it may also be the case that both Patañjali and the *Mahābhārata* authors drew on a body of earlier literature that is no longer extant.

We noted that at the end of the *Adhyātma-kathanam* that there is a rather surprising dearth of soteriological remarks, which we would expect as a natural conclusion to a discourse on Sāṁkhya. This can be more easily explained if we accept that the *Adhyātma-kathanam* and the *Dhyāna-yoga* are contiguous pieces rather than discrete treatises, for the opening verses here are given over to describing the soteriological orientation of the Yoga system being referred to. This is a significant point, which reminds us again that from the outset Yoga was regarded not as a means of gaining good health, relaxation, or peace of mind, but as a series of techniques that had the sole aim of granting the practitioner release from the cycle of rebirth. That is not to say that relaxation, good health, and mental serenity are not attained through the practice, but these are not the primary goals of the system. We may note that the term used here to designate that state of release is *nirvāṇa*, which is more often associated with Buddhism than with Sāṁkhya and Yoga (where *kaivalya* is the more usual term employed). It is not that uncommon, however, to find the term *nirvāṇa* used by Hindu texts, as is illustrated by the *Bhagavad-gītā*'s usage in 2.72 and in Chapter 5. We can also note that the treatise here seems to accept the idea of a *jīvan-mukta*, a person who has attained this state of release even whilst continuing to dwell in the world, as seems apparent from verse 4.

As mentioned above, the Yoga teachings presented herein are rather limited in scope and focus almost exclusively on gaining control over the fluctuations of the mind. The wandering, restless mind is to be brought under control by the regular practice of fixing it on a single point. The senses, which act as agents of the mind (*manas*), are withdrawn from their normal mode of perception and are taken back into the mind where they remain as a single substance. Thus the conventional processes of seeing, hearing, feeling, smelling, and tasting cease to operate; the mental processes are stilled. When this has been achieved, the controlled mind can then be directed inwards so as to gain direct knowledge of one's own being. At this point, in verse 10, we are informed that this is the first phase on the path of *dhyāna* (*dhyāna-pathaḥ pūrvaḥ*), but the treatise does not really carry the discussion any further. Rather it moves on to emphasise the difficulties involved in carrying out the process it has described, insisting that the practitioner must be prepared for setbacks and have the determination to start again when the mind slips from his control. This point is made in verses 11 to 14 and then again in 16 to 20 but then the discourse draws to an abrupt close with the final two verses simply proclaiming that the practitioner who is successful in his endeavours will experience great joy and finally *nirvāṇa* by ending the cycle of birth and death.

Verse 15, however, provides an interlude in this line of discussion and here the *Dhyāna-yoga* names three states of consciousness that begin to appear (*upajāyate*) in this early stage of the practice, the *prathamaṁ dhyānam*. These are given as *vicāra*, *vitarka*, and *viveka*, all of which are familiar notions within the wider of context of Yoga discourse. No details are given here of what these states involve or amount to, but they are also discussed in the *Yoga-sūtras*. Patañjali presents *vicāra* and *vitarka* as forms of concentration to be undertaken as a part of the beginning stages of the practice (1.17) in which one attempts contemplation, analysis, and inquiry into the true nature of one's own identity (1.42–45). It appears that the practice of intense concentration through *vitarka* and *vicāra* involves the absorption of the mind in a single object; when this technique is mastered, one is then able to progress to a higher state referred to as *nir-vicāra* concentration in which there is no need for a specific object as a focus for the concentrated mind (1.45). The term *viveka* usually has the meaning of discrimination, or the power of discrimination, and this is also included in the teachings of the *Yoga-sūtras*. The discrimination inherent in *viveka* forms a part of the Sāṁkhya ideology through which the spiritual entity, *puruṣa*, is recognised as being wholly distinct from its material embodiment in *prakṛti*. Hence the *Yoga-sūtras* refers to *viveka* as the means by which *avidyā* (ignorance) is destroyed, for *avidyā* is defined as being the inability to distinguish between the true self and matter, between the seer and the seen (2.21–26). And *viveka* is also noted in Chapter 3 of the *Yoga-sūtras* as being the source of realised knowledge, *viveka-jaṁ jñānam* (3.53, 55) and hence the means by which the practitioner gains liberation from rebirth.

This discussion highlights the fact that the type of Yoga touched upon briefly in the *Dhyāna-yoga* appears to be virtually identical to that outlined in the *Yoga-sūtras* and in Chapter 6 of the *Bhagavad-gītā*. Here there is no mention whatsoever of any of the physical aspects that have come to predominate in the later schools of Yoga practice. There is no reference to *āsana* or *prāṇāyāma* and the focus is placed entirely on gaining mastery over the fluctuating mind and senses, the *citta-vṛtti-nirodha* presented by Patañjali as the defining characteristic of Yoga practice (1.2). Of course, the treatise here is very short and limited in scope, so it would be unwise to base far-reaching conclusions upon it, but it does appear that at this point Yoga was very closely related to Sāṁkhya teachings and that the practice was designed exclusively to give realisation of the distinction between *prakṛti* and *puruṣa*, body and soul. We cannot say that the *haṭha* and tantric Yoga practices were unknown during this early period, but it seems apparent that for the *Mahābhārata* and the *Bhagavad-gītā* this is not what Yoga is about.

1. *bhīṣma uvāca*
hanta vakṣyāmi te pārtha dhyāna-yogaṁ catur-vidham
yaṁ jñātvā śāśvatīṁ siddhiṁ gacchanti paramarṣayaḥ

Bhīṣma said: Now, Pārtha, I will teach you about *dhyāna-yoga*, the Yoga of meditation, which can be divided into four types. After understanding this science, the highest amongst the *rishis* attain a state of perfection that never ends.

2. *yathā sv-anuṣṭhitaṁ dhyānaṁ tathā kurvanti yoginaḥ*
maharṣayo jñāna-tṛptā nirvāṇa-gata-mānasāḥ

The great *rishis* who are *yogins* are satisfied by wisdom alone and their minds are focused on reaching the state of *nirvāṇa*. They always behave in such a way that their meditation can be successfully performed.

3. *nāvartante punaḥ pārtha muktāḥ saṁsāra-doṣataḥ*
janma-doṣa-parikṣīṇāḥ sva-bhāve paryavasthitāḥ

When they are liberated from the miseries of repeated birth and death, Pārtha, they never return to this world. With the miseries of rebirth cast aside, they can then exist in accordance with their true nature.

4. *nirdvaṁdvā nitya-sattva-sthā vimuktā nityam āśritāḥ*
asaṅgīny avivādīni manaḥ-śānti-karāṇi ca

They are liberated beings, free from worldly dualities, who never deviate from the quality of *sattva*. They always dwell in places where there are no material entanglements or disputations and which create a tranquil state of mind.

5. *tatra svādhyāya-saṁśliṣṭam ekāgraṁ dhārayen manaḥ*
piṇḍī-kṛtyendriya-grāmam āsīnaḥ kāṣṭhavan muniḥ

There, absorbed in silent recitation, the sage fixes his mind in meditation on a single point. He sits like a log of wood, compressing all his senses into a single substance.

6. *śabdaṁ na vindec chrotreṇa sparśaṁ tvacā na vedayet*
rūpaṁ na cakṣuṣā vidyāj jihvayā na rasāṁs tathā

With his ear he perceives no sound; with his skin he is unaware of any touch. With his eye he sees no form; with his tongue he perceives no taste.

7. *ghreyāṇy api ca sarvāṇi jahyād dhyānena yoga-vit*
pañca-varga-pramāthīni necchec cetāni vīryavān

During his practice of meditation, one who knows the path of Yoga will also remain unaware of any aroma. Filled with spiritual potency, he no longer desires any object that agitates the five senses.

8. *tato manasi saṁsajya pañca-vargaṁ vicakṣaṇaḥ*
samādadhyān mano bhrāntam indriyaiḥ saha pañcabhiḥ

Having brought the five senses together within his mind, the man of wisdom should then take control of the wandering mind as well as the five senses within it.

9. *visaṁcārī nirālambaṁ pañca-dvāraṁ calācalam*
pūrve dhyāna-pathe dhīraḥ samādadhyān mano 'ntaram

The mind does not depend on anything but itself. It has five gates and is always restless. From the outset, the wise man who is undeviating on the path of meditation should direct the mind inwards.

10. *indriyāṇi manaś caiva yadā piṇḍī karoty ayam*
eṣa dhyāna-pathaḥ pūrvo mayā samanuvarṇitaḥ

When the practitioner combines the senses and the mind together as one substance, this marks the first stage of the path of meditation I am teaching.

11. *tasya tat pūrva-saṁruddhaṁ manaḥ-ṣaṣṭham anantaram*
sphuriṣyati samudbhrāntaṁ vidyud ambu-dhare yathā

Although the adept's mind, the sixth element, has previously been brought under complete control, it may ignite once more into a state of agitation just like lightning flashing from within a cloud.

12. *jala-bindur yathā lolaḥ parṇa-sthaḥ sarvataś calaḥ*
evam evāsya tac cittaṁ bhavati dhyāna-vartmani

The consciousness of one on the path of meditation is just like a drop of water moving in all directions as it sits trembling on a leaf.

13. *samāhitaṁ kṣaṇaṁ kiṁcid dhyāna-vartmani tiṣṭhati*
punar vāyu-pathaṁ bhrāntaṁ mano bhavati vāyu-vat

The mind remains fixed on its course of meditation for a short time but then it takes off once more, just like the wind as it sweeps along its course.

14. *anirvedo gata-kleśo gata-tandrīr amatsaraḥ*
samādadhyāt punaś ceto dhyānena dhyāna-yoga-vit

Without disappointment at the setback and setting aside his distress and all sense of hostility, one who understands this *dhyāna-yoga* should remain calm and bring his mind under control once more through renewed practice of meditation.

15. *vicāraś ca vitarkaś ca vivekaś copajāyate*
muneḥ samādadhānasya prathamaṁ dhyānam āditaḥ

In the beginning stage, the powers of reflection, deliberation and discrimination (*vicāra, vitarka*, and *viveka*) progressively appear as the primary meditation for the sage who is practising inner contemplation.

16. *manasā kliśyamānas tu samādhānaṁ ca kārayet*
na nirvedaṁ munir gacchet kuryād evātmano hitam

Even when disturbed by the mind, he must continue his practice of inward contemplation. The sage should never fall prey to disappointment but should continue to make the endeavours that will ultimately bestow great benefit.

17. *pāṁsu-bhasma-karīṣāṇāṁ yathā vai rāśayaś citāḥ*
sahasā vāriṇā siktā na yānti paribhāvanām

Piled-up heaps of soil, ashes, and dung do not immediately become merged together when they are soaked by water.

18. *kiṁcit snigdhaṁ yathā ca syāc chuṣka-cūrṇam abhāvitam*
kramaśas tu śanair gacchet sarvaṁ tat paribhāvanam

Slowly and gradually they all merge into one substance, but while they are only partially moistened there will still be parts that are dry like powder and devoid of water.

19. *evam evendriya-grāmaṁ śanaiḥ saṁparibhāvayet*
saṁharet kramaśaś caiva sa samyak praśamiṣyati

In the same way one should slowly draw together all the senses into one combined substance and gradually withdraw them from their objects. When held together in this way that group of senses will then become pacified.

20. *svayam eva manaś caiva pañca-vargaś ca bhārata*
pūrvaṁ dhyāna-pathaṁ prāpya nitya-yogena śāmyati

When, through his own resolve, he is able to keep his mind and five senses fixed on the path of meditation, O Bhārata, the adept then pacifies them by means of constant Yoga practice.

21. *na tat puruṣa-kāreṇa na ca daivena kenacit*
sukham eṣyati tat tasya yad evaṁ saṁyatātmanaḥ

Neither through human endeavour nor any gift of destiny can one obtain joy like that of one who controls his mind.

22. *sukhena tena saṁyukto raṁsyate dhyāna-karmaṇi*
gacchanti yogino hy evaṁ nirvāṇaṁ tan nirāmayam

Filled with this joy, *yogins* will then take further delight in their practice of meditation. In this way they reach the state of *nirvāṇa* that is free from any blemish.

The Jāpakopākhyānam

Śānti-parvan, Adhyāya 189–193

THE *JĀPAKOPAKHYĀNAM* or *Jāpaka Upākhyānam*, literally the tale of the *jāpaka*, is the only passage of the *Mokṣa-dharma-parvan* in which the practice of *japa* is praised or advocated. *Japa* is the silent or murmured recitation of a particular prayer, hymn, or divine name that is still frequently undertaken by contemporary Hindus, although today it is for the most part a devotional practice based on the name of the Deity worshipped or a short prayer dedicated to that Deity. This passage consists of five chapters, the first three of which are devoted to an exposition of the merits and possible pitfalls faced by those who practise *japa* as their main form of religious exercise. These three chapters are all quite brief and in Chapter 4, at Yudhiṣṭhira's request, Bhīṣma begins to recount the story of an incident that occurred at the end of the life of a *jāpaka* of most excellent accomplishment. This is a slightly whimsical tale that involves the presence of personified forms of Dharma, Death, Heaven, Time, and Yama, who is the god of death and the son of Vivasvān, the sun god. A lengthy conversation ensues between these characters and the *jāpaka*, although most of the debate takes place between the *jāpaka* and King Ikṣvāku, another son of the sun god, who also appears on the scene.

Most of their discussion is devoted to a debate concerning the giving away of any benefits that have been achieved through spiritual or religious practice, which is only resolved through the intervention of two further characters, named as Desire and Anger. Chapter 5 of the treatise then provides an account of how the *jāpaka* and Ikṣvāku achieved liberation from this world by entering into the Deity Brahmā, both sharing equally the merit of the spiritual practices they have undertaken. The passage draws to a conclusion with Bhīṣma asserting that when it is performed with full concentration *japa* is as efficacious as Yoga practice in bringing the practitioner to the highest spiritual position that can be achieved.

Śānti-parvan, Adhyāya 189

The first chapter of the *Jāpakopākhyānam* opens with a series of questions from Yudhiṣṭhira on the subject of *japa*, as he asks about how it is to be practised and the nature of the rewards to be gained from its performance. In response, Bhīṣma indicates that *japa* forms a part of both the path of Vedic ritualism and that of renunciation, *pravṛtti* and *nivṛtti*. Verses 9 and 10 offer a brief account of the lifestyle of ritualists who practise *japa*, before Bhīṣma turns to discuss the manner in which those who have renounced the world to perform *japa* must live and adhere to their discipline. It is clear from these verses that *japa* is to be understood as a form of concentration on mantras from the Veda, which are continuously repeated either by speech or purely within the mind. From this description, we are given to understand that *japa* is a form of the *dhāraṇā*, concentration, of Patañjali's *Yoga Sūtras*, serving as a preliminary to the practice of *dhyāna*, meditation, as indicated in verses 14 and 15.

1. *yudhiṣṭhira uvāca*
cātur āśramyam uktaṁ te rāja-dharmās tathaiva ca
nānāśrayāś ca bahava itihāsāḥ pṛthag vidhāḥ

Yudhiṣṭhira said: You have spoken about the four stages of life and about the *dharma* of a king. You have also narrated a number of different stories that refer to various points of instruction.

2. *śrutās tvattaḥ kathāś caiva dharma-yuktā mahā-mate*
saṁdeho 'sti tu kaścin me tad bhavān vaktum arhati

O learned teacher, several narrations have now been heard from you which reflect upon the idea of *dharma*. However, a specific doubt still afflicts me and you should now kindly address this topic.

3. *jāpakānāṁ phalāvāptiṁ śrotum icchāmi bhārata*
kiṁ phalaṁ japatām uktaṁ kva vā tiṣṭhanti jāpakāḥ

O Bhārata, I wish to hear about the result attained by the *jāpakas*. What is said to be the fruit of *japa*? What is the position of *jāpakas* in the next life?

4. *japasya ca vidhiṁ kṛtsnaṁ vaktum arhasi me 'nagha*
jāpakā iti kiṁ caitat sāṁkhya-yoga-kriyā-vidhiḥ

O sinless one, could you also describe in full the discipline that governs the practice of *japa*. When we speak of 'the *jāpakas*' does this refer to persons who adhere to the rules of conduct of the Sāṁkya and Yoga systems?

5. *kiṁ yajña-vidhir evaiṣa kim etaj japyam ucyate*
etan me sarvam ācakṣva sarva-jño hy asi me mataḥ

Is this practice spoken of as a form of sacrificial ritual? What is laid down as the sacred formula to be recited? Teach me everything about this practice; instruct me now, for you are all-knowing.

6. *bhīṣma uvāca*
atrāpy udāharantīmam itihāsaṁ purātanam
yamasya yat purā vṛttaṁ kālasya brāhmaṇasya ca

Bhīṣma said: In this connection, they narrate this ancient history about an encounter that took place long ago between Yama, Time, and a certain Brahmin.

7. *saṁnyāsa eva vedānte vartate japanam prati*
veda-vādābhinirvṛttā śāntir brahmaṇy avasthitau
mārgau tāv apy ubhāv etau saṁśritau na ca saṁśritau

Within the Vedānta, renunciation with regard to *japa* is to the fore, whilst inner tranquillity is the result of following the teachings of the Veda. Both these two paths are based on Brahman. The practice of *japa* may or may not form a part of them.

8. *yathā saṁśrūyate rājan kāraṇaṁ cātra vakṣyate*
manaḥ-samādhir atrāpi tathendriya-jayaḥ smṛtaḥ

I will now explain the reason for this, O king, as I have understood it from others. It is recognised that this concerns the fixing of the mind on one point and the control of the senses.

9. *satyam agni-paricāro viviktānāṁ ca sevanam*
dhyānaṁ tapo damaḥ kṣāntir anasūyā mitāśanam

Truthfulness, tending the sacred fire, and living alone in deserted places; meditation, austerity, self-control, patience, freedom from malice, moderation in eating;

10. *viṣaya-pratisaṁhāro mita-jalpas tathā śamaḥ*
eṣa pravṛttako dharmo nivṛttakam atho śṛṇu

Renunciation of the objects of sensory pleasure, control of one's speech, and equanimity; these constitute the *dharma* of the active religious life, now hear about the *dharma* for the religious life based on the renunciation of action.

11. *yathā nivartate karma japato brahmacāriṇaḥ*
etat sarvam aśeṣeṇa yathoktaṁ parivarjayet
tri-vidhaṁ mārgam āsādya vyaktāvyaktam anāśrayam

This is how action is abandoned by the celibate practitioner of *japa*: he must completely renounce everything in this world in the manner described above. He then applies himself to the threefold path, of which the first stage is easy to perceive, the next stage is imperceptible, and the final stage is that in which one needs no external support.

12. *kuśoccayaniṣaṇṇaḥ san kuśa-hastaḥ kuśaiḥ śikhī*
cīraiḥ parivṛttas tasmin madhye channaḥ kuśais tathā

He should be seated on a mat of plucked *kuśa* grass, with *kuśa* grass in his hands and on top of his head. He should dress in ragged clothes that have garments of *kuśa* grass inside them.

13. *viṣayebhyo namaskuryād viṣayān na ca bhāvayet*
sāmyam utpādya manaso manasy eva mano dadhat

He should offer his respect to the objects of sensory enjoyment and then never concern himself with them again. After bringing his mind to a state of equanimity, he should then fix the mind upon the mind alone.

14. *tad dhiyā dhyāyati brahma japan vai saṁhitāṁ hitām*
saṁnyasyaty atha vā tāṁ vai samādhau paryavasthitaḥ

By concentrating his mind in this way he is able to meditate upon Brahman, whilst reciting to himself an auspicious passage from the Veda. When his mind is absorbed in total concentration he gives up this recitation.

15. *dhyānam utpādayaty atra saṁhitā-bala-saṁśrayāt*
śuddhātmā tapasā dānto nivṛtta-dveṣa-kāmavān

He takes to the practice of meditation based on the power of Vedic mantras he recites. By undertaking acts of austerity he becomes pure at heart and self-controlled, and turns away from both loathing and longing.

16. *arāga-moho nirdvaṁdvo na śocati na sajjate*
na kartākaraṇīyānāṁ na kāryāṇām iti sthitiḥ

He is free from attachment and illusion, he has transcended the dualities of the world, he does not lament and he does not long for anything. Hence his position is such that he is the doer of neither forbidden nor prescribed actions.

17. *na cāhaṁkāra-yogena manaḥ prasthāpayet kvacit*
na cātma-grahaṇe yukto nāvamānī na cākriyaḥ

He should never allow his mind to dwell on any subject that invokes a sense of personal pride. He never indulges in any selfish pursuits, nor does he feel contempt for others, and he does not give up his religious duties.

18. *dhyāna-kriyā-paro yukto dhyānavān dhyāna-niścayaḥ*
dhyāne samādhim utpādya tad api tyajati kramāt

He undertakes the disciplines of meditation with great diligence, pursuing this practice with close attention and firm resolve. But when his meditation reaches the stage of total concentration, he then gives up such regulated practice.

19. *sa vai tasyām avasthāyāṁ sarva-tyāga-kṛtaḥ sukhī*
nirīhas tyajati prāṇān brāhmīṁ saṁśrayate tanum

In that state, his renunciation of the world is complete and he is filled with joy. Free from desire, he casts off the breath of life and exists in a form that is entirely spiritual.

20. *atha vā necchate tatra brahma-kāya-niṣevaṇam*
utkrāmati ca mārga-stho naiva kvacana jāyate

Or if he does not wish to exist in this way by taking on a spiritual form, then he continues on his upward journey and never takes birth anywhere again.

21. *ātma-buddhiṁ samāsthāya śāntī-bhūto nirāmayaḥ*
amṛtaṁ virajaḥ-śuddham ātmānaṁ pratipadyate

Having attained true self-knowledge, and being peaceful at heart and free from affliction, he finally attains the immortal *ātman*, which is pure and without blemish.

Śānti-parvan, Adhyāya 190

This short chapter focuses on the various ways in which practitioners of *japa* may fall short in their endeavours and the consequences of such failure. Bhīṣma repeatedly asserts that shortcomings in the performance of *japa* will lead the *jāpaka* to a destination in hell, *niraya*, although it is made apparent that this is not a form of hell in the more usual meaning of the term. What is meant by the word *niraya* is indicated in some of the verses here and made even more evident at the end of the next chapter where Bhīṣma states that any form of rebirth must be regarded as a type of hell in comparison to the absolute joy of liberation attained by practitioners of *japa* who are fully dedicated to their recitation and free from materialistic aspirations.

1. *yudhiṣṭhira uvāca*
gatīnām uttamā prāptiḥ kathitā jāpakeṣv iha
ekaivaiṣā gatis teṣām uta yānty aparām api

Yudhiṣṭhira said: You have stated that in this world the *jāpakas* may attain the highest goal. Is this their only destination or do they go to any other abode?

2. *bhīṣma uvāca*
śṛṇuṣvāvahito rājañ jāpakānāṁ gatiṁ vibho
yathā gacchanti nirayam anekaṁ puruṣarṣabha

Bhīṣma replied: O mighty king, O best of men, listen carefully as I tell you about the destination of the *jāpakas* and the various forms of damnation they must undergo.

3. *yathoktam etat pūrvaṁ yo nānutiṣṭhati jāpakaḥ*
eka-deśa-kriyaś cātra nirayaṁ sa nigacchati

Any *jāpaka* who does not pursue the course I previously described and fails to move on from the beginning stage of his practice will enter hell.

4. *avajñānena kurute na tuṣyati na śocati*
īdṛśo jāpako yāti nirayaṁ nātra saṁśayaḥ

The *jāpaka* who performs his recitation without respect for the practice, and hence is neither satisfied by progress nor troubled by failure, certainly goes to hell. There is no doubt about this.

5. *ahaṁkāra-kṛtaś caiva sarve niraya-gāminaḥ*
parāvamānī puruṣo bhavitā nirayopagaḥ

All those *jāpakas* whose works are tainted by pride are condemned to hell. A person who bears malice towards others is certainly destined for hell.

6. *abhidhyā-pūrvakaṁ japyaṁ kurute yaś ca mohitaḥ*
yatrābhidhyāṁ sa kurute taṁ vai nirayam ṛcchati

Under the spell of illusion, a person may recite his prayer with the aim of fulfilling some previous desire. Whatever desire he pursues becomes the particular form of hell he must experience.

7. *athaiśvarya-pravṛttaḥ sañjāpakas tatra rajyate*
sa eva nirayas tasya nāsau tasmāt pramucyate

The *jāpaka* who seeks to gain opulence is satisfied by its acquisition. This is certainly his hell and such a person never becomes free from that damnation.

8. *rāgeṇa jāpako japyaṁ kurute tatra mohitaḥ*
yatrāsya rāgaḥ patati tatra tatropajāyate

The *jāpaka* executes his recitation with attachment in his heart and therein lies his illusion. Wherever his attachment happens to descend, it is there that he will take his next birth.

9. *durbuddhir akṛta-prajñaś cale manasi tiṣṭhati*
calām eva gatiṁ yāti nirayaṁ vādhigacchati

Such an unintelligent *jāpaka* of limited wisdom remains with his mind always unsteady. Hence he attains either an unsteady destination or else a place in hell.

10. *akṛta-prajñako bālo mohaṁ gacchati jāpakaḥ*
sa mohān nirayaṁ yāti tatra gatvānuśocati

The foolish *jāpaka* who is devoid of wisdom thus sinks into a state of delusion. Because of his delusion he goes to hell and after going there he can only lament.

11. *dṛḍha-grāhī karomīti japyaṁ japati jāpakaḥ*
na saṁpūrṇo na vā yukto nirayaṁ so 'dhigacchati

If a *jāpaka* who performs his recitation with constant dedication subsequently fails to complete his practice, or is inattentive in its execution, then he goes to hell.

12. *yudhiṣṭhira uvāca*
animittaṁ paraṁ yat tad avyaktaṁ brahmaṇi sthitam
sad-bhūto jāpakaḥ kasmāt sa śarīram athāviśet

Yudhiṣṭhira said: That which is causeless and supreme is imperceptible to the senses and is located entirely in Brahman. So how is it that a righteous *jāpaka* must take on another body?

13. *bhīṣma uvāca*
duṣprajñānena nirayā bahavaḥ samudāhṛtāḥ
praśastaṁ jāpakatvaṁ ca doṣāś caite tadātmakāḥ

Bhīṣma said: Many forms of hell are said to be the result of inadequate knowledge. The process of *japa* is widely praised but it is also beset by these inherent shortcomings.

Śānti-parvan, Adhyāya 191

Chapter 3 of the *Jāpakopākhyānam* is given over in part to a description of the worlds of the gods and other members of the celestial host. Although these appear to be wonderful abodes in which to be reborn, Bhīṣma says here that they are to be regarded as no more than hell in comparison to the position of the *paramātman*, the *sthānasya paramātmanaḥ* (verse 6), a phrase that is not exactly clear but which must refer to the state of liberation from all forms of rebirth. The numbers referred to in verses 7 and 8 can be interpreted in different ways, but the main point is evident enough, revealing that liberation means an escape from all the sufferings that prevail in this world. In contrast, any form of rebirth, even if it be amongst the celestial beings, is to be regarded as a form of hell.

1. *yudhiṣṭhira uvāca*
kīdṛśo jāpako yāti nirayaṁ varṇayasva me
kautūhalaṁ hi me jātaṁ tad bhavān vaktum arhati

Yudhiṣṭhira said: Please describe to me the particular type of *jāpaka* who goes to hell. A keen interest in this topic has arisen within me so kindly explain it now.

2. *bhīṣma uvāca*
dharmasyāṁśaḥ prasūto 'si dharmiṣṭho 'si sva-bhāvataḥ
dharma-mūlāśrayaṁ vākyaṁ śṛṇuṣvāvahito 'nagha

Bhīṣma said: You were born as a part of Dharma and you are completely devoted to *dharma*. Listen attentively to this discourse, O sinless one, for it embodies the very root of *dharma*.

3. *amūni yāni sthānāni devānāṁ paramātmanām*
nānā-saṁsthāna-varṇāni nānā-rūpa-phalāni ca

Those worlds in which the great-minded gods exist have different levels and manifestations, and they appear in various forms, offering different rewards.

4. *divyāni kāma-cārīṇi vimānāni sabhās tathā*
ākrīḍā vividhā rājan padminyaś cāmalodakāḥ

There are celestial carriages, O king, that move through the sky according to one's will, as well as palaces, numerous parks and pleasure grounds, ponds filled with lotus flowers, and lakes of pure water.

5. *caturṇāṁ loka-pālānāṁ śukrasyātha bṛhaspateḥ*
marutāṁ viśvadevānāṁ sādhyānāṁ aśvinor api

These are the worlds of the four guardians of creation, of Śukra, Bṛhaspati, the Maruts, the Viśvadevas, the Sādhyas, and the two Aśvins.

6. *rūdrāditya-vasūnāṁ ca tathānyeṣāṁ divaukasām*
ete vai nirayās tāta sthānasya paramātmanaḥ

There are also the worlds of the Rudras, the Ādityas, and the Vasus, and many other gods besides. But in truth, my dear boy, these are forms of hell in comparison to the realm of the *paramātman.*

7. *abhayaṁ cānimittaṁ ca na ca kleśa-bhayāvṛtam*
dvābhyāṁ muktaṁ tribhir muktam aṣṭābhis tribhir eva ca

This is free from fear and has no external cause. In this existence, there is neither affliction nor anxiety for one is free from duality, free from the three, free from the eight, and free from the other three as well.

8. *catur-lakṣaṇa-varjaṁ tu catuṣ-kāraṇa-varjitam*
apraharṣam anānandam aśokaṁ vigata-klamam

That existence is free from the four attributes and the four causes. No feelings of pleasure are experienced there, nor joy, grief, or exhaustion.

9. *kālaḥ saṁpacyate tatra na kālas tatra vai prabhuḥ*
sa kālasya prabhū rājan svargasyāpi tatheśvaraḥ

There the influence of time is destroyed, for time has no dominion there. The Lord is indeed the master of time, O king, as he is master of the heavens of the gods.

10. *ātma-kevalatāṁ prāptas tatra gatvā na śocati*
īdṛśaṁ paramaṁ sthānaṁ nirayās te ca tādṛśāḥ

When one attains equality of existence with the *ātman* and reaches that domain, then one does not grieve. This is the topmost state of being and by comparison all other forms of existence are hell.

11. *ete te nirayāḥ proktāḥ sarva eva yathātatham*
tasya sthāna-varasyeha sarve niraya-saṁjñitāḥ

Now everything about these hells has been accurately described to you. In comparison to that highest position, all others are regarded as hell.

Śānti parvan, Adhyāya 192

Chapter 4 of the *Jāpakopākhyānam* is by far the longest of the five and it is here that we find the actual *upākhyānam*, the narrative, being related by Bhīṣma. The story is that of a certain Brahmin who followed the path of renunciation and dedicated his life to the practice of *japa*. It is indicated in verse 6 that the intention behind his practice was liberation from rebirth by reaching the state of Brahman, and the first of his several encounters is with the goddess Sāvitrī who assures him that he will remain dedicated to his practice and that his desire for liberation will be fulfilled. Following on from this meeting, it is the deity Dharma who next appears, urging the *jāpaka* to give up his present body and ascend to the realms of the gods. Yama, the god of death and rebirth, then comes there along with personified forms of Time, Death, and Heaven, and all of them press the *jāpaka* to follow Dharma's instruction. Unmoved by their urgings, however, he rejects their advice, stating that he gains so much inner joy from his *japa* that he is unwilling to give up his present bodily identity through which he experiences that joy.

From verse 34, the narrative takes another turn, as King Ikṣvāku enters upon the scene. A lengthy debate between Ikṣvāku and the *jāpaka* follows over whether it is appropriate for them to receive gifts from each other in the form of the results they have gained through their spiritual practices. This debate is punctuated by a eulogy of *satyam* (truth or truthfulness), spoken by the *jāpaka* in verses 60 to 69 as he attempts to persuade Ikṣvāku to accept the results he has attained from his practice of *japa*, which the king initially asked for but is now refusing to accept. Resolution is finally reached through the appearance of two further characters, named as Vikṛti and Virūpa, which mean agitation and disfiguration respectively. These two, who are later revealed to be personified forms of Anger and Desire, are having a similar debate to that going on between the *jāpaka* and Ikṣvāku, and when the king gives his verdict on who is in the right, it is made apparent that he cannot refuse the *jāpaka*'s gift if he is to be consistent in his judgement. The final agreement is then made that they will share the acquired merit of each other's spiritual endeavours and with that the matter is finally settled.

It might be said that this extended narrative tells us little about the practice of *japa*, although it is made clear that the benefits of *japa* may include both liberation from rebirth and elevation to the realm of the gods. The *jāpaka* also indicates that he seeks no result at all from his practice, as he is filled with joy simply by the recitation of the mantras and is not particularly concerned about gaining any reward for his endeavours. In other words, *japa* itself fills one with a sense of spiritual beatitude. In his conclusion to the chapter, Bhīṣma then reasserts his earlier point that liberation is a far superior goal to strive for than any form of elevated rebirth in this world, which is to be regarded as existence in hell by comparison.

1. *yudhiṣṭhira uvāca*
kāla-mṛtyu-yamānāṁ ca brāhmaṇasya ca sattama
vivādo vyāhṛtaḥ pūrvaṁ tad bhavān vaktum arhati

Yudhiṣṭhira said: O best of men, you previously referred to a debate that took place between a Brahmin, Time, Yama, and Death. You should now tell me about this incident.

2. *bhīṣma uvāca*
atrāpy udāharantīmam itihāsaṁ purātanam
ikṣvākoḥ sūrya-putrasya yad vṛttaṁ brāhmaṇasya ca

Bhīṣma said: In this connection they narrate this ancient history of an encounter that took place between Ikṣvāku, who was the son of the sun god, a Brahmin,

3. *kālasya mṛtyoś ca tathā yad vṛttaṁ tan nibodha me*
yathā sa teṣāṁ saṁvādo yasmin sthāne 'pi cābhavat

Time, and Death. Now learn from me about this incident in terms of the discussion that took place between them and the place where this occurred.

4. *brāhmaṇo jāpakaḥ kaścid dharma-vṛtto mahā-yaśaḥ*
ṣaḍ-aṅga-vin mahā-prājñaḥ paippalādiḥ sa kauśikaḥ

There was a certain Brahmin *jāpaka* who was widely renowned for his dedication to *dharma*. An adherent of the Pippalāda school and a descendent of Kuśika, he was learned in the six sub-branches of Vedic knowledge and was a man of deep wisdom.

5. *tasyāparokṣaṁ vijñānaṁ ṣaḍ-aṅgeṣu tathaiva ca*
vedeṣu caiva niṣṇāto himavat-pāda-saṁśrayaḥ

His deep understanding of the six sub-branches was plain to behold. Residing at the foot of the Himavat range, he was equally well versed in the texts of the Vedas.

6. *so 'ntyaṁ brāhmaṁ tapas tepe saṁhitāṁ saṁyato japan*
tasya varṣa-sahasraṁ tu niyamena tathā gatam

With Brahman as his ultimate goal, he performed austerities whilst reciting a passage from the Vedas with perfect self-control. A thousand years passed by as he was engaged in this discipline.

7. *sa devyā darśitaḥ sākṣāt prītāsmīti tadā kila*
japyam āvartayaṁs tūṣṇīṁ na ca tāṁ kiṁcid abravīt

He was then granted direct sight of the Goddess as she appeared before him saying, 'I am pleased with you.' Silently continuing his *japa*, he said nothing at all in reply.

8. *tasyānukampayā devī prītā samabhavat tadā*
veda-mātā tatas tasya taj japyaṁ samapūjayat

Filled with compassion for him, the Goddess was delighted by his dedication. That Mother of the Vedas then offered her respects to the words he was reciting.

9. *samāpta-japyas tūtthāya śirasā pādayos tathā*
papāta devyā dharmātmā vacanaṁ cedam abravīt

After completing his *japa*, he arose and fell with his head at the feet of the Goddess. Dedicated to *dharma*, he then spoke these words.

10. *diṣṭyā devi prasannā tvaṁ darśanaṁ cāgatā mama*
yadi vāpi prasannāsi japye me ramatāṁ manaḥ

'By good fortune, O Goddess, you have become pleased with me and appeared before my eyes. If you are truly satisfied with me, may my mind find pleasure in my *japa*.'

11. *sāvitry uvāca*
kiṁ prārthayasi viprarṣe kiṁ ceṣṭaṁ karavāṇi ca
prabrūhi japatāṁ śreṣṭha sarvaṁ tat te bhaviṣyati

Sāvitrī said: 'What is it that you are seeking, O Brahmin *rishi*, what is the desire that I should satisfy? Tell me now for you are the best of those who practise *japa* and all that you wish for will be granted.'

12. *bhīṣma uvāca*
ity uktaḥ sa tadā devyā vipraḥ provāca dharma-vit
japyaṁ prati mameccheyaṁ vardhatv iti punaḥ punaḥ

When he was addressed by the Goddess in this way, the Brahmin who understood *dharma* replied to her, saying, 'May my inclination towards *japa* grow ever stronger.

13. *manasaś ca samādhir me vardhetāhar ahaḥ śubhe*
tat tatheti tato devī madhuraṁ pratyabhāṣata

And day by day may the absorption of my mind in total concentration increase, O auspicious one.' To this the Goddess replied with sweet words, saying, 'It shall be so.'

14. *idaṁ caivāparaṁ prāha devī tat priya-kāmyayā*
nirayaṁ naiva yātāsi yatra yātā dvijarṣabhāḥ

With a desire to please him the Goddess then spoke something more: 'You will never go to that hell which the most exalted Brahmins must enter.

15. *yāsyasi brahmaṇaḥ sthānam animittam aninditam*
sādhaye bhavitā caitad yat tvayāham ihārthitā

You will attain the position of Brahman which has no external cause and is without blemish, and I will ensure that what you have asked for will come to pass.

16. *niyato japa caikāgro dharmas tvāṁ samupaiṣyati*
kālo mṛtyur yamaś caiva samāyāsyanti te 'ntikam
bhavitā ca vivādo 'tra tava teṣāṁ ca dharmataḥ

Controlling your mind and fixing it on one point you should continue with your *japa*. Then Dharma will come to you, and Time, Death, and Yama will meet with you in this place. There will be a debate here between you and them with regard to *dharma*.'

17. *evam uktvā bhagavatī jagāma bhavanaṁ svakam*
brāhmaṇo 'pi japann āste divyaṁ varṣa-śataṁ tadā

After speaking in this way, the Goddess departed for her own abode. The Brahmin then continued to practise his *japa* for one hundred years of the gods.

18. *samāpte niyame tasminn atha viprasya dhīmataḥ*
sākṣāt prītas tadā dharmo darśayāmāsa taṁ dvijam

When the wise Brahmin had completed his regulated practice, Dharma, being pleased with him, then revealed himself to that Brahmin.

19. *dharma uvāca*
dvijāte paśya māṁ dharmam ahaṁ tvāṁ draṣṭum āgataḥ
japyasya ca phalaṁ yat te saṁprāptaṁ tac ca me śṛṇu

Dharma said: Look upon me now, O Brahmin, for I am Dharma come here to see you. Hear from me what you have attained as the fruit of your *japa*.

20. *jitā lokās tvayā sarve ye divyā ye ca mānuṣāḥ*
devānāṁ nirayān sādho sarvān utkramya yāsyasi

You have attained all the worlds, both divine and human. Avoiding all the hells of the gods, you may now depart, O righteous one.

21. *prāṇa-tyāgaṁ kuru mune gaccha lokān yathepsitān*
tyaktvātmanaḥ śarīraṁ ca tato lokān avāpsyasi

Give up your life, O sage, and go to whatever worlds you desire. You will reach these worlds after you have given up your present body.

22. *brāhmaṇa uvāca*
kṛtaṁ lokair hi me dharma gaccha ca tvaṁ yathā sukham
bahu-duḥkha-sukhaṁ dehaṁ notsṛjeyaṁ ahaṁ vibho

The Brahmin said: I have no interest in these worlds, O Dharma, so go now wherever you please. I will not give up this body which causes me much suffering but also great joy, O Lord.

23. *dharma uvāca*
avaśyaṁ bhoḥ śarīraṁ te tyaktavyaṁ muni-puṁgava
svarga ārohyatāṁ vipra kiṁ vā te rocate 'nagha

Dharma said: Alas, O best of sages, this body must inevitably be given up. Now ascend to the world of the gods, O sinless Brahmin. What else is so attractive to you?'

24. *brāhmaṇa uvāca*
na rocaye svarga-vāsaṁ vinā dehād ahaṁ vibho
gaccha dharma na me śraddhā svargaṁ gantuṁ vinātmanā

The Brahmin said: My Lord, without my present body I have no desire for a place in heaven. Go from here, O Dharma. If it means giving up my present form then I have no aspiration to enter the realm of the gods.

25. *dharma uvāca*
alam dehe manaḥ kṛtvā tyaktvā dehaṁ sukhī bhava
gaccha lokān arajaso yatra gatvā na śocasi

Dharma said: Stop being so preoccupied with your body. You should put aside this physical form and become joyful. Go to those worlds which are free from passion, for after going there you will never again feel sorrow.

26. *brāhmaṇa uvāca*
rame japan mahā-bhāga kṛtaṁ lokaiḥ sanātanaiḥ
sa-śarīreṇa gantavyo mayā svargo na vā vibho

The Brahmin said: I feel intense pleasure whilst reciting prayers, O exalted one, so let us hear no more of these eternal worlds. In truth, my Lord, I would not go to heaven even with my body.

27. *dharma uvāca*
yadi tvaṁ necchasi tyaktuṁ śarīraṁ paśya vai dvija
eṣa kālas tathā mṛtyur yamaś ca tvāṁ upāgatāḥ

Dharma said: If you do not wish to give up your body, O Brahmin, then look now as Time, Death, and Yama all come to confront you.

28. *bhīṣma uvāca*
atha vaivasvataḥ kālo mṛtyuś ca tritayaṁ vibho
brāhmaṇaṁ taṁ mahā-bhāgam upāgamyedam abruvan

Bhīṣma said: Thereupon, O Lord, those three – the son of Vivasvān, Time, and Death – approached that exalted Brahmin and spoke the following words.

29. *tapaso 'sya sutaptasya tathā sucaritasya ca*
phala-prāptis tava śreṣṭhā yamo 'ham tvām upabruve

'As a result of the austerity you have devotedly endured and your constant good conduct, you have won the highest reward. It is I, Yama, who speaks to you.'

30. *yathāvadasya japyasya phalaṁ prāptas tvam uttamam*
kālas te svargam ārodhuṁ kālo 'haṁ tvām upāgataḥ

'You have also attained a matchless reward in accordance with the *japa* you have recited. The time has come for you to ascend to heaven. It is I, Time, who has approached you.'

31. *mṛtyuṁ mā viddhi dharma-jña rūpiṇaṁ svayam āgatam*
kālena coditaṁ vipra tvām ito netum adya vai

'You are fully conversant with *dharma* and hence, O Brahmin, you must know me as Death, come here today under the impulse of time to take you away.'

32. *brāhmaṇa uvāca*
svāgataṁ sūrya-putrāya kālāya ca mahātmane
mṛtyave cātha dharmāya kiṁ kāryaṁ karavāṇi vaḥ

The Brahmin said: A respectful welcome to the son of the Sun God, to that great soul who is Time itself, to Death, and also to Dharma. What service can I perform for you?

33. *bhīṣma uvāca*
arghyaṁ pādyaṁ ca dattvā sa tebhyas tatra samāgame
abravīt parama-prītaḥ sva-śaktyā kiṁ karomi vaḥ

Bhīṣma said: After offering water for washing the mouths and feet of his assembled guests, the Brahmin was filled with joy and said to them, 'What service do I have the power to perform for you?'

34. *tasminn evātha kāle tu tīrtha-yātrām upāgataḥ*
ikṣvākur agamat tatra sametā yatra te vibho

But at that precise moment Ikṣvāku, who was visiting various pilgrimage sites, arrived at the place where they were assembled, my Lord.

35. *sarvān eva tu rājarṣiḥ saṁpūjyābhipraṇamya ca*
kuśala-praśnam akarot sarveṣāṁ rāja-sattamaḥ

That royal *rishi*, who was the finest man amongst the royal order, offered his respects, bowed down to each of them, and made inquiries as to their welfare.

36. *tasmai so 'thāsanaṁ dattvā pādyam arghyaṁ tathaiva ca*
abravīd brāhmaṇo vākyaṁ kṛtvā kuśala-saṁvidam

After offering him a seat and water for washing his feet and mouth, the Brahmin then addressed King Ikṣvāku with courteous words to greet him.

37. *svāgataṁ te mahārāja brūhi yad yad ihecchasi*
sva-śaktyā kiṁ karomīha tad bhavān prabravītu me

'You are welcome, great king. You must tell me what it is you are seeking here and let me know what service I have the power to perform for you.'

38. *rājovāca*
rājāhaṁ brāhmaṇaś ca tvaṁ yadi ṣaṭ-karma-saṁsthitaḥ
dadāmi vasu kiṁcit te prārthitaṁ tad vadasva me

The king said: I am a king and if you are a Brahmin dedicated to performing your six duties then I must give you some valuable gift. Tell me what you desire.

39. *brāhmaṇa uvāca*
dvi-vidhā brāhmaṇā rājan dharmaś ca dvi-vidhaḥ smṛtaḥ
pravṛttaś ca nivṛttaś ca nivṛtto 'smi pratigrahāt

The Brahmin said: There are two types of Brahmin, O king, and it is accepted that they follow two separate forms of *dharma*. Some strictly observe ritual practices whilst others give up such rituals. I follow the way of renunciation and so never accept gifts.

40. *tebhyaḥ prayaccha dānāni ye pravṛttā narādhipa*
ahaṁ na pratigṛhṇāmi kim iṣṭaṁ kiṁ dadāni te
brūhi tvaṁ nṛpati-śreṣṭha tapasā sādhayāmi kim

Give your gifts to those who adhere to ritual actions, O lord of men, for I will not accept them. But what is it that you desire? What can I give to you? Tell me your wish, O best of kings, and I will fulfil it through the strength of my austerity.

41. *rājovāca*
kṣatriyo 'haṁ na jānāmi dehīti vacanaṁ kvacit
prayaccha yuddham ity evaṁ vādinaḥ smo dvijottama

The king said: I am a *kṣatriya* and so I do not know the words, 'Give me'. 'Give me battle', is the only request we ever make, O best of Brahmins.

42. *brāhmaṇa uvāca*
tuṣyasi tvaṁ sva-dharmeṇa tathā tuṣṭā vayaṁ nṛpa
anyonyasyottaraṁ nāsti yad iṣṭaṁ tat samācara

The Brahmin said: You find satisfaction in the performance of your personal *dharma*, just as we renunciants do, O king. One is not superior to the other, so you should act as you see fit.

43. *rājovāca*
sva-śaktyāhaṁ dadānīti tvayā pūrvaṁ prabhāṣitam
yāce tvāṁ dīyatāṁ mahyaṁ japyasyāsya phalaṁ dvija

The king said: Earlier you said to me, 'What can I give you on the strength of my own unique power?' So now I ask you to bestow upon me the fruit of your *japa*, O Brahmin.

44. *brāhmaṇa uvāca*
yuddhaṁ mama sadā vāṇī yācatīti vikatthase
na ca yuddhaṁ mayā sārdhaṁ kim arthaṁ yācase punaḥ

The Brahmin said: Previously you boasted, 'Battle is the only thing I ever make a request for.' So how is it that you are not asking for battle with me?

45. *rājovāca*
vāg-vajrā brāhmaṇāḥ proktāḥ kṣatriyā bāhu-jīvinaḥ
vāg-yuddhaṁ tad idaṁ tīvraṁ mama vipra tvayā saha

The king said: It is said that Brahmins have words as their weapons whilst *kṣatriyas* live by the strength of their arms. O Brahmin, this is indeed a fierce battle of words that you are conducting against me.

46. *brāhmaṇa uvāca*
saivādyāpi pratijñā me sva-śaktyā kiṁ pradīyatām
brūhi dāsyāmi rājendra vibhave sati māciram

The Brahmin said: Today I have an immovable resolve; what should I give to you through the power I have gained? Tell me, O king of kings, and I will give it to your lordship. Let there be no delay.

47. *rājovāca*
yat tad varṣa-śataṁ pūrṇaṁ japyaṁ vai japatā tvayā
phalaṁ prāptaṁ tat prayaccha mama ditsur bhavān yadi

The king said: For one hundred years you have engaged in *japa*. Now, if you are willing to do so, bestow upon me the reward you have gained for that *japa*.

48. *brāhmaṇa uvāca*
paramaṁ gṛhyatāṁ tasya phalaṁ yaj japitaṁ mayā
ardhaṁ tvam avicāreṇa phalaṁ tasya samāpnuhi

The Brahmin said: You may take the unrivalled fruit of the *japa* I have recited. Without any hesitation take half of that reward.

49. *atha vā sarvam eveha japyakaṁ māmakaṁ phalam*
rājan prāpnuhi kāmaṁ tvaṁ yadi sarvam ihecchasi

If, however, you want to fulfil every desire, you may take the entire reward I have gained from my *japa*, O king.

50. *rājovāca*
kṛtaṁ sarveṇa bhadraṁ te japyaṁ yad yācitaṁ mayā
svasti te 'stu gamiṣyāmi kiṁ ca tasya phalaṁ vada

The king said: May good fortune come to you. In truth, I want nothing to do with the fruits of your *japa* that I begged for. So may your path be always auspicious and I will now depart, but tell me, what is the reward you have won?

51. *brāhmaṇa uvāca*
phala-prāptiṁ na jānāmi dattaṁ yaj japitaṁ mayā
ayaṁ dharmaś ca kālaś ca yamo mṛtyuś ca sākṣiṇaḥ

The Brahmin said: I do not know what reward I have gained from my *japa*, but I have now given it away. Here are Dharma, Time, Yama, and Death who will serve as witnesses.

52. *rājovāca*
ajñātam asya dharmasya phalaṁ me kiṁ kariṣyati
prāpnotu tat phalaṁ vipro nāham icche sasaṁśayam

The king said: What can the reward for this *dharma* do for me when its very nature is unknown? Let the Brahmin take back his reward, I have no desire for such a doubtful acquisition.

53. *brāhmaṇa uvāca*
nādade 'para-vaktavyaṁ dattaṁ vācā phalaṁ mayā
vākyaṁ pramāṇaṁ rājarṣe mamāpi tava caiva hi

The Brahmin said: I will not accept any other decision. In plain speech I have given away the fruit of my *japa*. My words and yours as well, O royal *rishi*, should always be true.

54. *nābhisaṁdhir mayā japye kṛta-pūrvaḥ kathaṁcana*
japyasya rāja-śārdūla kathaṁ jñāsyāmy ahaṁ phalam

Never in the past did I form any aspiration to gain anything from my *japa*, so how could I know, O best of kings, what the fruit of such *japa* might be?

55. *dadasveti tvayā coktaṁ dadāmīti tathā mayā*
na vācaṁ dūṣayiṣyāmi satyaṁ rakṣa sthiro bhava

You said, 'Give it to me', and I replied, 'I give it away.' I will never allow my words to be false, so protect the truth and remain firm.

56. *athaivaṁ vadato me 'dya vacanaṁ na kariṣyasi*
mahān adharmo bhavitā tava rājan mṛṣā-kṛtaḥ

If you do not fulfil the words you have spoken to me today, O king, this will be a great act of *adharma* on your part, dishonestly performed.

57. *na yuktaṁ tu mṛṣā vāṇī tvayā vaktuṁ ariṁdama*
tathā mayāpy abhyadhikaṁ mṛṣā vaktuṁ na śakyate

It is inappropriate for you to speak words that are false, O subduer of the foe, and it is even more inappropriate for me to do so, for I cannot say anything that is untrue.

58. *saṁśrutaṁ ca mayā pūrvaṁ dadānīty avicāritam*
tad gṛhṇīṣvāvicāreṇa yadi satye sthito bhavān

You have previously heard me unhesitatingly say, 'I will give it to you.' So if you are dedicated to the truth you must accept this gift without any hesitation.

59. *ihāgamya hi māṁ rājañ jāpyaṁ phalam ayācithāḥ*
tan man-nisṛṣṭaṁ gṛhṇīṣva bhava satye sthiro 'pi ca

Having come to me here, O king, you begged for the reward I had won for my *japa*. Now you must take what I am giving you and be firm in your devotion to the truth.

60. *nāyaṁ loko 'sti na paro na ca pūrvān sa tārayet*
kuta evāvarān rājan mṛṣā-vāda-parāyaṇaḥ

One who indulges in dishonest words gains neither this world nor the world to come and cannot deliver his forefathers. How then can such a person guide his juniors, O king?

61. *na yajñādhyayane dānaṁ niyamās tārayanti hi*
tathā satyaṁ pare loke yathā vai puruṣarṣabha

Neither sacrifice, study of the Veda, charity, nor religious vows can deliver one in the next world in the same way that truthfulness can, O best of men.

62. *tapāṁsi yāni cīrṇāni cariṣyasi ca yat tapaḥ*
samāḥ śataiḥ sahasraiś ca tat satyān na viśiṣyate

Whatever austerities you have undertaken and whatever austerity you may execute in the future, even for hundreds and thousands of years, can never be as efficacious as the truth.

63. *satyam ekākṣaraṁ brahma satyam ekākṣaraṁ tapaḥ*
satyam ekākṣaro yajñaḥ satyam ekākṣaraṁ śrutam

Truth alone is the imperishable Brahman; truth alone is the imperishable austerity. Truth alone is the imperishable sacrifice; truth alone is the imperishable scripture.

64. *satyaṁ vedeṣu jāgarti phalaṁ satye paraṁ smṛtam*
satyād dharmo damaś caiva sarvaṁ satye pratiṣṭhitam

Truth is awake within the Vedas, and it is stated that the highest reward is gained through truth. Both *dharma* and self control come from truth; all things have truth as their basis.

65. *satyaṁ vedās tathāṅgāni satyaṁ yajñas tathā vidhiḥ*
vratacaryās tathā satyam oṁkāraḥ satyam eva ca

Truth is the Vedas and their sub-branches; truth is the sacrifice and the ritual that governs it. Truth is adherence to religious vows and truth is *oṁ*.

66. *prāṇināṁ jananaṁ satyaṁ satyaṁ saṁtatir eva ca*
satyena vāyur abhyeti satyena tapate raviḥ

Truth is the origin of all that lives and truth is the line of succession through which life passes. It is through truth that the wind blows, and through truth that the sun gives heat.

67. *satyena cāgnir dahati svargaḥ satye pratiṣṭhitaḥ*
satyaṁ yajñas tapo vedāḥ stobhā mantrāḥ sarasvatī

It is through truth that fire burns and the existence of heaven is based on truth. Truth is sacrifice, austerity, the Vedas, the Sāma hymns, the sacred prayers, and the Vedic wisdom.

68. *tulām āropito dharmaḥ satyaṁ caiveti naḥ śrutam*
samāṁ kakṣāṁ dhārayato yataḥ satyaṁ tato 'dhikam

We have heard that truth and *dharma* were once placed on a set of scales. Although *dharma* was weighed in an equal measure, truth still surpassed it.

69. *yato dharmas tataḥ satyaṁ sarvaṁ satyena vardhate*
kim artham anṛtaṁ karma kartuṁ rājaṁs tvam icchasi

Wherever there is *dharma* there will also be truth; all things flourish through truth. So for what reason, O king, do you wish to perform a dishonest act?

70. *satye kuru sthiraṁ bhāvaṁ mā rājann anṛtaṁ kṛthāḥ*
kasmāt tvam anṛtaṁ vākyaṁ dehīti kuruṣe 'śubham

Remain firm in your dedication to truth, O king, and do not act dishonestly. 'Give it to me', you said. So why do you perform an impure deed by making these words false?

71. *yadi japya-phalaṁ dattaṁ mayā neṣiṣyase nṛpa*
sva-dharmebhyaḥ parisbhraṣṭā lokān anucariṣyasi

If you do not accept the fruits of *japa* that I have given you, O king, then you will have deviated from your *dharma* and will continue to move from one world to another.

72. *saṁśrutya yo na ditseta yācitvā yaś ca necchati*
ubhāv ānṛtikāv etau na mṛṣā kartum arhasi

Both the person who fails to give after making a pledge and one who does not accept a gift after asking for it are guilty of dishonesty. You should not indulge in such falsehood.

73. *rājovāca*
yoddhavyaṁ rakṣitavyaṁ ca kṣatra-dharmaḥ kila dvija
dātāraḥ kṣatriyāḥ proktā gṛhṇīyāṁ bhavataḥ katham

The king said: Waging war and protecting his people constitute *kṣatriya-dharma*, O Brahmin. It is ordained that *kṣatriyas* should be givers of charity, so how can I take this gift from you?

74. *brāhmaṇa uvāca*
na chandayāmi te rājan nāpi te gṛham āvrajam
ihāgamya tu yācitvā na gṛhṇīṣe punaḥ katham

The Brahmin said: I did not solicit you, O king, and I did not make the journey to your house. But having come here and made such a request, how can you not accept what I have offered?

75. *dharma uvāca*
avivādo 'stu yuvayor vittaṁ māṁ dharmam āgatam
dvijo dāna-phalair yukto rājā satya-phalena ca

Dharma said: Now let us have the final word in this debate between you and let it be known that it is I, Dharma, who now comes forth. The Brahmin will be blessed with the fruits of his charity and the king will enjoy the fruit of his truthfulness.

76. *svarga uvāca*
svargaṁ mā viddhi rājendra rūpiṇaṁ svayam āgatam
avivādo 'stu yuvayor ubhau tulya-phalau yuvām

Heaven said: O king of kings, know me as Heaven itself come here in my own form. Let there be no more disputation between you, for you have both gained equal rewards.

77. *rājovāca*
kṛtaṁ svargeṇa mekāryaṁ gaccha svarga yathāsukham
vipro yadīcchate dātuṁ pratīcchatu ca me dhanam

The king said: I will have nothing to do with heaven. You may go, O Heaven, wherever it pleases you. If the Brahmin is determined to give, then he in turn must accept the wealth that is due to me.

78. *brāhmaṇa uvāca*
bālye yadi syād ajñānān mayā hastaḥ prasāritaḥ
nivṛtti-lakṣaṇaṁ dharmam upāse saṁhitāṁ japan

The Brahmin said: In my childhood, I might have stretched forth my hand for alms due to ignorance, but now I devote myself to the religious path marked by renunciation, performing *japa* with the words of the Veda.

79. *nivṛttaṁ māṁ ciraṁ rājan chipraṁ lobhayase katham*
svena kāryaṁ kariṣyāmi tvatto necche phalaṁ nṛpa
tapaḥ-svādhyāya-śīlo 'haṁ nivṛttaś ca pratigrahāt

O king, I am a Brahmin who has followed the way of renunciation for a long time, so how can you try to rouse my desires in this way? I will continue to perform the rites I have adopted; I do not desire the rewards you have won, my lord. I devote myself to austerity and recitation of the Veda and have renounced the custom of accepting charity.

80. *rājovāca*
yadi vipra nisṛṣṭaṁ te japyasya phalam uttamam
āvayor yat phalaṁ kiṁcit sahitaṁ nau tad astv iha

The king said: If, O Brahmin, you are giving away the supreme reward you have gained from your *japa*, then let both of us enjoy a share of the fruit of the religious acts each of us has performed.

81. *dvijāḥ pratigrahe yuktā dātāro rāja-vaṁśa-jāḥ*
yadi dharmaḥ śruto vipra sahaiva phalam astu nau

Brahmins live by accepting charity whilst those born in royal families are the givers of such gifts. If you have learned about *dharma*, O Brahmin, then let the fruits of our religion come to both of us.

82. *mā vā bhūt saha-bhojyaṁ nau madīyaṁ phalam āpnuhi*
pratīccha mat-kṛtaṁ dharmaṁ yadi te mayy anugrahaḥ

Or if you will not enjoy the fruits of our religious acts jointly with me, then take the reward that I have won. If you have any regard for me, please accept the *dharma* I have performed.

83. *bhīṣma uvāca*
tato vikṛta-ceṣṭau dvau puruṣau samupasthitau
gṛhītvānyonyam āveṣṭya kucelāv ūcatur vacaḥ

Bhīṣma said: At that moment two more people arrived there. They were moving awkwardly, holding on to each other for support, and were dressed in ragged clothes. They spoke the following words.

84. *na me dhārayasīty eko dhārayāmīti cāparaḥ*
ihāsti nau vivādo 'yam ayaṁ rājānuśāsakaḥ

One of them said, 'You do not owe me anything', but the other replied, 'I do owe it to you. This king can give us direction regarding this dispute of ours.'

85. *satyaṁ bravīmy aham idaṁ na me dhārayate bhavān*
anṛtaṁ vadasīha tvam ṛṇaṁ te dhārayāmy aham

'What I am saying is true, you do not owe me anything.' 'You are speaking dishonestly to me about this matter, for I am indeed indebted to you.'

86. *tāv ubhau bhṛśa-saṁtaptau rājānam idam ūcatuḥ*
parīkṣyatāṁ yathā syāva nāvām iha vigarhitau

These two intensely agitated persons then addressed the king with the following words, 'Kindly determine how we should act so that neither of us will be at fault.'

87. *virūpa uvāca*
dhārayāmi nara-vyāghra vikṛtasyeha goḥ phalam
dadataś ca na gṛhṇāti vikṛto me mahī-pate

Virūpa said: O tiger amongst men, this dispute has arisen because I owe Vikṛta the reward to be gained from his cow. Although I am offering it to him, Vikṛta will not accept it, O lord of the earth.

88. *vikṛta uvāca*
na me dhārayate kiṁcid virūpo 'yaṁ narādhipa
mithyā bravīty ayaṁ hi tvā mithyābhāsaṁ narādhipa

Vikṛta said: This Virūpa does not owe me anything at all, O lord of men. He is speaking dishonestly, presenting you with a distorted version of events, O lord of men.

89. *rājovāca*
virūpa kiṁ dhārayate bhavān asya vadasva me
śrutvā tathā kariṣyāmīty evaṁ me dhīyate matiḥ

The king said: Virūpa, tell me what it is you owe him. After hearing this I will proceed as I deem appropriate. That is my decision.

90. *virūpa uvāca*
śṛṇuṣvāvahito rājan yathaitad dhārayāmy aham
vikṛtasyāsya rājarṣe nikhilena nararṣabha

Virūpa said: O king, O royal *rishi*, O best of men, listen attentively as I explain in full how it is that I am indebted to Vikṛta.

91. *anena dharma-prāpty-arthaṁ śubhā dattā purānagha*
dhenur viprāya rājarṣe tapaḥ-svādhyāya-śīline

O sinless one, O royal *rishi*, for the sake of fulfilling his *dharma*, this man previously gave away a cow devoid of any fault to a Brahmin who devoted his life to austerity and recitation of the Veda.

92. *tasyāś cāyaṁ mayā rājan phalam abhyetya yācitaḥ*
vikṛtena ca me dattaṁ viśuddhenāntarātmanā

And, O king, when I approached him and asked for the reward that he had won for that act, it was granted to me by the pure-hearted Vikṛta.

93. *tato me sukṛtaṁ karma kṛtam ātma-viśuddhaye*
gāvau hi kapile krītvā vatsale bahu-dohane

Sometime later, in order to purify my heart, I performed a righteous act by purchasing two Kapila cows that were with their calves and full of milk.

94. *te coñcha-vṛttaye rājan mayā samapavarjite*
yathā-vidhi yathā-śraddhaṁ tad asyāhaṁ punaḥ prabho

O king, I presented these cows to a holy man who lived on the discarded grains that fall in the fields. Moreover, my lord, I made that gift to him according to the proper rituals and with faith in my heart.

95. *ihādya vai gṛhītvā tat prayacche dvi-guṇaṁ phalam*
ekasyāḥ puruṣa-vyāghra kaḥ śuddhaḥ ko 'tra doṣavān

Having accepted his gift, I am offering here and now to give to Vikṛta a reward that is twice what he gained from the one cow he gave away. So in this dispute, O tiger amongst men, who is pure and who is at fault?

96. *evaṁ vivadamānau svas tvām ihābhyāgatau nṛpa*
kuru dharmam adharmaṁ vā vinaye nau samādhaya

Arguing in this way, O king, we have come here before you. Determining what is *dharma* or *adharma*, please set us on the path of proper conduct.

97. *yadi necchati me dānaṁ yathā dattam anena vai*
bhavān atra sthiro bhūtvā mārge sthāpayatu prabhuḥ

If he does not wish to accept the gift I have offered him in return, then, as the lord, you must be firm with him and force him to follow the proper path.

98. *rājovāca*
dīyamānaṁ na gṛhṇāsi ṛṇaṁ kasmāt tvam adya vai
yathaiva te 'bhyanujñātaṁ tathā gṛhṇīṣva māciram

The king said: Why are you refusing to accept the repayment of this debt when it is offered to you? You are certainly entitled to this gift and so you should accept it without any further delay.

99. *vikṛta uvāca*
dīyatām ity anenoktaṁ dadānīti tathā mayā
nāyaṁ me dhārayaty atra gamyatāṁ yatra vāñchati

Vikṛta said: This man said, 'Give it to me', and I replied, 'I will certainly give it to you.' He is not indebted to me for this request, so he should now go wherever he wants.

100. *rājovāca*
dadato 'sya na gṛhṇāsi viṣamaṁ pratibhāti me
daṇḍyo hi tvaṁ mama mato nāsty atra khalu saṁśayaḥ

The king said: He will give it to you, but you will not accept it. This appears to me to be an act of perversity and it is my opinion that I should punish you for it; there can be no possible doubt about this.

101. *vikṛta uvāca*
mayāsya dattaṁ rājarṣe gṛhṇīyāṁ tat kathaṁ punaḥ
kāmam atrāparādho me daṇḍam ājñāpaya prabho

Vikṛta said: I made him a gift, O royal *rishi*, so how can I take it back from him again? If this inclination is an offence on my part, you should certainly command that I be punished for it, my lord.

102. *virūpa uvāca*
dīyamānaṁ yadi mayā neṣiṣyasi kathaṁcana
niyaṁsyati tvā nṛpatir ayaṁ dharmānuśāsakaḥ

Virūpa said: If you do not accept anything I offer, this king, who is an arbiter of *dharma*, will bring force to bear upon you.

103. *vikṛta uvāca*
svaṁ mayā yāciteneha dattaṁ katham ihādya tat
gṛhṇīyāṁ gacchatu bhavān abhyanujñāṁ dadāni te

Vikṛta said: How is it possible for me to take back my own property when I have already given it away at your request? You should go now, I give you leave to depart.

104. *brāhmaṇa uvāca*
śrutam etat tvayā rājann anayoḥ kathitaṁ dvayoḥ
pratijñātaṁ mayā yat te tad gṛhāṇāvicāritam

The Brahmin said: O king, you have heard the account given by these two and should now accept what I offered you without further hesitation.

105. *rājovāca*
prastutaṁ su-mahat kāryam āvayor gahvaraṁ yathā
jāpakasya dṛḍhī-kāraḥ katham etad bhaviṣyati

The king said: The affair of these two men that has now been introduced is as deep as an abyss. It certainly confirms the view of the *jāpaka*. How will this business now turn out?

106. *yadi tāvan na gṛhṇāmi brāhmaṇenāpavarjitam*
kathaṁ na lipyeyam ahaṁ doṣeṇa mahatādya vai

If I do not accept what the Brahmin is offering me in the same way that I have ordered here, how can I now avoid being besmirched by a great act of wrongdoing?

107. *bhīṣma uvāca*
tau covāca sa rājarṣiḥ kṛta-kāryau gamiṣyathaḥ
nedānīṁ mām ihāsādya rāja-dharmo bhaven mṛṣā

Bhīṣma said: The royal *rishi* then said to the two companions, 'Both of you will go from here having achieved your aim. Having come here to me in this way, you will not find the *dharma* of a king dishonestly executed.

108. *sva-dharmaḥ paripālyaś ca rājñām eṣa viniścayaḥ*
vipra-dharmaś ca su-gurur mām anātmānam āviśat

It is ordained that the *dharma* of the royal order must be maintained, and now the full weight of a Brahmin's *dharma* has descended on my unfortunate person.'

109. *brāhmaṇa uvāca*
gṛhāṇa dhāraye 'haṁ te yācitaṁ te śrutaṁ mayā
na ced grahīṣyase rājañ śāpiṣye tvāṁ na saṁśayaḥ

The Brahmin said: I owe you whatever I heard you begging for and you must now accept it. If you do not take this gift, O king, then I will surely curse you.

110. *rājovāca*
dhig rāja-dharmaṁ yasyāyaṁ kāryasyeha viniścayaḥ
ity arthaṁ me grahītavyaṁ kathaṁ tulyaṁ bhaved iti

The king said: How burdensome is the *dharma* of a king! This is indeed the correct conclusion as to how my duty must be performed in this instance. It is for this reason alone that I will accept what you offer; what else could makes things equal?

111. *eṣa pāṇir apūrvaṁ bho nikṣepārthaṁ prasāritaḥ*
yan me dhārayase vipra tad idānīṁ pradīyatām

Sir, this hand of mine is generally stretched forth in order to give and has never before been extended in this way. Now you may present me with the precise amount you owe me, O Brahmin.

112. *brāhmaṇa uvāca*
saṁhitāṁ japatā yāvān mayā kaścid guṇaḥ kṛtaḥ
tat sarvaṁ pratigṛhṇīṣva yadi kiṁcid ihāsti me

The Brahmin said: The specific nature of the reward generated is dependent upon the number of times I have performed *japa* of the Veda. Accept everything that I have attained.

113. *rājovāca*
jalam etan nipatitaṁ mama pāṇau dvijottama
samam astu sahaivāstu pratigṛhṇātu vai bhavān

The king said: O best of Brahmins, this water has dropped onto my hand. Let us partake of that water in equal measures. Kindly take what I am offering.

114. *virūpa uvāca*
kāma-krodhau viddhi nau tvam āvābhyāṁ kārito bhavān
sameti ca yad uktaṁ te samā lokās tavāsya ca

Virūpa said: You should know that we are Desire and Anger and it is because of us that you have acted like this. You said, 'Let us be equal'; so you and the Brahmin will now enjoy the same worlds.

115. *nāyaṁ dhārayate kiṁcij jijñāsā tvat-kṛte kṛtā*
kālo dharmas tathā mṛtyuḥ kāma-krodhau tathā yuvām

This man does not owe anything; the inquiry we made was for your sake alone. Time, Dharma, and Death, as well as Desire and Anger were present before you both.

116. *sarvam anyonya-nikaṣe nighṛṣṭaṁ paśyatas tava*
gaccha lokāñ jitān svena karmaṇā yatra vañchasi

As you ground against each other, all the issues were thoroughly examined so that they were clear for you to see. Now go as you wish to the worlds you have won through your own actions.

117. *bhīṣma uvāca*
jāpakānāṁ phalāvāptir mayā te saṁprakīrtitā
gatiḥ sthānaṁ ca lokāś ca jāpakena yathā jitāḥ

Bhīṣma said: I have now described the means by which *jāpakas* obtain their reward, as well as the destination, the status, and the worlds gained by the *jāpaka*.

118. *prayāti saṁhitādhyāyī brahmāṇaṁ parameṣṭhinam*
atha vāgniṁ samāyāti sūryam āviśate 'pi vā

One who silently recites a hymn from the Veda goes to Brahmā, the highest of the gods, or else he goes to Agni, the God of Fire, or enters the sun.

119. *sa taijasena bhāvena yadi tatrāśnute ratim*
guṇāṁs teṣāṁ samādatte rāgeṇa pratimohitaḥ

If he finds pleasure in that abode through its luminous state of being, he becomes deluded by this attachment to the qualities of those regions.

120. *evaṁ some tathā vāyau bhūmy-ākāśa-śarīra-gaḥ*
sa-rāgas tatra vasati guṇāṁs teṣāṁ samācaran

Be it within the moon or in the air, whether his body moves on the earth or through the sky, he lives there with attachment in his heart, existing in accordance with the qualities of those regions.

121. *atha tatra virāgī sa gacchati tv atha saṁśayam*
param avyayam icchan sa tam evāviśate punaḥ

One who is free of attachment goes to such an abode but remains dubious about its worth. Being desirous of the supreme domain that never changes, he then moves on to that highest destination.

122. *amṛtāc cāmṛtaṁ prāptaḥ śītī-bhūto nirātmavān*
brahma-bhūtaḥ sa nirdvaṁdvaḥ sukhī śānto nirāmayaḥ

Gaining immortality from that immortal existence, he is then liberated and free from any personal identity. His exists as Brahman, beyond the dualities of this world. Thus he is joyful, at peace, and free from affliction.

123. *brahma-sthānam anavartam ekam akṣara-saṁjñakam*
aduḥkham ajaraṁ śāntaṁ sthānaṁ tat pratipadyate

This is the Brahman state of being from which one never returns, the one abode that is known as undecaying. He attains that state which is free from sorrow, ageless, and tranquil.

124. *caturbhir lakṣaṇair hīnaṁ tathā ṣaḍbhiḥ sa-ṣoḍaśaiḥ*
puruṣaṁ samatikramya ākāśaṁ pratipadyate

Transcending the four marks of existence, as well as the six, and the sixteen, he leaves his individual personality behind and enters into the sky.

125. *atha vecchati rāgātmā sarvaṁ tad adhitiṣṭhati*
yac ca prārthayate tac ca manasā pratipadyate

Or if he still has attachments in his heart and nurtures desires, he may then gain everything he wants. Whatever it is he seeks to attain, he realises it through his mind.

126. *atha vā vīkṣate lokān sarvān niraya-saṁsthitān*
niḥspṛhaḥ sarvato muktas tatraiva ramate sukhī

Or if he beholds all those worlds that are equivalent to hell, the liberated person is completely unmoved and remains contented, finding joy even in such places.

127. *evam eṣā mahārāja jāpakasya gatir yathā*
etat te sarvam ākhyātaṁ kiṁ bhūyaḥ śrotum icchasi

Now, great king, everything concerning the destination attained by a *jāpaka* has been described to you. What would you like to learn about now?

Śānti-parvan, Adhyāya 193

The fifth and final chapter of *Jāpakopākhyānam* offers a slightly confusing account of how both the *jāpaka* and King Ikṣvāku attain the highest spiritual goal of emancipation from rebirth. It begins with the *jāpaka* saying once again that he desires nothing more than to be left to continue his recitation of the Veda. He is, however, persuaded by Ikṣvāku that they should take an equal share of the reward he has won through his previous practice. A great assembly of the celestial host then gathers in that place to witness the events that are unfolding there, including the Brahmā who appears here as the Supreme Deity and an embodiment of the absolute Brahman that is the object of liberation from this world.

Verses 15 to 19 offer a fascinating insight into the practice of a type of Yoga that is notably distinct from that taught by Patañjali and by other treatises on Yoga in the *Mokṣa-dharma-parvan*. One might even suggest that the practices undertaken by the *jāpaka* and King Ikṣvāku are more akin to *haṭha-yoga* than to the Yoga of the mind typically encountered in this early period of the development of Yoga techniques. As a result of this practice, the life force of the *jāpaka* is able to leave its embodiment through the palate and enter into the deity Brahmā. Ikṣvāku then follows the path taken by the *jāpaka* and also enters into Brahmā. The idea seems to be that liberation is achieved by entering into the existence of Brahman, which is here personified by the Supreme Deity named as Brahmā.

The conclusion of the chapter and of the passage as a whole is then presented as the assertion that *japa* is as efficacious as Yoga as a means by which liberation is attained. This is the message conveyed by the *upākhyānam* of the *jāpaka* that Bhīṣma has now recited in full as a response to Yudhiṣṭhira's questions.

1. *yudhiṣṭhira uvāca*
kim uttaraṁ tadā tau sma cakratus tena bhāṣite
brāhmaṇo vātha vā rājā tan me brūhi pitāmaha

Yudhiṣṭhira said: What more did those two say in their conversation with each other? Tell me what happened, O grandfather, when either the Brahmin or the king spoke next.

2. *atha vā tau gatau tatra yad etat kīrtitaṁ tvayā*
saṁvādo vā tayoḥ ko 'bhūt kiṁ vā tau tatra cakratuḥ

Or else tell me where they went from there in terms of the various destinations you have referred to. Or tell me what conversation took place between them, or what else they did in that place.

3. *bhīṣma uvāca*
tathety evaṁ pratiśrutya dharmaṁ saṁpūjya cābhibho
yamaṁ kālaṁ ca mṛtyuṁ ca svargaṁ saṁpūjya cārhataḥ

Bhīṣma said: Saying, 'Let it be so', and thereby assenting to the conclusion they had reached, my lord, he worshipped first Dharma and then Yama, Time, Death, and Heaven as was appropriate.

4. *pūrvaṁ ye cāpare tatra sametā brāhmaṇarṣabhāḥ*
sarvān saṁpūjya śirasā rājānaṁ so 'bravīd vacaḥ

Previously a number of other Brahmins of the highest order had assembled there and he worshipped them as well, bowing his head before them. He then spoke the following words to the king,

5. *phalenānena saṁyukto rājarṣe gaccha puṇyatām*
bhavatā cābhyanujñāto japeyaṁ bhūya eva hi

'Endowed with this reward, O royal *rishi*, now enter that auspicious state of being. With your permission I will commence my *japa* once more.

6. *varaś ca mama pūrvaṁ hi devyā datto mahā-bala*
śraddhā te japato nityaṁ bhaviteti viśāṁ pate

O mighty lord of your race, I previously received a blessing given by the Goddess, who said to me, "Your dedication to *japa* will remain constant." '

7. *rājovāca*
yady evam aphalā siddhiḥ śraddhā ca japituṁ tava
gaccha vipra mayā sārdhaṁ jāpakaṁ phalam āpnuhi

The king said: Now the perfection you have gained will be devoid of any reward, and yet you are still dedicated to the practice of *japa*. O Brahmin, you should accompany me and enjoy half the fruit of your *japa*.

8. *brāhmaṇa uvāca*
kṛtaḥ prayatnaḥ su-mahān sarveṣāṁ saṁnidhāv iha
saha tulya-phalau cāvāṁ gacchāvo yatra nau gatiḥ

The Brahmin said: In the presence of all these individuals, you have made a great effort. So let us now depart for the destination due to us and have an equal share of the reward.

9. *bhīṣma uvāca*
vyavasāyaṁ tayos tatra viditvā tri-daśeśvaraḥ
saha devair upayayau loka-pālais tathaiva ca

Bhīṣma said: Understanding their resolve, the lord of the thirty gods then appeared there along with the gods and the guardians of the world.

10. *sādhyā viśve 'tha maruto jyotīṁṣi sumahānti ca*
nadyaḥ śailāḥ samudrāś ca tīrthāni vividhāni ca

These included the Sādhyas, the Viśvadevas, and the Maruts, as well as the great luminaries. Also present were the rivers, mountains, and oceans, as well as the various places of pilgrimage.

11. *tapāṁsi saṁyoga-vidhir vedāḥ stobhāḥ sarasvatī*
nāradaḥ parvataś caiva viśvāvasur hahā huhūḥ

Austerities and the disciplines of Yoga were also there and so were the Vedas with their hymns, and Sarasvatī. Nārada and Parvata were present and so were Viśvāvasu, Hahā, and Huhū.

12. *gandharvāś citrasenaś ca parivāra-gaṇair yutaḥ*
nāgāḥ siddhāś munayo deva-devaḥ prajāpatiḥ
viṣṇuḥ sahasra-śīrṣaś ca devo 'cintyaḥ samāgamat

There were *gandharvas* and Citrasena along with his retinue. There were also divine serpents, Siddhas, and sages; Prajāpati, the god of the gods, was also present. Then the thousand-headed Viṣṇu, the inconceivable Deity, also appeared there.

13. *avādyantāntarikṣe ca bheryas tūryāṇi cābhibho*
puṣpa-varṣāṇi divyāni tatra teṣāṁ mahātmanām
nanṛtuś cāpsaraḥ-saṁghās tatra tatra samantataḥ

Throughout the heavens, my lord, kettle drums and musical instruments resounded, whilst showers of celestial flowers fell upon the great personalities gathered there and groups of *apsarases* moved here and there all around that place.

14. *atha svargas tathā rūpī brāhmaṇaṁ vākyam abravīt*
saṁsiddhas tvaṁ mahā-bhāga tvaṁ ca siddhas tathā nṛpa

Then Heaven itself in an embodied form spoke these words to the Brahmin, 'You have attained complete success, O fortunate one, and you have reached a similar state of perfection, O king.'

15. *atha tau sahitau rājann anyonyena vidhānataḥ*
viṣaya-pratisaṁhāram ubhāv eva pracakratuḥ

Acting together according to the agreement they had reached, both those persons, O king, achieved a state of detachment from the objects of sensory pleasure.

16. *prāṇāpānau tathodānaṁ samānaṁ vyānam eva ca*
evaṁ tān manasi sthāpya dadhatuḥ prāṇayor manaḥ

Having situated the bodily airs known as *prāṇa*, *apāna*, *udāna*, *samāna*, and *vyāna* within the mind, they then placed their mind within the *prāṇa*, the breath of life in each of them.

17. *upasthita-kṛtau tatra nāsikāgram adho bhruvau*
kuṅkuṇyāṁ caiva manasā śanair dhārayataḥ sma tau

They then brought the *prāṇa* to the top point of the nose just below the eyebrows. Gradually, by concentration of the mind, they then fixed it upon the place known as the *kuṅkuṇī*.

18. *niśceṣṭābhyāṁ śarīrābhyāṁ sthira-dṛṣṭī samāhitau*
jitāsanau tathādhāya mūrdhany ātmānam eva ca

With their bodies motionless, they kept their vision steady and perfectly controlled, whilst completely mastering the sitting postures (*āsana*). In this condition they held the *ātman* within the head.

19. *tālu-deśam athoddālya brāhmaṇasya mahātmanaḥ*
jyotir-jvālā sumahatī jagāma tri-divaṁ tadā

A great radiant effulgence burst forth through the palate of that Brahmin, a great soul, and then passed into the threefold regions of heaven.

20. *hāhā-kāras tato dikṣu sarvāsu su-mahān abhūt*
taj jyotiḥ stūyamānaṁ sma brahmāṇaṁ prāviśat tadā

When this happened there was a great cry of astonishment throughout all the heavens. Being highly praised, that effulgence then entered into Brahmā.

21. *tataḥ svāgatam ity āha tat tejaḥ sa pitāmahaḥ*
prādeśa-mātraṁ puruṣaṁ pratyudgamya viśāṁ pate

The grandfather said to that effulgence, 'You are welcome.' He then came forward to meet that being that was the size of the span of a hand.

22. *bhūyaś caivāparaṁ prāha vacanaṁ madhuraṁ sma saḥ*
jāpakais tulya-phalatā yogānāṁ nātra saṁśayaḥ

He then spoke further, using the sweetest words, 'There is no doubt that the *jāpakas* gain a reward equal to that attained through Yoga.

23. *yogasya tāvad etebhyaḥ phalaṁ pratyakṣa-darśanam*
jāpakānāṁ viśiṣṭaṁ tu pratyutthānaṁ samādhikam

The extent of the reward to be gained through Yoga is well known to those assembled here. But the particular eminence of *jāpakas* is recognised in this act of rising to greet them.

24. *uṣyatāṁ mayi cety uktvācetayat sa tataḥ punaḥ*
athāsya praviveśāsyaṁ brāhmaṇo vigata-jvaraḥ

Now you may reside within me.' After speaking these words, Brahmā restored him to a state of full consciousness. Now free from all afflictions, the Brahmin then entered the mouth of the Deity.

25. *rājāpy etena vidhinā bhagavantaṁ pitāmaham*
yathaiva dvija-śārdūlas tathaiva prāviśat tadā

Then the king also entered the worshipful grandfather of creation, following the same course as that taken by that most eminent Brahmin.

26. *svayaṁbhuvam atho devā abhivādya tato 'brūvan*
jāpakārtham ayaṁ yat nas tad arthaṁ vayam āgatāḥ

After first offering their respects to him, the gods then addressed the Lord who has no origin but himself, saying, 'Our purpose in coming here was to see this result gained by the *jāpaka*.

27. *kṛta-pūjāv imau tulyaṁ tvayā tulya-phalāv imau*
yoga-jāpakayor dṛṣṭaṁ phalaṁ su-mahad adya vai
sarvāḷ lokān atītyaitau gacchetāṁ yatra vāñchitam

These two have been shown equal respect by you and have received the same reward. Today we have seen how great are the fruits gained by the practitioners of Yoga and the *jāpakas*, for these two have transcended all the worlds and can now go wherever they desire.'

28. *brahmovāca*
mahā-smṛtiṁ paṭhed yas tu yathaivānusmṛtiṁ śubhām
tāv apy etena vidhinā gacchetāṁ mat-salokatām

Brahmā said: Both one who recites the great scripture and one who recites a secondary scripture that is pure may attain the same world as myself by following this discipline.

29. *yaś ca yoge bhaved bhaktaḥ so 'pi nāsty atra saṁśayaḥ*
vidhinānena dehānte mama lokān avāpnuyāt
gamyatāṁ sādhayiṣyāmi yathā-sthānāni siddhaye

Likewise there is no doubt that when his life comes to an end, one who devotes himself to Yoga practice also attains my worlds through that process. I will now depart and you should also go to your own places in order to achieve success.

30. *bhīṣma uvāca*
ity uktvā sa tadā devas tatraivāntar adhīyata
āmantrya taṁ tato devā yayuḥ svaṁ svaṁ niveśanam

Bhīṣma said: When the Lord had thus concluded his speech, he disappeared from that place. After respectfully taking their leave of him the gods then departed, each to his own abode.

31. *te ca sarve mahātmāno dharmaṁ sat-kṛtya tatra vai*
pṛṣṭhato 'nuyayū rājan sarve su-prīta-mānasāḥ

After offering due reverence to Dharma, O king, all those great souls followed on behind him with joy in their hearts.

32. *etat phalaṁ jāpakānāṁ gatiś caiva prakīrtitā*
yathā-śrutaṁ mahā-rāja kiṁ bhūyaḥ śrotum icchasi

I have now described to you the reward that is gained by *jāpakas* and also the destination they reach, just as I heard it from my teachers, great king. So what subject would you care to hear about now?

The Manu-Bṛhaspati-Saṁvāda

Śānti-parvan, Adhyāya 194–199

It is probably correct to identify the *Manu-Bṛhaspati-Saṁvāda*, literally the conversation between Manu and Bṛhaspati, as another of *Mahābhārata*'s treatises on Sāṁkhya and Yoga although again it falls well short of being a full exposition of either of these systems. Here the principal teacher is Manu and his interlocutor is Bṛhaspati, both of whom are well known both within and beyond the *Mahābhārata*. Indian cosmology reveals that the duration of a single creation is divided into fourteen eras, in each of which the original progenitor of human beings is given the title Manu. The most commonly referred to is Manu Svayaṁbhu, who is regarded as the author of the Hindu law book known as the *Manu Smṛti*, although we are given no indication here as to which of the Manus it is who is speaking. Bṛhaspati is well known from the

Vedas, the *Mahābhārata*, and Purāṇic literature as the priest and guide of the gods who uses his wisdom and ritual expertise to assist them in their conflicts with the *asuras*. He is thus qualified as a teacher in his own right, although here he appears as a ritualist who has not yet fully reached the highest spiritual realisations and hence feels the need to seek guidance from Manu on such topics.

As already mentioned, the teachings Manu gives him are very clearly based on Sāṁkhya and Yoga, but there is no systematic Sāṁkhya analysis of the elements of matter or any form of detailed exposition on the practice of Yoga. The six chapters of the treatise focus overwhelmingly on two principal topics: first, on establishing the true nature of a living being, then on showing that this spiritual identity can be perceived when the outward focus of the mind is suspended. In that sense, it might be more accurate to represent the *Manu-Bṛhaspati-Saṁvāda* as a further passage on the subject of *adhyātma*, although that term is never used in the text. We are thus informed about the mental faculties, perception through the senses, and analysis within the mind and intellect. The main emphasis, however, is on establishing the existence of a transcendent principle, the true self or *ātman*, which is beyond the range of the senses and remains untouched by the changing conditions of this world. The mind and senses are focused outwards towards the external world, but if this mode of perception can be stilled and suspended it becomes possible to gain insight into the inner reality of the true self. And when this higher vision is achieved, one ceases to exist within the constraints of this world and attains to the domain of Brahman. Hence it is quite apparent that the treatise is expounding the fundamental precepts of Sāṁkhya and Yoga, but refrains from laying out the details of those systems, perhaps leaving that task to other speakers.

Śānti-parvan, Adhyāya 194

The first chapter of the *Manu-Bṛhaspati-Saṁvāda* opens in the manner routinely employed throughout this section of *Mahābhārata*, with Yudhiṣṭhira posing questions and Bhīṣma responding by referring to a previous discussion on the same subject in which a renowned authority provided words of instruction. Here Yudhiṣṭhira asks specifically about the result that is achieved through *jñāna-yoga*, the Yoga of knowledge, and that which is achieved through the Vedic ritual and the observance of specific vows. He then asks how the *bhūtātman*, the soul within each being, can be known, which one might feel is a little redundant given the instruction on Yoga he has already received. When Bhīṣma relates these questions to a prior conversation in which Bṛhaspati sought guidance from Manu, it is the division between the way of knowledge and ritual action that dominates the opening phase of the discussion; this can clearly be traced back to Yudhiṣṭhira's questions.

The preliminaries are completed in the first nine verses and when Manu begins to speak he immediately emphasises the superiority of knowledge over ritual action, a point reasserted by Śaṅkarācārya centuries later. Manu's point is that ritual action is based on material desire; in order to attain the Supreme one must give up all such desires and attempt to cultivate spiritual realisation, the *jñāna* that leads to the Supreme. Although the Vedic ritual is not rejected outright, it is said to be predominated by the influence of the *guṇas* and hence the results obtained through *karma*, ritual action, will always be mixed, sometimes bringing pleasure but also being a cause of distress. This assertion, in verse 20, leads naturally on to a brief outline of the doctrine of karma and the manner in which one's actions inevitably yield future consequences of different types. In the final three verses, Manu announces that he has now discussed the nature of ritual action and will turn instead to the realisation of higher knowledge. The true object of this knowledge is designated simply as *param*, meaning the Supreme or that which is higher. This is described as being wholly devoid of attributes and yet also the source of the world and of all living beings. Although it is wholly transcendent, those persons who possess higher knowledge are able to perceive it, *paśyanti yad brahma-vido manuṣyāḥ* (verse 20), and this is the way of knowledge.

What we have in this chapter is essentially a rehearsal of the longstanding tension between knowledge and ritual action that is frequently encountered in the revelation of the *Upaniṣads*. It also forms one of the principal lines of argumentation pursued by Śaṅkarācārya in his writings, as exemplified by his famous debate with Mandana Miśra, an *ācārya* of the Mīmāṁsa school. It might also be said that the *Bhagavad-gītā* aims at offering a compromise between the two paths by presenting a doctrine of *karma-yoga*. In our text, however, there is no attempt whatsoever at compromise between the two forms of religion, as ritual action is placed clearly within the domain of karma (and hence rebirth) whilst knowledge of the higher reality is shown to be the path to enlightenment and freedom from the misery of worldly existence.

1. *yudhiṣṭhira uvāca*
kiṁ phalaṁ jñāna-yogasya vedānāṁ niyamasya ca
bhūtātmā vā kathaṁ jñeyas tan me brūhi pitāmaha

Yudhiṣṭhira said: Tell me this, grandfather, what reward is gained from the Yoga of knowledge, from following the instruction of the Vedas, or from observing religious vows? How can the true self in all beings be known?

2. *bhīṣma uvāca*
atrāpy udāharantīmam itihāsaṁ purātanam
manoḥ prajāpater vādaṁ maharṣeś ca bṛhaspateḥ

Bhīṣma said: In this connection they recite this ancient account of a conversation that took place between Manu, the progenitor of living beings, and the great *rishi* Bṛhaspati.

3. *prajāpatiṁ śreṣṭhatamaṁ pṛthivyāṁ*
devarṣi-saṁgha-pravaro maharṣiḥ
bṛhaspatiḥ praśnam imaṁ purāṇaṁ
papraccha śiṣyo 'tha guruṁ praṇamya

Manu was foremost amongst all the progenitors of living beings on earth. The great *rishi* Bṛhaspati was the leader of a host of other celestial *rishis*, but taking the role of a disciple and offering homage as to his teacher, he put this question to Manu concerning the origins of the world.

4. *yat kāraṇaṁ mantra-vidhiḥ pravṛtto*
jñāne phalaṁ yat pravadanti viprāḥ
yan mantra-śabdair akṛta-prakāśaṁ
tad ucyatāṁ me bhagavan yathāvat

'My lord, please properly explain the following subjects to me: the cause of the world, the origin of the ritual practices of the Vedas, the reward that Brahmins say is to be gained only from knowledge, and those subject matters that are not revealed by the Vedic hymns.

5. *yad artha-śāstrāgama-mantra-vidbhir*
yajñair anekair vara-go-pradānaiḥ
phalaṁ mahadbhir yad upāsyate ca
tat kiṁ kathaṁ vā bhavitā kva vā tat

Tell me about the reward pursued by great persons who possess knowledge of the *Artha-śāstras*, *Āgamas*, and Vedic hymns, and who perform various sacrifices and make gifts of the most excellent cows to achieve that reward. What is the goal they seek, how is it attained, and where will it be enjoyed?

6. *mahī mahī-jāḥ pavano 'ntarikṣaṁ*
jalaukasaś caiva jalaṁ divaṁ ca
divaukasaś caiva yataḥ prasūtās
tad ucyatāṁ me bhagavan purāṇam

Tell me about that from which the earth came into being, as well as all living entities born on earth, in the wind and in space, the creatures that live in the water, the water itself, the heavens and the heavenly beings. Teach me, my lord, that ancient history of the world.

7. *jñānaṁ yataḥ prārthayate naro vai*
tatas tad arthā bhavati pravṛttiḥ
na cāpy ahaṁ veda paraṁ purāṇaṁ
mithyā-pravṛttiṁ ca kathaṁ nu kuryām

It is knowledge that forms the basis for a man's desires and that then provides a motivation for the actions he undertakes. I do not know the highest principle, the ancient one, so how can I address my unworthy inclinations towards action?

8. *ṛk-sāma-saṁghāṁś ca yajūṁṣi cāhaṁ*
chandāṁsi nakṣatra-gatiṁ niruktam
adhītya ca vyākaraṇaṁ sakalpaṁ
śikṣāṁ ca bhūta-prakṛtiṁ na vedmi

Even after studying all parts of the *Ṛk* and the *Sāma*, and the *Yajus* as well, the sacred hymns, the path of the stars, the science of words, grammar, ritual conduct, and the art of pronouncing sacred texts, still I have no knowledge of the true nature of a living being.

9. *sa me bhavāñ śaṁsatu sarvam etaj*
jñāne phalaṁ karmaṇi vā yad asti
yathā ca dehāc cyavate śarīrī
punaḥ śarīraṁ ca yathābhyupaiti

Please explain all these things to me as well: the result attained through knowledge and that which is gained through ritual action; how the embodied soul leaves the body and how it subsequently takes on another bodily form.'

10. *manur uvāca*
yad yat priyaṁ yasya sukhaṁ tad āhus
tad eva duḥkhaṁ pravadanty aniṣṭam
iṣṭaṁ ca me syād itarac ca na syād
etat kṛte karma-vidhiḥ pravṛttaḥ
iṣṭaṁ tv aniṣṭaṁ ca na māṁ bhajet-
ety etat kṛte jñāna-vidhiḥ pravṛttaḥ

Manu said: Whenever anything pleasing occurs they call that happiness and similarly when something displeasing occurs they call that misery. When I act in such a way that pleasing circumstances will come to me and their opposites will not, the way of action arises. When I act in such a way that neither pleasing nor displeasing circumstances can ever possess me then the way of knowledge arises.

11. *kāmātmakāś chandasi karma-yogā*
ebhir vimuktaḥ param aśnuvīta
nānā-vidhe karma-pathe sukhārthī
naraḥ pravṛtto na paraṁ prayāti
paraṁ hi tat-karma-pathād apetaṁ
nirāśiṣaṁ brahma-paraṁ hy avaśyam

Material desire is the basis of the various forms of ritual action taught by the Vedic hymns. When a person transcends these he may then attain the Supreme. The man who longs for material happiness pursues undertakings of various types on the path of ritual action, but he does not attain the Supreme, for the Supreme exists in a realm apart from the path of ritual action. It is beyond materialistic desire, for it is indeed the Supreme Brahman.

12. *prajāḥ sṛṣṭā manasā karmaṇā ca*
dvāv apy etau sat-pathau loka-juṣṭau
dṛṣṭvā karma śāśvataṁ cāntavac ca
manas-tyāgaḥ kāraṇaṁ nānyad asti

Living beings are created by the mind and by action; these two are both proper paths praised throughout the world. Observing that action may be either eternal or temporary, renunciation of desire within the mind is the only means.

13. *svenātmanā cakṣur iva praṇetā*
niśātyaye tamasā saṁvṛtātmā
jñānaṁ tu vijñāna-guṇena yuktaṁ
karmāśubhaṁ paśyati varjanīyam

At daybreak the eye, which was previously covered by darkness, becomes one's guide once more through its own power of vision. In the same way, when knowledge is joined with the quality of realisation it then identifies the impurity inherent in action, which must therefore be given up.

14. *sarpān kuśāgrāṇi tathodapānaṁ*
jñātvā manuṣyāḥ parivarjayanti
ajñānatas tatra patanti mūḍhā
jñāne phalaṁ paśya yathā viśiṣṭam

If they know the places where snakes, sharp grasses, or a well are found, men can then avoid such dangers, whilst fools who lack such understanding fall down amongst them. You can see, therefore, how the best result is derived from knowledge.

15. *kṛtsnas tu mantro vidhi-vat prayukto*
yajñā yathoktās tv atha dakṣiṇāś ca
anna-pradānaṁ manasaḥ samādhiḥ
pañcātmakaṁ karma-phalaṁ vadanti

They say that five factors yield the result of ritual action: the prayer enunciated in accordance with the rule, sacrifices performed according to injunctions, the gifts made to the priests, the distribution of food, and the fixed concentration of the mind.

16. *guṇātmakaṁ karma vadanti vedās*
tasmān mantrā mantra-mūlaṁ hi karma
vidhir vidheyaṁ manasopapattiḥ
phalasya bhoktā tu yathā śarīrī

The Vedas assert that ritual actions are imbued with the *guṇas* and this must include the hymns of the Veda, for the ritual is derived from these hymns. It is through the mind that the rules of practice are employed in the execution of the ritual; the embodied living being is then the enjoyer of the fruit of the ritual.

17. *śabdāś rūpāṇi rasāś ca puṇyāḥ*
sparśāś ca gandhāś ca śubhās tathaiva
naro na saṁsthāna-gataḥ prabhuḥ syād
etat phalaṁ sidhyati karma-loke

So although action is the controlling factor in this world, a man can still be the controller of his own destiny without giving up his present position and attain the fruits of his actions in the form of pleasant sounds, sights, and tastes, as well as tactile sensations and sweet aromas.

18. *yad yac charīreṇa karoti karma*
śarīra-yuktaḥ samupāśnute tat
śarīram evāyatanaṁ sukhasya
duḥkhasya cāpy āyatanaṁ śarīram

It is through his bodily existence that a person experiences the results of the various actions he performs with his body. The body alone is the abode of pleasure but the body is also the abode of misery.

19. *vācā tu yat karma karoti kiṁcid*
vācaiva sarvaṁ samupāśnute tat
manas tu yat karma karoti kiṁcin
manaḥ-stha evāyam upāśnute tat

It is through words themselves that one experiences the results of action performed with words. Similarly it is within one's own mind that one experiences the results of mental action.

20. *yathā guṇaṁ karma-gaṇaṁ phalārthī*
karoty ayaṁ karma-phale niviṣṭaḥ
tathā tathāyaṁ guṇa-saṁprayuktaḥ
śubhāśubhaṁ karma-phalaṁ bhunakti

One who aspires to enjoy the fruits of his actions performs activities of different types, and the quality of each action performed shapes the nature of the result derived from it. Therefore a person who exists in association with the *guṇas* enjoys both the delightful and loathsome fruits of his previous actions.

21. *matsyo yathā srota ivābhipātī*
tathā kṛtaṁ pūrvam upaiti karma
śubhe tv asau tuṣyati duṣkṛte tu
na tuṣyate vai paramaḥ śarīrī

As a fish moves through the current of a river, so any action previously undertaken gravitates towards the performer. The transcendent embodied being thus enjoys pleasure if the action is righteous, but if the action is wicked it finds no satisfaction at all.

22. *yato jagat sarvam idaṁ prasūtaṁ*
jñatvātmavanto vyatiyānti yat tat
yan mantra-śabdair akṛta-prakāśaṁ
tad ucyamānaṁ śṛṇu me paraṁ yat

I will now speak about the source from which this whole world has arisen, about that which is not revealed in the words of the Vedic hymns, and on knowing which those who have found their true self go beyond this existence. Now hear from me about that which is beyond this world.

23. *rasair viyuktaṁ vividhaiś ca gandhair*
aśabdam asparśam arūpavac ca
agrāhyam avyaktam avarṇam ekaṁ
pañca-prakāraṁ sasṛje prajānām

It is devoid of any flavour or aroma, without sound, touch, or form, inconceivable to the mind, never manifest to the senses, and without colour. This alone created the five elements from which living beings are formed.

24. *na strī pumān vāpi napuṁsakaṁ ca*
na san na cāsat sad-asac ca tan na
paśyanti yad brahma-vido manuṣyās
tad akṣaraṁ na kṣaratīti viddhi

It is neither female nor male, nor indeed hermaphrodite. It is neither existent nor non-existent, nor that which is both existent and non-existent. It is this that persons who possess knowledge of Brahman are able to perceive. It is the one principle that does not decay, for you must understand that this never decays.

Śānti-parvan, Adhyāya 195

Chapter 2 continues with essentially the same theme encountered in the first chapter, noting the basic elements of which matter is comprised and insisting that the *param*, the Supreme, is wholly transcendent to them. The senses perceive the outer world whilst the *param* remains beyond perception, even though it is the all-pervasive causal factor that allows the world to exist. This is the true knower, the focus of all knowledge, invisible and yet predominant over the entire world. Verses 9 to 14 offer a series of metaphors through which Manu attempts to explain the existence of the soul within this world. The senses go forth and bring back knowledge in the form of sensory impressions, but the Supreme remains always aloof and transcendent. The Supreme cannot be perceived in this way, as fire cannot be perceived within the wood from which it bursts forth, but if the senses are united with the *buddhi* then it becomes possible for an enlightened person, a *budha*, to perceive the *param*. Here undoubtedly we have a reference to the sort of Yoga practice we have encountered in other passages, but at this point Manu decides not to discuss the subject in any further detail.

Verse 16 uses the word *ātman* to make it clear that the *param*, which is the main topic of discussion, is in fact the true self within all beings. Bodies appear and disappear but this *ātman* remains unchanged and unaffected, moving on from one form to another. At the end of the chapter (verses 19–21), we have a brief rehearsal of the Sāṁkhya view that each of the five great elements has a particular quality that is the object of perception for one of the senses. Thus space is linked to sound, aroma is a quality of earth, form is a quality of fire, flavour is a quality of water, and touch is a quality of air. This understanding of the relationship between the elements, the senses, and the objects of perception is a typical feature of Sāṁkhya analysis, but here it is established only in brief, with no attempt made to provide a full enumeration of the evolved elements of matter – the emphasis remains consistently on the transcendence of the *ātman*.

1. *manur uvāca*
akṣarāt khaṁ tato vāyur vāyor jyotis tato jalam
jalāt prasūtā jagatī jagatyāṁ jāyate jagat

Manu said: Space arose from the undecaying principle (*akṣara*) and from space came air. From the air came light and from light came water. The earth emerged from out of the water and the whole world originates on the earth.

2. *ime śarīrair jalam eva gatvā*
jalāc ca tejaḥ pavano 'ntarikṣam
khād vai nivartanti na-bhāvinas te
ye bhāvinas te param āpnuvanti

Due to their embodiment, these living beings enter the state of water; from water they become heat and then air and space. Those who have not succeeded in life return once more from space but those who are successful attain the Supreme.

3. *noṣṇaṁ na śītaṁ mṛdu nāpi tīkṣṇaṁ*
nāmlaṁ kaṣāyam madhuraṁ na tiktam
na śabda-van nāpi ca gandha-vat tan
na rūpa-vat tat param asva-bhāvam

It is neither hot nor cold, it is neither soft nor hard, nor is it sour, astringent, sweet or bitter. It makes no sound and it has neither aroma nor form. That is the Supreme, which is thus devoid of any identifiable form of existence.

4. *sparśaṁ tanur veda rasaṁ tu jihvā*
ghrāṇaṁ ca gandhāñ śravaṇe ca śabdān
rūpāṇi cakṣur na ca tat paraṁ yad
gṛhṇanty anadhyātma-vido manuṣyāḥ

The body recognises sensations of touch, the tongue recognises taste, the nose recognises odours, the ear recognises sound, and the eye recognises forms. Hence without knowledge of the *adhyātma* whatever men perceive is not the Supreme.

5. *nivartayitvā rasanaṁ rasebhyo*
ghrāṇaṁ ca gandhāc chravaṇe ca śabdāt
sparśāt tanuṁ rūpa-guṇāt tu cakṣus
tataḥ paraṁ paśyati svaṁ sva-bhāvam

After withdrawing the sense of taste from the tastes it perceives, the nose from aromas, the ear from sounds, the body from touch, and the eye from the quality of form, one then sees the Supreme, which is one's own true nature.

6. *yato gṛhītvā hi karoti yac ca*
yasmiṁś ca tām ārabhate pravṛttim
yasmiṁś ca yad yena ca yaś ca kartā
tat kāraṇaṁ taṁ samupāyam āhuḥ

The Supreme is the causal factor in this world. It is that through which the perception is made, that which then performs the action, the arena in which it commences the undertaking, the time at which it occurs, the force through which it is achieved, and the agent that is the doer. They say that these constitute the means by which an end is attained.

7. *yac cābhibhūḥ sādhakaṁ vyāpakaṁ ca*
yan mantra-vac chaṁsyate caiva loke
yaḥ sarva-hetuḥ paramārtha-kārī
tat kāraṇaṁ kāryam ato yad anyat

In this world, the Supreme is glorified by the Vedic hymns as that which is superior to everything else, the all-pervasive motive force. This is the source of all things, the creator of the original object in creation; it is the primal cause and everything else is simply the effect of that cause.

8. *yathā ca kaścit sukṛtair manuṣyaḥ*
śubhāśubhaṁ prāpnute 'thāvirodhāt
evaṁ śarīreṣu śubhāśubheṣu
sva-karma-jair jñānam idaṁ nibaddham

Desirable and undesirable circumstances can exist together and so a man obtains such varying results from the actions he performs. In the same way, knowledge of the Supreme may be sustained in both the pure and the degraded bodily forms generated by one's previous actions.

9. *yathā pradīpaḥ purataḥ pradīptaḥ*
prakāśam anyasya karoti dīpyan
tatheha pañcendriya-dīpa-vṛkṣā
jñāna-pradīptāḥ paravanta eva

When a lamp is lit it illuminates everything in its presence and makes other objects visible. In the same way, each of the lanterns of the five senses illuminates its object of perception with the light of knowledge.

10. *yathā hi rājño bahavo hy amātyāḥ*
pṛthak pramāṇaṁ pravadanti yuktāḥ
tadvac charīreṣu bhavanti pañca
jñānaika-deśaḥ paramaḥ sa tebhyaḥ

A king has numerous ministers and when they are called upon each one presents his own conclusion. In the same way, five senses are found in all bodies and there is a single point of knowledge that stands above them.

11. *yathārciṣo 'gneḥ pavanasya vegā*
marīcayo 'rkasya nadīṣu cāpaḥ
gacchanti cāyānti ca tanyamānās
tadvac charīrāṇi śarīriṇāṁ tu

The flames of a fire, the strength of the wind, the rays of the sun, and the water in rivers all go away and then return once more in a constantly recurring sequence. In the same way, the bodies of embodied beings ceaselessly come and go.

12. *yathā ca kaścit paraśuṁ gṛhītvā*
dhūmaṁ na paśyej jvalanaṁ ca kāṣṭhe
tadvac charīrodara-pāṇi-pādaṁ
chittvā na paśyanti tato yad anyat

When a person uses an axe he does not see the smoke or the fire within the wood he is cutting. In the same way when people cut open the belly, hands, or feet of a body they do not see any separate entity existing within it.

13. *tāny eva kāṣṭhāni yathā vimathya*
dhūmaṁ ca paśyej jvalanaṁ ca yogāt
tadvat subuddhiḥ samam indriyatvād
budhaḥ paraṁ paśyati svaṁ sva-bhāvam

When such pieces of wood are ground together one can see the smoke and fire within them made visible through this contact. In the same way, when the higher intellect (*subuddhi*) is brought to a state of union with the senses, the enlightened person sees the Supreme, which is his own true nature.

14. *yathātmano 'ṅgaṁ patitaṁ pṛthivyāṁ*
svapnāntare paśyati cātmano 'nyat
śrotrādi-yuktaḥ sumanāḥ subuddhir
liṅgāt tathā gacchati liṅgam anyat

In a dream one sees one's own body lying on the ground as if it were different from oneself. In the same way, one progresses from one bodily form to another with the mind and intellect still active and still in possession of the sense of hearing and other senses.

15. *utpatti-vṛddhi-kṣaya-saṁnipātair*
na yujyate 'sau paramaḥ śarīrī
anena liṅgena tu liṅgam anyad
gacchaty adṛṣṭaḥ pratisaṁdhi-yogāt

This transcendent embodied entity is not affected by birth, growth, decline, and death; it departs unseen from its present body and by uniting with another womb it takes on a different bodily form.

16. *na cakṣuṣā paśyati rūpam ātmano*
na cāpi saṁsparśam upaiti kiṁcit
na cāpi taiḥ sādhayate 'tha kāryaṁ
te taṁ na paśyanti sa paśyate tān

No one can perceive the form of the *ātman* with his eye, nor can anyone touch it. It does not execute its actions through senses such as these. The senses cannot perceive the *ātman* but it perceives them.

17. *yathā pradīpe jvalato 'nalasya*
saṁtāpa-jaṁ rūpam upaiti kiṁcit
na cāntaraṁ rūpa-guṇaṁ bibharti
tathaiva tad dṛśyate rūpam asya

When placed within a lamp an object assumes a blazing fiery form generated by the heat of the fire although it does not sustain this quality of form within itself. It is in the same way that the *ātman* is perceived to have a form.

18. *yathā manuṣyaḥ parimucya kāyam*
adṛśyam anyad viśate śarīram
visṛjya bhūteṣu mahatsu dehaṁ
tad āśrayaṁ caiva bibharti rūpam

Giving up his previous identity, a man enters another bodily form without being seen. After casting off his body, which then merges into the great elements, he adopts a new form composed from those same elements.

19. *khaṁ vāyum agniṁ salilaṁ tathorvīṁ*
samantato 'bhyāviśate śarīrī
nānāśrayāḥ karmasu vartamānāḥ
śrotrādayaḥ pañca guṇāñ śrayante

The embodied being thus enters into a form of existence composed entirely of space, air, fire, water, and earth. In executing their respective functions, the sense of hearing and other senses perceive various sensations as they come to rest upon the five qualities of the elements.

20. *śrotraṁ khato ghrāṇam atho pṛthivyās*
tejo-mayaṁ rūpam atho vipākaḥ
jalāśrayaḥ sveda ukto rasaś ca
vāyv-ātmakaḥ sparśa-kṛto guṇaś ca

Thus hearing is based on space, scent is based on earth, whilst form is assimilated when it is illuminated by light. Perspiration is said to be dependent on water as is the sense of taste, whilst the sense of touch operates on the quality inherent in air.

21. *mahatsu bhūteṣu vasanti pañca*
pañcendriyārthāś ca tathendriyeṣu
sarvāṇi caitāni mano 'nugāni
buddhiṁ mano 'nveti manaḥ sva-bhāvam

The five senses thus reside within the five great elements of matter, whilst the five objects of sensory perception exist within the senses. All such perceptions follow the directions of the mind. The mind is guided by the *buddhi*; one's inherent nature is then based upon the mind.

22. *śubhāśubhaṁ karma kṛtaṁ yad asya*
tad eva pratyādadate sva-dehe
mano 'nuvartantiparāvarāṇi
jalaukasaḥ srota ivānukūlam

The embodied being then takes back into this new body the virtuous or wicked actions previously executed. Whether they were performed recently or in the distant past, all actions follow the mind, just like fish drawn along by the current of a stream.

23. *calaṁ yathā dṛṣṭi-pathaṁ paraiti*
sūkṣmaṁ mahad-rūpam ivābhipāti
sva-rūpam ālocayate ca rūpaṁ
paraṁ tathā buddhi-pathaṁ paraiti

One may fix a moving object within the range of one's vision, one may observe a minute object by enlarging it, and one may perceive one's own form by seeing a reflection. In the same way, one can eventually bring the form of the Supreme within the range of the *buddhi*.

Śānti-parvan, Adhyāya 196

The third chapter of the *Manu-Bṛhaspati-Saṁvāda* continues with the same theme by again emphasising the invisible presence of the *ātman* within the body and its absolute transcendence over the material domain. The *ātman* does not have a direct influence over the world but remains as the invisible seer, using the senses for external perception whilst itself remaining beyond the range of the senses. In the previous chapters, this higher self was referred to by the term *param*, which simply means the supreme; here in verse 5 the word *kṣetrajña* is used, which literally means the 'knower of the field', and is a term commonly employed in Sāṁkhya discourse, as well as in the thirteenth chapter of the *Bhagavad-gītā*. In the main, however, the *ātman* is referred to by the term *śarīrin*, which simply means 'the embodied one'.

There is no doubt that the treatise as a whole functions within the purview of Sāṁkhya and Yoga teachings but it is unusual in the sense that it does not seek to pursue either of these philosophies in any kind of detail. Rather, it remains firmly focused on the single idea of the existence of the *ātman* within the material body, before moving on to consider how knowledge of this true self can be realised. In verses 9 and 10, it is stated that men of wisdom, the *budhas* and *su-vipaścits*, are able to perceive the self as the life within the body for, like fishermen catching fish, they are able to employ the proper techniques. This would seem to be an oblique reference to the Yoga techniques discussed elsewhere in the *Mokṣa-dharma-parvan* but the point is not expanded upon: we are simply told that this perception is based on *jñāna* (higher knowledge), which could simply be derived from inference. The final verses of the chapter employ the metaphor of the moon's appearances and disappearances to emphasise the point. On the first night of the new moon, the moon becomes invisible but we are certain by inference that the moon still exists. In the same way, although the soul cannot be seen with the eyes, its existence can be established by inference when we observe the existence of life within a bodily form comprised of lifeless matter.

1. *manur uvāca*
yad indriyais tūpakṛtān purastāt
prāptān guṇān saṁsmarate cirāya
teṣv indriyeṣūpahateṣu paścāt
sa buddhi-rūpaḥ paramaḥ sva-bhāvaḥ

Manu said: Generally one calls to mind at a later time the qualities of objects previously encountered by the senses. But when the activity of the senses is suspended, the higher nature of the living being takes on the form of the *buddhi*.

2. *yathendriyārthān yugapat samastān*
nāvekṣate kṛtsnam atulya-kālam
yathābalaṁ saṁcarate sa vidvāṁs
tasmāt sa ekaḥ paramaḥ śarīrī

The different objects are simultaneously perceived by the senses all together and so the embodied being cannot perceive them all at another time. Still, however, it is full of knowledge as it moves without directly influencing the world. Therefore this embodied being is the supreme principle that stands alone.

3. *rajas tamaḥ sattvam atho tṛtīyaṁ*
gacchaty asau jñāna-guṇān virūpān
tathendriyāṇy āviśate śarīrī
hutāśanaṁ vāyur ivendhana-stham

There are *rajas* and *tamas* and then *sattva* is the third. This embodied being thus encounters these distinctive forms of knowledge as it occupies and activates each of the senses in the way that wind activates the fire latent within kindling wood.

4. *na cakṣuṣā paśyati rūpam ātmano*
na paśyati sparśanam indriyendriyam
na śrotra-liṅgaṁ śravaṇe nidarśanaṁ
tathāgataṁ paśyati tad vinaśyati

One cannot perceive the form of the *ātman* with the sense of sight; the sense of touch does not have the power to perceive it, and if one hears something it is never the *ātman* that is perceived in this way as an object of hearing, for any object one perceives has come into being at some point and any such object must also meet with destruction.

5. *śrotrādīni na paśyanti svaṁ svam ātmānam ātmanā*
sarva-jñaḥ sarva-darśī ca kṣetra-jñas tāni paśyati

Hearing and the other senses cannot perceive themselves through their own powers of perception. The *kṣetrajña*, however, is all knowing and all seeing; it perceives the senses.

6. *yathā himavataḥ pārśvaṁ pṛṣṭhaṁ candramaso yathā*
na dṛṣṭa-pūrvaṁ manujair na ca tan nāsti tāvatā

Human beings have never seen the far slopes of the Himavat range or the other side of the moon, but it cannot be said that these do not exist.

7. *tadvad bhūteṣu bhūtātmā sūkṣmo jñānātmavān asau*
adṛṣṭa-pūrvaś cakṣurbhyāṁ na cāsau nāsti tāvatā

In the same way, the *bhūtāman* within all living beings, which is subtle and by its very nature endowed with knowledge, has never been seen with the eyes, but still it cannot be said that it does not exist.

8. *paśyann api yathā lakṣma jagat some na vindati*
evam asti na vety etan na ca tan na parāyaṇam

Even though the whole world can see the marks on the moon, nobody knows what they really are. In the same way, people can understand neither this world nor the end that awaits them.

9. *rūpavantam arūpatvād udayāstamaye budhāḥ*
dhiyā samanupaśyanti tad gatāḥ savitur gatim

Because objects have form when the sun rises and become formless when the sun sets, wise men can use their intelligence to note the movement of the sun.

10. *tathā buddhi-pradīpena dūra-sthaṁ su-vipaścitaḥ*
pratyāsannaṁ ninīṣanti jñeyaṁ jñānābhisaṁhitam

In the same way, men of vast learning make the self the object of their understanding. They use the illumination of their intellect, seeking to draw the true self near to them from its remote position and bring it within the purview of their knowledge.

11. *na hi khalv anupāyena kaścid artho 'bhisidhyati*
sūtra-jālair yathā matsyān badhnanti jala-jīvinaḥ

No goal can ever be reached without employing the proper techniques, just as fishermen must make use of nets made of string in order to catch fish.

12. *mṛgair mṛgāṇāṁ grahaṇaṁ pakṣiṇāṁ pakṣibhir yathā*
gajānāṁ ca gajair evaṁ jñeyaṁ jñānena gṛhyate

As beasts are captured by using other beasts as bait, as birds are taken by using other birds, and as elephants are seized with other elephants, so knowledge is the means by which realisation of the true object of knowledge is gained.

13. *ahir eva hy aheḥ pādān paśyatīti nidarśanam*
tadvan mūrtiṣu mūrti-sthaṁ jñeyaṁ jñānena paśyati

It is said that only a snake can see the feet of a snake. In the same way, the living being perceives its own self by means of knowledge. It is then understood as the embodied entity in all bodily forms.

14. *notsahante yathā vettum indriyair indriyāṇy api*
tathaiveha parā buddhiḥ paraṁ buddhyā na paśyati

One is never able to comprehend the senses by use of the senses. In the same way, the *buddhi*, which is superior to the senses, cannot perceive the Supreme through its intellectual capacity.

15. *yathā candro hy amāvāsyām aliṅgatvān na dṛśyate*
na ca nāśo 'sya bhavati tathā viddhi śarīriṇam

Because it has no form then, the moon is not seen on the first night of a new moon, although it has certainly not been destroyed. In the same way, you should understand that the embodied soul is not absent even though it cannot be seen.

16. *kṣīṇa-kośo hy amāvāsyāṁ candramā na prakāśate*
tadvan mūrti-viyuktaḥ sañ śarīrī nopalabhyate

On the first night of a new moon, the moon is divested of its external form and does not appear. In the same way, the existence of the embodied being cannot be perceived when it is separated from its embodied form.

17. *yathā kośāntaraṁ prāpya candramā bhrājate punaḥ*
tadval liṅgāntaraṁ prāpya śarīrī bhrājate punaḥ

When it has entered into a new phase, the moon shines forth once more. In the same way, the appearance of the embodied being shines forth again when it enters a new embodiment.

18. *janma-vṛddhi-kṣayaś cāsya pratyakṣeṇopalabhyate*
sā tu candramaso vyaktir na tu tasya śarīriṇaḥ

The birth, growth, and disappearance of the moon can be recognised by direct perception. This is the external, manifest form of the moon, but such changes never affect the embodied being.

19. *utpatti-vṛddhi-vyayato yathā sa iti gṛhyate*
candra eva tv amāvāsyāṁ tathā bhavati mūrtimān

The moon is subject to birth, growth, and then disappearance, but on the night of the new moon it is still the same luminary. So it is for the embodied entity.

20. *nābhisarpad vimuñcad vā śaśinaṁ dṛśyate tamaḥ*
visṛjaṁś copasarpaṁś ca tadvat paśya śarīriṇam

The dark planet remains unseen whilst it is approaching or moving away from the moon. You should see that in the same way the embodied being invisibly approaches and then departs from the body.

21. *yathā candrārka-saṁyuktaṁ tamas tad upalabhyate*
tadvac charīra-saṁyuktaḥ śarīrīty upalabhyate

The dark planet can be observed when it is in conjunction with the moon or the sun. In the same way, the existence of the embodied being can be ascertained when it is in conjunction with the body.

22. *yathā candrārka-nirmuktaḥ sa rāhur nopalabhyate*
tadvac charīra-nirmuktaḥ śarīrī nopalabhyate

And when the planet Rāhu is detached from the sun and the moon it can no longer be observed. In the same way, the existence of the embodied being cannot be ascertained when it is detached from the body.

23. *yathā candro hy amāvāsyāṁ nakṣatrair yujyate gataḥ*
tadvac charīra-nirmuktaḥ phalair yujyati karmaṇaḥ

When it departs on the new moon night, the moon maintains its conjunction with the constellations. In the same way, when the embodied being departs from the body it retains its connection with the fruits of the actions that body has performed.

Śānti-parvan, Adhyāya 197

In Chapter 4, Manu begins to move his teachings on, and here the verses are predominated by Yoga doctrine. In fact, the whole chapter is broadly commensurate with Chapter 2, the *Sādhana-pāda*, of Patañjali's *Yoga Sūtras*, though one would hesitate to suggest any direct link between the two texts. The first verse indicates that after death existence continues like that of a dream, presumably indicating that the mind remains active even though the body is still; Manu then turns to Yoga discourse with his assertion that the soul can be perceived when the senses are made still. Here the word *jñeyam* (that which is to be known) is used to indicate the soul, the *param* or *śarīrin* that has been the main subject of the previous chapters.

Here the emphasis is much more on providing a solution to the problem of the soul's embodiment. The cause of the problem is again presented in terms of Yoga teachings: the root cause is ignorance, which leads to a loss of intelligence and then contamination of the mind, so that the *ātman* remains *adṛṣṭa*, unseen and hence unknown. In this state of ignorance, we seek pleasure through the senses so our perception is projected outwards onto the world rather than inwards in pursuit of the *jñeyam*, the true object of knowledge. Only when the senses are withdrawn and sinful action abandoned is there any possibility that the true self can be known. And it is further to be noted that in this chapter Manu refers for the first time to *mokṣa* as the result achieved through the teachings he is presenting; the words used are *amṛtam aśnute*, 'he achieves immorality', which is a fairly unequivocal statement (verse 12).

Also to be noted here is the 'chain' established by the text, starting with what it refers to as the *avyakta*. Literally meaning 'non-manifest' or 'invisible', the word is used in Sāṁkhya treatises to indicate *prakṛti* in its non-evolved state. Here, however, one must take *avyakta* to mean the spiritual element within a living being, which Manu has gone to great lengths to show is beyond the range of conventional perception. From the *avyakta* (spiritual self) comes knowledge, from knowledge the *buddhi* (intellect), from the *buddhi* comes *manas* (mind), from *manas* come the senses, and then the objects perceived by the senses: taste, sound, aroma, flavour, and touch sensations. This idea is presented in verses 10 and 11; then in verse 19 the process advocated is described as a reversal of this 'chain' with the senses taken back into the mind, the mind into the intellect, the intellect into knowledge, and then knowledge back into the *avyakta*, referred to in this verse as *param* (the Supreme). In this process of reversal, we can again detect strong indications that the *Manu-Bṛhaspati-Saṁvāda* is making extensive use of Yoga philosophy in establishing its own conclusions. This suggestion is further reinforced by the way in which verses 16 to 18 assert that restraint of the senses is naturally achieved when the Supreme is realised, in line with the statement of 1.16 of the *Yoga Sūtras* ('A superior form of renunciation is the lack of hankering for material attributes that arises from realisation of *puruṣa*.').

1. *manur uvāca*
yathā vyaktam idaṁ śete svapne carati cetanam
jñānam indriya-saṁyuktaṁ tadvat pretya bhavābhavau

Manu said: Whilst the body lies down to sleep, the consciousness in conjunction with the senses continues its pursuit of knowledge through dreams. In the same way, after death there is both existence and non-existence.

2. *yathāmbhasi prasanne tu rūpaṁ paśyati cakṣuṣā*
tadvat prasannendriyavāñ jñeyaṁ jñānena paśyati

When water is still, one can use one's sense of sight to perceive a form reflected in it. In the same way, one whose senses are stilled can use knowledge to perceive the true object of knowledge.

3. *sa eva lulite tasmin yathā rūpaṁ na paśyati*
tathendriyākulī-bhāve jñeyaṁ jñāne na paśyati

And when the water is disturbed one cannot perceive a form reflected in it. In the same way, when the senses become agitated one cannot perceive the object of knowledge within his field of knowledge.

4. *abuddhir ajñāna-kṛtā abuddhyā duṣyate manaḥ*
duṣṭasya manasaḥ pañca sampraduṣyanti mānasāḥ

Loss of intelligence is caused by ignorance and the mind is corrupted by the absence of intelligence. When the mind is corrupted the five senses existing within the mind are also degraded.

5. *ajñāna-tṛpto viṣayeṣv avagāḍho na dṛśyate*
adṛṣṭvaiva tu pūtātmā viṣayebhyo nivartate

As long as one is satisfied with such ignorance and absorbed in the objects of pleasure, the pure self is not perceived. And as long as it remains beyond perception it repeatedly returns to the objects of sensual enjoyment.

6. *tarṣacchedo na bhavati puruṣasyeha kalmaṣāt*
nivartate tathā tarṣaḥ pāpam antaṁ gataṁ yathā

Because of this contamination, there is no cessation of such a person's hankerings. Desire fades only when the wickedness of the mind is terminated.

7. *viṣayeṣu ca saṁsargāc chāśvatasya na saṁśrayāt*
manasā cānyad ākāṅkṣan paraṁ na pratipadyate

Because of his association with the objects of pleasure and his dissociation from that which is eternal, a person does not attain the Supreme whilst the longings of his mind are focused elsewhere.

8. *jñānam utpadyate puṁsāṁ kṣayāt pāpasya karmaṇaḥ*
athādarśa-tala-prakhye paśyaty ātmānam ātmani

Knowledge arises in human beings as a direct result of giving up sinful actions. One then perceives the *ātman* within oneself, as if on the bright surface of a mirror.

9. *prasṛtair indriyair duḥkhī tair eva niyataiḥ sukhī*
tasmād indriya-rūpebhyo yac chedātmānaṁ ātmanā

When the senses become active one is afflicted by suffering, but one finds joy when they are restrained. Therefore, by means of self-control, the pacified mind should be withdrawn from the objects on which the senses focus.

10. *indriyebhyo manaḥ pūrvaṁ buddhiḥ paratarā tataḥ*
buddheḥ paratararṁ jñānaṁ jñānāt paratararṁ param

The mind (*manas*) is beyond the senses and the intellect (*buddhi*) is superior to the mind. Knowledge is superior to *buddhi* and the Supreme is superior to knowledge.

11. *avyaktāt prasṛtaṁ jñānaṁ tato buddhis tato manaḥ*
manaḥ śrotrādibhir yuktaṁ śabdādīn sādhu paśyati

Knowledge arises from the non-manifest source (*avyakta*), *buddhi* arises from knowledge, and *manas* arises from *buddhi*. Existing in conjunction with hearing and the other senses, the *manas* accurately perceives sound and the other objects of perception.

12. *yas tāṁs tyajati śabdādīn sarvāś ca vyaktayas tathā*
vimuñcaty ākṛti-grāmāṁs tān muktvāmṛtam aśnute

One who renounces sound and the other objects of sensory perception and all things manifest in this world goes beyond the various forms that appear here. After freeing himself from these, he then attains immortality.

13. *udyan hi savitā yadvat sṛjate raśmi-maṇḍalam*
sa evāstam upāgacchaṁs tad evātmani yacchati

The rising sun casts a circle of light across the world but when it reaches its final point in the west it holds the light within itself once more.

14. *antarātmā tathā dehaṁ āviśyendriya-raśmibhiḥ*
prāpyendriya-guṇān pañca so 'stam āvṛtya gacchati

In the same way, when it enters the body the *ātman* reaches out to the five objects of perception through the light of the senses and then withdraws that light within itself once more.

15. *praṇītaṁ karmaṇā mārgaṁ nīyamānaḥ punaḥ punaḥ*
prāpnoty ayaṁ karma-phalaṁ pravṛddhaṁ dharmam ātmavān

Over and over again, the *ātman* is thus led along the path prepared by its previous actions. In this way a prudent man attains the ripened fruits of action performed in accordance with his dharma.

16. *viṣayā vinivartante nirāhārasya dehinaḥ*
rasa-varjaṁ raso 'py asya paraṁ dṛṣṭvā nivartate

The objects of pleasure cannot touch the embodied soul when it abstains from them. Although one can restrict one's inclination in this way the attraction still remains, but after perceiving the Supreme one completely renounces such attraction.

17. *buddhiḥ karma-guṇair hīnā yadā manasi vartate*
tadā sampadyate brahma tatraiva pralayaṁ gatam

And when the *buddhi*, thus freed from the consequences of previous action, comes to rest within the *manas* it then attains Brahman; at that time the *manas* becomes still.

18. *asparśanam aśṛṇvānam anāsvādam adarśanam*
aghrāṇam avitarkaṁ ca sattvaṁ prativiśate param

It then enters the higher form of existence that is imperceptible to the senses of touch, hearing, taste, sight and scent, and is beyond the range of one's thoughts as well.

19. *manasy ākṛtayo magnā manas tv atigataṁ matim*
matis tv atigatā jñānaṁ jñānaṁ tv abhigataṁ param

Perceived forms are immersed within the *manas* and then one's intellectual activity overwhelms the *manas*. Intellectual activity is itself overwhelmed by knowledge and knowledge is subsumed by the Supreme.

20. *indriyair manasaḥ siddhir na buddhiṁ budhyate manaḥ*
na buddhir budhyate 'vyaktaṁ sūkṣmas tv etāni paśyati

Manas fulfils its function by means of the senses, but *manas* cannot comprehend the *buddhi*. The *buddhi* cannot comprehend the non-manifest entity (*avyakta*), but this subtle entity perceives all of these.

Śānti-parvan, Adhyāya 198

The first half of the fifth chapter continues with the exposition of Yoga philosophy, though again it does not move beyond this theme into the realm of Yoga practice. Here it is asserted that once the senses have been taken back into the mind (*manas*), the mind itself must then be united with the *buddhi*, the intellect that possesses the capacity for judgement and discrimination. In line with the teachings of the *Yoga Sūtras*, it is here again asserted that intellectual activity can be directed in one of two directions. The normal process is outward perception via the active mind and senses, but if these external processes are suspended then it is possible for the *buddhi* to turn its perception inwards and ultimately perceive the true self, the transcendent *ātman*, which here again is designated as *param* and *avyakta*, the supreme or higher identity that cannot be perceived through the senses. Only when the senses are withdrawn and the mind united with the *buddhi* does such higher perception become possible through the process of *dhyāna*, fixed meditation on a specific object. And such meditation is possible only if the outward perception via the senses is suspended as the two are deemed to be incompatible. Here one may readily identify parallels with Patañjali's definition of Yoga as *citta-vṛtti-nirodha*, 'the stilling of the movements of the mind'.

From verse 11, the chapter moves on to a rather different theme, firstly insisting that the practitioner pursuing this higher goal must maintain his dedication to the dharmic practices of his social order, for these bring about the state of purity required, and then reiterating the earlier theme of the absolute distinction between matter and spirit. The Yoga practice referred to is to be undertaken so that the practitioner can attain the Supreme Brahman and thereby avoid returning to this world. Again the utter transcendence of the true self is emphasised, but now the major themes of Manu's discourse are drawn together. It is because the *ātman* is distinct from its material embodiment that the senses should be withdrawn and material perception suspended; only in this way can the artificial connection between matter and spirit be severed. In this way Manu shows that an understanding of the true nature of a living being is to be combined with the classical Yoga practices that bring about realisation of the true self.

1. *manur uvāca*
jñānaṁ jñeyābhinirvṛttaṁ viddhi jñāna-guṇaṁ manaḥ
prajñā-karaṇa-saṁyuktaṁ tato buddhiḥ pravartate

Manu said: Knowledge arises from the object that should be known, and you should understand that the mind (*manas*) is an attribute of knowledge. When the *manas* exists in conjunction with the process of discrimination, the intellect (*buddhi*) appears from this combination.

2. *yadā karma-guṇopetā buddhir manasi vartate*
tadā prajñāyate brahma dhyāna-yoga-samādhinā

When the intellect previously endowed with qualities and action comes to exist within the mind, it is able to comprehend Brahman by the *samādhi* that arises from Yoga meditation.

3. *seyaṁ guṇavatī buddhir guṇeṣv evābhivartate*
avatārābhiniḥsrotaṁ gireḥ śṛṅgād ivodakam

Now if that same *buddhi* remains encumbered by material qualities, it then gravitates entirely towards the attributes of this world, just like water gushing down from the summit of a mountain.

4. *yadā nirguṇam āpnoti dhyānaṁ manasi pūrva-jam*
tadā prajñāyate brahma nikaṣyaṁ nikaṣe yathā

But when the *buddhi* is able to take the meditation begun previously within the mind to a level where it is entirely free of attributes, it then comprehends Brahman, just like the gold mark that appears on a stone used for testing gold.

5. *manas tv apahṛtaṁ buddhim indriyārtha-nidarśanam*
na samakṣaṁ guṇāvekṣi nirguṇasya nidarśanam

If the *manas* carries away the *buddhi* by becoming engrossed in the objects of the senses, then whilst it remains absorbed in observing whatever is present before it, it can never gain perception of that which is free of all attributes.

6. *sarvāṇy etāni saṁvārya dvārāṇi manasi sthitaḥ*
manasy ekāgratāṁ kṛtvā tat paraṁ pratipadyate

But after closing all these gateways of perception, the *buddhi* remains situated within *manas*. It then ensures that there is only one object of perception in the *manas*; this is the Supreme, which the *buddhi* attains thereby.

7. *yathā mahānti bhūtāni nivartante guṇa-kṣaye*
tathendriyāṇy upādāya buddhir manasi vartate

As the great elements are withdrawn when their associated qualities cease to exist, so after the senses are withdrawn the *buddhi* remains present within the *manas*.

8. *yadā manasi sā buddhir vartate 'ntara-cāriṇī*
vyavasāya-guṇopetā tadā saṁpadyate manaḥ

When the *buddhi* exists within the *manas*, it is inwardly active and also possesses the quality of firm resolve. It then enters a state of complete union with the *manas*.

9. *guṇavadbhir guṇopetaṁ yadā dhyāna-guṇaṁ manaḥ*
tadā sarva-guṇān hitvā nirguṇaṁ pratipadyate

The *manas* is endowed with material qualities by the senses, each of which focuses on a particular quality. But when its attributes are shaped by meditation, it then moves beyond all material qualities and focuses on that which is free from such qualities.

10. *avyaktasyeha vijñāne nāsti tulyaṁ nidarśanam*
yatra nāsti pada-nyāsaḥ kas taṁ viṣayam āpnuyāt

Apart from this there is no form of perception that can assist in gaining knowledge of that which is not manifest in this world. How else can one attain a goal that cannot be expressed in words?

11. *tapasā cānumānena guṇair jātyā śrutena ca*
ninīṣet tat paraṁ brahma viśuddhenāntarātmanā

Through austerity, contemplation, developing higher qualities, acting in accordance with one's social position, and listening to learned teachings, one should approach the Supreme Brahman, with one's innermost *ātman* thus made pure.

12. *guṇa-hīno hi taṁ mārgaṁ bahiḥ samanuvartate*
guṇābhāvāt prakṛtyā ca nistarkyaṁ jñeya-saṁmitam

One who is free of material qualities may also follow an external path. Because the true self is by its very nature devoid of qualities, it is beyond mundane logic and is designated as *jñeya*, that which one must endeavour to comprehend.

13. *nairguṇyād brahma cāpnoti sa-guṇatvān nivartate*
guṇa-prasāriṇī buddhir hutāśana ivendhane

When the intellect is free from material qualities it can attain Brahman, but when it is absorbed in material qualities one returns to this world. The *buddhi* roams through these qualities just like the fire of sacrifice engulfing kindling wood.

14. *yathā pañca vimuktāni indriyāṇi sva-karmabhiḥ*
tathā tat paramaṁ brahma vimuktaṁ prakṛteḥ param

When the five senses are withdrawn from the functions they perform, the Supreme Brahman is then completely liberated and exists beyond any contact with matter.

15. *evaṁ prakṛtitaḥ sarve prabhavanti śarīriṇaḥ*
nivartante nivṛttau ca sargaṁ naivopayānti ca

It is thus due to their contact with matter (*prakṛti*) that all these embodied beings are manifest in this world. When they turn away from *prakṛti* and no longer indulge in material actions they cease to partake of this material existence.

16. *puruṣaḥ prakṛtir buddhir viśeṣāś cendriyāṇi ca*
ahaṁkāro 'bhimānaś ca saṁbhūto bhūta-saṁjñakaḥ

Puruṣa, *prakṛti*, *buddhi*, the varied objects perceived and the senses that perceive them, self-awareness (*ahaṁkāra*), and personal identity are known collectively as the elements that comprise a living being.

17. *ekasyādyā pravṛttis tu pradhānāt saṁpravartate*
dvitīyā mithuna-vyaktim aviśeṣān niyacchati

The initial manifestation is of a single element, which arises from out of the *pradhāna*, the primal material substance. For the secondary manifestation, the distinction between male and female becomes manifest, imposing conditions on the living beings.

18. *dharmād utkṛṣyate śreyas tathāśreyo 'py adharmataḥ*
rāgavān prakṛtiṁ hy eti virakto jñānavān bhavet

Great benefit accrues from adherence to dharma whilst misfortune arises from *adharma*. One beset by attachments exists in conjunction with material nature, whilst one who is free from attachments becomes endowed with knowledge.

Śānti-parvan, Adhyāya 199

The sixth and final chapter of the *Manu-Bṛhaspati-Saṁvāda* draws the discussion to an effective conclusion as we find Manu at last placing his full emphasis on liberation from rebirth as the goal that can be achieved through the teachings he has presented herein. Again we see the same basic points being restated: firstly, the transcendent position of the soul that is beyond the range of sensory perception, then the Yoga philosophy, which asserts that the true self can in fact be perceived if the line of external perception is suspended and the mind thereby allowed to turn its perception inwards.

This line of discussion appears in the opening verses of the chapter as Manu explains that the soul in each body is identical, but the nature of the body is determined according to the law of karma. Yoga practice is next defined as the turning of the mind inwards so that perception of the true self is achieved. Then in the middle of the chapter we have a rather curious interlude in which the treatise appears to adopt a Vaiṣṇava identity by proclaiming that Viṣṇu is the supreme Brahman who stands above all the elements of the created world. He is entirely transcendent and is the abode and destination for those who achieve the state of transcendence by turning their perception away from the world. This brief theistic interlude is interesting as it sugggests again an early connection that appears to have existed between Yoga and Vaiṣṇava theism. This passage also serves to turn the discussion towards the result gained through attainment of the higher realisation Manu has been emphasising up until this point. The path of *nivṛtti*, the renunciation of ritual action, is above the religion of the

Veda and allows a person to reach the state of Brahman, the supreme abode previously identified with Viṣṇu.

The two paths of the mind take a person in different directions. Those whose perception is outwards via the senses remain absorbed in this world, but those who still the mind and turn their perception inwards 'reach the body of Brahman', *brahma-śarīram eti* (verse 27), or 'they enter Brahman that is devoid of attributes', *sa nirguṇaṁ brahma praviśanti* (verse 31). Hence at last the treatise reaches its *mokṣa*-dharmic conclusion by revealing the true purpose of the wisdom it has been expounding. The language again suggests that although the passage makes clear use of Yoga philosophy, and has parallels with the *Yoga Sūtras*, it is not strictly speaking a Yoga treatise. The equation of Viṣṇu with the Supreme Brahman suggests a wider context, which draws on a range of different sources and has no hesitation in seeking to bring together Vaiṣṇava, Sāṁkhya, and Yoga teachings. This tendency towards a free movement between what are usually regarded as distinctive schools of thought is a feature commonly encountered within the *Mokṣa-dharma-parvan* as a whole.

1. *manur uvāca*
yadā te pañcabhiḥ pañca vimuktā manasā saha
atha tad drakṣyase brahma maṇau sūtram ivārpitam

Manu said: When your five senses along with the *manas* are dissociated from the five objects of sensory perception, then you will see Brahman which is like the thread that passes through a gemstone.

2. *tad eva ca yathā sūtraṁ suvarṇe vartate punaḥ*
muktāsv atha pravāleṣu mṛnmaye rājate tathā

Such a thread may also be found in gold, pearls, coral beads, or clay, and thereby controls their position.

3. *tadvad goṣu manuṣyeṣu tadvad dhasti-mṛgādiṣu*
tadvat kīṭa-pataṅgeṣu prasaktātmā sva-karmabhiḥ

And in the same way, when beset by attachments, the *ātman* exists within cows or human beings, in elephants and other beasts, or within worms or flies, depending upon action previously performed.

4. *yena yena śarīreṇa yad yat karma karoty ayam*
tena tena śarīreṇa tat tat phalam upāśnute

According to the actions performed through the body it occupies, the *ātman* enjoys an appropriate reward to be experienced through that body.

5. *yathā hy eka-rasā bhūmir oṣadhy-ātmānusāriṇī*
tathā karmānugā buddhir antarātmānudarśinī

The earth receives one form of liquid, which is then transformed according to the individual nature of a plant. In the same way the *buddhi*, which is observed by the inner *ātman*, is shaped by the nature of actions previously performed.

6. *jñāna-pūrvodbhavā lipsā lipsāpūrvābhisaṁdhitā*
abhisaṁdhi-pūrvakaṁ karma karma-mūlaṁ tataḥ phalam

Desire arises from the knowledge one has previously acquired, and the formation of intent arises from a previous desire. Action is based on these previously formed intentions, and action is the root from which future results arise.

7. *phalaṁ karmātmakaṁ vidyāt karma jñeyātmakaṁ tathā*
jñeyaṁ jñānātmakaṁ vidyāj jñānaṁ sad-asad-ātmakam

Future results depend on actions performed and action is determined by what is known. What is known will depend upon the knowledge one acquires, and knowledge relates to both the permanent and the impermanent.

8. *jñānānāṁ ca phalānāṁ ca jñeyānāṁ karmaṇāṁ tathā*
kṣayānte tat phalaṁ divyaṁ jñānaṁ jñeya-pratiṣṭhitam

When the different types of knowledge one possesses and the results of one's previous actions come to an end, as well as the objects one comprehends and the actions one performs, the result one gains thereby is spiritual knowledge that makes the *ātman* its object.

9. *mahad dhi paramaṁ bhūtaṁ yuktāḥ paśyanti yoginaḥ*
abudhās taṁ na paśyanti hy ātma-sthā guṇa-buddhayaḥ

When the *yogins* are engaged in Yoga practice they perceive the *mahat*, the highest element. Self-absorbed persons who lack true intelligence and focus their intellect on the qualities of this world do not perceive the Supreme.

10. *pṛthivī-rūpato rūpam apām iha mahattaram*
adbhyo mahattaraṁ tejas tejasaḥ pavano mahān

By nature water is greater than earth. Heat is greater than water, and air is greater than heat.

11. *pavanāc ca mahad vyoma tasmāt parataraṁ manaḥ*
manaso mahatī buddhir buddheḥ kālo mahān smṛtaḥ

The sky is greater than air and *manas* is superior to the sky. *Buddhi* is greater than *manas* and time is recognised as greater than *buddhi.*

12. *kālāt sa bhagavān viṣṇur yasya sarvam idaṁ jagat*
nādir na madhyaṁ naivāntas tasya devasya vidyate

Greater than time is the exalted Lord Viṣṇu, the master of all the world. For that Deity there is no beginning, no middle, and no end.

13. *anāditvād amadhyatvād anantatvāc ca so 'vyayaḥ*
atyeti sarva-duḥkhāni duḥkhaṁ hy antavad ucyate

Because he has no beginning, middle, or end, he is not subject to decay or transformation. He transcends all miseries, for it is said that misery must have an end.

14. *tad brahma paramaṁ proktaṁ tad dhāma paramaṁ smṛtam*
tad gatvā kāla-viṣayād vimuktā mokṣam āśritāḥ

This is spoken of as the Supreme Brahman and is known as the highest abode. Those who have attained that position are free from the domain of time and exist in a state of liberation.

15. *guṇais tv etaiḥ prakāśante nirguṇatvāt tataḥ param*
nivṛtti-lakṣaṇo dharmas tathānantyāya kalpate

Objects are perceived through the qualities they possess but the Supreme stands above other objects because it is devoid of such qualities. There is a dharma that involves renunciation of ritual action and through it one gains the state of immortality.

16. *ṛco yajūṁṣi sāmāni śarīrāṇi vyapāśritāḥ*
jihvāgreṣu pravartante yatna-sādhyā vināśinaḥ

The chants of the *Ṛk*, *Yajus*, and *Sāma* Vedas make their abode in the bodies of human beings. These hymns are produced by physical exertion as they issue from the tip of the tongue of their reciters and hence they perish when the chant is complete.

17. *na caivam iṣyate brahma śarīrāśraya-saṁbhavam*
na yatna-sādhyaṁ tad brahma nādi-madhyaṁ na cāntavat

Brahman has a dwelling place within the body but it cannot be sought out in this way. Brahman is not attained through physical exertion for it has no beginning, middle, or end.

18. *ṛcām ādis tathā sāmnām yajuṣām ādir ucyate*
antaś cādi-matāṁ dṛṣṭo na cādir brahmaṇaḥ smṛtam

It is said that the hymns of the *Ṛk Sāma*, and *Yajur* Vedas all have a point of origin, and one can see that there must be an end to anything that has a beginning. But Brahman is known to have no beginning.

19. *anāditvād anantatvāt tad anantam athāvyayam*
avyayatvāc ca nirdvaṁdvaṁ dvaṁdvābhāvāt tataḥ param

Because it has no beginning and no end, it is unlimited and also unchanging. Because it never changes, it is free from duality and beyond all forms of existence based on duality.

20. *adṛṣṭato 'nupāyāc cāpy abhisaṁdheś ca karmaṇaḥ*
na tena martyāḥ paśyanti yena gacchanti tat param

Because of destiny, because they do not know the proper techniques, or because of the nature of the intent that underlies their actions, mortal beings do not develop the form of perception that would allow them to approach the Supreme.

21. *viṣayeṣu ca saṁsargāc chāśvatasya ca darśanāt*
manasā cānyad ākāṅkṣan paraṁ na pratipadyate

Because of indulgence in the objects of pleasure, visions of eternal life in heaven, and the mind hankering after other things, one fails in the attempt to attain the Supreme.

22. *guṇān yad iha paśyanti tad icchanty apare janāḥ*
paraṁ naivābhikāṅkṣanti nirguṇatvād guṇārthinaḥ

Then there are persons who see the material qualities of an object and long to possess it. Because they are attracted by material qualities, such persons do not even desire the Supreme, which is by nature devoid of qualities.

23. *guṇair yas tv avarair yuktaḥ kathaṁ vidyād guṇān imān*
anumānād dhi gantavyaṁ guṇair avayavaiḥ saha

How can a person who occupies himself with inferior qualities comprehend these other qualities? Only by inferred knowledge may that which possesses attributes of a different substance be reached.

24. *sūkṣmeṇa manasā vidmo vācā vaktuṁ na śaknumaḥ*
mano hi manasā grāhyaṁ darśanena ca darśanam

We may come to know the Supreme through the most subtle application of the mind (*manas*), but we can never describe it with words. The mind grasps only what can be conceived of and sight perceives only what is visible.

25. *jñānena nirmalī-kṛtya buddhiṁ buddhyā tathā manaḥ*
manasā cendriya-grāmam anantaṁ pratipadyate

When the *buddhi* is made pure by knowledge, *manas* is made pure by *buddhi*, and all the senses are made pure by *manas*, one then attains that which has no limit.

26. *buddhi-prahīṇo manasāsamṛddhas*
tathā nirāśīr guṇatām upaiti
paraṁ tyajantīha vilobhyamānā
hutāśanaṁ vāyur ivendhana-stham

One devoid of intelligence, who falls short in his mental endeavours, loses his spiritual aspirations and turns instead to things that possess material qualities. Beguiled by these temptations such persons turn away from the Supreme, as the wind never fans the fire dormant in wood.

27. *guṇādāne viprayoge ca teṣāṁ*
manaḥ sadā buddhi-parāvarābhyām
anenaiva vidhinā saṁpravṛtto
guṇādāne brahma-śarīram eti

The mind can either draw material qualities to itself or separate itself from them. These two tendencies always cause the degradation and elevation of the *buddhi*. But when one fully adopts the mental discipline referred to above and draws the higher qualities to oneself in that process, then one enters the body of Brahman.

28. *avyaktātmā puruṣo 'vyakta-karmā*
so 'vyaktatvaṁ gacchati hy anta-kāle
tair evāyaṁ cendriyair vardhamānair
glāyadbhir vā vartate karma-rūpaḥ

The true self of each person is by nature imperceptible and performs no perceptible action. Hence at the time of death it enters a state that is entirely beyond perception. But when the *ātman* exists in association with the senses, which expand and withdraw in relation to their objects, its action takes on a manifest form.

29. *sarvair ayaṁ cendriyaiḥ saṁprayukto*
dehaḥ prāptaḥ pañca-bhūtāśrayaḥ syāt
nāsāmarthyād gacchati karmaṇeha
hīnas tena parameṇāvyayena

When it exists in conjunction with all the senses, the *ātman* is endowed with a body composed of the five principal elements. Eventually, because of bodily weakness, it no longer performs action, and then it is deprived of this body by the Supreme who does not change.

30. *pṛthvyā naraḥ paśyati nāntam asyā*
hy antaś cāsyā bhavitā ceti viddhi
paraṁ nayantīha vilobhyamānaṁ
yathā plavaṁ vāyur ivārṇava-stham

No man ever sees the end of the world, but you know that its end will come. In this world, the senses lead one who is beguiled by their perceptions to the world beyond, just as the wind blows a boat across the surface of the ocean.

31. *divākaro guṇam upalabhya nirguṇo*
yathā bhaved vyapagata-raśmi-maṇḍalaḥ
tathā hy asau munir iha nirviśeṣavān
sa nirguṇaṁ praviśati brahma cāvyayam

When it gains a specific quality the sun manifests the daylight, and when it is devoid of that quality the spread of its rays fades away. In the same way, any sage who makes no distinctions between the various objects he finds in this world enters into the unchanging Brahman that is itself devoid of material qualities.

32. *anāgatiṁ sukṛtimatāṁ parāṁ gatiṁ*
svayaṁbhuvaṁ prabhava-nidhānam avyayam
sanātanaṁ yad amṛtam avyayaṁ padaṁ
vicārya taṁ śamam amṛtatvam aśnute

Brahman is the highest goal attained by the righteous, the abode from which one does not return. It does not depend on any other substance, for it is the origin and resting place of everything that exists and is unchanging and eternal. Having approached that immortal, unchanging position, one enters a state of complete peace and immortality.

The Keśava-Māhātmyam

Śānti–parvan, Adhyāya

FOLLOWING ON from the *Manu-Bṛhaspati-Saṁvāda*, we find three chapters containing three discrete treatises which at first glance appear to be rather out of place within the *Mokṣa-dharma-parvan*, as they have little or nothing to say about the subject of gaining liberation from the cycle of rebirth. The first, the *Keśava Māhātmyam*, is clearly a Vaiṣṇava tract probably derived from an early phase of the Pañcarātra sect. This is followed by the *Dik-Pālaka-Kīrtanam*, which is not a Vaiṣṇava piece at all but rather deals with Brahmā's creation of the gods, the *rishis*, and the progenitors of living beings, a topic that is frequently considered in the major Purāṇas. The third of the three is the *Viṣṇoḥ Varāha-Rūpam*, which provides an account of Viṣṇu's appearance in the form of a boar in order to assist the gods in their struggles against the *asuras*, essentially an *avatāra* narrative that is also found in several of the major Purāṇas.

The question therefore naturally arises as to why these passages have been included within the *Mokṣa-dharma-parvan* when they appear to be notably 'off subject'. It appears likely that their inclusion was inspired by the references made to Viṣṇu in the final chapter of the *Manu-Bṛhaspati-Saṁvāda*, which allowed the redactor to then add passages of a Vaiṣṇava orientation, which of course he does again towards the end of the *Mokṣa-dharma-parvan* with the lengthy *Nara-Nārāyaṇīyam*. There may be, however, some further significance in this choice of material that could reflect on the idea that early Sāṁkhya and Yoga had a theistic tendency, a point emphasised by Surendranath Dasgupta in Volume One of his *History of Indian Philosophy*. We might suppose that Sāṁkhya and Vaiṣṇavism are rather distinct strands of Indian religious thought, but a close study of the *Mokṣa-dharma-parvan* reveals that they are in many ways quite closely related. This became apparent in the final chapter of the *Manu-Bṛhaspati-Saṁvāda*, and the presence of these chapters here in the midst of the *Mokṣa-dharma-parvan* would seem to re-emphasise the point. Although we might regard the presentation of these ideas here as aberrant, we should not presume that they were regarded as such in this early period. It is quite apparent from numerous sources that early Sāṁkhya and Yoga doctrines were often closely aligned with Vaiṣṇava teachings, such as those found in the second chapter of the first book of the *Viṣṇu Purāṇa*, which can probably be dated to a few centuries after most of the passages in the *Mokṣa-dharma-parvan*.

It is also interesting to reflect on the Purāṇic nature of the material encountered here. Anyone familiar with the content of the eighteen major Purāṇas will immediately identify the subject matter covered in these chapters as being of a similar type, and indeed verse 7 of the *Keśava Māhātmyam* and verse 5 of the *Dik-Pālaka-Kīrtanam* directly refer to their teachings as being related to or derived from Purāṇa. It is natural therefore to examine whether or not these passages are to be found in any of the extant Purāṇas – most likely in the *Viṣṇu Purāṇa*, both because of its Vaiṣṇava orientation and because it is believed to be the earliest example of Purāṇic literature to which we now have access. In this endeavour, however, there will be disappointment, for there is nothing within the extant *Viṣṇu Purāṇa* that displays commonality with the three treatises. It is in fact notable that the *Viṣṇu Purāṇa*'s telling of the story of the Varāha *avatāra*, in particular, emphasises the raising of the earth from the waters, whilst here this element of the story is alluded to only briefly and the central theme of the narrative is the destruction of the *asuras*.

Hence we are forced to consider what type of work the *Mahābhārata* is here referring to as *Purāṇa*. The use of the singular *purāṇe* in verse 5 of the *Dik-Pālaka-Kīrtanam* might indicate that at the time of the *Mahābhārata* there was only a single *Purāṇa* or a single body of literature designated as *Purāṇa*, which was subsequently re-edited and expanded upon so as to form the eighteen or more works we are familiar with today. This is certainly possible and perhaps likely, but given the very limited evidence all that we can say with certainty is that at the time in which the *Mokṣa-dharma-parvan* was compiled there was in existence a body of literature designated as *Purāṇa* and that this material appears to bear a clear resemblance to passages that appear consistently in the eighteen extant *Purāṇas* we possess today. For his own reasons, the compiler has decided that some of this Purāṇic material is relevant to the line of discourse being followed here in the *Mokṣa-dharma-parvan*, presumably because of the way in which some of the Sāṁkhya and Yoga treatises identify the spiritual principle with the Deity Viṣṇu.

The first of these three treatises is the *Keśava Māhātmyam*, the glorification of Keśava, Viṣṇu, and the request from Yudhiṣṭhira for teachings about the greatness of Viṣṇu, must be seen as a response to the references to Viṣṇu in the final chapter of the *Manu-Bṛhaspati-Saṁvāda*. As noted above, the passage displays similarities with material typically encountered in Purāṇic literature, and in verse 7 here Bhīṣma admits that the glorification of Viṣṇu he will present is identical to that given by people who are *purāṇa-vid* (learned in the *Purāṇa*). After listing the names of the *rishis* who teach this wisdom (interestingly including Vālmīki, the author of the *Rāmāyaṇa*), Bhīṣma begins his discourse with a few verses about the divine identity of Viṣṇu before moving on to the main topic of the chapter, the Vaiṣṇava version of the creation of the world. And in verse 8, we see a significant designation of Viṣṇu that links the Vaiṣṇavism of this chapter with the previous discourses on Sāṁkhya, as the Deity is here referred to as the *bhūtātman* (the self of the living being) who instigates the process of creation by bringing forth the five *mahā-bhūtas*, the great elements familiar from the Sāṁkhya teachings.

The treatise then turns to its account of the creation. First the Deity manifests his form as Saṁkarṣaṇa, one of the four forms of Viṣṇu usually associated with the Pañcarātra school of Vaiṣṇavism, which suggests that this passage may be a product of Pañcarātric sources. This is followed by a brief retelling of the creation story, with Brahmā appearing from the lotus flower and the work of creation interrupted by the *asura* Madhu who is destroyed by Viṣṇu. The middle portion of the chapter then gives an account of the appearance of different orders of living beings as the offspring and descendants of Brahmā in a manner that is again typical of Purāṇic discourse. Verse 29 appears to mark a change in the line of discussion, possibly indicating that the author has moved on to another source, although the subject is still that of the creation of the world. Now, however, Viṣṇu is shown to be the creator of the phases of time and of the world and its various manifestations, including the four *varṇas* (social classes). The passage concludes with a brief consideration of the four *yugas* (the great ages), and the idea that at the beginning of the world people were of a higher order and more inherently righteous. Thus although the title *Keśava-Māhātmyam* suggests a eulogy of Viṣṇu as the Supreme Deity, the main subject presented by the treatise is the Purāṇic understanding of the creation of the world with Viṣṇu placed in the role of creator and primal instigator.

1. *yudhiṣṭhira uvāca*
pitāmaha mahā-prājña puṇḍarīkākṣam acyutam
kartāram akṛtaṁ viṣṇuṁ bhūtānāṁ prabhavāpyayam

2. *nārāyaṇaṁ hṛṣīkeśaṁ govindam aparājitam*
tattvena bharata-śreṣṭha śrotum icchāmi keśavam

Yudhiṣṭhira said: O grandfather your wisdom is vast. O greatest of the Bharata dynasty, I wish to hear the truth about the infallible lotus-eyed Viṣṇu, the creator who is not created, the beginning and end of all beings, who is known also as Nārāyaṇa, Hṛṣīkeśa, Govinda, and Keśava and who is unsurpassed by any other being.

3. *bhīṣma uvāca*
śruto 'yam artho rāmasya jāmadagnyasya jalpataḥ
nāradasya ca devarṣeḥ kṛṣṇa-dvaipāyanasya ca

Bhīṣma said: I have learned about this topic from the discourses of Rāma Jāmadgnya, the divine *rishi* Nārada, and from Kṛṣṇa Dvaipāyana.

4. *asito devalas tāta vālmīkiś ca mahā-tapāḥ*
mārkaṇḍeyaś ca govinde kathayaty adbhutaṁ mahat

My dear boy, Asita, Devala, the great ascetic Vālmīki, and Mārkaṇḍeya have also presented truly wonderful teachings concerning Govinda.

5. *keśavo bharata-śreṣṭha bhagavān īśvaraḥ prabhuḥ*
puruṣaḥ sarvam ity eva śrūyate bahudhā vibhuḥ

O best of the Bharata dynasty, I have heard Keśava described in many different ways, as the exalted one, the Lord, the master, the *puruṣa*, the sum total of all existence, the all-pervasive one.

6. *kiṁ tu yāni vidur-loke brāhmaṇāḥ śārṅga-dhanvanaḥ*
māhātmyāni mahā-bāho śṛṇu tāni yudhiṣṭhira

So now, O mighty Yudhiṣṭhira, listen to the glories of the Deity who bears the bow named Śārṅga, which Brahmins recite in the realm inhabited by men of wisdom.

7. *yāni cāhur manuṣyendra ye purāṇa-vido janāḥ*
aśeṣeṇa hi govinde kīrtayiṣyāmi tāny aham

O lord of men, I will describe to you in full all those attributes that persons who possess knowledge of the *Purāṇa* say are to be found within Govinda.

8. *mahā-bhūtāni bhūtātmā mahātmā puruṣottamaḥ*
vāyur jyotis tathā cāpaḥ khaṁ gāṁ caivānvakalpayat

He is the *ātman* within all beings, the great soul, and the supreme person. He alone caused the emergence of the great elements air, light, water, space, and earth, one after the other.

9. *sa dṛṣṭvā pṛthivīṁ caiva sarva-bhūteśvaraḥ prabhuḥ*
apsv eva śayanaṁ cakre mahātmā puruṣottamaḥ

He is the mighty lord of all beings, the great soul, the supreme person. After glancing over the earth, he then made his bed upon the waters.

10. *sarva-tejomayas tasmiñ śayānaḥ śayane śubhe*
so 'gra-jaṁ sarva-bhūtānāṁ saṁkarṣaṇam acintayat

He is imbued with all the energy of the world. Whilst lying on that wonderful bed, he thought of Saṁkarṣaṇa, the first born of all living beings.

11. *āśrayaṁ sarva-bhūtānāṁ manaseti viśuśruma*
sa dhārayati bhūtātmā ubhe bhūta-bhaviṣyatī

We have heard that Saṁkarṣaṇa is manifested through his mind as the abode of all beings. He is the soul of all beings who bears within himself both those who lived in the past and those who are yet to be.

12. *tatas tasmin mahā-bāho prādur-bhūte mahātmani*
bhāskara-pratimaṁ divyaṁ nābhyāṁ padmam ajāyata

O mighty king, when that great soul had thus come into being, a celestial lotus flower as effulgent as the sun then sprouted from his navel.

13. *sa tatra bhagavān devaḥ puṣkare bhāsayan diśaḥ*
brahmā samabhavat tāta sarva-bhūta-pitāmahaḥ

My dear boy, on that very lotus the exalted Deity Brahmā, the grandfather of all beings, took his birth, spreading light in all directions.

14. *tasminn api mahā-bāho prādur-bhūte mahātmani*
tamasaḥ pūrva-jo jajñe madhur nāma mahāsuraḥ

O mighty king, when that great soul had thus come into being, a powerful *asura* named Madhu, who had been born previously from out of the darkness, appeared there.

15. *tam ugram ugra-karmāṇam ugrāṁ buddhiṁ samāsthitam*
brahmaṇopacitiṁ kurvañ jaghāna puruṣottamaḥ

He was ferocious by nature, he acted with ferocity, and his mind was set on aggression. Acting for the benefit of Brahmā, the supreme person slew him.

16. *tasya tāta vadhāt sarve deva-dānava-mānavāḥ*
madhusūdanam ity āhur vṛṣabhaṁ sarva-sātvatām

My dear boy, because of his killing this demon, all the gods, Dānavas, and human beings speak of him as Madhusūdana, the killer of Madhu, who is the leader of all virtuous beings (*sātvatas*).

17. *brahmā tu sasṛje putrān mānasān dakṣa-saptamān*
marīcim atry-aṅgirasau pulastyaṁ pulahaṁ kratum

Brahmā then created seven sons from his mind, of whom Dakṣa was the seventh. The other six were Marīci, Atri, Aṅgiras, Pulastya, Pulaha, and Kratu.

18. *marīciḥ kaśyapaṁ tāta putraṁ cāsṛjad agra-jam*
mānasaṁ janayāmāsa taijasaṁ brahma-sattamam

My dear boy, Marīci produced Kaśyapa as his first-born son. Kaśyapa was born from his father's mind; he was full of spiritual potency and was the best of all Brahmins.

19. *aṅguṣṭhād asṛjad brahmā marīcer api pūrva-jam*
so 'bhavad bharata-śreṣṭha dakṣo nāma prajāpatiḥ

Before the birth of Marīci, Brahmā created another son from out of his thumb. His name was Dakṣa, O best of the Bharata dynasty, and he was a Prajāpati, a progenitor of many living beings.

20. *tasya pūrvam ajāyanta daśa-tisraś ca bhārata*
prajāpater duhitaras tāsāṁ jyeṣṭhābhavad ditiḥ

First to be born from that Prajāpati, O Bhārata, were thirteen daughters, of whom Diti was the eldest.

21. *sarva-dharma-viśeṣa-jñaḥ puṇya-kīrtir mahā-yaśāḥ*
mārīcaḥ kaśyapas tāta sarvāsām abhavat patiḥ

Kaśyapa the son of Marīci understood all the different forms of dharma. He was celebrated for his virtue and widely renowned. My dear boy, it was Kaśyapa who became the husband of all those thirteen daughters of Dakṣa.

22. *utpādya tu mahā-bhāgas tāsām avara-jā daśa*
dadau dharmāya dharma-jño dakṣa eva prajāpatiḥ

Dakṣa, that exalted Prajāpati, fully understood the principles of dharma. When he subsequently produced ten more daughters, he gave them to Dharma to be his wives.

23. *dharmasya vasavaḥ putrā rudrāś cāmita-tejasaḥ*
viśvedevāś ca sādhyāś ca marutvantaś ca bhārata

The Vasus were the sons of Dharma and so were the Rudras whose energy is without limit. O Bhārata, the Viśvedevas, the Sādhyas, and the wind gods were also sons of Dharma.

24. *aparās tu yavīyasyas tābhyo 'nyāḥ sapta-viṁśatiḥ*
somas tāsāṁ mahā-bhāgaḥ sarvāsām abhavat patiḥ

And later on Dakṣa begot twenty-seven other daughters, younger than those mentioned before. The exalted Soma, the god of the moon, became the husband of them all.

25. *itarās tu vyajāyanta gandharvāṁs turagān dvijān*
gāś ca kiṁpuruṣān matsyān audbhidāṁś ca vanaspatīn

Now it was his other daughters who gave birth to the *gandharvas*, horses, birds, cows, *kiṁpuruṣas*, fish, sprouting plants, and trees.

26. *ādityān aditir jajñe deva-śreṣṭhān mahā-balān*
teṣāṁ viṣṇur vāmaṇo 'bhūd govindaś cābhavat prabhuḥ

Aditi gave birth to the greatest of the gods, the mighty Ādityas. Taking the form of a dwarf, Viṣṇu appeared as one of them and thus Govinda became their lord.

27. *tasya vikramaṇād eva devānāṁ śrīr vyavardhata*
dānavāś ca parābhūtā daiteyī cāsurī prajā

Simply because of Viṣṇu's might, the prosperity of the gods expanded and the Dānavas were vanquished. Those progeny who were *asuras* were the descendants of Diti.

28. *vipracitti-pradhānāṁś ca dānavān asṛjad danuḥ*
ditis tu sarvān asurān mahā-sattvān vyajāyata

Danu brought forth the Dānavas, the foremost of whom was Vipracitti, whilst Diti gave birth to all the powerful *asuras*.

29. *aho-rātraṁ ca kālaṁ ca yathartu madhusūdanaḥ*
purvāhṇaṁ cāparāhṇaṁ ca sarvam evānvakalpayat

Madusūdana arranged the sequences of day and night, the passage of time, and the morning and afternoon, with each in its appropriate position.

30. *buddhyāpaḥ so 'sṛjan meghāṁs tathā sthāvara-jaṅgamān*
pṛthivīṁ so 'sṛjad viśvāṁ sahitāṁ bhūri-tejasā

Through his intelligence, he created water, and then the clouds, and the moving and stationary beings. Through his vast potency, he created the earth and all that exists upon it.

31. *tataḥ kṛṣṇo mahā-bāhuḥ punar eva yudhiṣṭhira*
brāhmaṇānāṁ śataṁ sreṣṭhaṁ mukhād asṛjata prabhuḥ

Then, Yudhiṣṭhira, Kṛṣṇa, the mighty lord, further manifested one hundred of the most elevated Brahmins from out of his mouth.

32. *bāhubhyāṁ kṣatriya-śataṁ vaiśyānām ūrutaḥ śatam*
padbhyāṁ śūdra-śataṁ caiva keśavo bharatarṣabha

O best of the Bharata dynasty, Keśava also produced one hundred *kṣatriyas* from his arms, one hundred *vaiśyas* from his thighs, and one hundred *śūdras* from his feet.

33. *sa evaṁ caturo varṇān samutpādya mahāyaśāḥ*
adhyakṣaṁ sarva-bhūtānāṁ dhātāraṁ akarot prabhuḥ

The fame of the Lord is spread far and wide. When he had thus generated the four social classes, he then created the Ordainer who has power over all living beings.

34. *yāvad yāvad abhūc chraddhā dehaṁ dhārayituṁ nṛṇām*
tāvat tāvad ajīvaṁs te nāsīd yama-kṛtaṁ bhayam

At that time people lived for as long as they had the desire to sustain their body, and there was no fear due to Yama, the god of death.

35. *na caiṣāṁ maithuno dharmo babhūva bharatarṣabha*
saṁkalpād eva caiteṣām apatyam udapadyata

Furthermore, O best of the Bharatas, at that time there were no sexual relations between people for they could produce offspring simply by willing them to exist.

36. *tatra tretā-yuge kāle saṁkalpāj jāyate prajā*
na hy abhūn maithuno dharmas teṣām api janādhipa

In the era known as the Tretā Yuga, children were born from the desire of the parents. Hence, O lord of men, sexual relations between people never occurred.

37. *dvāpare maithuno dharmaḥ prajānām abhavan nṛpa*
tathā kali-yuge rājan dvaṁdvam āpedire janāḥ

In the Dvāpara Yuga, my lord, sexual relations were practised in order to produce offspring, whilst in the Kali Yuga, O king, people entered into marriage relationships.

38. *eṣa bhūta-patis tāta svadhyakṣaś ca prakīrtitaḥ*
niradhyakṣāṁs tu kaunteya kīrtayiṣyāmi tān api

My dear boy, the lord of all beings has now been described to you as well as the wonderful way in which he manages the creation. Now, Kaunteya, I shall speak about those living beings who oppose his rule.

39. *dakṣiṇā-patha-janmānaḥ sarve talavarāndhrakāḥ*
utsāḥ pulindāḥ śabarāś cūcupā maṇḍapaiḥ saha

Those born in the lands of the south include all the Talavaras, Andhrakas, Utsas, Pulindas, Śabaras, Cūcupas, and the Maṇḍapas as well.

40. *uttarā-patha-janmānaḥ kīrtayiṣyāmi tān api*
yauna-kāmboja-gāndhārāḥ kirātā barbaraiḥ saha

Now I shall speak of those born in the lands of the north. These include the Yaunas, Kāmbojas, Gāndhāras, Kirātas, and the Barbaras as well.

41. *ete pāpa-kṛtas tāta caranti pṛthivīm imām*
śva-kāka-bala-gṛdhrāṇāṁ sadharmāṇo narādhipa

My dear boy, lord of men, these wrongdoers roam across this earth adhering to the ways of life pursued by dogs, crows, ravens, and vultures.

42. *naite kṛta-yuge tāta caranti pṛthivīm imām*
tretā-prabhṛti vartante te janā bharatarṣabha

But in the age known as the Kṛta Yuga they did not roam across the earth. O best of the Bharata dynasty, such people have only existed since the onset of the Tretā Yuga.

43. *tatas tasmin mahā-ghore saṁdhyā-kāle yugāntike*
rājānaḥ samasajjanta samāsādyetaretaram

Then at the terrible time when the *yuga* ends and two ages meet, the kings of the earth gathered together and engaged one another in battle.

44. *evam eṣa kuru-śreṣṭha prādurbhāvo mahātmanaḥ*
deva-devarṣir ācaṣṭa nāradaḥ sarva-loka-dṛk

The divine sage Nārada has knowledge of all the worlds. O lord of the Kurus, it was he who revealed the things I have spoken of concerning the creation of the world by the supreme soul.

45. *nārado 'py atha kṛṣṇasya paraṁ mene narādhipa*
śāśvatatvaṁ mahā-bāho yathāvad bharatarṣabha

O mighty king, lord of the Bharatas, Nārada himself accepted this truth about the eternal nature of Kṛṣṇa and his transcendence of this world.

46. *evam eṣa mahā-bāhuḥ keśavaḥ satya-vikramaḥ*
acintyaḥ puṇḍarīkākṣo naiṣa kevala-mānuṣaḥ

So the mighty Keśava is powerful indeed, for he is no mere mortal but is in truth that inconceivable Deity with lotus-like eyes.

The Dik-Pālaka-Kīrtanam

Śānti-parvan, Adhyāya 201

THE *KEŚAVA-MĀHĀTMYAM* is followed by a passage entitled the *Dik-Pālaka-Kīrtanam*, literally 'the account of the guardians of the directions', apparently inspired by a question from Yudhiṣṭhira on that very subject. The middle section of the *Keśava-Māhātmyam* had included a brief discussion of the original progeny begotten by Brahmā as a part of the creative process, and this next passage must be seen as an expansion on that theme. It is, however, interesting to note that this treatise does not display the same Vaiṣṇava orientation as its predecessor and that here Brahmā himself is represented as being the one Supreme Deity, as the words *ekaḥ svayaṁbhūr bhagavān ādyo brahmā sanātanaḥ* make clear (verse 3).

The discussion begins by referring to the seven *rishis* who were the original offspring of Brahmā. This is a well known idea that has Vedic antecedents, although the Vedic versions usually differ from Purāṇic accounts in relation to the naming of the seven. Hence, for example, the *Jaiminīya Brāhmaṇa* (2.218–221) gives us the names Vasiṣṭha, Bharadvāja, Jamadagni, Gautama, Atri, Viśvāmitra, and Agastya, whilst the *Bṛhadāraṇyaka Upaniṣad* (2.2.4) offers the same list except that Kaśyapa appears at the expense of Agastya. The seven names listed here, however, are those typically found in Purāṇic sources and indeed verse 5 clearly states that this is an account derived from *Purāṇa* (see, for example, *Viṣṇu Purāṇa* 1.7.5, although there Bhṛgu and Dakṣa are added to make a list of nine). It is also worth noting that whilst the *Keśava-Māhātmyam* includes Dakṣa in its list of seven, here the name of Vasiṣṭha appears and Dakṣa is referred to as being the grandson of Atri.

The passage then recounts the names of the offspring of some of these seven *rishis* as well as the descendants of Śaśabindu and the principal deities of the Vedic tradition, the Ādityas who are the sons of Kaśyapa and Aditi. Verses 22 to 25 present the rather unusual view that the deities are also divided according to the four *varṇas*, the social classes prevalent in human society, with the Āṅgirases designated as Brahmins, the Ādityas as *kṣatriyas*, the Maruts as *vaiśyas*, and the two Aśvins as *śūdras*. It is then only in the final ten verses (26–35) that the subject of the *dik-pālakas* is addressed, with the names given of the *rishis* who are said to reside in each of the four main directions, all of whom are referred to as descendants of the seven original *rishis* born as the sons of Brahmā.

1. *yudhiṣṭhira uvāca*
ke pūrvam āsan patayaḥ prajānāṁ bharatarṣabha
ke carṣayo mahā-bhāgā dikṣu pratyekaśaḥ smṛtāḥ

Yudhiṣṭhira said: O lord of the Bharatas, who were those persons who produced offspring at the beginning of the creation? Who were those exalted *rishis* each of whom is known in various regions of the world?

2. *bhīṣma uvāca*
śrūyatāṁ bharata-śreṣṭha yan mā tvaṁ paripṛcchasi
prajānāṁ patayo ye sma dikṣu pratyekaśaḥ smṛtāḥ

Bhīṣma said: Listen now, O best of the Bharata dynasty, as I explain the subject you have asked me about concerning the progenitors of living beings, each of whom is known in various regions of the world.

3. *ekaḥ svayaṁbhūr bhagavān ādyo brahmā sanātanaḥ*
brahmaṇaḥ sapta putrā vai mahātmānaḥ svayaṁbhuvaḥ

There was one original Deity, the eternal, self-born Brahmā. From the self-born Brahmā came seven sons, all of whom were great persons.

4. *marīcir atry-aṅgirasau pulastyaḥ pulahaḥ kratuḥ*
vasiṣṭhaś ca mahā-bhāgaḥ sadṛśā vai svayaṁbhuvā

These were Marīci, Atri, Aṅgiras, Pulastya, Pulaha, Kratu, and the exalted Vasiṣṭha, all of whom were equal in potency to the self-born Brahmā.

5. *sapta brāhmaṇa ity eṣa purāṇe niścayo gataḥ*
ata ūrdhvaṁ pravakṣyāmi sarvān eva prajāpatīn

This is the group known as 'the seven Brahmins', as is made clear within the *Purāṇa*. I shall now discuss the progenitors who followed after them.

6. *atri-vaṁśa-samutpanno brahma-yoniḥ sanātanaḥ*
prācīnabarhir bhagavāṁs tasmāt prācetaso daśa

The deathless Prācīnabarhi was born as a descendent of Atri with Brahman as his womb. The ten Prācetases took birth from him.

7. *daśānāṁ tanayas tv eko dakṣo nāma prajāpatiḥ*
tasya dve nāmanī loke dakṣaḥ ka iti cocyate

One son was born in the line of the ten Prācetases. This was the Prajāpati named Dakṣa. It is said that he was known in the world by two names, Dakṣa and Ka.

8. *marīceḥ kaśyapaḥ putras tasya dve nāmanī śrute*
ariṣṭanemir ity ekaṁ kaśyapety aparaṁ viduḥ

The son of Marīci was Kaśyapa and two names are recorded for him as well. One of these is Ariṣṭanemi and they also know him by his other name of Kaśyapa.

9. *aṅgaś caivaurasaḥ śrīmān rājā bhaumaś ca vīryavān*
sahasraṁ yaś ca divyānāṁ yugānāṁ paryupāsitā

Aṅga, the son born from the body of Kaśyapa, was a glorious and mighty ruler of the earth who performed acts of worship for a thousand ages of the gods.

10. *aryamā caiva bhagavān ye cānye tanayā vibho*
ete pradeśāḥ kathitā bhuvanānāṁ prabhāvanāḥ

My lord, it is recorded that the exalted Aryaman and others born in his line were generators of living beings and givers of instruction as well.

11. *śaśabindoś ca bhāryāṇāṁ sahasrāṇi daśācyuta*
ekaikasyāṁ sahasraṁ tu tanayānām abhūt tadā

O infallible one, there were ten thousand wives of Śaśabindu and from each one of them a thousand descendants came into being.

12. *evaṁ śata-sahasrāṇāṁ śataṁ tasya mahātmanaḥ*
putrāṇāṁ na ca te kaṁcid icchanty anyaṁ prajāpatim

So ten million sons were born from that great person and none of them acknowledge anyone but Śaśabindu as a Prajāpati.

13. *prajām ācakṣate viprāḥ paurāṇīṁ śāśabindavīm*
sa vṛṣṇi-vaṁśa-prabhavo mahān vaṁśaḥ prajāpateḥ

Brahmins make a statement about this ancient line of descent from Śaśabindu. They say that the huge number of descendants begotten by that Prajāpati gave rise to the Vṛṣṇi dynasty.

14. *ete prajānāṁ patayaḥ samuddiṣṭā yaśasvinaḥ*
ataḥ paraṁ pravakṣyāmi devāṁs tri-bhuvaneśvarān

These celebrated progenitors of living beings have thus been revealed to you. I shall now go on to describe the gods who are the lords of the three worlds.

15. *bhago 'ṁśaś cāryamā caiva mitro 'tha varuṇas tathā*
savitā caiva dhātā ca vivasvāṁś ca mahā-balaḥ

These include Bhaga, Aṁśa, and Aryaman, Mitra and Varuṇa, Savitṛ, Dhātṛ, and the mighty Vivasvān as well.

16. *puṣā tvaṣṭā tathaivendro dvādaśo viṣṇur ucyate*
ta ete dvādaśādityāḥ kaśyapasyātma-saṁbhavāḥ

Then we have Puṣan, Tvaṣṭṛ, and Indra, and Viṣṇu is said to be the twelfth of this group. These then are the twelve Ādityas who are the sons of Kaśyapa.

17. *nāsatyaś caiva dasraś ca smṛtau dvāv aśvināv api*
mārtaṇḍasyātma-jāv etāv aṣṭamasya prajāpateḥ

Nāsatya and Dasra are known as the two Aśvins. They are the sons of Mārtaṇḍa, the eighth Prajāpati.

18. *tvaṣṭuś caivātmajaḥ śrīmān viśvarūpo mahā-yaśāḥ*
ajaikapād ahirbudhnyo virūpākṣo 'tha raivataḥ

The renowned and illustrious Viśvarūpa was the son Tvaṣṭṛ, as were Ajaikapād, Ahir-budhnya, Virūpākṣa, and Raivata.

19. *haraś ca bahurūpaś ca tryambakaś ca sureśvaraḥ*
sāvitraś ca jayantaś ca pinākī cāparājitaḥ
pūrvam eva mahā-bhāgā vasavo 'ṣṭau prakīrtitāḥ

The other sons of Tvaṣṭṛ were Hara, Bahurūpa, Tryambaka, who is the lord of the gods, Sāvitra, Jayanta, and Pinākin of matchless prowess. The names of the eight illustrious Vasus have already been mentioned.

20. *eta evaṁ-vidhā devā manor eva prajāpateḥ*
te ca pūrve surāś ceti dvi-vidhāḥ pitaraḥ smṛtāḥ

These are the various types of divinities who prevailed during the period of Prajāpati Manu. In the beginning of creation, a twofold division was identified amongst them, and thus they were designated as the gods and the forefathers.

21. *śīla-rūpa-ratās tv anye tathānye siddha-sādhyayoḥ*
ṛbhavo marutaś caiva devānāṁ coditā gaṇāḥ

The Siddhas and Sādhyas are differentiated in terms of their good conduct and beautiful forms. The Ṛbhus and the Maruts are said to be associates of the gods.

22. *evam ete samāmnātā viśvedevās tathāśvinau*
ādityāḥ kṣatriyās teṣāṁ viśas tu marutas tathā

These then are all the different types of gods traditionally referred to, including the Aśvins as well. Amongst these gods the Ādityas are *kṣatriyas* whilst the Maruts are *vaiśyas.*

23. *aśvinau tu matau śūdrau tapasy ugre samāhitau*
smṛtās tv aṅgiraso devā brāhmaṇā iti niścayaḥ
ity etat sarva-devānāṁ cātur-varṇyaṁ prakīrtitam

The two Aśvins who dedicated themselves to severe penances are considered to be *śūdras*, but it has been determined that the gods descended from Aṅgiras should recognised as Brahmins. The division of all the gods into the four *varṇas* has thus been explained.

24. *etān vai prātar utthāya devān yas tu prakīrtayet*
sva-jād anya-kṛtāc caiva sarva-pāpāt pramucyate

One who rises at daybreak and recites the names of these gods is released from all sins, both those he has performed himself and those performed by others on his behalf.

25. *yavakrīto 'tha raibhyaś ca arvāvasu-parāvasū*
auśijaś caiva kakṣīvān nalaś cāṅgirasaḥ sutāḥ

Yavakrīta, Raibhya, Arvāvasu, Parāvasu, Auśija, Kakṣīvat, and Nala are the sons of Aṅgiras.

26. *ṛṣer medhātitheḥ putraḥ kaṇvo barhiṣadas tathā*
trai-lokya-bhāvanās tāta prācyāṁ saptarṣayas tathā

Kaṇva who is the son of the *rishi* Medhātithi, as well as Barhiṣada, and the seven *rishis* who generated progeny throughout the three worlds, all reside in the east, my son.

27. *unmuco vimucaś caiva svastyātreyaś ca vīryavān*
pramucaś cedhmavāhaś ca bhagavāṁś ca dṛḍha-vrataḥ

Unmuca, Vimuca, and Svastyātreya who possesses great power; Pramuca, Idhmavāha, and the exalted Dṛḍhavrata;

28. *mitrāvaruṇayoḥ putras tathāgastyaḥ pratāpavān*
ete brahmarṣayo nityam āśritā dakṣiṇāṁ diśam

The glorious Agastya who is the son of Mitra and Varuṇa; all these holy *rishis* reside constantly in the regions of the south.

29. *ruṣadguḥ kavaṣo dhaumyaḥ parivyādhaś ca vīryavān*
ekataś ca dvitaś caiva tritaś caiva maharṣayaḥ

Ruṣadgu, Kavaṣa, Dhaumya, and Parivyādha who possesses great power; the illustrious *rishis* Ekata, Dvita, and Trita;

30. *atreḥ putraś ca bhagavāṁs tathā sārasvataḥ prabhuḥ*
ete nava mahātmānaḥ paścimām āśritā diśam

The exalted son of Atri and the mighty Sārasvata as well; these nine great persons reside in the regions of the west.

31. *ātreyaś ca vasiṣṭhaś ca kaśyapaś ca mahān ṛṣiḥ*
gautamaḥ sa-bharadvājo viśvāmitro 'tha kauśikaḥ

Ātreya, Vasiṣṭha, and the great *rishi* Kaśyapa; Gautama, Bharadh-vāja, and Viśvāmitra who is descended from Kuśika;

32. *tathaiva putro bhagavān ṛcīkasya mahātmanaḥ*
jamadagniś ca saptaite udīcīṁ diśam āśritāḥ

And Jamadagni, the exalted son of Ṛcīka who is a great personality in his own right; these seven reside in the regions of the north.

33. *ete pratidiśaṁ sarve kīrtitās tigma-tejasaḥ*
sākṣi-bhūtā mahātmāno bhuvanānāṁ prabhāvanāḥ

Now I have described all those persons endowed with burning potency as they exist in each of the directions. These great souls are witnesses to all that comes to pass and they are the progenitors of the living beings.

34. *evam ete mahātmānaḥ sthitāḥ pratyekaśo diśaḥ*
eteṣāṁ kīrtanaṁ kṛtvā sarva-pāpaiḥ pramucyate

These then are the great persons and the positions they hold in each of the directions. When one recites the names of these great souls one is released from all sins.

35. *yasyāṁ yasyāṁ diśi hy ete tāṁ diśaṁ śaraṇaṁ gataḥ*
mucyate sarva-pāpebhyaḥ svastimāṁś ca gṛhān vrajet

If one seeks refuge in any of the places where they reside, one is released from all sins and returns joyfully to his own dwelling place.

The Viṣṇoḥ Varāha-Rūpam

Śānti-parvan, Adhyāya 202

THE THIRD OF THESE THREE PASSAGES, the *Viṣṇoḥ Varāha-Rūpam*, offers an account of the descent of Viṣṇu in the form of the Varāha (boar) *avatāra* (though the term *avatāra* is not encountered within the *Mahābhārata*). A consideration of Purāṇic accounts would seem to indicate that there were two versions of this story, with emphasis placed either on the vanquishing of the *asuras* or on the raising of the earth from out of the vast ocean. Most of the Purāṇic accounts combine these two themes; in the *Bhāgavata Purāṇa* the asuric adversary is named as Hiraṇyākṣa, the elder brother of Hiraṇyakaśipu who is killed by the Narasiṁha *avatāra*. In the south of India it appears that most emphasis is placed on the raising of the earth and Viṣṇu is often shown with two consorts, one of whom is Bhūdevī, the Earth Goddess, who stands alongside Śrī, the Goddess of Prosperity. It is also interesting to note that the *asura* named Naraka is said in some accounts to be the son of the Earth Goddess begotten by Viṣṇu in his Varāha form, though here Naraka is said to be the leader of the Dānavas who triumph over the gods.

In fact, the account of Viṣṇu's appearance as a boar presented here is very similar to the *avatāra* stories found in the *Mahābhārata* to explain the divinity of Kṛṣṇa and in Vālmīki's *Rāmāyaṇa* to explain the divinity of Rāma. The gods are oppressed by the rising power of their adversaries, the *asuras* led by Naraka and others, and appeal to Brahmā for help. Brahmā informs them that Viṣṇu himself will appear to address the situation, which he does by assuming the form of a boar and launching an irresistible assault on the *asuras*. The mighty roars of that boar terrify the world and confuse even the gods, but when the *asuras* are destroyed and the natural order of the created world restored, the gods and *rishis* offer prayers and worship to glorify the Deity. The idea of the earth being in a state of distress due to the burden of the *asuras* on her surface is mentioned in verse 10 but it is a secondary theme, and the raising of the earth from the depths of the water, a prominent element in Purāṇic renditions of the Varāha story, is not referred to at all. As for there being any connection with the wider context of the *Mokṣa-dharma-parvan*, the only point we might note here is the fact that Brahmā refers to the Deity to as *mahā-yogī bhūtātmā bhūta-bhāvanaḥ* (verses 29 and 31), thereby asserting the identity of Viṣṇu as a great *yogin* who is the inner self of all beings and the origin of all beings. The connection is, however, a tenuous one, and in truth these passages stand out as something of an aberration in the ongoing discourse on liberation from rebirth.

1. *yudhiṣṭhira uvāca*
pitāmaha mahā-prājña yudhi satya-parākrama
śrotum icchāmi kārtsnyena kṛṣṇam avyayam īśvaram

Yudhiṣṭhira said: O grandfather, your wisdom is extensive and in battle you attack with great strength. I wish now to hear in full about Kṛṣṇa, the unchanging lord of the world.

2. *yac cāsya tejaḥ su-mahad yac ca karma purātanam*
tan me sarvaṁ yathā-tattvaṁ prabrūhi bharatarṣabha

Explain to me in full the precise nature of his vast potency and also the actions he performed in times gone by, O best of the Bharata race.

3. *tiryag-yoni-gataṁ rūpaṁ kathaṁ dhāritavān hariḥ*
kena kārya-visargeṇa tan me brūhi pitāmaha

Tell me, grandfather, how was it that Hari took on a form that came from the womb of a beast; what purpose did he seek to accomplish thereby?

4. *bhīṣma uvāca*
purāhaṁ mṛgayāṁ yāto mārkaṇḍeyāśrame sthitaḥ
tatrāpaśyaṁ muni-gaṇān samāsīnān sahasraśaḥ

Bhīṣma said: Once whilst pursuing the hunt I rested for a while in the *āśrama* of Mārkaṇḍeya. There I saw thousands of sages all sitting together.

5. *tatas te madhuparkeṇa pūjāṁ cakrur atho mayi*
pratigṛhya ca tāṁ pūjāṁ pratyanandam ṛṣīn aham

They worshipped me by offering milk mixed with honey and after accepting their worship I offered my respects to those *rishis.*

6. *kathaiṣā kathitā tatra kaśyapena maharṣiṇā*
manaḥ-prahlādinīṁ divyāṁ tām ihaika-manāḥ śṛṇu

It was there that this narration was recited by the great *rishi* Kaśyapa. Now listen with undivided attention to these divine words, which will fill your mind with joy.

7. *purā dānava-mukhyā hi krodha-lobha-samanvitāḥ*
balena mattāḥ śataśo narakādyā mahāsurāḥ

Long ago the leaders of the Dānavas became overwhelmed by anger and greed. They were accompanied by hundreds of powerful *asuras* who were commanded by Naraka and intoxicated with their own strength.

8. *tathaiva cānye bahavo dānavā yuddha-durmadāḥ*
na sahante sma devānāṁ samṛddhiṁ tām anuttamām

There were numerous other Dānavas as well who were ferocious in battle. They could not tolerate the unrivalled prosperity enjoyed by the gods.

9. *dānavair ardyamānās tu devā devarṣayas tathā*
na śarma lebhire rājan viśamānās tatas tataḥ

When they were attacked by these Dānavas, the gods and celestial *rishis* could find no place of refuge and wandered here and there.

10. *pṛthivīṁ cārta-rūpāṁ te samapaśyan divaukasaḥ*
dānavair abhisaṁkīrṇāṁ ghora-rūpair mahā-balaiḥ
bhārārtām apakṛṣṭāṁ ca duḥkhitāṁ saṁnimajjatīm

The gods beheld the afflicted condition of the earth, now swarming with Dānavas who were dreadful to look at and possessed of invincible prowess. Overwhelmed by this burden, the earth was in a distressed condition as it was pushed down and submerged beneath the waters.

11. *athāditeyāḥ saṁtrastā brahmāṇam idam abruvan*
kathaṁ śakyāmahe brahman dānavair upamardanam

So, with fear in their hearts, the sons of Aditi addressed these words to Brahmā, 'O Brahmā, how can we resist the afflictions imposed upon us by the Dānavas?'

12. *svayaṁbhūs tān uvācedaṁ nisṛṣṭo 'tra vidhir mayā*
te vareṇābhisaṁmattā balena ca madena ca

The self-born Brahmā replied to them, 'I have allowed these events to take place.These Dānavas are intoxicated by a boon they have been granted and because of their strength and arrogance.

13. *nāvabhotsyanti saṁmūḍhā viṣṇum avyakta-darśanam*
varāha-rūpiṇaṁ devam adhṛṣyam amarair api

Viṣṇu is always hidden from their sight. Because they are so deluded they will not recognise the lord when he assumes the form of a boar that is invincible even for the immortals.

14. *eṣa vegena gatvā hi yatra te dānavādhamāḥ*
antar-bhūmi-gatā ghorā nivasanti sahasraśaḥ
śamayiṣyati śrutvā te jahṛṣuḥ sura-sattamāḥ

Thousands of the vilest of those fearsome Dānavas have penetrated through to the interior of the earth and are now residing there. After forcefully entering that place, the lord will put an end to them.' On hearing these words the leaders of the gods felt great joy.

15. *tato viṣṇur mahā-tejā vārāhaṁ rūpam āśritaḥ*
antar-bhūmiṁ saṁpraviśya jagāma diti-jān prati

Then Viṣṇu, who is endowed with vast potency, assumed the form of a boar. Penetrating through to the interior of the earth, he advanced towards the descendants of Diti.

16. *dṛṣṭvā ca sahitāḥ sarve daityāḥ sattvam amānuṣam*
prasahya sahasā sarve saṁtasthuḥ kāla-mohitāḥ

When all those Daityas saw that being in a non-human form, they came forward with great ferocity to do battle, deluded as they were by the force of time.

17. *sarve ca samabhidrutya varāhaṁ jagṛhuḥ samam*
saṁkruddhāś ca varāhaṁ taṁ vyakarṣanta samantataḥ

Rushing at the boar, all of them together seized hold of it. Filled with rage, they then surrounded that boar and sought to drag it down.

18. *dānavendrā mahā-kāyā mahā-vīryā balocchritāḥ*
nāśaknuvaṁś kiṁcit te tasya kartuṁ tadā vibho

Despite their powerful bodies, immense physical prowess, and tremendous strength, the leaders of the Dānavas were unable to do anything at all to that creature, my lord.

19. *tato 'gaman vismayaṁ te dānavendrā bhayāt tadā*
saṁśayaṁ gatam ātmānaṁ menire ca sahasraśaḥ

The lords of the Dānavas then became perplexed due to the fear that afflicted them. Although there were thousands of them, they were convinced that they were in danger of losing their lives.

20. *tato devādi-devaḥ sa yogātmā yoga-sārathiḥ*
yogam āsthāya bhagavāṁs tadā bharata-sattama

That exalted lord who is the original Deity, who has Yoga as his very self, and Yoga as his constant associate then entered a mystical state of Yoga, O best of the Bharata race.

21. *vinanāda mahā-nādaṁ kṣobhayan daitya-dānavān*
saṁnāditā yena lokāḥ sarvāś caiva diśo daśa

He sounded forth a cacophonous roar that filled the worlds with its vibration in all ten directions and caused great agitation amongst the Daityas and Dānavas.

22. *tena saṁnāda-śabdena lokāḥ saṁkṣobham āgaman*
saṁbhrāntāś ca diśaḥ sarvā devāḥ śakra-purogamāḥ

All the worlds were disturbed by the sound of his roaring and all directions were agitated, as indeed were the gods with Śakra at their head.

23. *nirviceṣṭaṁ jagac cāpi babhūvātibhṛśaṁ tadā*
sthāvaraṁ jaṅgamaṁ caiva tena nādena mohitam

All living entities, both moving and stationary, became utterly motionless, held spellbound by his mighty roars.

24. *tatas te dānavāḥ sarve tena śabdena bhīṣitāḥ*
petur gatāsavaś caiva viṣṇu-tejo-vimohitāḥ

All those Dānavas were terrified by that sound. They fell to the ground with their life expiring, confounded by the power of Viṣṇu.

25. *rasātala-gatāṁś caiva varāhas tri-daśa-dviṣaḥ*
khuraiḥ saṁdārayāmāsa māṁsa-medosthi-saṁcayam

With his hooves the boar ripped apart the flesh, fat, and bones of those enemies of the thirty gods who had entered the underworld.

26. *nādena tena mahatā sanātana iti smṛtaḥ*
padmanābho mahā-yogī bhūtācāryaḥ sa bhūta-rāṭ

He sprouts a lotus from his navel, his Yoga powers are vast, he is the teacher of all beings and their master as well. It is because of the mighty roar he emitted that he is also known as 'Sanātana'.

27. *tato deva-gaṇāḥ sarve pitāmaham upābruvan*
nādo 'yaṁ kīdṛśo deva nainaṁ vidma vayaṁ vibho
ko 'sau hi kasya vā nādo yena vihvalitaṁ jagat

Then the gods all spoke to Brahmā, the grandfather of the world, saying, 'O mighty lord, what kind of sound is this? We cannot comprehend it. Who is this? Who has made this sound that is disturbing the entire world?'

28. *etasminn antare viṣṇur vārāhaṁ rūpam āsthitaḥ*
udatiṣṭhan mahādevaḥ stūyamāno maharṣibhiḥ

Viṣṇu, the Supreme Deity, still assuming the form of a boar, then appeared amongst them surrounded by great *rishis* offering prayers of glorification.

29. *pitāmaha uvāca*
nihatya dānava-patīn mahā-varṣmā mahā-balaḥ
eṣa devo mahā-yogī bhūtātmā bhūta-bhāvanaḥ

The grandfather said: This Deity of vast proportions and mighty power possesses great mystic potency. He is the true self within all beings and he is the creator of all beings as well. Now he has destroyed the lords of the Dānavas.

30. *sarva-bhūteśvaro yogī yonir-ātmā tathātmanaḥ*
sthirī-bhavata kṛṣṇo 'yaṁ sarva-pāpa-praṇāśanaḥ

He is the master of all beings, the *yogin*, the original *ātman* that is the source of the *ātman* in each creature. So now compose yourselves for this is Kṛṣṇa, the destroyer of all evil.

31. *kṛtvā karmātisādhv etad aśakyam amita-prabhaḥ*
samāyātaḥ svam ātmānaṁ mahā-bhāgo mahā-dyutiḥ
padmanābho mahā-yogī bhūtātmā bhūta-bhāvanaḥ

His power is without limit and now that he has performed this wonderful act, impossible for anyone else, he will resume his true form of existence. His glory and splendour are magnificent, he is the one who sprouts a lotus from his navel, he is the great *yogin*, he is the true self within all beings and he is the creator of all beings as well.

32. *na saṁtāpo na bhīḥ kāryā śoko vā sura-sattamāḥ*
vidhir eṣa prabhāvaś ca kālaḥ saṁkṣaya-kārakaḥ
lokān dhārayatānena nādo mukto mahātmanā

O best of the gods, there will be no more suffering and nothing remains that will give rise to fear or grief. He is destiny, he is the source of creation, he is time, the bringer of destruction, and he is also the maintainer of the worlds. The terrible roar you heard was emitted by this great soul.

33. *sa eva hi mahā-bhāgaḥ sarva-loka-namaskṛtaḥ*
acyutaḥ puṇḍarīkākṣaḥ sarva-bhūta-samudbhavaḥ

He is indeed the illustrious lord to whom the whole world pays homage. He is infallible, his eyes are like lotus petals, and he is original source of all living beings.

The Guru-Śiṣya-Saṁvāda

Śānti-parvan, Adhyāya 203–210

THE *GURU-ŚIṢYA-SAṀVĀDA*, the conversation between a teacher and his student, consistently presents the translator with a series of problems, primarily because the meaning of many of the verses is highly obscure. Hence at times one is forced into a surmise as to the intended meaning and then one cannot be sure that the rendition is entirely accurate. Whilst we were discussing the difficulties posed by some of the verses, Professor Narasimhachary commented to me that the passage as a whole appears to be not so much a systematic treatise as the notes taken by a student in a lecture, the meaning of which may be apparent to the note taker but is very hard for anyone else to comprehend. And on reading the passage, one does have a sense of immediacy and authenticity: one suspects that this may in fact be an approximate record of a real discourse delivered by a teacher to a group of celibate students endeavouring to control their passions and focus their attention on the pursuit of higher knowledge.

Despite the difficulties of meaning, the passage presents us with a number of interesting features. It appears likely that the redactor of the *Mokṣa-dharma-parvan* has included it at this point because it starts with a continuation of the Vaiṣṇava orientation that was the main feature of the chapters immediately preceding it. Here though we are not encountering the Purāṇic Vaiṣṇavism but rather what appears to be a further expression of the theistic Sāṁkhya that is such a salient feature of these passages. The highest principle, the Supreme Puruṣa, is identified with Viṣṇu who is present in every being, but crucially there is no idea of *mokṣa* being achieved through the grace or love of God. Rather, the teacher insists that knowledge based on renunciation is the key to liberation from rebirth.

Although the passage does lead eventually to a consideration of the attainment of *mokṣa* and refers to ideas derived from both Sāṁkhya and Yoga, the main emphasis here is on renunciation and restraint of the senses. If we accept that these teachings do represent the authentic voice of a teacher addressing the young men who are his students, then we can readily understand why this theme is addressed so completely and so ardently in a manner that is uncharacteristic of other treatises within the *Mokṣa-dharma-parvan*. Here we find injunctions on sexual restraint which adopt an unusually misogynistic tone, as women are condemned as witches who have the power to break a young man's vows. The discussion also turns towards the problem of passion arising in the dreaming state and how this can be avoided by remaining awake and vigilant. It is this emphasis on restraint of the senses and the passions that is the defining characteristic of the *Guru-Śiṣya-Saṁvāda*. The teacher speaks about the supremacy of Viṣṇu, about Sāṁkhya and Yoga doctrine, and about knowledge as the path to liberation, but his primary concern is to instil in his student an appreciation of the importance of suppressing the *guṇas* of *rajas* and *tamas*, adhering to rigid vows of celibacy, and restraining the senses from seeking out the objects they are prone to enjoy.

Śānti-parvan, Adhyāya 203

As is usual for the various treatises of the *Mokṣa-dharma-parvan*, this new passage opens with Yudhiṣṭhira putting a further question to his grandfather. This time the question is a very simple one: what is the highest form of Yoga, *yogam paramam*, which will bring liberation from rebirth. In reply, Bhīṣma refers to an ancient account of a conversation between a disciple and his *guru*, which apparently dealt with the same subject as Yudhiṣṭhira has inquired about. In fact any congruence in the inquiries is far from apparent; Yudhiṣṭhira had inquired about a form of Yoga practice whilst the disciple's questions are purely philosophical concerning the origin of the world and why living beings have different births. It may be the case therefore that the redactor shapes Yudhiṣṭhira's question in relation to the discussion contained in the later chapters, which do deal with religious practice, whilst the earlier chapters, perhaps the first two, represent the response to the disciple's initial inquiries.

Beginning from verse 7, the *guru* presents his response to the first of these questions, and it is clear from the outset that although the passage makes extensive use of Sāṁkhya thought, there is a significant Vaiṣṇava orientation to his teachings. The source of this world is Viṣṇu who is all things and is the soul of every being. He has now appeared as Kṛṣṇa in the Vṛṣṇi family but he is the creator of all beings, the creator of the Vedas, and at the end of the age (here referred to as a *yuga*) he draws the world back into himself. It was he who gave the *rishis* access to the knowledge of the Vedas; different *rishis* are learned in different areas of Vedic knowledge but Nārāyaṇa alone has knowledge of Brahman and he alone is the teacher of this knowledge.

From verse 23, the discussion moves towards an exposition of Sāṁkhya doctrine concerning the evolution of the different elements from out of the *avyakta*, the non-manifest state of matter. The *avyakta* is the first in the list, which is followed by *buddhi*, *ahaṁkāra*, the five great elements, five senses of perception, five organs of action, five objects of perception, and finally *manas*, the mind, which rather unusually is here placed as the final element in the usual Sāṁkhya enumeration of twenty-four. Following the characteristic dualism of Sāṁkhya discourse, from verse 33 the chapter turns towards a consideration of *puruṣa*, the soul or spiritual element that gives life to the living beings. We are reminded again in verse 34, however, that it is a theistic Sāṁkhya being referred to, for the supreme principle from which all the elements come into being is the *deva*, the Supreme Deity. With this in mind, we are then told that the *puruṣa* is ageless and untouched by death; this inner self pervades the whole body and, because knowledge is its very nature, all the knowledge we can acquire arises only because of the presence of *puruṣa*. The *puruṣa* performs action through its contact with the body; because of the action performed it becomes covered with the effects of karma and as a result is propelled forward to a new bodily form.

1. *yudhiṣṭhira uvāca*
yogaṁ me paramaṁ tāta mokṣasya vada bhārata
tam ahaṁ tattvato jñātum icchāmi vadatāṁ vara

Yudhiṣṭhira said: O Bhārata, my dear grandfather, please speak to me about the highest form of Yoga, that which leads to liberation. I wish to properly understand that subject, O best of teachers.

2. *bhīṣma uvāca*
atrāpy udāharantīmam itihāsaṁ purātanam
saṁvādaṁ mokṣa-saṁyuktaṁ śiṣyasya guruṇā saha

Bhīṣma said: In this connection they recite this ancient account of a discussion about liberation from rebirth that took place between a disciple and his teacher.

3. *kaścid brāhmaṇam āsīnam ācāryam ṛṣi-sattamam*
śiṣyaḥ parama-medhāvī śreyorthī su-samāhitaḥ
caraṇāv upasaṁgṛhya sthitaḥ prāñjalir abravīt

That teacher was a Brahmin who was the best amongst *rishis*. His highly intelligent disciple was intent on attaining something truly beneficial and possessed great determination. Coming to where his teacher was sitting, he first touched his feet and then spoke to him with his palms joined together as a mark of respect.

4. *upāsanāt prasanno 'si yadi vai bhagavan mama*
saṁśayo me mahān kaścit tan me vyākhyātum arhasi

'My lord, if you are satisfied with the devotion I have shown you, kindly address a great doubt that I have.

5. *kutaś cāhaṁ kutaś ca tvaṁ tat samyag brūhi yat param*
kathaṁ ca sarva-bhūteṣu sameṣu dvija-sattama
samyag-vṛttā nivartante viparītāḥ kṣayodayāḥ

From what source of origin have both you and I come into being? Explain to me properly about that highest principle. O best of Brahmins, when all living beings are identical, how is it that their death and rebirth are found to occur in such a variety of different ways?

6. *vedeṣu cāpi yad vākyaṁ laukikaṁ vyāpakaṁ ca yat*
etad vidvan yathā-tattvaṁ sarvaṁ vyākhyātum arhasi

Teach me the ideas contained in the Vedas and also the different doctrines current amongst ordinary people. O learned teacher, kindly explain to me the whole truth about this subject.'

7. *gurur uvāca*
śṛṇu śiṣya mahā-prājña brahma-guhyam idaṁ param
adhyātmaṁ sarva-bhūtānām āgamānāṁ ca yad vasu

The teacher said: You are a student of great wisdom. Listen now to the highest knowledge that is concealed within the Vedas. This concerns the self of all beings and represents the true worth of the *Āgamas*.

8. *vāsudevaḥ sarvam idaṁ viśvasya brahmaṇo mukham*
satyaṁ dānam atho yajñas titikṣā dama ārjavam

Vāsudeva is everything that exists; he is the mouth through which all the Vedas emerge. He is truth, charity, sacrifice, tolerance, restraint, and honesty.

9. *puruṣaṁ sanātanaṁ viṣṇuṁ yat tad veda-vido viduḥ*
sarga-pralaya-kartāram avyaktaṁ brahma śāśvatam
tad idaṁ brahma vārṣṇeyam itihāsaṁ śṛṇuśva me

Those who fully comprehend the Vedas know that Viṣṇu is the timeless *puruṣa*, the non-manifest eternal Brahman who brings about both the creation and destruction of the world. Now hear from me the story of how he who is Brahman appeared as a member of the Vṛṣṇi tribe.

10. *brāhmaṇo brāhmaṇaiḥ śrāvyo rājanyaḥ kṣatriyais tathā*
māhātmyaṁ deva-devasya viṣṇor amita-tejasaḥ
arhas tvam asi kalyāṇa vārṣṇeyaṁ śṛṇu yat param

Viṣṇu is the god of gods and his power is without limit. When Brahmins recite his glories the account should be heard by other Brahmins, but if a *kṣatriya* recites them it should be attended to by other *kṣatriyas*. You are righteous and thus also worthy, so now hear about that member of the Vṛṣṇi race who is in truth the Supreme.

11. *kāla-cakram anādyantaṁ bhāvābhāva-sva-lakṣaṇam*
trailokyaṁ sarva-bhūteṣu cakra-vat parivartate

He is the wheel of time that has neither beginning nor end and is marked by alternating states of being and non-being. Just like a wheel, he moves around the three worlds amongst all the living beings that exist therein.

12. *yat tad akṣaram avyaktam amṛtaṁ brahma śāśvatam*
vadanti puruṣa-vyāghraṁ keśavaṁ puruṣarṣabham

He is the eternal Brahman which never decays, is never manifest in this world, and never meets with death. They say that Keśava, who is a tiger amongst men and the greatest of all persons, is in fact that Brahman.

13. *pitṝn devān ṛṣīṁś caiva tathā vai yakṣa-dānavān*
nāgāsura-manuṣyāṁś ca sṛjate paramo 'vyayaḥ

That Supreme Being, the unchanging one, creates the forefathers, gods, *rishis*, *yakṣas*, *dānavas*, celestial serpents, *asuras*, and human beings.

14. *tathaiva veda-śāstrāṇi loka-dharmāṁś ca śāśvatān*
pralaye prakṛtiṁ prāpya yugādau sṛjate prabhuḥ

The lord is also the creator of the Vedas and other scriptures, as well as the eternal forms of dharma practised within the world. At the time of destruction, he absorbs *prakṛti* and at the beginning of the *yuga* he manifests it once again.

15. *yathartuṣv ṛtu-liṅgāni nānā-rūpāṇi paryaye*
dṛśyante tāni tāny eva tathā brahmāha-rātriṣu

As the seasons revolve one after the other, the various features that distinguish each season can be observed. In the same way, it can be seen that the days and nights of Brahmā continually revolve.

16. *atha yad yad yadā bhāvi kāla-yogād yugādiṣu*
tat tad utpadyate jñānaṁ loka-yātrā-vidhāna-jam

And whatever the state of existence that prevails due to the disposition of time at the beginning of each *yuga*, an appropriate form of knowledge arises, shaped by the prescribed way of life that people in that *yuga* must follow.

17. *yugānte 'ntarhitān vedān setihāsān maharṣayaḥ*
lebhire tapasā pūrvam anujñātāḥ svayaṁbhuvā

In the beginning of creation, with the consent of the self-born Brahmā, the great *rishis* by dint of their penances gained access to the Vedas and histories that had become concealed at the end of the previous *yuga*.

18. *veda-vid veda bhagavān vedāṅgāni bṛhaspatiḥ*
bhārgavo nīti-śāstraṁ ca jagāda jagato hitam

The illustrious Bṛhaspati, who has full knowledge of the Vedas, also comprehends the various sub-branches of Vedic knowledge. For the welfare of the world, Bhārgava proclaimed the *nīti-śāstra*, the scripture that teaches proper conduct.

19. *gāndharvaṁ nārado vedaṁ bharadvājo dhanur-graham*
devarṣi-caritaṁ gārgyaḥ kṛṣṇātreyaś cikitsitam

Nārada teaches the science of music, Bharadvāja teaches knowledge of weapons, Gārgya teaches about the conduct of the celestial *rishis*, and Kṛṣṇātreya teaches the science of medicine.

20. *nyāya-tantrāṇy anekāni tais tair uktāni vādibhiḥ*
hetv-āgama-sadācārair yad uktaṁ tad upāsyate

Various different *rishis* deliver the numerous doctrines based on logic. Whatever they teach concerning reason, scripture and proper conduct is to be respected.

21. *anādyaṁ yat paraṁ brahma na devā narṣayo viduḥ*
ekas tad veda bhagavān dhātā nārāyaṇaḥ prabhuḥ

Neither the gods nor *rishis* can fully comprehend Brahman, the supreme principle which has no beginning. Bhagavān Nārāyaṇa is the Ordainer, the master of the world. He alone possessed knowledge of Brahman.

22. *nārāyaṇād ṛṣi-gaṇās tathā mukhyāḥ surāsurāḥ*
rājarṣayaḥ purāṇāś ca paramaṁ duḥkha-bheṣajam

Knowledge of Brahman is the highest, for it is the remedy that ends all misery. The *rishis*, the leaders of the gods and *asuras*, and the royal *rishis* who reigned in ancient times all received this knowledge from Nārāyaṇa.

23. *puruṣādhiṣṭhitaṁ bhāvaṁ prakṛtiḥ sūyate sadā*
hetu-yuktam ataḥ sarvaṁ jagat saṁparivartate

Prakṛti constantly brings forth this existence, which exists under the direction of the *puruṣa*. It is from this cause alone that the entire world proceeds on its course.

24. *dīpād anye yathā dīpāḥ pravartante sahasraśaḥ*
prakṛtiḥ sṛjate tadvad ānantyān nāpacīyate

From a single lamp thousands of other lamps can be lit. In the same way, *prakṛti* brings forth this world but remains undiminished because its extent is without limit.

25. *avyakta-karma-jā buddhir ahaṁkāraṁ prasūyate*
ākāśaṁ cāpy ahaṁkārād vāyur ākāśa-saṁbhavaḥ

Buddhi, the intellect, is created when matter in its non-manifest state becomes active; *buddhi* gives rise to *ahaṁkāra*, self-awareness. Space comes into being from *ahaṁkāra* and air is born from space.

26. *vāyos tejas tataś cāpas tv adbhyo hi vasudhodgatā*
mūla-prakṛtayo 'ṣṭau tā jagad etāsv avasthitam

Heat appears from air, water arises from heat, and earth comes into being from water. These eight are the primal elements of *prakṛti*; the entire world rests upon them.

27. *jñānendriyāṇy ataḥ pañca pañca karmendriyāṇy api*
viṣayāḥ pañca caikaṁ ca vikāre ṣoḍaśaṁ manaḥ

From this group of eight come the five knowledge-acquiring senses, the five organs through which action is performed, and the five objects perceived by the senses. Their constant interactions produce the single entity that is *manas*, the mind; hence this list is sixteen in total.

28. *śrotraṁ tvak-cakṣuṣī jihvā ghrāṇaṁ pañcendriyāṇy api*
pādau pāyur upasthaś ca hastau vāk karmaṇām api

The ear, the skin, the eyes, the tongue, and the nose are the five senses. The feet, the anus, the genitals, the hands, and the voice are the five organs through which action is performed.

29. *śabdaḥ sparśo 'tha rūpaṁ ca raso gandhas tathaiva ca*
vijñeyaṁ vyāpakaṁ cittaṁ teṣu sarva-gataṁ manaḥ

Sound, touch, form, flavour, and aroma are the objects perceived by the senses. Roaming everywhere amongst them, *manas* should be understood as the consciousness that pervades all of these.

30. *rasa-jñāne tu jihveyaṁ vyāhṛte vāk tathaiva ca*
indriyair vividhair yuktaṁ sarvaṁ vyastaṁ manas tathā

When flavour is an object of knowledge *manas* is the tongue, and when one speaks it is the voice. Acting in conjunction with the different senses, *manas* extends to all the objects of perception and all actions performed.

31. *vidyāt tu ṣoḍaśaitāni daivatāni vibhāgaśaḥ*
deheṣu jñāna-kartāram upāsīnam upāsate

Each one of these sixteen elements may be understood as a deity. They render service to the entity that exists within all bodies as the creator of knowledge.

32. *tadvat soma-guṇā jihvā gandhas tu pṛthivī-guṇaḥ*
śrotraṁ śabda-guṇaṁ caiva cakṣur agner guṇas tathā
sparśaṁ vāyu-guṇaṁ vidyāt sarva-bhūteṣu sarvadā

The sense of taste is the quality of liquid, aroma is the quality of earth, hearing is the quality of sound, sight is the quality of fire, and touch is the quality of air. It should be understood that these are always present in all living beings.

33. *manaḥ sattva-guṇaṁ prāhuḥ sattvam avyakta-jaṁ tathā*
sarva-bhūtātma-bhūta-sthaṁ tasmād budhyeta buddhimān

They say that *manas* is the quality of the manifest world and this manifestation arises from the non-manifest state. A wise man should understand that the *ātman* of all beings is situated in each living being.

34. *ete bhāvā jagat sarvaṁ vahanti sa-carācaram*
śritā virajasaṁ devaṁ yam āhuḥ paramaṁ padam

It is these elements that sustain the entire creation with its moving and stationary beings. They in turn are dependent upon the Deity who is free from any impurity. They say that he represents the topmost state of existence.

35. *nava-dvāraṁ puraṁ puṇyaṁ etair bhāvaiḥ samanvitam*
vyāpya śete mahān ātmā tasmāt puruṣa ucyate

This excellent city (*pura*) of nine gates is composed of these elements. After spreading throughout the body, the great *ātman* comes to rest (*śete*). Therefore it is known as *puruṣa.*

36. *ajaraḥ so 'maraś caiva vyaktāvyaktopadeśavān*
vyāpakaḥ saguṇaḥ sūkṣmaḥ sarva-bhūta-guṇāśrayaḥ

The *puruṣa* does not age or succumb to death and has insight into both the manifest and non-manifest. It pervades the body and hence it is endowed with qualities though it is subtle by nature. All the elements and *guṇas* rest upon it.

37. *yathā dīpaḥ prakāśātmā hrasvo vā yadi vā mahān*
jñānātmānaṁ tathā vidyāt puruṣaṁ sarva-jantuṣu

Whether it be tiny or great in size, a lamp will be effulgent because that is its essential nature. In the same way, it should be understood that the *puruṣa* in all creatures has knowledge as its essential nature.

38. *so 'tra vedayate vedyaṁ sa śṛṇoti sa paśyati*
kāraṇaṁ tasya deho 'yaṁ sa kartā sarva-karmaṇām

It is the *puruṣa* within the body that causes the comprehension of what is known; thus the *puruṣa* hears and the *puruṣa* sees. Using the body as its means, it is the performer of all actions.

39. *agnir dāru-gato yadvad bhinne dārau na dṛśyate*
tathaivātmā śarīra-stho yogenaivātra dṛśyate

The fire present within wood cannot be seen even when the wood is split open. In the same way, the *ātman* present within the body can only be seen by means of Yoga practice.

40. *nadīṣv āpo yathā yuktā yathā sūrye marīcayaḥ*
saṁtanvānā yathā yānti tathā dehāḥ śarīriṇām

Water exists in conjunction with rivers, particles of light exist in conjunction with the sun, and they both go forth in a continuous line of progression. In the same way, bodies exist in relation to the embodied *ātman*.

41. *svapna-yoge yathaivātmā pañcendriya-samāgataḥ*
deham utsṛjya vai yāti tathaivātropalabhyate

Whilst one is asleep the *ātman* in combination with the five senses leaves the body behind and goes away. It is precisely in this way that another body is attained by the disembodied *ātman*.

42. *karmaṇā vyāpyate pūrvaṁ karmaṇā copapadyate*
karmaṇā nīyate 'nyatra sva-kṛtena balīyasā

The *ātman* is covered by its previous actions and on the basis of this action it approaches a specific bodily form. Thus it is led to its destination by the strength of actions it has performed elsewhere.

43. *sa tu dehād yathā dehaṁ tyaktvānyaṁ pratipadyate*
tathā taṁ saṁpravakṣyāmi bhūta-grāmaṁ sva-karma-jam

I shall now explain how the *ātman* moves on from its body, how it takes on another form after leaving its previous body, and how each living being is born as a result of its previous actions.

Śānti-parvan, Adhyāya 204

In this second chapter, the teacher expands his explanation of the concept of the soul, or life force, which was begun at the end of the first chapter. The discussion is loosely based on Sāṁkhya ideas but falls short of being a fully developed Sāṁkhya discourse. We are told that the living being itself, here designated by the term *kṣetrajña*, is not subject to perception by the senses and becomes manifest in this world only when it comes to exist in association with the material elements. Before this world became manifest, the life force, the *jīva*, existed alone, but because of the force of ignorance it became a performer of action and thus entered the realm of causality in which karma and rebirth prevail. Thus the cycle of life progresses due to attachment and desire for enjoyment. However, despite its embodiment and its entanglement with matter, the *kṣetrajña* remains untouched by causality; it is always aloof, existing within this world but never forming a part of it. Its higher identity is never impinged upon by its embodied state. After giving this brief explanation of the nature of the living being, the teacher appears to conclude his instruction in the final three verses of the chapter; as suggested above, it may be that this was the full extent of an original work, which has been combined with other material to form the passage included here as the *Guru-Śiṣya-Saṁvāda*. The final point made is that a wise man who understands this distinction between the life force and its physical embodiment frees himself from this condition and never again comes to exist in the realm of matter, *na gacchet prakṛtiṁ punaḥ*.

1. *gurur uvāca*
catur-vidhāni bhūtāni sthāvarāṇi carāṇi ca
avyakta-prabhavāny āhur avyakta-nidhanāni ca
avyakta-nidhanaṁ vidyād avyaktātmātmakaṁ manaḥ

The teacher said: Stationary and moving beings are of four kinds. They say that living beings are imperceptible before their appearance and are again imperceptible after their death. Hence it should be understood that the mind is not manifest after death, for the mind shares a common identity with the imperceptible *ātman*.

2. *yathāśvattha-kaṇīkāyām antar-bhūto mahā-drumaḥ*
niṣpanno dṛśyate vyaktam avyaktāt saṁbhavas tathā

Like the mighty tree that exists within each tiny banyan seed, the living entity can be perceived only when it has come into being, emerging from the state of non-manifestation.

3. *abhidravaty ayas-kānta-mayo niścetanāv ubhau*
sva-bhāva-hetu-jā bhāvā yadvad anyad apīdṛśam

Even though both are devoid of consciousness, a lodestone draws near to an object containing iron. The fundamental identity of objects arises due to their own inherent nature, although they are essentially different from one another.

4. *tadvad avyakta-jā bhāvāḥ kartuḥ kāraṇa-lakṣaṇāḥ*
acetanāś cetayituḥ kāraṇād abhisaṁhitāḥ

It is in the same way that various forms of existence emerge from a state of non-manifestation due to the action of the creator and become subject to the laws of causality. Thus it is to be accepted that non-sentient objects appear from a sentient cause.

5. *na bhūḥ khaṁ dyaur na bhūtāni narṣayo na surāsurāḥ*
nānyad āsīd ṛte jīvam āsedur na tu saṁhitam

In the beginning there was no earth, no space, and no heavens. Neither were there living beings, *rishis*, gods, or *asuras*. Nothing else existed apart from the living force. Life was thus present but it did not exist in conjunction with anything else.

6. *sarva-nītyā sarva-gataṁ mano-hetu sa-lakṣaṇam*
ajñāna-karma nirdiṣṭam etat kāraṇa-lakṣaṇam

As the universal guiding force, life pervades all things. When it acquires attributes it is the origin of the mind. It is declared that it performs action only due to ignorance and it then becomes subject to the laws of causality.

7. *tat kāraṇair hi saṁyuktaṁ kārya-saṁgraha-kārakam*
yenaitad vartate cakram anādi-nidhanaṁ mahat

When life is combined with the various causal factors in this world, it performs action and draws objects to itself. In this way the vast wheel of life goes on with no beginning or end.

8. *avyakta-nābhaṁ vyaktāraṁ vikāra-parimaṇḍalam*
kṣetra-jñādhiṣṭhitaṁ cakraṁ snighdākṣaṁ vartate dhruvam

This wheel has matter in its non-manifest state as its hub, matter in its manifest state as the spokes, and the transformations of matter as its rim. Impelled by the *kṣetrajña*, the wheel moves on relentlessly with attachment as its axle.

9. *snigdhatvāt tilavat sarvaṁ cakre 'smin pīḍyate jagat*
tila-pīḍair ivākramya bhogair ajñāna-saṁbhavaiḥ

Because of the state of attachment, the entire world is crushed like sesame seeds on this wheel of life. The world is possessed by the objects of pleasure that arise from ignorance and act just like grinding presses.

10. *karma tat kurute tarṣād ahaṁkāra-parigraham*
kārya-kāraṇa-saṁyoge sa hetur upapāditaḥ

Accepting the sense of self, the world then performs action based on desire. Thus the process of causality is generated from the union of cause, which is desire, and effect, which is selfish action.

11. *nātyeti kāraṇaṁ kāryaṁ na kāryaṁ kāraṇaṁ tathā*
kāryāṇāṁ tūpakaraṇe kālo bhavati hetumān

In this process the effect does not enter into the cause, nor does the cause enter the effect. And in the generation of effects, time is the ultimate cause.

12. *hetu-yuktāḥ prakṛtayo vikārāś ca parasparam*
anyonyam abhivartante puruṣādhiṣṭhitāḥ sadā

The primary elements of matter and their transformation are themselves the causal factors for each other. They constantly exist in conjunction with one another whilst being presided over by the *puruṣa*.

13. *sa-rajas-tāmasair bhāvaiś cyuto hetu-balānvitaḥ*
kṣetrajñam evānuyāti pāṁsur vāterito yathā
na ca taiḥ spṛśyate bhāvo na te tena mahātmanā

Just as dust follows the wind that blows it, so this existence follows the *kṣetrajña* along with the power of causality and those things associated with *rajas* and *tamas*. But the *kṣetrajña* is never touched by them and they are never touched by that great soul.

14. *sa-rajasko 'rajaskaś ca sa vai vāyur yathā bhavet*
tathaitad antaraṁ vidyāt kṣetra-kṣetrajñayor budhaḥ
abhyāsāt sa tathā yukto na gacchet prakṛtiṁ punaḥ

As the wind may sometimes be full of dust but is without dust in itself, so the enlightened man should understand the distinction between *kṣetra* and *kṣetrajña*. Such a person who is properly engaged through regulated practices is never again embroiled in *prakṛti*.

15. *saṁdeham etam utpannam acchinad bhagavān ṛṣiḥ*
tathā vārtāṁ samīkṣeta kṛta-lakṣaṇa-saṁmitām

In this way the exalted *rishi* cut through this doubt that had arisen. Based on this understanding, one should observe the path of life that is in accordance with the proper rules.

16. *bījāny agny-upadagdhāni na rohanti yathā punaḥ*
jñāna-dagdhais tathā kleśair nātmā saṁbadhyate punaḥ

Seeds scorched by fire never germinate again. In the same way, the *ātman* is never again bound to the torments of this world once these have been scorched by the fire of knowledge.

Śānti-parvan, Adhyāya 205

The third chapter appears to carry on from verse 15 of the previous chapter, which refers to following the proper path in accordance with the prescribed rules, for now the discussion turns to the way of life to be followed by renunciants. First of all, the teacher points out that there are two forms of dharma, one based on ritual acts and the other centring on the pursuit of knowledge; these two can of course be recognised as forming the division between the *karma-kāṇḍa* and the *jñāna-kāṇḍa* of the Veda or the paths of *pravṛtti* and *nivṛtti* mentioned frequently within the *Mahābhārata*. Here the teacher seems to share the view of the *Bhagavad-gītā*, insisting on the acceptance of ritual dharma; *adharma*, the opposite, is based on illusion and leads to attachment. Desires of that kind must be transcended, and it is this point that leads us into the discussion of the lifestyle to be adopted by the renunciants who are seeking the higher knowledge referred to at the beginning. This consists of accepting the simple uncooked food available from the forest, practising austerities, and showing forbearance whilst accepting whatever fortune fate may bring.

From verse 19, the teacher begins to make use of the Sāṁkhya concept of the three *guṇas* as a basis for perfecting one's conduct. All living beings are subject to the influence of these *guṇas*; the student should observe himself and his own conduct, noting the way in which each of the *guṇas* has an influence over his character and actions. It is by means of this detached observation that one's own faults can be understood and ultimately transcended. At this point (verse 25) the student asks for further clarification as to the nature of these faults and the means by which they can be overcome, and the teacher responds by expanding further on the previous idea of the effect the *guṇas* have upon a person. It is *rajas* that gives rise to acts of violence both in the Vedic ritual and in the ardent pursuit of prosperity. From *tamas* come greed, anger, aggression, and idleness, but *sattva* produces purity and frees a person from contamination. It is interesting to note how the teacher here elevates the quality of *sattva* and appears to make it a part of the quest for higher knowledge. In Sāṁkhya teachings all three *guṇas* are a part of *prakṛti*, the material manifestation an aspirant must seek to detach himself from, but here it seems that *sattva* is also a part of the solution, a view that can also be detected in the teachings of the final chapter of the *Bhagavad-gītā*.

1. *gurur uvāca*
pravṛtti-lakṣaṇo dharmo yathāyam upapadyate
teṣāṁ vijñāna-niṣṭhānām anyat tattvaṁ na rocate

The teacher said: There is one form of dharma that consists of ritual performances, but for those dedicated to the pursuit of knowledge no other doctrine is acceptable.

2. *durlabhā veda-vidvāṁso vedokteṣu vyavasthitāḥ*
prayojanam atas tv atra mārgam icchanti saṁstutam

Scholars who are learned in the Vedas and who adhere strictly to the teachings of the Vedas are rarely found. But those who pursue knowledge seek out the path that is praised because it leads to a higher goal.

3. *sadbhir ācaritatvāt tu vṛttam etad agarhitam*
iyaṁ sā buddhir anyeyaṁ yayā yāti parāṁ gatim

Because it is followed by virtuous men, that way of life should never be condemned. This is one form of understanding whilst the other is that by which one gains the highest destination.

4. *śarīravān upādatte mohāt sarva-parigrahān*
kāma-krodhādibhir bhāvair yukto rājasa-tāmasaiḥ

It is due to illusion that the living being in its embodied form pursues all the objects it seeks in life. It is beset by desire, anger, and other propensities that arise from the qualities of *rajas* and *tamas*.

5. *nāśuddham ācaret tasmād abhīpsan deha-yāpanam*
karmaṇo vivaraṁ kurvan na lokān āpnuyāc chubhān

One seeking the end of bodily existence should never perform an impure action. One who is negligent in carrying out his duties never attains the pure realms of this creation.

6. *loha-yuktaṁ yathā hema vipakvaṁ na virājate*
tathāpakva-kaṣāyākhyaṁ vijñānaṁ na prakāśate

When it is mixed with copper, the pure form of gold cannot shine. In the same way, knowledge that is still touched by contaminations does not spread its illumination.

7. *yaś cādharmaṁ caren mohāt kāma-lobhāv anu plavan*
dharmyaṁ panthānam ākramya sānubandho vinaśyati

Due to illusion one may then pursue *adharma*, moving in accordance with desire and greed. After abandoning the path of dharma, such a person becomes attached to this world and meets with destruction.

8. *śabdādīn viṣayāṁs tasmād asaṁrāgād anuplavet*
krodha-harṣau viṣādaś ca jāyante hi parasparam

Therefore one should adopt a mood of complete detachment and renounce sound and the other objects enjoyed through the senses, for anger, delight, and despair all appear in turn, each one being a product of the others.

9. *pañca-bhūtātmake dehe sattva-rājasa-tāmase*
kam abhiṣṭhuvate cāyaṁ kaṁ vā krośati kiṁ vadet

When this body is composed of five elements and permeated by the qualities of *sattva*, *rajas*, and *tamas*, who can one praise and who can one condemn? How can one speak any such words?

10. *sparśa-rūpa-rasādyeṣu saṅgaṁ gacchanti bāliśāḥ*
nāvagacchanty avijñānād ātma-jaṁ pārthivaṁ guṇam

Foolish people develop attachment for touches, forms, tastes, and other objects enjoyed through the senses. Because of their lack of wisdom, they do not understand that the body is of the quality of earth and comes into being due to the presence of the *ātman*.

11. *mṛn-mayaṁ śaraṇaṁ yadvan mṛdaiva parilipyate*
pārthivo 'yaṁ tathā deho mṛd-vikārair vilipyate

A dwelling place built from earth has its structure held in place by a smearing of earth on its exterior. In the same way, this body, which is composed of earth, is held intact by transformations of earth.

12. *madhu tailaṁ payaḥ sarpir māṁsāni lavaṇaṁ guḍaḥ*
dhānyāni phala-mūlāni mṛd-vikārāḥ sahāmbhasā

Honey, sesame oil, milk, ghee, meat, salt, sugar, grains, fruits, and roots are all transformations of earth combined together with water.

13. *yadvat kāntāram ātiṣṭhan nautsukyaṁ samanuvrajet*
śramād āhāram ādadyād asvādv api hi yāpanam

One who dwells in the forest can never indulge in the satisfaction of his desires. Because of his austere lifestyle he accepts any food that will maintain his life, even though it be unpalatable to the taste.

14. *tadvat saṁsāra-kāntāram ātiṣṭhañ śrama-tat-paraḥ*
yātrārtham adyād āhāraṁ vyādhito bheṣajaṁ yathā

Similarly, one who dwells in the forest of worldly existence should also follow a renounced way of life. He should take proper food just to facilitate his passage through life in the same way that a person afflicted by disease takes medicine.

15. *satya-śaucārjava-tyāgair yaśasā vikrameṇa ca*
kṣāntyā dhṛtyā ca buddhyā ca manasā tapasaiva ca

Using truthfulness, purity, honesty, renunciation, honour, inner strength, forbearance, determination, the intellect, the mind, and austerity,

16. *bhāvān sarvān yathā vṛttān saṁvaseta yathākramam*
śāntim icchann adīnātmā saṁyacched indriyāṇi ca

The superior person must accept all the circumstances that arise in life, as they follow one after another. Seeking true peace, he must restrain the actions of the senses.

17. *sattvena rajasā caiva tamasā caiva mohitāḥ*
cakravat parivartante hy ajñānāj jantavo bhṛśam

Living beings are deluded by the qualities of *sattva*, *rajas*, and *tamas*, and because of this ignorance they revolve constantly through the cycle of existence.

18. *tasmāt samyak parīkṣeta doṣān ajñāna-saṁbhavān*
ajñāna-prabhavaṁ nityam ahaṁkāraṁ parityajet

He should therefore closely observe the faults that arise within himself due to ignorance, and he must always give up the sense of ego, the *ahaṁkāra* that is born of ignorance.

19. *mahā-bhūtānīndriyāṇi guṇāḥ sattvaṁ rajas tamaḥ*
trai-lokyaṁ seśvaraṁ sarvam ahaṁkāre pratiṣṭhitam

The great elements, the senses, the qualities of *sattva*, *rajas*, and *tamas*, as well as the three levels of the universe and the Deity who is its master all rest on this *ahaṁkāra*.

20. *yatheha niyataṁ kālo darśayaty ārtavān guṇān*
tadvad bhūteṣv ahaṁkāraṁ vidyād bhūta-pravartakam

In this world time exerts its control over everything, causing the qualities of each season to appear in turn; similarly, one should understand that the *ahaṁkāra* present in all creatures is the factor that causes them to proceed through life.

21. *saṁmohakaṁ tamo vidyāt kṛṣṇam ajñāna-saṁbhavam*
prīti-duḥkha-nibaddhāṁś ca samastāṁs trīn atho guṇān
sattvasya rajasaś caiva tamasaś ca nibodha tān

One should know *tamas* as the dark quality that deludes the living beings; it is born of ignorance. All the joy and misery that such beings encounter are bound to the three *guṇas*. Now you may learn about these as they pertain to *sattva*, *rajas*, and *tamas*.

22. *pramoho harṣa-jaḥ prītir asaṁdeho dhṛtiḥ smṛtiḥ*
etān sattva-guṇān vidyād imān rājasa-tāmasān

The infatuation that comes from delight, happiness, freedom from doubt, determination, and memory are known as the qualities of *sattva*. The following are the qualities of *rajas* and *tamas*:

23. *kāma-krodhau pramādaś ca lobha-mohau bhayaṁ klamaḥ*
viṣāda-śokāv aratir māna-darpāv anāryatā

These are lust, anger, negligence, greed, stupidity, fear, indolence, despondency, grief, dissatisfaction, arrogance, contempt, and vulgarity.

24. *doṣāṇām evam ādīnāṁ parīkṣya guru-lāghavam*
vimṛśed ātma-saṁsthānām ekaikam anusaṁtatam

When one has considered the severity or weakness of these faults and others as well, one should review them one by one, noting the extent of their presence within oneself.

25. *śiṣya uvāca*
ke doṣā manasā tyaktāḥ ke buddhyā śithilī-kṛtāḥ
ke punaḥ punar āyānti ke mohād aphalā iva

The disciple said: Which of these faults can be subjugated by mental exertion and which of them must be detached by means of the intellect? Which of them constantly recur and which of them appear to offer no reward whatsoever and arise only because of illusion?

26. *keṣāṁ balābalaṁ buddhyā hetubhir vimṛśed budhaḥ*
etat sarvaṁ samācakṣva yathā vidyām ahaṁ prabho

What are the faults the wise man should review with his intellect and powers of reason, considering their strength or weakness? Tell me all of this, my lord, as I should properly understand it.

27. *gurur uvāca*
doṣair mūlād avacchinnair viśuddhātmā vimucyate
vināśayati saṁbhūtam ayasmaya-mayo yathā
tathākṛtātmā saha-jair doṣair naśyati rājasaiḥ

The teacher said: One who is pure in heart gains liberation by cutting these faults down to their very root. When it strikes against something else made of iron, an iron tool is itself destroyed. In the same way, a person who is spiritually immature is destroyed by the faults arising from the quality of *rajas* that are a part of his own identity.

28. *rājasaṁ tāmasaṁ caiva śuddhātmā-karma-saṁbhavam*
tat sarvaṁ dehināṁ bījaṁ sarvam ātma-vataḥ samam

The seed from which these embodied beings arise consists entirely of the manifestations of *rajas* and *tamas* combined with those created by pure actions. For one who is spiritually advanced all things are viewed equally,

29. *tasmād ātma-vatā varjyaṁ rajaś ca tama eva ca*
rajas-tamobhyāṁ nirmuktaṁ sattvaṁ nirmalatām iyāt

And hence the qualities of *rajas* and *tamas* are shunned by a person who is spiritually advanced. When liberated from *rajas* and *tamas*, *sattva* becomes free from contamination.

30. *atha vā mantra-vad brūyur māṁsādānāṁ yajuṣ-kṛtam*
hetuḥ sa evānādāne śuddha-dharmānupālane

On this subject they speak of the ceremonies performed with sacred prayers and the rituals of sacrifice that allow one to acquire meat. The only reason for this, however, is to protect the purity of dharma and to remove the motive of personal gain.

31. *rajasā dharma-yuktāni kāryāṇy api samāpnuyāt*
artha-yuktāni cātyarthaṁ kāmān sarvāṁś ca sevate

It is on the basis of the quality of *rajas* that a person performs such rituals as a form of dharma. It is also through *rajas* that one seeks to an excessive degree those things associated with prosperity (*artha*) and the fulfilment of all sensual desires (*kāma*).

32. *tamasā lobha-yuktāni krodha-jāni ca sevate*
hiṁsā-vihārābhiratas tandrī-nidrā-samanvitaḥ

It is through the quality of *tamas* that one performs actions based on greed and those that are born of anger. Such a person enjoys aggression and idle pleasure and indulges in laziness and sleep.

33. *sattva-sthaḥ sāttvikān bhāvāñ śuddhān paśyati saṁśritaḥ*
sa dehī vimalaḥ śrīmāñ śuddho vidyā-samanvitaḥ

A person situated in *sattva* observes the pure ways of life that arise from the quality of *sattva* and conducts himself accordingly. Such an embodied being is no longer defiled, for he is glorious, he is pure, and he is blessed with knowledge.

Śānti-parvan, Adhyāya 206

In the fourth chapter, the teacher's principal topic is the causes of rebirth, which, perhaps rather predictably, he reveals to be ignorance and attachment. The chapter begins, however, with one of the few references to liberation from rebirth that we find in this passage. It is the two lower *guṇas* of *rajas* and *tamas* that must be subjugated in order for a state of purity to be achieved;

and it is this state of purity that allows the person to enter into Viṣṇu, the Supreme Deity. This second verse of the chapter reminds us again of the Vaiṣṇava orientation of the passage; the manner in which *mokṣa* is described as entering into the existence of the Deity is interesting and somewhat unusual, although the idea is also to be found in the *Bhagavad-gītā* (11.54) and in Pañcarātra literature. Where this state of purity is not achieved then *māyā* (illusion) prevails and the human being is preoccupied with pleasure, anger, and conceit; it is these that give rise to the performance of action, which in turn leads to continued rebirth.

From verse 6, the discussion takes another unusual turn as we find the sort of misogynistic teaching that is very rarely encountered in the *Mokṣa-dharma-parvan*, a factor which tends to reinforce the suspicion that this passage is a genuine record of teachings given by a particular individual. The person who does not attain purity and so does not enter the Deity is placed in the womb of a woman. Such women are witches with hideous forms (*ghora-rūpa*); one must cast off association with wife and children just as one would cast aside worms living on one's body. After this rather extraordinary diatribe, the teacher seems to recover his composure and return to a more philosophical line of discourse. In verses 12 to 21, he provides a more technical explanation of the process of rebirth that seems to be loosely based on the Yoga philosophy encountered in Patañjali's *sūtras* and to some extent in the *Bhagavad-gītā* as well. Ignorance, *ajñāna*, emerges from the state of knowledge because the *buddhi* displays *ahaṁkāra* and it is this ignorance covering the living being which perpetuates the process of rebirth. The nature of this rebirth is shaped by the state of the mind, which in turn is dependent upon the previous actions performed; in the Yoga philosophy, action is not merely physical but is a reflection of the state of consciousness that impels action. And this state of consciousness remains impressed upon the psyche as a *vāsanā* that will yield a future result. The senses then develop once more to become the living being's organs of perception, but the appearance of the senses is a facet of the mind because the mind carries with it a desire to experience the objects of perception.

The final verses reinforce the imperative towards seeking liberation from the process of rebirth. Life in this world is inevitably beset by misery, hence one should practice *tyāga* (renunciation), for where there is no desire the senses will cease to be active. We were told earlier that the senses appear in relation to the living being because of the desire for their objects that exists within the mind, and hence renunciation of desire can end this process. And only if one gains an understanding of this teaching on the causes of rebirth can one act against the causes and prevent them from producing effects.

1. *gurur uvāca*
rajasā sādhyate mohas tamasā ca nararṣabha
krodha-lobhau bhayaṁ darpa eteṣāṁ sādhanāc chuciḥ

The teacher said: Delusion appears as a result of *rajas*, O best of men, whilst anger, greed, fear, and contempt arise due to *tamas*. When these sentiments are subjugated purity prevails.

2. *paramaṁ paramātmānaṁ devam akṣayam avyayaṁ*
viṣṇum avyakta-saṁsthānaṁ viśante deva-sattamam

And those who are pure enter into Viṣṇu who is the supreme principle. He is the supreme soul, the Deity who never changes or deteriorates, whose position is never manifest in this world and who is foremost amongst the gods.

3. *tasya māyā-vidagdhāṅgā jñāna-bhraṣṭā nirāśiṣaḥ*
mānavā jñāna-saṁmohāt tataḥ kāmaṁ prayānti vai

Because their knowledge is covered by illusion, human beings possess forms dominated by his *māyā*, his deluding power. When their wisdom is thus nullified and their hopes vanquished, they turn to the pursuit of sensual pleasure.

4. *kāmāt krodham avāpyātha lobha-mohau ca mānavāḥ*
māna-darpād ahaṁkāram ahaṁkārāt tataḥ kriyāḥ

Anger arises as a result of this desire and human beings then fall prey to greed and illusion. Egotism arises from their arrogance and conceit, and the actions they perform are based on this egotistical pride.

5. *kriyābhiḥ sneha-saṁbandhaḥ snehāc chokam anantaram*
sukha-duḥkha-samārambhāj janmājanma-kṛta-kṣaṇāḥ

It is due to actions that the bondage of attachment develops and from such attachment comes limitless misery. And due to actions that bring both joy and suffering there is the constant recurrence of birth and death.

6. *janmato garbha-vāsaṁ tu śukra-śoṇita-saṁbhavam*
purīṣa-mūtra-vikleda-śoṇita-prabhavāvilam

And as a result of rebirth, an abode for the embryo is formed arising from the combination of semen and blood. This is a fetid environment composed of stool, urine, foul liquids, and blood.

7. *tṛṣṇābhibhūtas tair baddhas tān evābhipariplavan*
saṁsāra-tantra-vāhinyas tatra budhyeta yoṣitaḥ

In this state of bondage, the embryo covered by these substances feels terrible thirst because of them. Hence one should understand that it is women who sustain the mechanism of repeated birth and death.

8. *prakṛtyā kṣetra-bhūtās tā narāḥ kṣetrajña-lakṣaṇāḥ*
tasmād etā viśeṣeṇa naro 'tīyur vipaścitaḥ

By their essential nature women represent the *kṣetra,* the domain that is known, whilst men have the quality of the *kṣetrajña*, the knower of that domain. Therefore a man of discrimination should completely shun the company of women.

9. *kṛtyā hy etā ghora-rūpā mohayanty avicakṣaṇān*
rajasy antarhitā mūrtir indriyāṇāṁ sanātanī

They are just like witches who use their frightful bodily forms to enchant the minds of foolish men. Submerged in the quality of *rajas*, woman is the eternal manifestation of sensory indulgence.

10. *tasmāt tarṣātmakād rāgād bījāj jāyanti jantavaḥ*
sva-deha-jān asva-saṁjñān yadvad aṅgāt kṛmīṁs tyajet
sva-saṁjñān asva-jāṁs tadvat suta-saṁjñān kṛmīṁs tyajet

Living beings are thus born from passion based on lust in the form of semen. Even though worms may be born on one's own body they are not regarded as related to oneself and so are cast aside. In the same way, one should discard the worms known as sons that are regarded as one's own even though they are not truly born from oneself.

11. *śukrato rasataś caiva snehāj jāyanti jantavaḥ*
sva-bhāvāt karma-yogād vā tān upekṣeta buddhimān

It is due to attachment that these living beings are born from one's semen or from one's perspiration. This happens either because of the inherent nature of the living being or because of the link with previous actions. An intelligent man should abandon all such offspring.

12. *rajas tamasi paryastaṁ sattvaṁ tamasi saṁsthitam*
jñānādhiṣṭhānam ajñānaṁ buddhy-ahaṁkāra-lakṣaṇam

The quality of *rajas* pervades *tamas*, and *sattva* likewise is present within *tamas*. Ignorance has its basis in knowledge and is a feature of the *buddhi* when it is in contact with *ahaṁkāra*.

13. *tad bījaṁ dehināṁ āhus tad bījaṁ jīva-saṁjñitam*
karmaṇā kāla-yuktena saṁsāra-parivartakam

They say that this ignorance is the seed of embodied beings, and the seed of ignorance is known as *jīva*. And so it is that the cycle of rebirth is perpetuated through a combination of the actions living beings perform and the influence of time.

14. *ramaty ayaṁ yathā svapne manasā deha-vān iva*
karma-garbhair guṇair dehī garbhe tad upapadyate

In a dream the living being acts through the mind and thereby enjoys various pleasures as if it were actually employing the body. In the same way, it is through the qualities acquired from previous actions that the embodied entity takes up its position within the womb.

15. *karmaṇā bīja-bhūtena codyate yad yad indriyam*
jāyate tad ahaṁkārād rāga-yuktena cetasā

Previous action then becomes the seed of the senses one acquires. When each of the senses is thus activated by previous actions, it comes into being from out of the sense of ego (*ahaṁkāra*) as the mind is combined with various kinds of desire.

16. *śabda-rāgāc chotram asya jāyate bhāvitātmanaḥ*
rūpa-rāgāt tathā cakṣur ghrāṇaṁ gandha-cikīrṣayā

When the living being has begun its new existence, its sense of hearing arises because of the attachment to sound it carries with it. Similarly, the sense of sight arises from its attachment to forms and the sense of smell comes into being through its desire for pleasant aromas.

17. *sparśanebhyas tathā vāyuḥ prāṇāpāna-vyapāśrayaḥ*
vyānodānau samānaś ca pañcadhā deha-yāpanā

It is due to sensations of touch that the element of air appears in the body, making its abode in the *prāṇa* and *apāna* and in the *vyāna*, *udāna*, and *samāna*, the five airs that sustain life within the body.

18. *saṁjātair jāyate gātraiḥ karma-jair brahmaṇā vṛtaḥ*
duḥkhādyantair duḥkha-madhyair naraḥ śārīra-mānasaiḥ

Encased by Brahman, the living being then takes birth endowed with the limbs that develop in accordance with its previous actions. Thus at the beginning and end of life, and in the middle as well, a man must endure misery through his body and his mind.

19. *duḥkhaṁ vidyād upādānād abhimānāc ca vardhate*
tyāgāt tebhyo nirodhaḥ syān nirodha-jño vimucyate

One should understand that such misery comes from accepting existence in this world and increases as a result of one's sense of ego. When one abandons such conceptions there is an end of suffering, and one who comprehends the way to end suffering gains liberation.

20. *indriyāṇāṁ rajasy eva prabhava-pralayāv ubhau*
parīkṣya saṁcared vidvān yathāvac chāstra-cakṣuṣā

After observing both the activation and withdrawal of the senses that takes place within the domain of *rajas*, a wise man should conduct himself properly in accordance with the guidance of scriptures.

21. *jñānendriyāṇīndriyārthān nopasarpanty atarṣulam*
jñātaiś ca kāraṇair dehī na dehaṁ punar arhati

Even when the senses that acquire knowledge encounter the objects of the senses, they do not approach one who has no desire for such objects. When these causes of rebirth are properly understood, the embodied entity will never again acquire a body.

Śānti-parvan, Adhyāya 207

In the fifth chapter, the teacher returns to the subject of restricting desire and practising celibacy as he insists that this is what sets the highest aspirants apart from the rest. The chapter opens with a brief hierarchy of living beings, concluding with the view that a learned Brahmin who possesses full knowledge of the Veda is the highest of all. Verse 5 refers to there being two paths, which share many of the same characteristics. The meaning of this and the following verses is not entirely apparent, but it seems that what is being referred to here is the two paths of *pravṛtti*, adherence to the Vedic ritual, and *nivṛtti*, the way of renunciation. Both are considered admirable, but it is *brahmacarya*, the rigid vow of celibacy, which separates the highest aspirants from all others. And to practise this vow one must not only avoid sexual contact with women but entirely shun all forms of interaction, even through hearing and thinking about them.

From verse 15, the teacher begins to expound further on why celibacy is such an important part of the process by which spiritual perfection is achieved. Here perhaps we have an early indication of the Tantric ideas about the nature of the body that become such a prominent feature of the later Yoga teachings but are rarely encountered in the earlier works and are wholly absent from the *Bhagavad-gītā* and the *Yoga-sūtras*. In the midst of the network of veins running throughout the body is a major duct known as the *manovahā*, in which a man's semen is produced when sexual desires arise within the mind. It is because mental arousal is crucial to the production of semen that ejaculation can occur in the course of dreams. And here perhaps we again need to be aware of the context of this discourse in which a teacher is giving instruction on spiritual practice to a young man who is likely to be experiencing the consequences of sexual desire that are being described here. When such desires arise, one must undertake austere vows in order to master them and one may also attempt to move the bodily airs into the *manovahā* in order to prevent the movement of semen. But above all one must gain mastery over the inclinations of the mind and minimise the influence of *rajas* and *tamas*;

this is achieved by cultivating higher knowledge, which is the means by which spiritual perfection is achieved.

1. *gurur uvāca*
atropāyaṁ pravakṣyāmi yathāvac chāstra-cakṣuṣā
tad-vijñānāc caran prājñaḥ prāpnuyāt paramāṁ gatim

The teacher said: I will now explain the means by which this is achieved according to the guidance of scripture. By acting on the basis of scriptural knowledge a wise man can attain the highest goal.

2. *sarveṣām eva bhūtānāṁ puruṣaḥ śreṣṭha ucyate*
puruṣebhyo dvijān āhur dvijebhyo mantra-vādinaḥ

The human being is said to be the best of all living entities and amongst humans they say that the Brahmins are the best. And amongst Brahmins, the best are those who can recite the Vedic hymns.

3. *sarva-bhūta-viśiṣṭās te sarva-jñāḥ sarva-darśinaḥ*
brāhmaṇā veda-tattva-jñās tattvārtha-gati-niścayāḥ

The greatest of all living entities are those all-knowing, all-seeing Brahmins who comprehend the true meaning of the Vedas and have ascertained the goal that is the object of this teaching.

4. *netra-hīno yathā hy ekaḥ kṛcchrāṇi labhate 'dhvani*
jñāna-hīnas tathā loke tasmāj jñāna-vido 'dhikāḥ

A man who has no sense of sight encounters difficulties whilst travelling down a road alone. In the same way, a man devoid of knowledge encounters difficulties whilst travelling through this world. Therefore those who possess knowledge are superior persons.

5. *tāṁs tān upāsate dharmān dharma-kāmā yathāgamam*
na tv eṣām artha-sāmānyam antareṇa guṇān imān

Those who pursue the way of dharma dedicate themselves to various types of dharma according to the instruction of scripture. But these paths are not identical and differ in relation to the following characteristics.

6. *vāg-deha-manasāṁ śaucaṁ kṣamā satyaṁ dhṛtiḥ smṛtiḥ*
sarva-dharmeṣu dharma-jñā jñāpayanti guṇān imān

The teachers who properly understand the different forms of dharma all advocate the following attributes: purity of speech, body and mind, tolerance, truthfulness, determination, and understanding.

7. *yad idaṁ brahmaṇo rūpaṁ brahmacaryam iti smṛtam*
paraṁ tat sarva-bhūtebhyas tena yānti parāṁ gatim

But the practice of the vow of *brahmacarya* is known as the manifest form of Brahman. It is the highest expression of religious life for all living beings, for through this vow they attain the highest goal.

8. *liṅga-saṁyoga-hīnaṁ yac charīra-sparśa-varjitam*
śrotreṇa śravaṇaṁ caiva cakṣuṣā caiva darśanam

In the practice of *brahmacarya* there must be no sexual union and one must avoid contact with the body of a woman. One must also give up hearing pleasant sounds with the ears and beholding sights with the eyes.

9. *jihvayā rasanaṁ yac ca tad eva parivarjitam*
buddhyā ca vyavasāyena brahmacaryam akalmaṣam

Similarly, the enjoyment of tastes by the tongue must be completely avoided. Such unblemished practice of *brahmacarya* can only be performed with resolute intelligence.

10. *samyag vṛttir brahma-lokaṁ prāpnuyān madhyamaḥ surān*
dvijāgryo jāyate vidvān kanyasīṁ vṛttim āsthitaḥ

When this practice is strictly adhered to one attains the realm of Brahman and by moderate adherence one attains a position amongst the gods. A wise man who adheres to this practice even to a small degree is born as one of the foremost of the Brahmins.

11. *suduṣkaraṁ brahmacaryam upāyaṁ tatra me śṛṇu*
saṁpravṛttam udīrṇaṁ ca nigṛhṇīyād dvijo manaḥ

This vow of *brahmacarya* is extremely difficult to follow. Now hear from me the means by which this may be accomplished. A Brahmin must restrain his mind whenever it becomes active and when it is agitated.

12. *yoṣitāṁ na kathāḥ śrāvyā na nirīkṣyā nirambarāḥ*
kadācid darśanād āsāṁ durbalān āviśed rajaḥ

He must not listen to talk about women and should never look at women when they are undressed; whenever women are seen, passion enters the hearts of weak-minded men.

13. *rāgotpattau caret kṛcchram ahnas triḥ praviśed apaḥ*
magnaḥ svapne ca manasā trir japed aghamarṣaṇam

When such passion is aroused, he should undertake a *kṛcchra* vow involving painful austerity and enter water for three days. If such passion arises whilst he is dreaming, he should mentally recite three *aghamarṣaṇa* prayers.

14. *pāpmānaṁ nirdahed evam antar-bhūtaṁ rajo-mayam*
jñāna-yuktena manasā saṁtatena vicakṣaṇaḥ

In this way, the wise man should keep his mind constantly in touch with true knowledge and purge the sinful urges existing within himself that such passion arouses.

15. *kuṇapāmedhya-saṁyuktaṁ yadvad acchidra-bandhanam*
tadvad deha-gataṁ vidyād ātmānaṁ deha-bandhanam

The body and the stool passing through it exist together in a combination, without any division between them. It should be understood that the *ātman* that enters the body is similarly linked to that body with no apparent line of demarcation.

16. *vāta-pitta-kaphān raktaṁ tvaṅ māṁsaṁ snāyum asthi ca*
majjāṁ caiva sirājālais tarpayanti rasā nṛṇām

In the human body, liquids pass through the veins and replenish the bodily airs, bile, phlegm, blood, skin, flesh, sinew, bone, and marrow.

17. *daśa vidyād dhamanyo 'tra pañcendriya-guṇāvahāḥ*
yābhiḥ sūkṣmāḥ pratāyante dhamanyo 'nyāḥ sahasraśaḥ

You should know that there are ten ducts in the body that carry the qualities perceived by the five senses. Thousands of other smaller ducts spread out from these.

18. *evam etāḥ sirā-nadyo rasodā deha-sāgaram*
tarpayanti yathā-kālaṁ āpagā iva sāgaram

So these veins are like rivers bearing liquid to the bodily ocean, replenishing its different parts whenever it is required, exactly as rivers carry water to the sea.

19. *madhye ca hṛdayasyaikā sirā tv atra manovahā*
śukraṁ saṁkalpa-jaṁ nṝṇāṁ sarva-gātrair vimuñcati

In the midst of the body there is a single duct leading to the heart. This is the artery known as the *manovahā*. The semen that arises from sexual inclination in men flows into it from all parts of the body.

20. *sarva-gātra-pratāyinyas tasyā hy anugatāḥ sirāḥ*
netrayoḥ pratipadyante vahantyas taijasaṁ guṇam

Similar smaller ducts spread out from the *manovahā* to all parts of the body. Bearing the quality of heat throughout the body, these ducts reach the eyes as well.

21. *payasy antarhitaṁ sarpir yadvan nirmathyate khajaiḥ*
śukraṁ nirmathyate tadvad deha-saṁkalpa-jaiḥ khajaiḥ

The butter present within milk is extracted by the churning process. Similarly, semen is extracted by the internal churning caused by sexual desires in the body.

22. *svapne 'py evaṁ yathābhyeti manaḥ-saṁkalpa-jaṁ rajaḥ*
śukram asparśa-jaṁ dehāt sṛjanty asya manovahā

Hence even in dreams sexual arousal caused by mental desires manifests itself, and although there is no physical stimulation, the *manovahā* duct ejaculates semen from the body due to passion alone.

23. *maharṣir bhagavān atrir veda tac chukra-saṁbhavam*
tri-bījam indra-daivatyaṁ tasmād indriyam ucyate

It was Bhagavān Atri, the great *rishi*, who came to understand the way that semen is produced. Semen has three causes and Indra is the deity who controls this process. It is for this reason that the word '*indriya*' is used to refer to the senses.

24. *ye vai śukra-gatiṁ vidyur bhūta-saṁkara-kārikām*
virāgā dagdha-doṣās te nāpnuyur deha-saṁbhavam

Those who understand that unrestrained emission of semen gives rise to the merging of the different levels of society free themselves from passion and destroy the faults they possess. Such persons will never again receive a bodily form.

25. *guṇānāṁ sāmyam āgamya manasaiva manovaham*
deha-karma nudan prāṇān anta-kāle vimucyate

Using the power of the mind alone to bring the *guṇas* to a state of equilibrium and impelling the breaths into the *manovaha* duct, one who acts only to maintain the body can achieve liberation at the time of death.

26. *bhavitā manaso jñānaṁ mana eva pratāyate*
jyotiṣmad virajo divyam atra siddhaṁ mahātmanām

Knowledge will then take possession of the mind and the mind spreads its influence throughout one's existence, effulgent and now free from passion. This is the state of spiritual perfection attained by great persons.

27. *tasmāt tad avighātāya karma kuryād akalmaṣam*
rajas tamaś ca hitveha na tiryag-gatim āpnuyāt

So in order to overcome this obstacle one must act in a manner that is free from blemish. By thus removing the influence of *rajas* and *tamas* one will never be condemned to a lower form of life.

28. *taruṇādhigataṁ jñānaṁ jarā-durbalatāṁ gatam*
paripakva-buddhiḥ kālena ādatte mānasaṁ balam

The knowledge acquired in one's youth vanishes as the weakness of old age takes hold. But intelligence matured by time can reclaim the power of the mind.

29. *sudurgam iva panthānam atītya guṇa-bandhanam*
yadā paśyet tadā doṣān atītyāmṛtam aśnute

The path by which one breaks free from the bondage of the *guṇas* appears very hard to traverse. When a man recognises the faults that bind him, he can go beyond them and attain the state of immortality.

Śānti-parvan, Adhyāya 208

In Chapter 6, the teacher continues to lecture his disciple about the ideal lifestyle to be followed by a renunciant seeking the highest spiritual goals. Such a person should perceive the misery of worldly existence and therefore adopt a mood of indifference towards the objects of desire. Good action ensures good results and he should therefore act for the benefit of all beings whilst remaining silent and aloof. If he does speak to others it should only be with pleasing and truthful words and he should never speak under the influence of passion. The lower *guṇas* of *rajas* and *tamas* are to be shunned; he should undertake acts of austerity and eat only small amounts of food. The subject of food is revisited in verses 21 and 22 but before this there is a brief reference to the practice of Yoga, restraining the mind, fixing it on one point, withdrawing the senses back into the mind and thereby focusing on *īśvara*, which might refer to the *ātman* or, as this passage shows definite theistic tendencies, to Viṣṇu who is identified as the self of all beings. The final four verses of the chapter then provide an insight into the purpose behind this lifestyle of extreme renunciation. It is in order to develop the realised knowledge that dispels the ignorance that keeps all living beings in a state of bondage. Knowledge is the key to a higher state of being in which one attains what is referred to here as *brahma sanātanam*, the eternal Brahman.

1. *gurur uvāca*
duranteṣv indriyārtheṣu saktāḥ sīdanti jantavaḥ
ye tv asaktā mahātmānas te yānti paramāṁ gatim

The teacher said: Pursuit of the objects of the senses leads only to suffering. When living beings develop attachment for such objects they sink down to a lower state. But those great persons who are free from such attachment reach the highest goal.

2. *janma-mṛtyu-jarā-duḥkhair vyādhibhir manasaḥ klamaiḥ*
dṛṣṭvemaṁ saṁtataṁ lokaṁ ghaṭen mokṣāya buddhimān

Understanding that this world is filled with the miseries caused by birth, death, old age, diseases, and mental torments, an intelligent person should devote himself to the pursuit of liberation.

3. *vāṅ-manobhyāṁ śarīreṇa śuciḥ syād anahaṁkṛtaḥ*
praśānto jñānavān bhikṣur nirapekṣaś caret sukham

The religious mendicant (*bhikṣu*) must keep his words, thoughts, and body pure, and free himself from pride. At peace with the world, filled with wisdom, and free of desire, he should wander across the earth with joy in his heart.

4. *atha vā manasaḥ saṅgaṁ paśyed bhūtānukampayā*
atrāpy upekṣāṁ kurvīta jñātvā karma-phalaṁ jagat

And if he observes attachment growing within his mind due to feelings of compassion for other living beings, he should then develop a mood of indifference, understanding that this world is merely the result of previous actions.

5. *yat kṛtaṁ prāk śubhaṁ karma pāpaṁ vā tad upāśnute*
tasmāc chubāni karmāṇi kuryād vāg-buddhi-karmabhiḥ

The fortune that befalls one in life is determined by the righteous or wicked action one has previously performed. Therefore one should act righteously through one's words, thoughts, and deeds.

6. *ahiṁsā satya-vacanaṁ sarva-bhūteṣu cārjavam*
kṣamā caivāpramādaś ca yasyaite sa sukhī bhavet

This involves never harming others, speaking the truth, honesty in one's dealings with all living beings, tolerance, and vigilance. One who acts in this way becomes joyful.

7. *yaś cainaṁ paramaṁ dharmaṁ sarva-bhūta-sukhāvaham*
duḥkhān niḥsaraṇaṁ veda sa tattva-jñaḥ sukhī bhavet

This is the highest dharma, which involves bringing joy to all living beings and dispelling the miseries of this world. One who understands it as such has seen the truth and such a person will become joyful.

8. *tasmāt samāhitaṁ buddhyā mano bhūteṣu dhārayet*
nāpadhyāyen na spṛhayen nābaddhaṁ cintayed asat

Therefore when one focuses it on other living beings, one should control one's mind with the intellect. One should cultivate neither hatred nor attachment for them and one should never think of falsehoods or foolish ideas.

9. *avāg-yoga-prayogeṇa mano-jñaṁ sampravartate*
vivakṣatā vā sad-vākyaṁ dharmaṁ sūkṣmam avekṣatā
satyāṁ vācam ahiṁsrāṁ ca vaded anapavādinīm

It is by practising Yoga without speaking that the mind becomes filled with knowledge. If, however, a person is drawn towards speaking righteous words whilst adhering to a pure form of dharma, he should speak only words that are truthful, cause no pain, and are not critical of others.

10. *kalkāpetām aparuṣām anṛśaṁsām apaiśunām*
īdṛg alpaṁ ca vaktavyam avikṣiptena cetasā

Speech should be free from deceit, harshness, cruelty, and condemnation, and should be as concise as possible. One should speak only when one's mind is not disturbed.

11. *vāk-prabuddho hi saṁrāgād virāgād vyāhared yadi*
buddhyā hy anigṛhītena manasā karma tāmasam
rajo-bhūtair hi karaṇaiḥ karmaṇā pratipadyate

If a person brings forth words due to passion or hatred, with his mind unrestrained by the intellect, this is an action under the influence of *tamas*. Or it may arise due to action where the instigating factors are predominated by *rajas*.

12. *sa duḥkhaṁ prāpya loke 'smin narakāyopapadyate*
tasmān mano-vāk-śarīrair ācared dhairyam ātmanaḥ

Having gained only suffering in this world, he then passes on to hell. Therefore one should practise firm restraint of mind, speech, and body.

13. *prakīrṇa-meṣa-bhāro hi yadvad dhāryeta dasyubhiḥ*
pratilomāṁ diśaṁ buddhvā saṁsāram abuddhās tathā

Sheep that have strayed from the herd because they follow the wrong path become booty carried away by thieves. So it is with unintelligent persons as they traverse the cycle of rebirth.

14. *tān eva ca yathā dasyūn kṣiptvā gacchec chivāṁ diśam*
tathā rajas-tamaḥ-karmāṇy utsṛjya prāpnuyāt sukham

But if one evades these thieves one may then proceed along the proper route. Such is the lot of one who avoids actions based on *rajas* and *tamas* and thereby finds happiness.

15. *niḥsaṁdigdham anīho vai muktaḥ sarva-parigrahaiḥ*
vivikta-cārī laghv-āśī tapasvī niyatendriyaḥ

Such a person is free from doubt, is indifferent to the world, and is liberated from attachment to all possessions. He wanders alone, eating only small amounts, practising acts of austerity, with his senses completely controlled.

16. *jñāna-dagdha-parikleśaḥ prayoga-ratir ātmavān*
niṣpracāreṇa manasā paraṁ tad adhigacchati

Such a self-disciplined person burns away his suffering with the fire of knowledge and finds joy in applying himself to spiritual discipline. By keeping his mind fixed on one point, he attains the highest state.

17. *dhṛtimān ātmavān buddhiṁ nigṛhṇīyād asaṁśayam*
mano buddhyā nigṛhṇīyād viṣayān manasātmanaḥ

Without doubt, one who is resolute and self-controlled must master his intellect and then employ the intellect to subdue the mind. He may then use the mind to subdue his attraction for the objects of the senses.

18. *nigṛhītendriyasyāsya kurvāṇasya mano vaśe*
devatās tāḥ prakāśante hṛṣṭā yānti tam īśvaram

When one acts with his senses strictly under control and his mind thus restrained, those senses are then illuminated and joyfully transfer themselves to the *īśvara*.

19. *tābhiḥ saṁsakta-manaso brahma-vat saṁprakāśate*
etaiś cāpagataiḥ sarvair brahma-bhūyāya kalpate

When the mind is united with the senses, the nature of Brahman becomes manifest, and as the senses thus dwindle to nothing, he achieves the existence of Brahman.

20. *atha vā na pravarteta yoga-tantrair upakramet*
yena tantra-mayaṁ tantraṁ vṛttiḥ syāt tat tad ācaret

Or if he does not make progress in this way, he may proceed by means of the regulated practices of the Yoga system. He should adjust his lifestyle in line with these Yoga regulations and proceed in conducting himself in the appropriate manner.

21. *kaṇa-piṇyāka-kulmāṣa-śāka-yāvaka-saktavaḥ*
tathā mūla-phalaṁ bhaikṣaṁ paryāyeṇopayojayet

For his food he should partake of grains, sesame cakes, unripened corn, spinach, barley, flour, roots, and fruit obtained by begging.

22. *āhāraṁ niyataṁ caiva deśe kāle ca sāttvikam*
tat parīkṣyānuvarteta yat pravṛtty-anuvartakam

If the consumption of food is regulated in terms of place and time, then it is under the influence of *sattva*. Understanding this point, one should pursue the particular path one has adopted.

23. *pravṛttaṁ noparundheta śanair agnim ivendhayet*
jñānendhitaṁ tato jñānam arka-vat saṁprakāśate

One should not interrupt the gradual advancement of this spiritual discipline. Just as one gradually sparks a fire into life, so the fire of knowledge is lighted and such knowledge then spreads its illumination like the rising sun.

24. *jñānādhiṣṭhānam ajñānaṁ trīḷ lokān adhitiṣṭhati*
vijñānānugataṁ jñānam ajñānād apakṛṣyate

The ignorance that abides within knowledge dominates all three levels of the universe. The knowledge that arises from proper discrimination is destroyed by this ignorance.

25. *pṛthaktvāt saṁprayogāc ca nāsūyur veda śāśvatam*
sa tayor apavarga-jño vīta-rāgo vimucyate

Because of his false sense of separation and his false sense of unity, an envious person cannot comprehend that which is eternal. A person who knows how to divest himself of both these notions becomes free from passion and attains liberation.

26. *vayotīto jarā-mṛtyū jitvā brahma sanātanam*
amṛtaṁ tad avāpnoti yat tad akṣaram avyayam

He transcends the various stages of existence and having thus conquered old age and death, he then attains the eternal, immortal Brahman, which never decays and never changes.

Śānti-parvan, Adhyāya 209

In the seventh chapter, the teacher purports to continue his discussion on celibacy and renunciation but becomes rather distracted by the subject of dreams and how they come about. This begins from a concern that passions may arise whilst a celibate student is sleeping so that he becomes drawn towards sensuality in his dreams. The solution offered for this problem is simple but somewhat unsatisfactory: an aspiring renunciant should learn to abandon sleep altogether. From verse 4 onwards, the discussion turns towards the subject of dreaming. It is explained that when the senses become exhausted and cease to absorb sensations, the mind remains active and explores sensations that have been experienced previously. The impressions encountered in dreams may come from this or from previous lives and are a product of the influence of the *guṇas*. It is in this way that any object previously perceived by the senses may be encountered again in the dreaming state.

The course of the discussion turns once again from verse 13. Now we are told that beyond such mental states is the true self of all beings situated within a living being, the *sarva-bhūtātma-bhūta-sthaḥ* (verse 14). Realisation of this inner self requires great power which is acquired only through *tapas*, harsh acts of austerity. Here again we might detect a slightly unorthodox tendency within the treatise, which may reflect the personal views of an individual teacher. Throughout the *Guru-Śiṣya-Saṁvāda* we have seen an emphasis on celibacy, restraint, and renunciation that is unusually excessive in the context of the *Mokṣa-dharma-parvan* as a whole. And here again in the final verses of its seventh chapter we find *tapas* rather than knowledge or Yoga presented as the desired antithesis of *avidyā*, ignorance; Yoga is perhaps hinted at in verse 20, but it is no more than a slight indication that is not followed up with any direct instruction.

1. *gurur uvāca*
niṣkalmaṣaṁ brahmacaryam icchatā carituṁ sadā
nidrā sarvātmanā tyājyā svapna-doṣān avekṣatā

The teacher said: One who wishes to constantly observe a flawless vow of *brahmacarya* should utilise his entire being to abandon sleep, understanding the problems that occur whilst one is dreaming.

2. *svapne hi rajasā dehī tamasā cābhibhūyate*
dehāntaram ivāpannaś caraty apagata-smṛtiḥ

Whilst dreaming, the embodied entity is overwhelmed by the qualities of *rajas* and *tamas*. It then roams forth as if it had assumed a different bodily form, without any recollection of its previous existence.

3. *jñānābhyāsāj jāgarato jijñāsārtham anantaram*
vijñānābhiniveśāt tu jāgaraty aniśaṁ sadā

In his regulated pursuit of knowledge, the *brahmacārin* remains awake so that he may continue his endeavours for realisation without interruption. Indeed, because of his dedication to achieving such realisation he remains constantly awake without any sleep at all.

4. *atrāha ko nv ayaṁ bhāvaḥ svapne viṣaya-vān iva*
pralīnair indriyair dehī vartate deha-vān iva

Here one might ask, 'What is this state of existence when a person is dreaming and appears to be captivated by the objects of the senses? Whilst the senses are merged in sleep, the embodied entity continues its existence as if it still possessed a body.'

5. *atrocyate yathā hy etad veda yogeśvaro hariḥ*
tathaitad upapannārthaṁ varṇayanti maharṣayaḥ

And in reply it is stated that Hari, the Lord of Yoga, knows the answer to this and great *rishis* also declare that this explanation is the right one.

6. *indriyāṇāṁ śramāt svapnam āhuḥ sarva-gataṁ budhāḥ*
manasas tu pralīnatvāt tat tad āhur nidarśanam

Wise men say that dreams roam in all directions when the external senses become exhausted. They say that when the senses thus become dormant, various objects of perception enter the vision of the mind.

7. *kārya-vyāsakta-manasaḥ saṁkalpo jāgrato hy api*
yadvan mano-rathaiśvaryaṁ svapne tadvan mano-gatam

When a person is awake and has his mind focused on various actions, his desires are shaped by the strength of the attractions experienced by the mind. The same thing happens whilst he is dreaming as the mind follows whatever desires are aroused.

8. *saṁsārāṇām asaṁkhyānāṁ kāmātmā tad avāpnuyāt*
manasy antarhitaṁ sarvaṁ veda sottama-pūruṣaḥ

One whose heart is filled with desire receives impressions drawn from countless previous births, for the Supreme Soul is aware of everything that is concealed within the mind.

9. *guṇānām api yad yat tat karma jānāty upasthitam*
tat tac chaṁsanti bhūtāni mano yad bhāvitaṁ yathā

And whatever the form of action shaped by the *guṇas* he focuses attention upon is that which living beings are drawn to as the mind is affected accordingly.

10. *tatas tam upavartante guṇā rājasa-tāmasāḥ*
sāttviko vā yathā-yogam ānantarya-phalodayaḥ

So the qualities shaped by *rajas*, *tamas*, and *sattva* come before a living being as a result of the connection with actions previously performed. The results of each quality then appear to him in an unbroken succession.

11. *tataḥ paśyaty asaṁbaddhān vāta-pitta-kaphottarān*
rajas-tamo-bhavair bhāvais tad apy āhur duranvayam

In this state one perceives ideas that have no logical connection; thesere produced by the air, bile, and mucus in the body. These are the mental states generated by *rajas* and *tamas*. They say that this state of mind is hard to break free from.

12. *prasannair indriyair yad yat saṁkalpayati mānasam*
tat tat svapne 'py uparate mano-dṛṣṭir nirīkṣate

Whatever is fixed in the mind by the senses whilst their perceptions are clear, the mind's eye later perceives in dreams when the actual perception is finished.

13. *vyāpakaṁ sarva-bhūteṣu vartate 'pratighaṁ manaḥ*
manasy antarhitaṁ dvāraṁ deham āsthāya mānasam

The mind pervades all living beings and exists within them without restraint. Having assumed the mental body and traversed the gateway concealed within the mind,

14. *yat tat sad-asad-avyaktaṁ svapity asmin nidarśanam*
sarva-bhūtātma-bhūta-sthaṁ tad adhyātma-guṇaṁ viduḥ

One then enters a state of sleep that reveals the non-manifest conditions of being and non-being. They know that that which exists within the very self of all beings is of the quality of pure spirit.

15. *lipseta manasā yaś ca saṁkalpād aiśvaraṁ guṇam*
ātma-prabhāvāt taṁ vidyāt sarvā hy ātmani devatāḥ

And if due to continuing desire he wishes to acquire the attribute of exceptional mental strength, he must understand that this is to be derived from the power that resides within the *ātman*, for all the senses exist within the *ātman*.

16. *evaṁ hi tapasā yuktam arka-vat tamasaḥ param*
trai-lokya-prakṛtir dehī tapasā taṁ maheśvaram

This mental strength is absorbed through the practice of austerity. It is also through austerity that the embodied entity rises like the sun beyond this darkness. It gravitates towards the Supreme Deity, for it is the basis of the three worlds.

17. *tapo hy adhiṣṭhitaṁ devais tapo-ghnam asurais tamaḥ*
etad devāsurair guptaṁ tad āhur jñāna-lakṣaṇam

Austerity is the domain of the gods whilst the ignorance that destroys austerity is the domain of the *asuras*. And then there is that which is hidden from both the gods and the *asuras*. They say that this domain has knowledge as its attribute.

18. *sattvaṁ rajas tamaś ceti devāsura-guṇān viduḥ*
sattvaṁ deva-guṇaṁ vidyād itarāv āsurau guṇau

It is understood that *sattva*, *rajas*, and *tamas* are the qualities of existence for the gods and *asuras*. One should know *sattva* as the quality for the gods and the other two as the qualities for the *asuras*.

19. *brahma tat paramaṁ vedyam amṛtaṁ jyotir akṣaram*
ye vidur bhāvitātmānas te yānti paramāṁ gatim

Brahman is to be known as being beyond them all, the immortal light that never fades. Those who are absorbed in self-realisation comprehend Brahman and move on to the highest position.

20. *hetumac chakyam ākhyātum etāvaj jñāna-cakṣuṣā*
pratyāhāreṇa vā śakyam avyaktaṁ brahma veditum

Using reasoned arguments, it is possible to explain the subject to this extent through the vision that comes with knowledge. Or else one can comprehend Brahman, which is not manifest to sensory perception, by withdrawing one's senses from the world (*pratyārāra*).

Śānti-parvan, Adhyāya 210

In the eighth and final chapter of the *Guru-śiṣya-saṁvāda,* the teacher finally reaches the conclusion of his discourse by describing the ultimate goal of release from *saṁsāra*, the cycle of rebirth. This, however, does not occur until after verse 20; the chapter opens with an assertion of there being two paths, one of action, *pravṛtti*, and one of absolute renunciation, *nivṛtti*. This is a common theme found throughout the *Mahābhārata* and is used as a means by which teachers can emphasise renunciation of the world whilst at the same time not denying the value and efficacy of the Vedic ritual. We then have a brief passage of theistic Sāṁkhya, which seems rather similar to the ideas encountered in the final five verses of the fifteenth chapter of the *Bhagavad-gītā*, which in turn appear to be derived from the *Śvetāśvatara Upaniṣad.* Here we are informed that there are three eternal principles – matter, spirit, and the supreme spirit – which in the context of the theistic orientation of this passage must be taken as referring to Viṣṇu, the Supreme Deity (verses 6–7). The teacher then reverts to a more conventional form of Sāṁkhya discourse by describing the differences between *avyakta* and *puruṣa*, matter and spirit, and then explaining how *puruṣa* assumes a false identity through its association with matter. Hence one must identify the spiritual *puruṣa*, which is enshrouded by the three *guṇas* even though it has no real relationship with them. From verse 14, the *guru* reverts to one of the main themes of the earlier chapters by insisting on the power of *tapas* in overcoming obstacles. The reference to *tapas* of body and mind is interesting and has certain similarities to a passage in the *Bhagavad-gītā* that deals with the same subject (17.14–16). Ultimately, though, the teacher returns to the more obvious concerns of his pupil by asserting that *tapas* is reflected in one's eating habits; hence one must eat only small amounts.

In the passage's final teachings on liberation from rebirth we find a return to the Vaiṣṇava orientation that has been an ongoing theme throughout the passage as a whole. This in itself is interesting as it reminds us once again of the close ties between early Vaiṣṇavism and the Yoga systems, which can also be observed in the ideas of Pāñcarātric texts such as the *Jayākhya Saṁhitā* and the *Ahirbudhnya Saṁhitā*. Here the Yoga system is represented as being a technique by which those who have attained a state of purity are able to absorb their minds in concentration on the Supreme Deity. If they are able to achieve this state at the time of death, they then transcend this world and attain the supreme destination. It is spiritual knowledge and freedom from desire that enable them to break free from this world, and the level of transcendence attained is dependent upon the depth of the knowledge they have come to achieve. The highest level is that of Viṣṇu who is situated within the heart of the *yogin*; and when Viṣṇu is reached one never returns to this world or to rebirth. It is desire that perpetuates our present existence and hence liberation through knowledge can come only by conquering desire in the manner that the teacher has been emphasising so steadfastly throughout the teachings he has given to his pupil.

1. *gurur uvāca*
na sa veda paraṁ dharmaṁ yo na veda catuṣṭayam
vyaktāvyakte ca yat tattvaṁ saṁprāptaṁ paramārṣiṇā

The teacher said: One who does not first comprehend the fourfold truth cannot understand the highest dharma. Nor can such a person understand the truth about the manifest and the non-manifest, as revealed by the supreme *rishi*.

2. *vyaktaṁ mṛtyu-mukhaṁ vidyād avyaktam amṛtaṁ padam*
pravṛtti-lakṣaṇaṁ dharmam ṛṣir nārāyaṇo 'bravīt

One should understand the manifest to be whatever is subject to death and the non-manifest as the domain of immortality. Nārāyaṇa Rishi gave instructions about the form of dharma that involves performance of ritual acts (*pravṛtti*).

3. *atraivāvasthitaṁ sarvaṁ trai-lokyaṁ sa-carācaram*
nivṛtti-lakṣaṇaṁ dharmaṁ avyaktaṁ brahma śāśvatam

Everything within this threefold creation with its moving and stationary beings exists in relation to this form of dharma. The dharma that involves the renunciation of acts (*nivṛtti*) exists in relation to Brahman, which is eternal and is not manifest.

4. *pravṛtti-lakṣaṇaṁ dharmaṁ prajāpatir athābravīt*
pravṛttiḥ punar āvṛttir nivṛttiḥ paramā gatiḥ

It was Prajāpati who gave instructions on the *pravṛtti* dharma that involves ritual acts. This *pravṛtti* dharma leads to rebirth but the dharma of renunciation, *nivṛtti*, leads to the highest destination.

5. *tāṁ gatiṁ paramām eti nivṛtti-paramo muniḥ*
jñāna-tattva-paro nityaṁ śubhāśubha-nidarśakaḥ

The sage who dedicates himself entirely to the path of *nivṛtti* attains that highest destination. Constantly devoted to knowledge and truth, he is able to perceive what is pure and also what is impure.

6. *tad evam etau vijñeyāv avyakta-puruṣāv ubhau*
avyakta-puruṣābhyāṁ tu yat syād anyan mahattaram

What this means is that both matter in its non-manifest state (*avyakta*) and *puruṣa* may be comprehended. But that which is distinct from both *avyakta* and *puruṣa* is the highest principle.

7. *taṁ viśeṣam avekṣeta viśeṣeṇa vicakṣaṇaḥ*
anādy-antāv ubhāv etāv aliṅgau cāpy ubhāv api

It is by his power of discrimination that the man of wisdom should identify that principle that is superior to them. Both *avyakta* and *puruṣa* have no beginning or end, and neither of them has any distinguishing qualities.

8. *ubhau nityau sūkṣmatarau mahadbhyaś ca mahattarau*
sāmānyam etad ubhayor evaṁ hy anyad viśeṣaṇam

Both are eternal, they are both minute in size and also greater than the greatest objects. These are the qualities common to both; I shall now describe the distinctive features that separate them.

9. *prakṛtyā sarga-dharmiṇyā tathā tri-vidha-sattvayā*
viparītam ato vidyāt kṣetrajñasya ca lakṣaṇam

The nature of *prakṛti* is to create, and its existence has three qualities. One should understand that the nature of the soul, the *kṣetrajña*, is quite different from that of *prakṛti.*

10. *prakṛteś ca vikārāṇāṁ draṣṭāram aguṇānvitam*
agrāhyau puruṣāv etāv aliṅgatvād asaṁhitau

Unaffected by these three qualities, the self is merely the observer of the transformations that matter undergoes. The two *puruṣas* within the body remain distinct from all aspects of matter and because they are devoid of qualities they cannot be perceived.

11. *saṁyoga-lakṣaṇotpattiḥ karma-jā gṛhyate yayā*
karaṇaiḥ karma-nirvṛttaiḥ kartā yad yad viceṣṭate
kīrtyate śabda-saṁjñābhiḥ ko 'ham eṣo 'py asāv iti

The self is seized by the development of different combinations of qualities arising from previous actions. According to the types of action the performer undertakes, in terms of the exertions he makes and the actions he completes, he is identified by a specific title when questions such as 'Who am I? Who is this?' and 'Who are these two?' are asked.

12. *uṣṇīṣavān yathā vastrais tribhir bhavati saṁvṛtaḥ*
saṁvṛto 'yaṁ tathā dehī sattva-rājasa-tāmasaiḥ

A person who wears a turban has three pieces of cloth wrapped around him. In the same way, the embodied being has the three qualities known as *sattva*, *rajas*, and *tamas* wrapped around it.

13. *tasmāc catuṣṭayaṁ vedyaṁ etair hetubhir ācitam*
yathā-saṁjño hy ayaṁ samyag anta-kāle na muhyati

This then is the fourfold truth that one must comprehend, using the explanations given here to understand it. To the extent that this subject has been properly absorbed, one will not be bewildered at the time of death.

14. *śriyaṁ divyām abhiprepsur brahma vāṅ-manasā śuciḥ*
śārīrair niyamair ugraiś caren niṣkalmaṣaṁ tapaḥ

One who is desirous of attaining the spiritual riches of Brahman must practise flawless vows of austerity, with his speech and mind kept pure and his bodily passions strictly controlled.

15. *trailokyaṁ tapasā vyāptam antar-bhūtena bhāsvatā*
sūryaś ca candramāś caiva bhāsatas tapasā divi

The threefold universe is pervaded by the energy of austerity, for it exists within all things, spreading its illumination. In the heavens above, both the sun and the moon become luminous through the energy of austerity.

16. *pratāpas tapaso jñānaṁ loke saṁśabditaṁ tapaḥ*
rajas-tamo-ghnaṁ yat karma tapasas tat sva-lakṣaṇam

Knowledge is the power that energises austerity. Austerity is glorified throughout the world. Where an action has the power to dispel the influence of *rajas* and *tamas* then it possesses the characteristic mark of austerity.

17. *brahmacaryam ahiṁsā ca śārīraṁ tapa ucyate*
vāṅ-mano-niyamaḥ sāmyaṁ mānasaṁ tapa ucyate

Celibacy and not harming others represent bodily austerity whilst control of one's speech and thoughts and being equal to all represent the austerity of the mind.

18. *vidhi-jñebhyo dvijātibhyo grāhyam annaṁ viśiṣyate*
āhāra-niyamenāsya pāpmā naśyati rājasaḥ

The best type of food is that which is received from Brahmins conversant with the proper rules of conduct. By regulating one's consumption of food, the sinful inclinations arising from *rajas* are dispelled.

19. *vaimanasyaṁ ca viṣaye yānty asya karaṇāni ca*
tasmāt tanmātram ādadyād yāvad atra prayojanam

Furthermore, each of the active senses will then enter a state of indifference towards its object of enjoyment. So one must accept only the small amount of food necessary to sustain one's life.

20. *anta-kāle vayotkarṣāc chanaiḥ kuryād anāturaḥ*
evaṁ yuktena manasā jñānaṁ tad upapadyate

At the end of one's life, remaining free of despair, one should continue with one's practice by gradually increasing one's mental strength. By engaging the mind in this way one at last attains a state of knowledge.

21. *rajasā cāpyayaṁ dehī deha-vāñ śabda-vac caret*
kāryair avyāhata-matir vairāgyāt prakṛtau sthitaḥ
ā dehād apramādāc ca dehāntād vipramucyate

Devoid of passion but still possessing a material form, the embodied being then roams free like sound passing through space. With his mental perception no longer impeded by bodily activities, he becomes situated within *prakṛti* because of his indifference to the created world. And because of his diligent practice in life he is liberated from the clutches of death after departing from the present body.

22. *hetu-yuktaḥ sadotsargo bhūtānāṁ pralayas tathā*
para-pratyaya-sarge tu niyataṁ nātivartate

The birth and disappearance of living beings are always governed by strict rules of causality. But at this point this control over one's existence no longer prevails.

23. *bhavānta-prabhava-prajñā āsate ye viparyayam*
dhṛtyā dehān dhārayanto buddhi-saṁkṣipta-mānasāḥ
sthānebhyo dhvaṁsamānāś ca sūkṣmatvāt tān upāsate

Those who understand the origin of birth and death remain intent on moving in the opposite direction. Sustaining their bodies with committed resolve, they use their intellect to control the mind. Moving away from the gross elements, they fix their attention on other things because of their subtle nature.

24. *yathāgamaṁ ca tat sarvaṁ buddhyā tan naiva budhyate*
dehāntaṁ kaścid anvāste bhāvitātmā nirāśrayaḥ
yukto dhāraṇayā kaścit sattāṁ kecid upāsate

One person concludes that the truth cannot be perceived by the intellect and accepts the teachings of scripture in full. Remaining pure at heart, he wanders without any abode until death comes upon him. Another person engages in Yoga practice with intense concentration, whilst others contemplate the Primordial Essence.

25. *abhyasyanti paraṁ devaṁ vidyut-saṁśabditākṣaram*
anta-kāle hy upāsannās tapasā dagdha-kilbiṣāḥ

At the end, when they are approaching death, with their sins destroyed by acts of austerity, they fix their concentration on the Supreme Deity who is described as a lightning flash that does not fade.

26. *sarva ete mahātmāno gacchanti paramāṁ gatim*
sūkṣmaṁ viśeṣaṇaṁ teṣām avekṣec chāstra-cakṣuṣā

All such great persons attain the highest goal. With the vision of scriptural insight, one should recognise the subtle distinctions that exist between them.

27. *dehaṁ tu paramaṁ vidyād vimuktam aparigraham*
antarikṣād anyataraṁ dhāraṇāsakta-mānasam

And one should also understand this higher bodily form that is free from this world and carries no possessions with it. It is distinct from the space through which it roams with its mind engaged in concentration.

28. *martya-lokād vimucyante vidyā-saṁyukta-mānasāḥ*
brahma-bhūtā virajasas tato yānti parāṁ gatim

With their minds thus absorbed in wisdom, they are liberated from this mortal world and exist on the level of Brahman, free from worldly passions. They then move on to the highest position.

29. *kaṣāya-varjitaṁ jñānaṁ yeṣām utpadyate 'calam*
te yānti paramāḷ lokān viśudhyanto yathā-balam

Persons who acquire this unwavering knowledge that is free of all contamination attain a state of purity. According to the depth of the knowledge they achieve, they then attain the higher worlds.

30. *bhagavantam ajaṁ divyaṁ viṣṇum avyakta-saṁjñitam*
bhāvena yānti śuddhā ye jñāna-tṛptā nirāśiṣaḥ

Through their elevated disposition, those who are pure at heart, satisfied by knowledge alone, and free from desires, approach that most glorious Deity, the unborn, divine Viṣṇu who is known as the one who is not manifest in this world.

31. *jñātvātma-sthaṁ hariṁ caiva nivartante na te 'vyayāḥ*
prāpya tat paramaṁ sthānaṁ modante 'kṣaram avyayam

And when they have fully realised the existence of Hari situated within their own self, those changeless beings never again return to this world. After attaining the topmost stage of existence, they then find joy in that changeless, unfading state of being.

32. *etāvad etad vijñānam etad asti ca nāsti ca*
tṛṣṇā-baddhaṁ jagat sarvaṁ cakra-vat parivartate

This knowledge consists of understanding that one thing truly exists and another thing does not. Bound by the ropes of desire, the entire world rotates through its cycle like a wheel.

33. *bisa-tantur yathaivāyam anta-sthaḥ sarvato bise*
tṛṣṇā-tantur anādy-antas tathā deha-gataḥ sadā

This lotus plant consists of fibres that spread everywhere throughout the lotus. In the same way, the fibre of desire is always present throughout the body with neither beginning nor end.

34. *sūcyā sūtraṁ yathā vastre saṁsārayati vāyakaḥ*
tadvat saṁsāra-sūtraṁ hi tṛṣṇā-sūcyā nibadhyate

The tailor passes the thread in and out of the cloth with his needle. In the same way, the thread of *saṁsāra* is woven in and out by the needle of desire.

35. *vikāraṁ prakṛtiṁ caiva puruṣaṁ ca sanātanam*
yo yathāvad vijānāti sa vitṛṣṇo vimucyate

One who properly understands the transformations of *prakṛti* and the eternally existing *puruṣa* becomes free from desire and is liberated from this world.

36. *prakāśaṁ bhagavān etad ṛṣir nārāyaṇo 'mṛtam*
bhūtānām anukampārthaṁ jagāda jagato hitam

Out of his compassion for all living beings and for the benefit of the world, the blessed Nārāyaṇa Rishi proclaimed this immortal wisdom for all to hear.

The Pañcaśikha-Janaka-Saṁvāda

Śānti-parvan, Adhyāya 211–212

The *Pañcaśikha-Janaka-Saṁvāda*, the conversation between Pañcaśikha and Janaka, is a fascinating passage of the *Mahābhārata*, though for historical rather than philosophical reasons. Its two chapters of almost equal length are very different in content; they may in fact have originally existed as distinct treatises which the redactor has brought together simply because they share the same two principal participants. Some confirmation of this view might be seen in Bhīṣma's statement that opens the second chapter, possibly included so as to provide a link between the two. The historical interest lies in the manner in which this relatively early piece establishes the succession of Sāṁkhya teachers and indicates their interaction with non-orthodox teachers. As is universally acknowledged, it is Kapila who is the founder of the Sāṁkhya system – but here we are informed that this preeminent position was later taken by Āsuri and then by Pañcaśikha, who is here said to be the disciple and adopted son of Āsuri. After this preliminary revelation about the background of Pañcaśikha as a leading exponent of the Sāṁkhya system, the focus of the discussion switches to the court of King Janaka, a setting that is familiar both from the *Upaniṣads* and from other passages of the *Mahābhārata*. Here we are told of how Janaka had fallen under the influence of various false teachers; this representation must surely reflect a historical context in which various kings and rulers of India were lured away from Vedic philosophy and practice by exponents of the Buddhist, Jain, and other non-orthodox creeds. The discussion here includes both the views of these false teachers and the refutation given to their ideas, although at times it is not entirely clear whose views are being represented and where the refutation begins.

The conclusion of this first chapter is exactly as one might anticipate, with Janaka accepting the shortcomings of his false teachers and being drawn to the orthodox views of Pañcaśikha who is shown to be a performer of Vedic ritual and one who accepts the truth of revealed scripture. Despite his apparent conversion, however, Janaka is still beset by the doubts that have been sown in his mind by his prior dalliance with false doctrines, and Pañcaśikha is therefore required to explain to him the essential precepts of Sāṁkhya teachings. Thus the second part of the treatise takes the form of a discourse on Sāṁkhya although it is considerably removed from the philosophy's classical form, focusing almost exclusively on the means by which perception takes place through the mind and senses. The conclusion, however, is archetypal Sāṁkhya with the emphasis firmly placed on the transcendent nature of the true self and the possibility of liberation from rebirth when knowledge of one's true identity is properly realised. To my mind, the most interesting features of this piece are, firstly, the way in which it outlines the relationship between the principal teachers of Sāṁkhya and, secondly, the manner in which an early text of this type seeks to represent what may well be the Buddhist position on the nature of rebirth whilst showing how the more orthodox followers of the Veda sought to refute this position. Almost certainly, one gains here some insight into the historical development of Indian religious thought, with different teachers and schools of philosophy competing against one another in staged debates and perhaps more especially seeking to gain the support and patronage granted by the rulers of the age. In this piece we are shown a triumph of orthodoxy, but of course the presentation here must be highly tendentious and no doubt the Buddhists had a very different perspective.

Śānti-parvan, Adhyāya 211

As noted above, the first of the *Pañcaśikha-Janaka-Saṁvāda*'s two chapters begins with a brief explanation of the line of progression amongst the major teachers of early Sāṁkhya. The question posed by Yudhiṣṭhira that prompts this discussion is somewhat unusual as it relates not to a matter of doctrine but is asked about a particular person and the spiritual path he followed, namely Janaka the King of Mithilā. Janaka of Mithilā is well known from a variety of different sources, most notably perhaps the *Rāmāyaṇa* of Vālmīki where he appears as the father of Sītā, the wife of Rāma. The earliest reference to Janaka, however, is probably in the *Bṛhadāraṇyaka Upaniṣad* in which he receives instruction from the famous sage Yājñavalkya, and at whose court Yājñavalkya emerges victorious from a debate between learned scholars. It may well be this Upaniṣadic context that has provided the setting for the present treatise as the situation is somewhat similar, with a teacher of true wisdom triumphing over his less insightful adversaries.

Bhīṣma begins his response to Yudhiṣṭhira's question by describing how the righteous Janaka was a seeker of truth whose mind had become bewildered due to the instruction given him by a hundred teachers of false religion, *pāṣaṇḍa-vādins*. It is not clear exactly who these *ācāryas* are, although it seems apparent from the later discussion that it is the sceptical logicians and perhaps the purveyors of Buddhist doctrine that the author of the *Pañcaśikha-Janaka-Saṁvāda* has in mind. This is the situation that Pañcaśikha encounters when he arrives in Mithilā and comes into Janaka's presence. At this point the discourse changes direction for a time in order to provide information as to exactly who this Pañcaśikha was. He is first referred to as a *kāpileya*, an adherent of the doctrines of Kapila, but the presentation becomes somewhat confused: there seems to be some suggestion that Pañcaśikha was in some way identical to that Kapila but at other times the name Kapila seems to be applied to him. One possible solution could be that the title of 'Kapila' was given to the head of the followers of the Sāṁkhya system, just as the title of Śaṅkarācārya is given to the heads of the *maths* founded by Ādi Śaṅkarācārya. In any case, these verses appear to be a little disjointed and perhaps corrupted so that it is not always apparent as to whether it is Pañcaśikha or the original Kapila who is being referred to. A further interesting point is that in verse 9 the original Kapila is referred to as Prajāpati, indicating that the idea that he was an *avatāra*, as is frequently mentioned in the *Purāṇas*, was current from an early date. We are then told that a teacher of religion named Āsuri succeeded Kapila as the leader of the latter's religious community, although he may not have been a direct disciple of Kapila himself. Pañcaśikha is then identified as the foremost disciple of Āsuri and his adopted son who was breastfed by the mother of the household; somewhat confusingly this woman is named as Kapilā, thereby suggesting another reason as to why Pañcaśikha is known as Kāpileya.

After thus locating Pañcaśikha in the line of great teachers of the Sāṁkhya system, the account returns to the court of Janaka and Pañcaśikha's encounter with the hundred *pāṣaṇḍa-vādins*. One significant point to note here is that both Janaka and Pañcaśikha are located within the purview of Vedic orthodoxy. Janaka is referred to in verse 5 as *āgama-stha*, fixed on the *Āgamas* or Vedas, whilst verses 10 and 12 indicate that both Āsuri and Pañcaśikha were performers of the Vedic ritual as well as being exponents of the true philosophy. This point is surely significant in terms of both the orthodox orientation of this passage and also in indicating the degree of ideological hostility existing between those who accepted and those who denied the authority of the Vedic revelation.

The teaching that Pañcaśikha initially presents to Janaka is a fairly simple doctrine of renunciation and world indifference, which we find in verses 20 and 21, but then verses 22 to 30 seem to represent the views of some of the *pāṣaṇḍa-vādins* although there is no overt statement that this is the case. Here one might detect some of the teachings of the Buddhists, and most notably the doctrine of *anātman*, but it seems more likely that the speaker is simply an adherent of a rationalist school of thought, which holds that direct perception must be the preeminent source of knowledge. Thus we find a forthright dismissal of the notion of a transcendent soul existing within the body, a concept fundamental to the Sāṁkhya doctrines of Kapila and his successors. Essentially the argument is that the notion of a soul or *ātman* cannot be accepted because no such entity can be identified by means of direct perception, the *pratyakṣa-pramāṇa*, and the other two accepted sources of knowledge, scripture and inference (the *śabda-* and *anumāna-pramāṇas*) are dismissed as being inferior. Scripture can only be taken as a valid source of knowledge where it is in harmony with perception whilst inference is of no use in this case because no meaningful comparison can be made between an eternal and a non-eternal entity.

From verse 31 we can detect the introduction of another school of thought, which may indeed be a reference to Buddhist teachings. The word *kecid* in verse 31 would seem to indicate that we now have the opinion of another group of teachers who accept the notion of rebirth but not perhaps the idea of the *ātman*, for in their view each new existence comes into being from the previous bodily form at the time of its destruction. This may be a reference to the Buddhist doctrine of *anātman* (no soul), with the passage beginning from verse 34 a refutation of this doctrine. This again is interesting, for I think it might be possible to identify the arguments here as representing the orthodox repost to the Buddhist critique of conventional Upaniṣadic wisdom. Essentially the question raised in these verses is whether there can be a viable doctrine of rebirth without the belief in a transcendent *ātman* that moves from one body to another. The point made is a relatively simple one. If there is no *ātman* then the being that experiences the results of actions performed in a previous life is a different entity to the performer of the action. In that case why should one be concerned about the future karma accruing from action and why should one perform any kind of charity or ritual to ensure future good fortune when the experiencer of the result will be a being different to oneself as the performer. Moreover, if rebirth is understood as a constant chain of causality without any spiritual component, then as with anything material there would be gradual decline and decay and hence such a process would eventually come to an end through natural progression.

This refutation appears to end at verse 41 as the final verses of the chapter conclude with a denial of the value of all such speculative systems of thought. They simply confuse the mind of the bewildered seeker and bestow no benefit whatsoever. The only meaningful truth one has to realise is that this body consists simply of the primary elements, and on the basis of this realisation one should develop a mood of renunciation in one's attitude towards the world. Hence if my reading is correct we can divide the speeches of this chapter as follows: verses 22 to 30 are the ideas of a sceptical rationalist who insists that nothing can be accepted as true unless it is subject to direct perception; verses 31 to 33 contain the view of other teachers who like the Buddhists accept the phenomenon of rebirth but not the notion of a transcendent soul; and verses 34 to 41 contain Pañcaśikha's refutation of this latter view on the grounds that it is wholly illogical to believe in rebirth but not in the *ātman*.

1. *yudhiṣṭhira uvāca*
kena vṛttena vṛtta-jño janako mithilādhipaḥ
jagāma mokṣaṁ dharma-jño bhogān utsṛjya mānuṣān

Yudhiṣṭhira said: Janaka, the King of Mithilā, understood both proper conduct and dharma. After giving up the pleasures of human existence what way of life did he adopt in order to pursue the goal of liberation?

2. *bhīṣma uvāca*
atrāpy udāharantīmam itihāsaṁ purātanam
yena vṛttena vṛtta-jñaḥ sa jagāma mahat sukham

Bhīṣma said: Janaka certainly understood proper conduct. Concerning this point, they recount this ancient history about the way of life he adopted when he pursued that highest form of happiness.

3. *janako jana-devas tu mithilāyāṁ janādhipaḥ*
aurdhva-dehika-dharmāṇām āsīd yukto vicintane

There was a king named Janaka Janadeva who was the ruler of the city of Mithilā. He used to absorb his mind in contemplating the different forms of dharma that focused on the afterlife.

4. *tasya sma śatam ācāryā vasanti satataṁ gṛhe*
darśayantaḥ pṛthag dharmān nānā pāṣaṇḍa-vādinaḥ

There were always a hundred teachers of religion residing in his house, revealing to him many different forms of dharma and advocating a variety of false doctrines.

5. *sa teṣāṁ pretya-bhāve ca pretya-jātau viniścaye*
āgama-sthaḥ sa bhūyiṣṭhaṁ ātma-tattve na tuṣyati

He sought a conclusion from them concerning one's existence after death and the nature of rebirth after death. But because he adhered to the teachings of the Veda, he was generally dissatisfied by their ideas on the nature of the *ātman*.

6. *tatra pañcaśikho nāma kāpileyo mahā-muniḥ*
paridhāvan mahīṁ kṛtsnāṁ jagāma mithilām api

There was a renowned sage named Pañcaśikha who was a follower of the teachings of Kapila. In the course of his wanderings throughout the world he eventually arrived at the city of Mithilā.

7. *sarva-saṁnyāsa-dharmāṇāṁ tattva-jñāna-viniścaye*
su-paryavasitārthaś ca nirdvaṁdvo naṣṭa-saṁśayaḥ

He had reached a final conclusion in ascertaining a true understanding of all the different forms of dharma that emphasise renunciation of the world. Thus he existed beyond the dualities of life and was free from doubt.

8. *ṛṣīṇām āhur ekaṁ yaṁ kāmād avasitaṁ nṛṣu*
śāśvataṁ sukham atyantam anvicchan sa sudurlabham

They speak of him as the one amongst the *rishis* who had broken free from the usual desires that exist amongst men. Instead he dedicated his life to gaining the eternal, endless joy that is so hard to attain.

9. *yam āhuḥ kapilaṁ sāṁkhyāḥ paramarṣiṁ prajāpatim*
sa manye tena rūpeṇa vismāpayati hi svayam

I think that he caused astonishment by the form he assumed which was that of the one whom the followers of Sāṁkhya speak of as Kapila, the great *rishi* who is indeed Prajāpati.

10. *āsureḥ prathamaṁ śiṣyaṁ yam āhuś cira-jīvinam*
pañca-srotasi yaḥ satram āste varṣa-sahasrikam

They say that he was the foremost disciple of Āsuri and that he lived for an incredible length of time. In the land of the five rivers, he performed a *satra* sacrifice that continued for a thousand years.

11. *taṁ samāsīnam āgamya maṇḍalaṁ kāpilaṁ mahat*
puruṣāvastham avyaktaṁ param arthaṁ nibodhayat

Approaching a large assembly of the followers of Kapila who had gathered together, Āsuri had instructed them about the supreme object of knowledge, which is the true nature of the *puruṣa* beyond the perception of the senses.

12. *iṣṭi-satreṇa saṁsiddho bhūyaś ca tapasā muniḥ*
kṣetra-kṣetrajñayor vyaktiṁ bubudhe deva-darśanaḥ

He had attained a state of perfect enlightenment by performing the *iṣṭi* and *satra* sacrifices and by undertaking acts of austerity. He was able to perceive the divine, and he understood the reality of both *kṣetra* and *kṣetrajña*, the body and the soul.

13. *yat tad ekākṣaraṁ brahma nānā-rūpaṁ pradṛśyate*
āsurir maṇḍale tasmin pratipede tad avyayam

In the midst of that gathering, Āsuri began to speak about the changeless Brahman, the one principle that never decays and which is perceived in an infinitude of different forms.

14. *tasya pañcaśikhaḥ śiṣyo mānuṣyā payasā bhṛtaḥ*
brāhmaṇī kapilā nāma kācid āsīt kuṭumbinī

Pañcaśikha became his disciple and had his belly filled with human milk. A certain Brahmin woman named Kapilā was the mother of the *guru*'s household.

15. *tasyāḥ putratvam āgamya striyāḥ sa pibati stanau*
tataḥ sa kāpileyatvaṁ lebhe buddhiṁ ca naiṣṭhikīm

After becoming her adopted son, he drank milk from her breast. So it was that he attained the status of Kapila and gained a conclusive understanding of the truth.

16. *etan me bhagavān āha kāpileyāya sambhavam*
tasya tat kāpileyatvaṁ sarva-vittvam anuttamam

It was the Lord himself who told me about how Pañcaśikha became the son of Kapilā, about his attaining the status of Kapila, and about his supreme understanding of all things.

17. *sāmānyaṁ kapilo jñātvā dharma-jñānām anuttamam*
upetya śatam ācāryān mohayāmāsa hetubhiḥ

This new Kapila understood with equal perfection the teachings of all those who claimed to possess a knowledge of dharma. Coming before those one hundred teachers, he perplexed them all with his reasoned arguments.

18. *janakas tv abhisaṁraktaḥ kāpileyānudarśanāt*
utsṛjya śatam ācāryān pṛṣṭhato 'nujagāma tam

After hearing the discourse of that disciple of Kapila, Janaka became intensely devoted to him. Abandoning his hundred teachers, he then became a devoted follower of Pañcaśikha.

19. *tasmai parama-kalyāya praṇatāya ca dharmataḥ*
abravīt paramaṁ mokṣaṁ yat tat sāṁkhyaṁ vidhīyate

Being submissive and devoted to dharma, Janaka was a suitable person to receive instructions. Therefore Pañcaśikha taught him about the highest path to liberation from rebirth, that which is known as the Sāṁkhya.

20. *jāti-nirvedam uktvā hi karma-nirvedam abravīt*
karma-nirvedam uktvā ca sarva-nirvedam abravīt

He first taught him indifference towards birth and status, and then indifference towards ritual acts. And after teaching indifference towards rituals, he then taught him complete indifference towards all things.

21. *yad arthaṁ karma-saṁsargaḥ karmaṇāṁ ca phalodayaḥ*
tad anāśvāsikaṁ moghaṁ vināśi calam adhruvam

He explained the reason behind ritual actions and the results gained from them, insisting that one can have no confidence in such results and that they are ultimately worthless, subject to destruction, constantly changing, and uncertain.

22. *dṛśyamāne vināśe ca pratyakṣe loka-sākṣike*
āgamāt param astīti bruvann api parājitaḥ

'The destruction of a living entity is apparent to the vision of the world. Even though it is asserted on the basis of scripture that there is life beyond death, this opinion can be defeated by rational argument.

23. *anātmā hy ātmano mṛtyuḥ kleśo mṛtyur jarāmayaḥ*
ātmānaṁ manyate mohāt tad asamyak paraṁ matam

Death means that the self (*ātman*) no longer exists; death is an affliction accompanied by old age. It is due to illusion that the existence of the *ātman* is conceived of; seeing this as an error is a superior understanding.

24. *atha ced evam apy asti yal loke nopapadyate*
ajaro 'yam amṛtyuś ca rājāsau manyate tathā

If people accept the existence of something that cannot be proven in this world then this king must be regarded as ageless and free from death!

25. *asti nāstīti cāpy etat tasminn asati lakṣaṇe*
kim adhiṣṭhāya tad brūyāl loka-yātrā-viniścayam

So the crux of the debate is, "It exists" or "It does not exist." But if we accept the existence of an object when there is no conclusive proof, tell me how we can be certain of anything in our worldly dealings.

26. *pratyakṣaṁ hy etayor mūlaṁ kṛtāntaitihyayor api*
pratyakṣo hy āgamo 'bhinnaḥ kṛtānto vā na kiṁcana

Direct perception is clearly the basis of the conclusions reached by the two other traditional means of acquiring knowledge. Indeed, scripture must never be in conflict with perception or its conclusion cannot be sustained.

27. *yatra tatrānumāne 'sti kṛtaṁ bhāvayate 'pi vā*
anyo jīvaḥ śarīrasya nāstikānāṁ mate smṛtaḥ

When inference is employed on any subject, it does not provide proof. Hence the idea that there is a living entity (*jīva*) separate from the body is known as the view of *nāstikas*.

28. *reto vaṭa-kaṇīkāyāṁ ghṛta-pākādhivāsanam*
jāti-smṛtir ayas-kāntaḥ sūrya-kānto 'mbu-bhakṣaṇam

The presence of life in semen and a tiny banyan seed, heating butter to make ghee, remembrance of past lives, the use of the loadstone, or the *sūryakānta* gem, the consumption of water by fire,

29. *pretya bhūtātyayaś caiva devatābhyupayācanam*
mṛte karma-nivṛttiś ca pramāṇaṁ iti niścayaḥ

The departure of the living being after death, going before the gods to offer prayers, and the cessation of action at the time of death are all arguments used to prove the existence of the *ātman* on the basis of inference.

30. *na tv ete hetavaḥ santi ye kecin mūrti-saṁsthitāḥ*
amartyasya hi martyena sāmānyaṁ nopapadyate

But although these arguments appear solid, they are not real proofs of the existence of the *ātman* and here is the reason: it is not a valid argument to draw an equivalence between an object subject to destruction and an immortal entity.

31. *avidyā-karma-ceṣṭānāṁ kecid āhuḥ punar bhavam*
kāraṇaṁ lobha-mohau tu doṣāṇāṁ ca niṣevaṇam

There are others who argue that those who act on the basis of ignorance gain continuous rebirth because the cause of rebirth is greed, folly, and addiction to various forms of wickedness.

32. *avidyāṁ kṣetram āhur hi karma bījaṁ tathā kṛtam*
tṛṣṇā saṁjananaṁ sneha eṣa teṣāṁ punar bhavaḥ

They say that ignorance is the field, action is the seed that is sown therein, and desire is the dampness in the soil that causes the seed to sprout. This, they contend, is the basis of rebirth for such persons.

33. *tasmin vyūḍhe ca dagdhe ca citte maraṇa-dharmiṇi*
anyo 'nyāj jāyate dehas tam āhuḥ sattva-saṁkṣayam

When life is drawn from the body and the corpse is consumed by fire, and when consciousness becomes subject to the law of death, a new body comes into being from the previous existence. This is what they teach about the end of life.

34. *yadā sa rūpataś cānyo jātitaḥ śrutito 'rthataḥ*
katham asmin sa ity eva saṁbandhaḥ syād asaṁhitaḥ

But as this new existence is different in terms of form, species, the things it has learned about, and the goals it pursues, how can there be any link between the two? There is no connection between them.

35. *evaṁ sati ca kā prītir dāna-vidyā-tapo-balaiḥ*
yad anyācaritaṁ karma sarvam anyaḥ prapadyate

And if this doctrine were true, how could any satisfaction be gained on the strength of one's acts of charity, learning, and austerity? A different person would gain all the results from action performed by someone else.

36. *yadā hy ayam ihaivānyaiḥ prākṛtair duḥkhito bhavet*
sukhitair duḥkhitair vāpi dṛśyo 'py asya vinirṇayaḥ

Furthermore, if this were the case, a person living now would be afflicted with miseries by others who existed previously, or else endowed with pleasures by those who suffered previously. This is the clear conclusion of this system of thought.

37. *tathā hi musalair hanyuḥ śarīraṁ tat punar bhavet*
pṛthag jñānaṁ yad anyac ca yenaitan nopalabhyate

According to this philosophy, one may batter the body to death with clubs but still it would exist. But this is a separate entity and its knowledge is different. Hence it is not the same existence.

38. *ṛtuḥ saṁvatsaras tithyaḥ śītoṣṇe ca priyāpriye*
yathātītāni paśyanti tādṛśaḥ sattva-saṁkṣayaḥ

They understand the destruction of one's existence in the same way that they observe the seasons, the years, the lunar days, heat and cold, and pleasing and displeasing events, all of which recur in constant cycles.

39. *jarayā hi parītasya mṛtyunā vā vināśinā*
durbalaṁ durbalaṁ pūrvaṁ gṛhasyeva vinaśyati

But that which is repeatedly seized by the destructive power of old age or death must surely become progressively weakened until, just like a house in a state of decay, it eventually succumbs to complete annihilation.

40. *indriyāṇi mano vāyuḥ śoṇitaṁ māṁsam asthi ca*
ānupūrvyā vinaśyanti svaṁ dhātum upayānti ca

The senses, the mind, bodily air, blood, flesh, and bone meet with destruction one after the other. Each of them then returns to its own basic element.

41. *loka-yātrā-vidhānaṁ ca dāna-dharma-phalāgamaḥ*
yad arthaṁ veda-śabdāś ca vyavahārāś ca laukikāḥ

The purpose of Vedic injunctions, rules that govern people's conduct, and the popular traditions, is to regulate the affairs of human society and to show the benefits derived from charity and the observance of dharma.

42. *iti saṁyaṅ manasy ete bahavaḥ santi hetavaḥ*
etad astīdam astīti na kiṁcit pratipadyate

The various opinions I have set forth here represent the many lines of argument that run through the mind of the seeker. "This is the truth, that is the truth", he thinks, but he never gets anywhere in this way.

43. *teṣāṁ vimṛśatām evaṁ tat tat samabhidhāvatām*
kvacin niviśate buddhis tatra jīryati vṛkṣavat

Such is the condition of those who fly after this or that speculative opinion. Eventually their understanding finds a permanent position and there it rots away like a decaying tree.

44. *evam arthair anarthaiś ca duḥkhitāḥ sarva-jantavaḥ*
āgamair apakṛṣyante hasti-pair hastino yathā

In this way all living beings are made to suffer by the proper and improper courses they pursue. They are restrained by the religious texts they follow just as elephants are held in check by their riders.

45. *arthāṁs tathātyanta-sukhāvahāṁś ca*
lipsanta ete bahavo viśulkāḥ
mahattaraṁ duḥkham abhiprapannā
hitvāmiṣaṁ mṛtyu-vaśaṁ prayānti

Many people who lack the currency to purchase such things hanker after acquisitions which they believe will bring unlimited happiness. In fact, they attain the greatest misery. They fail to achieve the object of their pleasure and then yield to the power of death.

46. *vināśino hy adhruva-jīvitasya*
kiṁ bandhubhir mitra-parigrahaiś ca
vihāya yo gacchati sarvam eva
kṣaṇena gatvā na nivartate ca

When one is destined to die and has such a fragile hold on life, what is the value of relatives, friends, and possessions? After renouncing all such things, one departs this world in an instant and after departing never again returns.

47. *bhū-vyoma-toyānala-vāyavo hi*
sadā śarīraṁ paripālayanti
itīdam ālakṣya kuto ratir bhaved
vināśino hy asya na śarma vidyate

It is earth, space, water, fire, and air that always sustain the body. Once one has understood this point, how can there still be attraction for a body that will meet with destruction and in which no happiness can be found.'

48. *idam anupadhi vākyam acchalaṁ*
parama-nirāmayam ātma-sākṣikam
nara-patir abhivīkṣya vismitaḥ
punar anuyoktum idaṁ pracakrame

Observing this forthright discourse that was free from deceit, completely faultless, and focused on the existence of the *ātman*, the king was astonished by what he had heard and began to ask the following questions.

Śānti-parvan, Adhyāya 212

For the second of the two chapters of the *Pañcaśikha-Janaka-Saṁvāda*, the situation has changed. Impressed by the way Pañcaśikha refuted the ideas of the *pāṣaṇḍa-vādins*, Janaka now wishes to be instructed by his new teacher. Residual doubts remain, however, presumably as a result of the instruction he had previously received. In the question he now puts to Pañcaśikha it is possible to detect a Buddhist argument against the notion that liberation from rebirth can occur without the cessation of individual existence and individual consciousness. Expressing a doubt on this issue, Janaka questions whether a state in which the existence of an individual persists can truly be accepted as liberation from rebirth. Initially Pañcaśikha responds to this doubt only very briefly, in the first line of verse 6, although he does return to the point towards the end of the chapter. His primary concern, however, is to give the king some preliminary grounding in Sāṁkhya doctrine and it is this line of discussion that takes up the bulk of the chapter.

As is usual, we have a listing of the great elements and then the five senses, the *indriya*, which perceive their respective objects, the *indriyārthas*. It is in this way that a living being gathers knowledge of the world. Ignorant persons regard this combination of elements and senses as the true self but a permanent cessation of suffering can be achieved only when this misapprehension is removed through the acquisition of true knowledge. In verse 17, this process is designated as *samyaṅ-manaḥ*, right-mindedness; when the truth about the world and one's own existence is properly perceived, then false teachings are abandoned and one develops a mood of renunciation. This alone can bring freedom from suffering. Again perhaps these verses represent something of a dialogue with Buddhist teachings, in particular the emphasis we find in Buddhism on finding a solution to the problem of suffering. Here, however, it is urged that the solution is to be found in the appreciation of Sāṁkhya wisdom and the spirit of absolute renunciation such realisation inevitably invokes. After this brief interruption, the discussion returns once again to the analysis of the world; from verse 20 we have a description of the organs of action, the *karmendriyas* designated as the hands, feet, voice, anus, and genitals, and then the processes by which the senses of perception acquire knowledge of the world.

This analysis is taken a step further with the introduction of the idea of the three *guṇas*, the essential and pervasive qualities of *prakṛti*. After the nature of the three *guṇas* is explained in verses 25 to 31, the discussion returns to the senses of perception, the relationship between the senses and the great elements, and how the senses function so as to facilitate the acquisition of knowledge. Here, however, an important point is made. The extent of perception achievable in this way is limited because the mind is flickering, hence the understanding gained through the senses is incomplete; this is due to the influence on a living being of the *guṇa* known as *tamas*. Because of the influence of *tamas*, the mind can never become steady leading to a limited perception and understanding. This idea can in fact be taken as a response to the insistence on the pre-eminence of perception as a means of acquiring knowledge, which we encountered in the previous chapter as a part of the discourse given by a teacher of false doctrines. It also gives some suggestion of Yoga techniques, which elsewhere are advocated as the means by which the mind can be stilled and perception of the higher self thereby attained.

Verses 40 to 43 mark the point at which Pañcaśikha directly addresses the question posed by Janaka at the beginning of this second chapter. Firstly, the true nature of a living being is defined through the dualistic terms *kṣetra* and *kṣetrajña*, the field and the knower of the field, which are familiar from Chapter 13 of the *Bhagavad-gītā* and other passages of the *Mokṣa-dharma-parvan*. The answer which is then given to Janaka's question could be seen as veering towards Vedānta rather than Sāṁkhya, particularly where it uses the example of rivers losing their identity as they merge into the ocean, which is used by Āruṇi in his teachings to Śvetaketu in the *Chāndogya Upaniṣad* (6.10.1–3). The passage, however, is slightly obscure and I think it unlikely that we are here encountering any form of reconciliation between Sāṁkhya and Vedānta. What Pañcaśikha most probably means is that when the soul is released from its state of embodiment, and hence its contact with the material elements, the sense of individual identity based on material designation, as referred to in verse 14, no longer prevails. So there is certainly some form of existence after liberation but it is not to be confused with the type of consciousness we experience in this present state of existence.

In the final verses of his teachings (verses 44–49), Pañcaśikha focuses directly on the subject of *mokṣa*, the ultimate goal of the Sāṁkhya system. When this is attained one can escape from the effects of past actions, from all suffering, and from old age and death. Unlike the *pāṣaṇḍa-vādins*, however, and indeed unlike the Buddhists, Pañcaśikha declares that this supreme goal is to be obtained by adherence to the *śruti*, the Vedic revelation. Here again we can detect an emphasis on freedom from suffering in the discussion of liberation, which one might see as a response to one of the major themes of Buddhist thought. Thus in this chapter we have another exposition of non-theistic Sāṁkhya, which does not exactly equate with classical Sāṁkhya but is entirely typical of the early forms encountered throughout the *Mokṣa-dharma-parvan* of the *Mahābhārata*.

1. *bhīṣma uvāca*
janako janadevas tu jñāpitaḥ paramarṣiṇā
punar evānupapraccha sāṁparāye bhavābhavau

Bhīṣma said: After receiving these instructions from that great *rishi*, Janaka Janadeva inquired from him once more about the question of existence or non-existence in the afterlife.

2. *bhagavan yad idaṁ pretya saṁjñā bhavati kasyacit*
evaṁ sati kim ajñānaṁ jñānaṁ vā kiṁ kariṣyati

'O blessed one, if it is the case that a person's consciousness persists after death then what distinction is there between ignorance and knowledge in terms of the results that each of them yields?

3. *sarvam uccheda-niṣṭhaṁ syāt paśya caitad dvijottama*
apramattaḥ pramatto vā kiṁ viśeṣaṁ kariṣyati

Everything would then be worthless; you must see this, O best of Brahmins. If what you say is so, then what difference does it make whether one is negligent or careful in one's practice?

4. *asaṁsargo hi bhūteṣu saṁsargo vā vināśiṣu*
kasmai kriyeta kalpena niścayaḥ ko 'tra tattvataḥ

Whether it involves becoming free of contact with the material elements or remaining in contact with the temporary things of this world, to what end is religious practice to be executed with such dedication? What is the correct resolution of this issue?'

5. *tamasā hi praticchannaṁ vibhrāntam iva cāturam*
punaḥ praśamayan vākyaiḥ kaviḥ pañcaśikho 'bravīt

It appeared that the king was overwhelmed by ignorance, being confused and also distressed. Therefore the wise Pañcaśikha instructed him once more, bringing relief through the words he spoke.

6. *uccheda-niṣṭhā nehāsti bhāva-niṣṭhā na vidyate*
ayaṁ hy api samāhāraḥ śarīrendriya-cetasām
vartate pṛthag anyonyam apy apāśritya karmasu

'The condition you refer to is not a state of complete annihilation and yet the state of being does not persist. What we see in this world is just the combination of body, senses, and mind, each of them separate though dependent on the others as they are absorbed in various types of action.

7. *dhātavaḥ pañca-śākho 'yaṁ khaṁ vāyur jyotir ambu bhūḥ*
te sva-bhāvena tiṣṭhanti viyujyante sva-bhāvataḥ

There are five branches to this present form of existence, which has space, air, fire, water, and earth as its constituent parts. Due to their inherent nature these can exist together, but in accordance with that same inherent nature they will eventually separate.

8. *ākāśaṁ vāyur ūṣmā ca sneho yac cāpi pārthivam*
eṣa pañca-samāhāraḥ śarīram iti naikadhā
jñānam ūṣmā ca vāyuś ca tri-vidhaḥ karma-saṁgrahaḥ

This body is not a single entity but is a combination of the five elements, space, air, heat, fluid, and that which is of an earthy nature. Action consists of a combination of three elements, knowledge, heat, and air.

9. *indriyāṇīndriyārthāś ca sva-bhāvaś cetanā manaḥ*
prāṇāpānau vikāraś ca dhātavaś cātra niḥsṛtāḥ

Knowledge is the senses, the objects they perceive, inherent nature, the intellect, and the mind; air is the incoming and outgoing breaths and their transformations; heat is seen to go out from the body when action is performed.

10. *śravaṇaṁ sparśanaṁ jihvā dṛṣṭir nāsā tathaiva ca*
indriyāṇīti pañcaite citta-pūrvaṁgamā guṇāḥ

Hearing, touch, the tongue, sight, and the nose are known as the senses. The qualities of these five senses follow behind the movements of the mind.

11. *tatra vijñāna-saṁyuktā tri-vidhā vedanā dhruvā*
sukha-duḥkheti yām āhur aduḥkhety asukheti ca

In the process of gaining experiences three states of perception constantly exist within the mind. They refer to these as happiness combined with misery, happiness untouched by misery, and misery without any happiness.

12. *śabdaḥ sparśaś ca rūpaṁ ca raso gandhaś ca mūrty atha*
ete hy āmaraṇāt pañca ṣaḍ-guṇā jñāna-siddhaye

Until one is overcome by death, the five senses distinguish six qualities in order to acquire knowledge of an object. These six are its sound, touch, colour, taste, scent, and form.

13. *teṣu karma nisargaś ca sarva-tattvārtha-niścayaḥ*
tam āhuḥ paramaṁ śukraṁ buddhir ity avyayaṁ mahat

The natural mode of action for the senses is to determine the truth about all forms of perception. They say that this is a pure form of perception that is the highest of all. It is known as the *buddhi*; it is changeless and it is the *mahat*, the great element.

14. *imaṁ guṇa-samāhāram ātma-bhāvena paśyataḥ*
asamyag-darśanair duḥkham anantaṁ nopaśāmyati

Whilst one adheres to false notions and considers this combination of elements to be the true self, the limitless suffering of this world never ceases.

15. *anātmeti ca yad dṛṣṭaṁ tenāhaṁ na mamety api*
vartate kim adhiṣṭhānā prasaktā duḥkha-saṁtatiḥ

But if it is seen that this is not the self and the sense of 'I and mine' no longer persists, then how could there be any basis for this causal progression of repeated suffering?

16. *tatra samyaṅ-mano nāma tyāga-śāstram anuttamam*
śṛṇu yat tava mokṣāya bhāṣyamāṇaṁ bhaviṣyati

Regarding this point, there is a most excellent teaching on the subject of renunciation, which is named *Samyaṅ-Manaḥ*, 'Right Mindedness'. Listen now to what I say in the cause of your liberation.

17. *tyāga eva hi sarveṣām uktānām api karmaṇām*
nityaṁ mithyā-vinītānāṁ kleśo duḥkhāvaho mataḥ

All the forms of action that have been spoken of here must be given up. It is understood that for those who have been taught false doctrines this is an affliction that brings only misery.

18. *dravya-tyāge tu karmāṇi bhoga-tyāge vratāny api*
sukha-tyāge tapo-yogaḥ sarva-tyāge samāpanā

The proper outcome of ritual acts is the renunciation of wealth, the outcome of religious vows is the renunciation of objects of pleasure. The conclusion of austerity and Yoga practice is the renunciation of material happiness. The true conclusion of religious duties is complete renunciation.

19. *tasya mārgo 'yam advaidaḥ sarva-tyāgasya darśitaḥ*
viprahāṇāya duḥkhasya durgatir hy anyathā bhavet

The direct path to this complete renunciation will now be revealed. This path brings the cessation of misery; any other path will bring only misfortune.

20. *pañca-jñānendriyāṇy uktvā manaḥ-ṣaṣṭhāni cetasi*
manaḥ-ṣaṣṭhāni vakṣyāmi pañca-karmendriyāṇi tu

In mental activity there are five knowledge-acquiring senses with *manas* as a sixth element in this group. These have already been described to you. I shall now speak about the five organs of action, which again have *manas* as the sixth factor.

21. *hastau karmendriyaṁ jñeyam atha pādau gatīndriyam*
prajanānandayoḥ śepho visarge pāyur indriyam

The hands are to be known as the organ for performing action and the feet are the means of movement. The genitals are the organ for reproduction and for pleasure, and the anus is the organ of evacuation.

22. *vāk tu śabda-viśeṣārthaṁ gatiṁ pañcānvitāṁ viduḥ*
evam ekādaśaitāni buddhyā tv avasṛjen manaḥ

Now speech has the function of conveying different types of sound. They recognise speech as the fifth of this group and so there are eleven elements altogether. One must cast aside the activity of the *manas* by means of the *buddhi*.

23. *karṇau śabdaś ca cittaṁ ca trayaḥ śravaṇa-saṁgrahe*
tathā sparśe tathā rūpe tathaiva rasa-gandhayoḥ

In the process of hearing there are three factors: the ears, the sound, and the mind. It is the same for touch and in the perception of form, taste, and aroma.

24. *evaṁ pañca-trikā hy ete guṇās tad upalabdhaye*
yena yas tri-vidho bhāvaḥ paryāyāt samupasthitaḥ

Hence five groups of three factors are involved in the process of perception by means of which this threefold existence is experienced, one quality after another.

25. *sāttviko rājasaś caiva tāmasaś caiva te trayaḥ*
tri-vidhā vedanā yeṣu prasūtā sarva-sādhanā

The three dimensions of existence are those influenced by *sattva*, by *rajas*, and by *tamas*. Thus there are three forms of perception and everything one experiences in life is based on these three factors.

26. *praharṣaḥ prītir ānandaḥ sukhaṁ saṁśānta-cittatā*
akutaścit kutaścid vā cittataḥ sāttviko guṇaḥ

Joy, contentment, bliss, happiness, and complete peace of mind, whether or not there be any cause for them, represent the mental state that arises due to the influence of the quality of *sattva*.

27. *atuṣṭiḥ paritāpaś ca śoko lobhas tathākṣamā*
liṅgāni rajasas tāni dṛśyante hetv-ahetutaḥ

Dissatisfaction, grief, sorrow, greed, and impatience, with or without any cause, are the characteristic emotions recognised as arising from the quality of *rajas*.

28. *avivekas tathā mohaḥ pramādaḥ svapna-tandritā*
kathaṁcid api vartante vividhās tāmasā guṇāḥ

However they may be caused, lack of discrimination, delusion, negligence, and the lethargy of sleep are the qualities that arise from the influence of *tamas.*

29. *tatra yat prīti-saṁyuktaṁ kāye manasi vā bhavet*
vartate sāttviko bhāva ity apekṣeta tat tathā

One should recognise that whenever there is a manifestation of contentment within one's body or mind the influence of *sattva* is present.

30. *yat tu saṁtāpa-saṁyuktam aprīti-karam ātmanaḥ*
pravṛttaṁ raja ity eva tatas tad abhicintayet

And whenever there is a manifestation of the distress that produces a dissatisfied state of mind, one should understand that *rajas* is active.

31. *atha yan moha-saṁyuktaṁ kāye manasi vā bhavet*
apratarkyam avijñeyaṁ tamas tad upadhārayet

And one should recognise that whenever there is a manifestation of delusion within one's body or mind this represents the presence of the incomprehensible, unknown quality of *tamas.*

32. *tad dhi śrotrāśrayaṁ bhūtaṁ śabdaḥ śrotraṁ samāśritaḥ*
nobhayaṁ śabda-vijñāne vijñānasyetarasya vā

The process of hearing depends upon its related element; sound is dependent on the sense of hearing. But neither of these two is the true cause of knowledge derived from sound or of any other perception.

33. *evaṁ tvak cakṣuṣī jihvā nāsikā caiva pañcamī*
sparśe rūpe rase gandhe tāni ceto manaś ca tat

The same consideration applies with regard to the skin, the eye, the tongue, and the fifth sense, which is the nose, as they engage in the perception of touch, form, taste, and aroma. Collectively these constitute an individual's mental process, which is the *manas.*

34. *sva-karma-yugapad-bhāvo daśasv eteṣu tiṣṭhati*
cittam ekādaśaṁ viddhi buddhir dvādaśamī bhavet

Each of the senses has its own mode of action but they exist together in a state of union. This is the condition of these ten elements. If you understand the mind (*citta*) as the eleventh factor, the *buddhi* will then be the twelfth.

35. *teṣām ayugapad-bhāve ucchedo nāsti tāmasaḥ*
āsthito yugapad-bhāve vyavahāraḥ sa laukikaḥ

If they existed as entirely distinct functions then the influence of *tamas* would never be removed, but as long as they operate simultaneously all the signs of normal life are evident.

36. *indriyāṇy avasṛjyāpi dṛṣṭvā pūrvaṁ śrutāgamam*
cintayan nānuparyeti tribhir evānvito guṇaiḥ

After setting the senses loose to gather perceptions and having perceived an object that had previously been heard about, one who is in contact with the three *guṇas* does not proceed through each sense individually whilst considering what has been perceived.

37. *yat tamopahataṁ cittam āśu saṁcāram adhruvam*
karoty uparamaṁ kāle tad āhus tāmasaṁ sukham

But the mind afflicted by *tamas* flits rapidly from one thing to another, without ever being steady. If one eventually stops the mind from acting in this way they call this the form of happiness that pertains to *tamas.*

38. *yad yad āgama-saṁyuktaṁ na kṛtsnam upaśāmyati*
atha tatrāpy upādatte tamo vyaktam ivānṛtam

Whenever a particular sensation arises, the mind can never become completely tranquil. Rather it is simply *tamas* that grasps the manifest impression and makes it appear unreal.

39. *evam eṣa prasaṁkhyātaḥ sva-karma-pratyayī guṇaḥ*
kathaṁcid vartate samyak keṣāṁcid vā na vartate

Now this *guṇa* has been explained along with its own specific function. For some it will be exactly in this way but for others there will be no such affliction.

40. *evam āhuḥ samāhāraṁ kṣetram adhyātma-cintakāḥ*
sthito manasi yo bhāvaḥ sa vai kṣetrajña ucyate

Those who comprehend the nature of the self speak of this combination of elements as the *kṣetra*. The entity situated within the mind is referred to as the *kṣetrajña*.

41. *evaṁ sati ka ucchedaḥ śāśvato vā kathaṁ bhavet*
sva-bhāvād vartamāneṣu sarva-bhūteṣu hetutaḥ

This being so, what could ever be destroyed, or how could such destruction be permanent? The reason for this is that it is the inherent nature of all beings to continue to exist.

42. *yathārṇava-gatā nadyo vyaktīr jahati nāma ca*
na ca svatāṁ niyacchanti tādṛśaḥ sattva-saṁkṣayaḥ

When rivers flow into the sea they relinquish both their form and name, and they no longer maintain their individual nature. So it is when material existence is brought to an end.

43. *evaṁ sati kutaḥ saṁjñā pretya-bhāve punar bhavet*
pratisaṁmiśrite jīve gṛhyamāṇe ca madhyataḥ

This being the case, how can consciousness continue in its present state after death, when the soul (*jīva*) is taken from the midst of these elements and its existence is merged into the total existence?

44. *imāṁ tu yo veda vimokṣa-buddhim*
ātmānam anvicchati cāpramattaḥ
na lipyate karma-phalair aniṣṭaiḥ
patraṁ bisasyeva jalena siktam

Now one who grasps this understanding of liberation from rebirth, and resolutely seeks out the *ātman*, is never touched by the unwanted results of his actions, as a lotus petal is untouched by the water in which it stands.

45. *dṛḍhaiś ca pāśair bahubhir vimuktaḥ*
prajā-nimittair api daivataiś ca
yadā hy asau sukha-duḥkhe jahāti
muktas tad āgryāṁ gatim ety aliṅgaḥ
śruti-pramāṇāgama-maṅgalaiś ca
śete jarā-mṛtyu-bhayād atītaḥ

When he breaks free from the multitude of strong ropes caused by attachment to one's children and by the gods as well, and when he goes beyond both joy and misery, the liberated person who is free of all designation then attains the topmost goal. It is through the auspicious results gained from the *śruti*, the philosophical works, and other scriptures that he finds repose beyond the fear of old age and death.

46. *kṣīṇe ca puṇye vigate ca pāpe*
tato nimitte ca phale vinaṣṭe
alepam ākāśam aliṅgam evam
āsthāya paśyanti mahad dhy asaktāḥ

When piety is exhausted and sin is removed and when the causal factor that gives rise to the results of action is thus destroyed, those who are without attachments attain a position like space that has no contamination and no material designation. They can then perceive the greater existence.

47. *yathorṇa-nābhiḥ parivartamānas*
tantu-kṣaye tiṣṭhati pātyamānaḥ
tathā vimuktaḥ prajahāti duḥkhaṁ
vidhvaṁsate loṣṭa ivādrimarcchan

The worm in its cocoon keeps moving round and round until the threads are broken and it gains control of its existence. In the same way, one who is liberated transcends the misery of this world. Indeed, his suffering is like a lump of earth that is smashed into fragments when it falls upon a rock.

48. *yathā ruruḥ śṛngam atho purāṇaṁ*
hitvā tvacaṁ vāpy urago yathāvat
vihāya gacchaty anavekṣamāṇas
tathā vimukto vijahāti duḥkham

After discarding its old horns, an antelope continues on its way without any consideration. Similarly, a snake will shed its skin and then move on without concern. In the same way one who is liberated leaves his suffering behind him.

49. *drumaṁ yathā vāpy udake patantam*
utsṛjya pakṣī prapataty asaktaḥ
tathā hy asau sukha-duḥkhe vihāya
muktaḥ parārddhyāṁ gatim ety aliṅgaḥ

Or again a bird will leave a tree that has fallen into a lake and fly away without any sense of attachment for it. In the same way, the liberated person who is free from material designations gives up both joy and misery and attains the topmost destination.'

50. *api ca bhavati maithilena gītaṁ*
nagaram upāhitam agninābhivīkṣya
na khalu mama tuṣo 'pi dahyate 'tra
svayam idam āha kila sma bhūmipālaḥ

And there is a verse sung by the Lord of Mithilā when he saw his city destroyed by fire. 'Not even the chaff from the rice that has been burned here was really mine.' It was truly the king himself who said this.

51. *idam amṛta-padaṁ videha-rājaḥ*
svayam iha pañcaśikhena bhāṣyamāṇaḥ
nikhilam abhisamīkṣya niścitārthaṁ
parama-sukhī vijahāra vīta-śokaḥ

The King of Videha was instructed by Pañcaśikha who presented him with these teachings on immortality. Having listened carefully to everything that was spoken, he reached the proper conclusion. He was then filled with joy and cast off his sorrow, which troubled him no more.

52. *imaṁ hi yaḥ paṭhati vimokṣa-niścayaṁ*
na hīyate satatam avekṣate tathā
upadravān nānubhavaty aduḥkhitaḥ
pramucyate kapilam ivaitya maithilaḥ

Any person who studies this treatise on liberation, who never turns away from its teachings, and always thinks about its instructions, becomes free from sorrow and never experiences life's great miseries. Thus he gains liberation just like the Lord of Mithilā after his encounter with the Kapila.

A Discourse on Proper Conduct

Śānti-parvan, Adhyāya 213–214

FOLLOWING ON from the *Pañcaśikha-janaka-saṁvāda*, the next major phase of the *Mokṣa-dharma-parvan* consists of a series of discussions held between Indra and one of his enemies whom he has vanquished and stripped of power and status. Before this section commences, however, we have an interlude consisting of two short chapters (213 and 214 of the *Śānti-parvan*) in which Bhīṣma responds briefly to a series of questions from Yudhiṣṭhira concerning proper conduct. There is no obvious reason why these chapters should be inserted at this point and one can only guess at the editor's motives; perhaps there is no reason at all as there is no rigid structure apparent within the *Mokṣa-dharma-parvan* as a whole. The discussion begins with Yudhiṣṭhira's opening question as to the type of actions that bring joy, misery, and success, to which Bhīṣma responds with a discourse on the quality of *dama* (which is to be understood as indicating restraint or self-control), making the point that the conduct of the self-controlled person (the *dānta*) is equal to any form of ritual and yields the result of rebirth in the higher worlds.

In the second of the two chapters, Yudhiṣṭhira asks first of all about eating meat from the offerings made in the Vedic ritual and then about the nature of *tapas*, a term which usually refers to acts of austerity and mortification of the body undertaken by renunciants in order to break free from attachment, or possibly to gain superhuman powers. Here, however, Bhīṣma discusses the ways in which a householder can perform *tapas* without abandoning human society rather than the extreme acts of mortification referred to elsewhere. In fact it is to be noted that, despite their location in this section of the *Mahābhārata*, these passages are not really about achieving liberation from rebirth at all, as it is quite clearly stated that the person who displays *dama* or performs the recommended acts of *tapas* will be reborn in higher worlds but apparently not escape from rebirth altogether.

Śānti-parvan, Adhyāya 213

The passage opens with a question from Yudhiṣṭhira about actions that bring either *sukha* or *duḥkha*, joy or misery, and about action through which one can live in the world without any fear. The question is not answered directly as Bhīṣma takes it as an opportunity to give a speech emphasising the importance of *dama*, self-control. *Dama* is the means by which passion is brought under control so that one can then live without performing sinful actions. The self-controlled person is happy and contented and causes no sense of fear to arise in others. In the second half of the chapter, from verse 9 to verse 12, Bhīṣma describes the attributes that jointly comprise *dama*, thereby adding depth to his analysis of this essential quality by showing how it becomes manifest in the day-to-day conduct of the self-controlled *dānta*. He concludes the chapter with a brief discourse on ideal human conduct, the elements of which are all manifestations of a single essential quality, *dama*, here defined as the ability to control the passions and the urges of mind and senses so that action is dictated by the enlightened intellect alone.

1. *yudhiṣṭhira uvāca*
kiṁ kurvan sukham āpnoti kiṁ kurvan duḥkham āpnute
kiṁ kurvan nirbhayo loke siddhaś carati bhārata

Yudhiṣṭhira said: Through what form of action does one find happiness and through what form of action will one attain misery? What is the form of action through which one becomes free of fear and lives successfully in this world, O Bhārata?

2. *bhīṣma uvāca*
damam eva praśaṁsanti vṛddhāḥ śruti-samādhayaḥ
sarveṣām eva varṇānāṁ brāhmaṇasya viśeṣataḥ

Bhīṣma said: The seers of ancient times who realised the Vedas within their minds praise self-control above all practices. They recommend such conduct for all the *varṇas* but for the Brahmins in particular.

3. *nādāntasya kriyā-siddhir yathāvad upalabhyate*
kriyā tapaś ca vedāś ca dame sarvaṁ pratiṣṭhitam

The rituals performed by one who lacks self-control are never completely successful, for ritual acts, austerity, and the Vedic rites are all based on such restraint.

4. *damas tejo vardhayati pavitraṁ dama ucyate*
vipāpmā nirbhayo dāntaḥ puruṣo vindate mahat

Self-control causes one's strength to increase for it is said that restraint is purity. That person who practises self-control becomes sinless and free from fear; he achieves great things.

5. *sukhaṁ dāntaḥ prasvapiti sukhaṁ ca pratibudhyate*
sukhaṁ loke viparyeti manaś cāsya prasīdati

One who is self-controlled sleeps easily and awakens with joy in his heart. He wanders happily across the world for his mind is always at peace.

6. *tejo damena dhriyate na tat tīkṣṇo 'dhigacchati*
amitrāṁś ca bahūn nityaṁ pṛthag ātmani paśyati

Passion can be held in check by self-control but one who is aggressive by nature cannot achieve such restraint. Hence the self-controlled person still sees many separate enemies as existing within himself.

7. *kravyādbhya iva bhūtānām adāntebhyaḥ sadā bhayam*
teṣāṁ vipratiṣedhārthaṁ rājā sṛṣṭaḥ svayaṁbhuvā

Just as they fear carnivorous beasts, living beings are always afraid of those who lack self-control. It was to control such persons that kingship was created by the self-born Deity.

8. *āśrameṣu ca sarveṣu dama eva viśiṣyate*
yac ca teṣu phalaṁ dharme bhūyo dānte tad ucyate

In all stages of life self-control is the highest quality; it is said that practising self-control brings a greater reward than the dharma of these *āśramas*.

9. *teṣāṁ liṅgāni vakṣyāmi yeṣāṁ samudayo damaḥ*
akārpaṇyam asaṁrambhaḥ saṁtoṣaḥ śraddadhānatā

I will now describe the characteristics that jointly comprise the practice of self-control. These are generosity, tranquillity, contentment, and being endowed with faith;

10. *akrodha ārjavaṁ nityaṁ nātivādo na mānitā*
guru-pūjānasūyā ca dayā bhūteṣv apaiśunam

Never becoming angry, always being honest, never quarrelling, and being free from pride; showing reverence to one's teacher, never displaying malice, compassion for other living beings, and never speaking ill of others;

11. *jana-vāda-mṛṣā-vāda-stuti-nindā-vivarjanam*
sādhu-kāmaś cāspṛhayan nāyāti pratyayaṁ nṛṣu

Avoiding gossip, dishonest speech, and words of flattery or condemnation. Seeking the company only of righteous persons and remaining free of hankering, he never again puts his faith in men.

12. *avaira-kṛt sūpacāraḥ samo nindā-praśaṁsayoḥ*
suvṛttaḥ śīla-saṁpannaḥ prasannātmātmavān budhaḥ
prāpya loke satkāraṁ svargaṁ vai pretya gacchati

The enlightened sage never acts out of enmity, he is gentle in all ways and is equally unmoved by condemnation or praise; his conduct is always righteous, he is virtuous by nature, he is satisfied at heart, self-possessed, and wise. After being honoured in this world, he then attains the heaven of the gods after death.

13. *sarva-bhūta-hite yukto na smayād dveṣṭi vai janam*
mahā-hrada ivākṣobhya prajñā-tṛptaḥ prasīdati

He devotes himself to the welfare of all living beings and never despises anyone out of a sense of pride. He is imperturbable like the vast ocean and is peaceful at heart because he finds satisfaction in the wisdom he has gained.

14. *abhayaṁ sarva-bhūtebhyaḥ sarveṣām abhayaṁ yataḥ*
namasyaḥ sarva-bhūtānāṁ dānto bhavati jñānavān

He has no fear of any living being, nor does he inspire fear in any other creature. Endowed with knowledge, the self-controlled sage is worthy of worship for all beings.

15. *na hṛṣyati mahaty arthe vyasane ca na śocati*
sa vai parimita-prajñaḥ sa dānto dvija ucyate

He does not delight in any great achievement nor does he lament if calamity overtakes him, and he shows moderation in his pursuit of knowledge. Such a self-controlled person is referred to as a Brahmin.

16. *karmabhiḥ śruta-saṁpannaḥ sadbhir ācaritaiḥ śubhaiḥ*
sadaiva dama-saṁyuktas tasya bhuṅkte mahat-phalam

Possessing extensive knowledge of the Veda, such a self-controlled person enjoys the wonderful results achieved by means of the auspicious ritual acts performed by righteous men.

17. *anasūyā kṣamā śāntiḥ saṁtoṣaḥ priya-vāditā*
satyaṁ dānam anāyāso naiṣa mārgo durātmanām

This path which demands freedom from malice, tolerance, peacefulness, contentment, gentle words, truthfulness, charity, and ease of endeavour will never be followed by evil-minded persons.

18. *kāma-krodhau vaśe kṛtvā brahmcārī jitendriyaḥ*
vikramya ghore tapasi brāhmaṇaḥ saṁśita-vrataḥ
kālākāṅkṣī carel lokān nirapāya ivātmavān

Having brought his desire and anger under control, maintained his vow of celibacy, and conquered his senses, and having successfully completed harsh austerities whilst remaining true to the vows he has made, the self-controlled Brahmin awaits the time of his death, moving amongst the people of this world like one who is free of any difficulty.

Śānti-parvan, Adhyāya 214

The second of these two chapters opens with a question from Yudhiṣṭhira regarding Brahmins, or perhaps any member of the three higher *varṇas*, who eat as their food the remnants of the offerings made in sacrifice. This might be taken as an inquiry as to the propriety of eating meat from animals slaughtered for ritual purposes, a topic considered in more detail later in the *Mokṣa-dharma-parvan*, and here it appears that Bhīṣma disapproves of such a practice, although if this is the case then he seems to contradict himself in verse 11 where he states that only eating meat of this type is the same as abstaining from meat entirely. Both the question and the answer here are somewhat obscure and it might even be that they have been inserted afterwards by a later editor who was unhappy with Bhīṣma's subsequent assertion.

After this brief response, Yudhiṣṭhira then raises the issue of *tapas* and asks for Bhīṣma's opinion on the subject. The word *tapas* is usually used to refer to acts of severe austerity such as extended fasts or standing on the toes with arms raised for a long period of time. It is recorded that such practices were often undertaken in order to achieve the favour of the gods (as Arjuna did when seeking the celestial weapons he needed to defeat the Kauravas) but were not necessarily equated with dharma or virtue. In the *Rāmāyaṇa*, for example, we are told how Rāvaṇa undertook a drastic form of *tapas* in order to acquire the power that enabled him to vanquish the gods. It is interesting to note that the biographies of the Buddha record how he practised severe mortifications of the body before realising the ultimate futility of such acts, and within the *Mahābhārata* attitudes are at best ambivalent. In the *Āśramavāsika-parvan* (Book 15), Dhṛtarāṣṭra, Gāndhārī, Vidura, and others are praised for the severe austerities they undertake, through which they gain entry into the realm of the gods, but in the seventeenth chapter of the *Bhagavad-gītā* we find that such practices are condemned as not being prescribed by scripture, and being performed on the basis of arrogance and conceit, or in pursuit of sensual desires (17.5). The *Gītā* also offers an alternative interpretation of *tapas* based on proper conduct, righteous speech, and gentility of mind, rather than bodily austerity, and it is this understanding of *tapas* that Bhīṣma reiterates here.

Explicitly rejecting extreme practices, Bhīṣma begins by defining *tapas* as *tyāga* and *sannati*, renunciation and humility. He then explains how the practice of celibacy and fasting may be understood as imposing limits on sexual activity and eating, rather than there being any absolute abstention. Similarly, if one eats only the meat left over from sacrificial offerings and never sleeps during the daylight hours, then he can be considered as accepting a vegetarian diet and abstaining from sleep. He should take his own food only after his family members, guests, and servants have been fed; he can then be understood as eating the *amṛta* consumed by the gods that bestows upon them the gift of immortality. Hence the harsh practices that sometimes comprise the act of *tapas* are here modified, and restraint is advocated in preference to abstention. We might also note that this passage is again somewhat out of place in a *mokṣa-dharma-parvan* as it is clearly stated that following the prescription given herein enables one to ascend to *svarga-loka*, the heaven of the gods, rather than attaining release from all forms of rebirth, the goal that both the Sāṁkhya and Yoga systems aspire towards.

1. *yudhiṣṭhira uvāca*
dvijātayo vratopetā yad idaṁ bhuñjate haviḥ
annaṁ brāhmaṇa-kāmāya katham etat pitāmaha

Yudhiṣṭhira said: Brahmins who adhere to religious ordinances consume the offerings made into the sacrificial fire in order to fulfil their desires. How can that be so, grandfather?

2. *bhīṣma uvāca*
avedokta-vratopetā bhuñjānāḥ kārya-kāriṇaḥ
vedokteṣu ca bhuñjānā vrata-luptā yudhiṣṭhira

Bhīṣma said: It is persons who perform the rituals without adhering strictly to the rules ordained by the Vedas who eat such food. If persons who do adhere to Vedic injunctions eat food in this way then their rules of conduct are broken, Yudhiṣṭhira.

3. *yudhiṣṭhira uvāca*
yad idaṁ tapa ity āhur upavāsaṁ pṛthag janāḥ
etat tapo mahārāja utāho kiṁ tapo bhavet

Yudhiṣṭhira said: The common people say that *tapas* means to undergo a fast. Is this what *tapas* means, O king? How would you define *tapas*?

4. *bhīṣma uvāca*
māsa-pakṣopavāsena manyante yat tapo janāḥ
ātma-tantropaghātaḥ sa na tapas tat satāṁ matam
tyāgaś ca sannatiś caiva śiṣyate tapa uttamam

Bhīṣma said: People think that undergoing a fast for a month or a fortnight is *tapas*, but the view of the righteous is that affliction of the substance of one's being is not truly *tapas*; rather it is taught that renunciation and humility are the highest form of *tapas*.

5. *sadopavāsī ca bhaved brahmacārī sadaiva ca*
muniś ca syāt sadā vipro daivataṁ ca sadā bhajet

One who accepts this *tapas* will always be fasting and will remain constantly celibate. And such a Brahmin will also be a sage who constantly worships the celestial host.

6. *kuṭumbiko dharma-kāmaḥ sadāsvapnaś ca bhārata*
amāṁsāśī sadā ca syāt pavitraṁ ca sadā japet

As a householder, he desires the way of dharma and always refrains from sleeping, O Bhārata. He will never eat meat and constantly recites prayers for purification.

7. *amṛtāśī sadā ca syān na ca syād viṣa-bhojanaḥ*
vighasāśī sadā ca syāt sadā caivātithi-priyaḥ

For his food he will always consume the nectar of the gods and never have to eat food that is like poison. He will always eat the food left over from the sacred offerings and he will always show affection to the guests he receives.

8. *yudhiṣṭhira uvāca*
kathaṁ sadopavāsī syād brahmacārī kathaṁ bhavet
vighasāśī kathaṁ ca syāt sadā caivātithi-priyaḥ

Yudhiṣṭhira said: How will such a person be constantly fasting and how can he follow a vow of celibacy? How will he eat the food left over from the offerings and how will he show affection to his guests?

9. *bhīṣma uvāca*
antarā prātar āśaṁ ca sāyam āśaṁ tathaiva ca
sadopavāsī ca bhaved yo na bhuṅkte kathaṁcana

Bhīṣma said: By refraining from eating between his morning meal and evening meal a person undertakes a permanent fast.

10. *bhāryāṁ gacchan brahmacārī ṛtau bhavati brāhmaṇaḥ*
ṛta-vādī sadā ca syāj jñāna-nityaś ca yo naraḥ

A Brahmin is a *brahmacārin* following the vow of celibacy if he approaches his wife only at the appropriate time of the month, always speaks the truth, and is constant in his dedication to knowledge.

11. *abhakṣayan vṛthā-māṁsam amāṁsāśī bhavaty uta*
dāna-nityaḥ pavitraś ca asvapnaś ca divāsvapan

If one never eats the flesh of animals unless they were slaughtered for sacrifice, that is the same as not eating meat at all. Always giving in charity is complete purity, and not sleeping in the daytime represents abstention from sleep.

12. *bhṛtyātithiṣu yo bhuṅkte bhuktavatsu sadā sa ha*
amṛtaṁ sakalaṁ bhuṅkta iti viddhi yudhiṣṭhira

You should understand, Yudhiṣṭhira, that one who eats only when his servants and guests are satisfied consumes food that is identical in every way to the nectar of the gods.

13. *abhuktavatsu nāśnānaḥ satataṁ yas tu vai dvijaḥ*
abhojanena tenāsya jitaḥ svargo bhavaty uta

A Brahmin who never eats whilst others are still unsatisfied wins a heavenly reward by abstaining from food in this way.

14. *devatābhyaḥ pitṛbhyaś ca bhṛtyebhyo 'tithibhiḥ saha*
avaśiṣṭaṁ tu yo 'śnāti tam āhur vighasāśinam

One who eats what is left after food has been presented to the gods, forefathers, servants, and guests is said to be one who eats the sacred offerings.

15. *teṣāṁ lokā hy aparyantāḥ sadane brahmaṇā saha*
upasthitāś cāpsarobhiḥ pariyānti divaukasaḥ

Such persons attain worlds without limit. The inhabitants of heaven including Brahmā himself and the *apsarases* come and situate themselves within their abodes.

16. *devatābhiś ca ye sārdhaṁ pitṛbhiś copabhuñjate*
ramante putra-pautraiś ca teṣāṁ gatir anuttamā

Those who set aside half the food they eat as an offering to the gods and forefathers enjoy life in the company of their sons and grandsons and then attain the highest abode of all.

The Indra-Prahrāda-Saṁvāda

Śānti-parvan, Adhyāya 215

Chapters 215 to 221 of the *Mahābhārata*'s *Śānti-parvan* form a discrete unit held together by the fact that they all focus on Indra, the lord of the Vedic gods, and the conversations he has either with vanquished adversaries or with the Goddess Śrī after she has deserted them. The theme of these discussions is not particularly philosophical and marks a return to the emphasis on dissociation from the world we noted in the opening chapters of the *Mokṣa-dharma-parvan*. The usual line of discussion takes the form of Indra seeking out a defeated adversary, inquiring about his change of fortune, and asking how the fallen enemy is adjusting to this transformation. We then discover that these individuals have overcome misfortune and grief by developing a detached state of mind that enables them to view the world dispassionately without feeling any sense of loss. The lesson offered is relatively simple, one should rise above the inevitable fluctuations of fortune, neither rejoicing in times of prosperity nor feeling grief in times of distress.

The persons who instruct Indra in these passages are well known from Purāṇic literature, namely Prahrāda (Chapter 215), his grandson Bali (Chapters 216–218), Namuci (Chapter 219), Bali again (Chapter 220), and finally the Goddess Śrī (Chapter 221). What we learn from them is that good fortune is never constant and will inevitably be followed by periods of tribulation. Hence one should take a philosophical view of life through which one can learn to tolerate these constant vicissitudes. Of some interest is the basis on which a mood of dispassionate acceptance may be developed. In the first three of the passages we find Prahrāda arguing that it is *sva-bhāva*, the inherent nature of a living being, which is the ultimate causal factor, while Bali contends that everything is subject to time alone, and then finally Namuci indicates that everything occurs as a result of predestination. It is not clear to what extent these different ideas represent distinctive philosophical perspectives, but in each case the conclusion is one of absolute determinism and the rejection of the efficacy of human endeavour in producing the results of action.

The first of these discussions is a short passage in which Indra encounters Prahrāda, a leader of the *asuras* who is well known from the Purāṇas and whom we have already encountered in an earlier passage describing the instruction on renunciation he received from a saint who followed the way of the python. In the Purāṇas, Prahrāda (or Prahlāda) is represented as being the son of Hiraṇyakaśipu, the *asura* king destroyed by Viṣṇu's Narasiṅgha *avatāra*. In some of these accounts, notably that in Book 7 of the *Bhāgavata Purāṇa*, Prahrāda is shown as being devoted to Viṣṇu; it is Hiraṇyakaśipu's persecution of his son that is the main reason for the descent of the *avatāra*. The *Mahābhārata* shows some awareness of this man-lion form of Viṣṇu but does not make the connection with Prahrāda as the son of Hiraṇyakaśipu or refer to his involvement in the Deity's descent.

In this passage, Prahrāda is presented as an adversary of the gods who has now been defeated and is living in a state of poverty. Bhīṣma gives this account as a response to a question from Yudhiṣṭhira about the existence or otherwise of free will in relation to the performance of action, and it is this subject that forms the main theme of Prahrāda's instruction to Indra (here referred to by the name of Śakra). We are first told of the good qualities displayed by Prahrāda and then encounter the usual exchange for these passages with Indra asking why it is that his humbled adversary does not lament over this change of fortune. Right away, Prahrāda takes up the line of discussion that dominates the presentation as a whole by insisting that whatever a person does is simply a reflection of his *sva-bhāva*, a phrase that indicates one's inherent nature or personal identity. This cannot be changed and the action we perform is not based on any choice we make or expression of free will, for all actions are simply unavoidable manifestations of that nature.

Hence what Prahrāda expresses here is an intensely deterministic view of human life and human conduct, arguing that there is no free will at all (verse 16) and that the course of action we choose to adopt is entirely circumscribed by the *sva-bhāva* of the individual. We do find some indication of this perspective in the *Bhagavad-gītā* (18.59), where Kṛṣṇa indicates that Arjuna has no real choice over whether or not to fight because his nature will force him to act in that way, but there the idea is very much in the background as Arjuna is also advised that he should acts as he chooses (18.63). Here, however, no such choices are possible, for even when we feel we are exercising free will this is merely an error and the apparent choice made is just a further manifestation of one's inherent nature. Hence a person should never feel pride in his success and should never lament over failure, for every action we perform and every success we achieve is predetermined in accordance with the *sva-bhāva* of each individual.

From verse 24, Prahrāda's discourse appears to take a different turn as he states that he also holds to the doctrine of karma, whereby our future destiny is shaped by the actions we are presently performing. This apparent support for the efficacy of personal endeavour is immediately countered, however, by his assertion that the actions we do perform are not undertaken out of any sense of free will but are merely an inevitable reflection of our inherent nature. The consequence of these ideas seems therefore to be a mood of absolute indifference to the world, whilst the implication would appear to be that there is no real meaning to *dharma* or moral values, though this line of discussion is not taken up in the present passage. The conversation concludes with Indra asking how it is possible to gain such wisdom, which can bring freedom from lamentation. Prahrāda then lists the qualities required to achieve such realisation: honesty, vigilance, generosity, respecting elders; but lest one think it can be gained through any personal endeavour he remains true to his fundamental thesis by insisting that such qualities do not represent any sort of personal achievement but are simply a further reflection of the *sva-bhāva* of the individual.

1. *yudhiṣṭhira uvāca*
yad idaṁ karma loke 'smiñ śubhaṁ vā yadi vāśubhaṁ
puruṣaṁ yojayaty eva phala-yogena bhārata

Yudhiṣṭhira said: In this world, O Bhārata, a person is beset by the good and evil actions he has previously performed, as the fruits of such action overtake him.

2. *kartā svit tasya puruṣa utāho neti saṁśayaḥ*
etad icchāmi tattvena tvattaḥ śrotuṁ pitāmaha

But is a person the true performer of his actions, or is this not the case? This is what I do not understand. So now, grandfather, I want to hear from you the proper resolution of this issue.

3. *bhīṣma uvāca*
atrāpy udāharantīmam itihāsaṁ purātanam
prahrādasya ca saṁvādam indrasya ca yudhiṣṭhira

Bhīṣma said: Concerning this point, Yudhiṣṭhira, they recite this ancient account of a discussion that took place between Prahrāda and Indra.

4. *asaktaṁ dhūta-pāpmānaṁ kule jātaṁ bahu-śrutam*
astambham anahaṁkāraṁ sattva-sthaṁ samaye ratam

Prahrāda had no worldly attachments, he was free from sin, born into a good family and well versed in the Vedic teachings. He was never arrogant or egotistical, he was firm in his adherence to the quality of *sattva*, and dedicated to following the rules of religious life.

5. *tulya-nindā-stutiṁ dāntaṁ śūnyāgāra-niveśanam*
carācarāṇāṁ bhūtānāṁ vidita-prabhavāpyayam

He was equal in blame or praise, he was self-controlled, and he lived in a solitary abode. He fully understood the origin and dissolution of this host of moving and stationary beings.

6. *akrudhyantam ahṛṣyantam apriyeṣu priyeṣu ca*
kāñcane vātha loṣṭe vā ubhayoḥ sama-darśanam

He never showed anger at any misfortune nor joy at anything pleasurable, regarding a piece of gold and a lump of earth with equal vision.

7. *ātma-niḥśreyasa-jñāne dhīraṁ niścita-niścayam*
parāvara-jñaṁ bhūtānāṁ sarva-jñaṁ sama-darśanam

He was fixed in his understanding of the *ātman* and its liberation, resolute in his philosophical convictions. He understood both the greatest and the least of living beings. He was all knowing and viewed all things equally.

8. *śakraḥ prahrādam āsīnam ekānte saṁyatendriyam*
bubhutsamānas tat prajñām abhigamyedam abravīt

Whilst Prahrāda was sitting in a solitary place with his senses completely controlled, Śakra approached him and spoke the following words, for he wished to understand the wisdom Prahrāda possessed.

9. *yaiḥ kaiścit saṁmato loke guṇaiḥ syāt puruṣo nṛṣu*
bhavaty anapagān sarvāṁs tān guṇāḷ lakṣayāmahe

'In this world there are specific qualities through which a person gains renown amongst men. We observe that all such qualities are present here, and there is no deviation from them.

10. *atha te lakṣyate buddhiḥ samā bāla-janair iha*
ātmānaṁ manyamānaḥ sañ śreyaḥ kim iha manyase

Your understanding appears to be just like that of children, for you are absorbed in contemplating the *ātman*. So what do you consider to be the best way of understanding the *ātman*.

11. *baddhaḥ pāśaiś cyutaḥ sthānād dviṣatāṁ vaśam āgataḥ*
śriyā vihīnaḥ prahrāda śocitavye na śocasi

You are bound by ropes, you have fallen from your position and are now in the power of your enemies. You have been deprived of your opulence, Prahrāda, and yet in this lamentable condition you do not lament.

12. *prajñā-lābhāt tu daiteya utāho dhṛtimattayā*
prahrāda svastha-rūpo 'si paśyan vyasanam ātmanaḥ

Is this due to the knowledge you have acquired, Daiteya, or is it due to your resolute state of mind? Even though you can see your own misfortune, Prahrāda, you have the appearance of complete contentment.'

13. *iti saṁcoditas tena dhīro niścita-niścayaḥ*
uvāca ślakṣṇayā vācā svāṁ prajñām anuvarṇayan

When challenged by Indra in this way, Prahrāda was unmoved and remained firm in his convictions. He then replied with gentle words, revealing the wisdom that he had gained.

14. *pravṛttiṁ ca nivṛttiṁ ca bhūtānāṁ yo na budhyate*
tasya stambho bhaved bālyān nāsti stambho 'nupaśyataḥ

'If a person does not comprehend the origin and conclusion of living beings he becomes bewildered because of his stupidity, but one who perceives this truth is never bewildered.

15. *sva-bhāvāt saṁpravartante nivartante tathaiva ca*
sarve bhāvās tathābhāvāḥ puruṣārtho na vidyate

It is because of their inherent nature that living beings come into existence and then disappear. All of them exist and then they cease to exist but personal endeavour plays no part in this process.

16. *puruṣārthasya cābhāve nāsti kaścit sva-kārakaḥ*
svayaṁ tu kurvatas tasya jātu māno bhaved iha

And as personal endeavour is not a factor, there is no one who truly performs his own actions. If, however, a person thinks for a moment that he is himself the doer, then pride inevitably arises.

17. *yas tu kartāram ātmānaṁ manyate sādhv-asādhunoḥ*
tasya doṣavatī prajñā sva-mūrty-ajñeti me matiḥ

One who regards himself as the enactor of his own virtue and wickedness displays a flawed understanding and does not comprehend his own nature. That is my opinion.

18. *yadi syāt puruṣaḥ kartā śakrātma-śreyase dhruvam*
ārambhās tasya sidhyeran na ca jātu parābhavet

If, O Śakra, a person was the creator of his destiny, then the attainment of his own prosperity would be certain. All his endeavours would meet with success and he would never experience failure.

19. *aniṣṭasya hi nirvṛttir anivṛttiḥ priyasya ca*
lakṣyate yatamānānāṁ puruṣārthas tataḥ kutaḥ

The truth of the matter can be seen if we observe persons who endeavour for the cessation of unpleasant circumstances and for the perpetuation of pleasant circumstances. What does their endeavour achieve?

20. *aniṣṭasyābhinirvṛttim iṣṭa-saṁvṛttim eva ca*
aprayatnena paśyāmaḥ keṣāṁcit tat sva-bhāvataḥ

We see that for some people the avoidance of what is undesirable and the attainment of what is desirable are achieved without exertion. This is simply due to the nature of the world.

21. *pratirūpa-dharāḥ kecid dṛśyante buddhi-sattamāḥ*
virūpebhyo 'lpa-buddhibhyo lipsamānā dhanāgamam

Some people of refined appearance and keen intelligence can be seen trying to get money from those who appear uncouth and have little intelligence.

22. *sva-bhāva-preritāḥ sarve niviśante guṇā yadā*
śubhāśubhās tadā tatra tasya kiṁ māna-kāraṇam

When all the qualities one acquires, be they good or evil, are developed because of the impulse of one's inherent nature, what reason can there be for taking pride in possessing them?

23. *sva-bhāvād eva tat sarvam iti me niścitā matiḥ*
ātma-pratiṣṭhitā prajñā mama nāsti tato 'nyathā

It is my firm conviction that all such attributes are due only to one's inherent nature. This is the wisdom established in my heart. There is nothing else other than one's nature.

24. *karma-jaṁ tv iha manye 'haṁ phala-yogaṁ śubhāśubham*
karmaṇāṁ viṣayaṁ kṛtsnam ahaṁ vakṣyāmi tac chṛṇu

But I also consider the good and bad rewards one encounters in life to be the result of previous actions. So now I will speak in full on the subject of action. Hear my words.

25. *yathā vedayate kaścid odanaṁ vāyaso vadan*
evaṁ sarvāṇi karmāṇi sva-bhāvasyaiva lakṣaṇam

As the cries of one bird reveal the presence of cooked rice to others, so the actions one performs are an indication of one's inherent nature.

26. *vikārān eva yo veda na veda prakṛtiṁ parām*
tasya stambho bhaved bālyān nāsti stambho 'nupaśyataḥ

One who knows only the transformations and does not perceive the higher identity of *prakṛti* becomes confused because of his stupidity. But one who perceives this higher nature is never confused.

27. *sva-bhāva-bhāvino bhāvān sarvān eveha niścaye*
budhyamānasya darpo vā māno vā kiṁ kariṣyati

When a person reaches the firm conviction that all forms of existence arise solely because of the influence of inherent nature, what purpose would conceit or pride then serve for such an enlightened one?

28. *veda dharma-vidhiṁ kṛtsnaṁ bhūtānāṁ cāpy anityatām*
tasmāc chakra na śocāmi sarvaṁ hy evedam antavat

I fully understand the rules of dharma and the temporary nature of living beings and so I never lament, Śakra. Everything in this world must come to an end.

29. *nirmamo nirahaṁkāro nirīho mukta-bandhanaḥ*
svastho 'vyapetaḥ paśyāmi bhūtānāṁ prabhavāpyayau

I have no sense of ownership, I am free of any sense of ego, I have no desires, and I am free from bondage. Cheerful and detached from the world, I observe the birth and death of living beings.

30. *kṛta-prajñasya dāntasya vitṛṣṇasya nirāśiṣaḥ*
nāyāso vidyate śakra paśyato loka-vidyayā

There is no trouble in life for a person who possesses wisdom, practises self-control, and is free from material longings and from aspirations, Śakra, for he observes the world with a true understanding of its nature.

31. *prakṛtau ca vikāre ca na me prītir na ca dveṣe*
dveṣṭāraṁ na ca paśyāmi yo mamādya mamāyate

I have no attraction for *prakṛti* or its transformations, and neither have I any aversion to it. I do not regard anyone as my enemy, nor anyone as belonging to me either now or in the future.

32. *nordhvaṁ nāvāṅ na tiryak ca na kvacic chakra kāmaye*
na vijñāne na vijñeye nājñāne śarma vidyate

I have no hankering for the world above, for the lower worlds, or for the intermediate region, Śakra. For me there is no satisfaction in knowledge, in the object that is known, or indeed in ignorance.'

33. *śakra uvāca*
yenaiṣā labhyate prajñā yena śāntir avāpyate
prabrūhi tam upāyaṁ me samyak prahrāda pṛcchate

Śakra said: Instruct me fully, Prahrāda, as I now ask you about the means by which such wisdom is acquired and this state of tranquillity attained.

34. *prahrāda uvāca*
ārjavenāpramādena prasādenātmavattayā
vṛddha-śuśrūṣayā śakra puruṣo labhate mahat

Prahrāda said: It is through sincerity, vigilance, generosity, composure, and showing reverence to his elders, O Śakra, that a person achieves greatness.

35. *sva-bhāvāl labhate prajñāṁ śāntim eti sva-bhāvataḥ*
sva-bhāvād eva tat sarvaṁ yat kiṁcid anupaśyasi

But it is because of his inherent nature that he acquires wisdom and it is due to his inherent nature that he finds tranquillity. In truth everything you see develops because of its inherent nature.'

36. *bhīṣma uvāca*
ity ukto daitya-patinā śakro vismayam āgamat
prītimāṁś ca tadā rājaṁs tad vākyaṁ pratyapūjayat

Bhīṣma said: After being addressed in this way by the lord of the Daityas, Śakra was filled with wonder. Being fully satisfied, O king, he then offered his respects to the words he had heard.

37. *sa tadābhyarcya daityendraṁ trai-lokya-patir īśvaraḥ*
asurendram upāmantrya jagāma svaṁ niveśanam

Though Prahrāda was the king of the Daityas and *asuras*, that Deity who is the lord of the three worlds then worshipped him and after taking his leave departed for his own abode.

The Bali-Vāsava-Saṁvāda

Śanti-parvan, Adhyāya 216–218

The second passage of this group records a conversation between Indra and Bali who, like Prahrāda, is also well known from Purāṇic literature. According to the *Purāṇas*, Prahrāda was the son of the *asura* king Hiraṇyakaśipu, slain by the Narasiṅgha *avatāra*, and Bali was the son of Virocana and grandson of Prahrāda. Bali is best known, however, from the stories concerning Viṣṇu's Vāmana or dwarf *avatāra* to whom Bali gave three paces of land; subsequently he was forced to give up his lordship over the universe when the Vāmana assumed a cosmic form and covered both heaven and earth with the paces given. In this passage, however, there is no mention of the *avatāra* story even though Bali is shown to have been defeated by the gods and cast down from his position as lord of all the worlds.

Although the basic premise is fundamentally the same, there is something of a difference of tone between this and the previous passage. First of all, Indra himself is more inimical towards his defeated adversary, his questions delivered in a haughty and mocking way, and he is still inclined to act violently against Bali. Similarly, despite his claim to be wholly detached from the changing fortunes of the world, Bali likewise retains his enmity towards Indra and at various points threatens to resume hostilities. The passage is divided into three chapters each of which has its own distinctive theme. In the first, Indra is directed to Bali's hiding place by Brahmā and then questions him about his state of mind following the dramatic change in fortune he has experienced. In the second, Bali replies to Indra, claiming like Prahrāda that he has no sense of grief or loss because he understands that everything occurs due to the progression of time and not through human endeavour. Then in the third chapter, Śrī, the Goddess of Prosperity, emerges from the body of Bali and takes refuge with Indra, explaining to him that she cannot be controlled by any living being but resides wherever virtue prevails. The principal idea here is very much the same as in the previous passage, presenting an intensely determinist view of life that emphasises the absolute precedence of destiny over human endeavour The types of action through which we seek prosperity in life are ultimately futile for all outcomes are determined by time alone. Hence one should develop a mood of detachment from the world, transcending both grief and celebration, recognising the inevitable progression of time.

Śānti-parvan, Adhyāya 216

The first chapter of the *Bali-vāsava-saṁvāda* does little more than to set the scene for the conversation between Bali and Indra, here referred to as Vāsava, which is presented in Chapter 2. The passage begins in the usual way with Yudhiṣṭhira putting a question to Bhīṣma, in this case as to how a king can continue living in the world when his opulence is lost. In reply, Bhīṣma tells of how Indra once came before Brahmā and asked him where Bali, the fallen king of the *asuras*, is to be found now that his wealth, good fortune, and dominion over the whole of creation is lost. Brahmā is unhappy at Indra's request and has to instruct him that Bali should not be molested in any way;

rather, instruction should be sought from him in order learn of the great wisdom he possesses.

We are then told of how Indra locates Bali who is now in hiding, having assumed the form of an ass. Indra inquires of the fallen king about his feelings and emotions both when he was in his exalted position and now that all his good fortune has vanished. One might take this as a genuine inquiry as to how a man of wisdom is able to come to terms with the inevitable misfortunes of life, but one gets the sense that Indra's primary aim is to mock his old adversary and thereby relish his triumph still further. Certainly, Bali sees Indra's words in this way, condemning him for the baseness of his sentiments in seeking to deride a person in distress. There is also a veiled threat from Bali who suggests that his degradation is not permanent and there will come a time in the future when he will rise once more to vanquish Indra and regain his lost status.

1. *yudhiṣṭhira uvāca*
yayā buddhyā mahī-pālo bhraṣṭa-śrīr vicaren mahīm
kāla-daṇḍa-viniṣpiṣṭas tan me brūhi pitāmaha

Yudhiṣṭhira said: By what form of understanding may a king continue his sojourn on earth when he has been stripped of his wealth and ground down by the rod of time? Teach me this, grandfather.

2. *bhīṣma uvāca*
atrāpy udāharantīmam itihāsaṁ purātanam
vāsavasya ca saṁvādaṁ baler vairocanasya ca

Bhīṣma said: Concerning this subject they recite this ancient account of a discussion that took place between Vāsava and Bali, the son of Virocana.

3. *pitāmaham upāgatya praṇipatya kṛtāñjaliḥ*
sarvān evāsurāñ jitvā baliṁ papraccha vāsavaḥ

After approaching the grandfather of the world and falling before him with his hands together, Vāsava, who had conquered all the *asuras*, questioned him concerning Bali.

4. *yasya sma dadato vittaṁ na kadācana hīyate*
taṁ baliṁ nādhigacchāmi brahmann ācakṣva me balim

'Although he gave away his wealth, Bali was never bereft of anything. I cannot find Bali anywhere, O Brahmā, so tell me where Bali is to be found.

5. *sa eva hy astam ayate sa sma vidyotate diśaḥ*
sa varṣati sma varṣāṇi yathā-kālam atandritaḥ
taṁ baliṁ nādhigacchāmi brahmann ācakṣva me balim

It was he who set at evening time and he alone who illuminated the directions. Paying careful attention, he poured down the rains at the appropriate time. But now I cannot find Bali anywhere, O Brahmā, so tell me where Bali is to be found.

6. *sa vāyur varuṇaś caiva sa raviḥ sa ca candramāḥ*
so 'gnis tapati bhūtāni pṛthivī ca bhavaty uta
taṁ baliṁ nādhigacchāmi brahmann ācakṣva me balim

He was Vāyu and Varuṇa, he was the sun and the moon, he was Agni who burns these living beings, and he was the earth as well. But now I cannot find Bali anywhere, O Brahmā, so tell me where Bali is to be found.'

7. *brahmovāca*
naitat te sādhu maghavan yad etad anupṛcchasi
pṛcchas tu nānṛtaṁ brūyāt tasmād vakṣyāmi te balim

Brahmā said: It is unrighteous of you, Maghavan, to make such an inquiry. But when asked about something one should never speak falsely, so I will inform you about Bali.

8. *uṣṭreṣu yadi vā goṣu khareṣv aśveṣu vā punaḥ*
variṣṭho bhavitā jantuḥ śūnyāgāre śacī-pate

Husband of Śacī, whether he is living with camels, cows, donkeys, or horses, he will be the best creature amongst them and will be found living in a solitary abode.

9. *śakra uvāca*
yadi sma balinā brahmañ śūnyāgāre sameyivān
hanyām enaṁ na vā hanyāṁ tad brahmann anuśādhi mām

Śakra said: If, O Brahmā, I should meet with Bali in that secluded place, tell me whether or not I should slay him.

10. *brahmovāca*
mā sma śakra baliṁ hiṁsīr na balir vadham arhati
nyāyāṁs tu śakra praṣṭavyas tvayā vāsava kāmyayā

Brahmā said: No indeed, Śakra, you should not harm Bali. He must not be slain. Rather he should be asked for instruction about the rules of religious life and whatever you wish to learn about, Vāsava.

11. *bhīṣma uvāca*
evam ukto bhagavatā mahendraḥ pṛthivīṁ tadā
cacārairavata-skandham adhiruhya śriyā vrtaḥ

Bhīṣma said: After receiving this instruction from the lord, Mahendra climbed onto the shoulders of Airāvata and journeyed across the earth, bedecked in all his finery.

12. *tato dadarśa sa baliṁ khara-veṣeṇa saṁvṛtam*
yathā-khyātaṁ bhagavatā śūnyāgāra-kṛtālayam

Eventually he saw Bali concealed within the form of a donkey, making his abode in a solitary place just as the lord had indicated.

13. *śakra uvāca*
khara-yonim anuprāptas tuṣa-bhakṣo 'si dānava
iyaṁ te yonir adhamā śocasy āho na śocasi

Śakra said: Having entered the womb of a donkey, Dānava, you now live by eating the chaff of the grain. Do you lament for the lowly birth you have taken, or does it not distress you?

14. *adṛṣṭaṁ bata paśyāmi dviṣatāṁ vaśam āgatam*
śriyā vihīnaṁ mitraiś ca bhraṣṭa-vīrya-parākramam

Never before have I seen what I now behold. You have fallen under the power of your enemies, you are bereft of wealth and friends, and your strength and courage are gone.

15. *yat tad yāna-sahasreṇa jñātibhiḥ parivāritaḥ*
lokān pratāpayan sarvān yāsy asmān avitarkayan

It was you who went forth with a thousand chariots, surrounded by your kinsmen. Whilst scorching all the worlds in this way, you paid us no heed at all.

16. *tvan-mukhāś caiva daiteyā vyatiṣṭhaṁs tava śāsane*
akṛṣṭa-pacyā pṛthivī tavaiśvarye babhūva ha
idaṁ ca te 'dya vyasanaṁ śocasy āho na śocasi

When you were their leader, the Daiteyas acted upon your commands and because of your power the earth produced crops without being ploughed. So do you lament for the terrible plight you now find yourself in, or does it not distress you at all?

17. *yadātiṣṭhaḥ samudrasya pūrva-kūle vilelihan*
jñātibhyo vibhajan vittaṁ tadāsīt te manaḥ katham

When you went as far as the eastern shore of the ocean, lapping everything up, what was your state of mind as you distributed shares of your riches to your kinsmen?

18. *yat te sahasra-samitā nanṛtur deva-yoṣitaḥ*
bahūni varṣa-pūgāni vihāre dīpyataḥ śriyā

Thousands of heavenly women gathered together and danced before you. Effulgent with opulence, you passed many years in succession indulging in such pastimes.

19. *sarvāḥ puṣkara-mālinyaḥ sarvāḥ kāñcana-saprabhāḥ*
katham adya tadā caiva manas te dānaveśvara

All of them were garlanded with lotus flowers and were effulgent like gold. What was your state of mind then, Lord of the Dānavas, and how do you feel now?

20. *chatraṁ tavāsīt sumahat sauvarṇaṁ maṇi-bhūṣitam*
nanṛtur yatra gandharvāḥ ṣaṭ-sahasrāṇi saptadhā

The huge parasol you possessed was made of gold and inlaid with gems. Forty-two thousand *gandharvas* used to dance before you.

21. *yūpas tavāsīt sumahān yajataḥ sarva-kāñcanaḥ*
yatrādadaḥ sahasrāṇām ayutāni gavāṁ daśa

The sacred post used in your sacrifices was huge in size and made completely of gold. At those sacrifices you gave away many millions of cows.

22. *yadā tu pṛthivīṁ sarvāṁ yajamāno 'nuparyayāḥ*
śamyā-kṣepeṇa vidhinā tadāsīt kiṁ nu te hṛdi

What feelings arose in your heart when you travelled round the earth performing sacrifices, casting your staff before you as ordained by the rules of scripture?

23. *na te paśyāmi bhṛṅgāraṁ na chatraṁ vyajanaṁ na ca*
brahma-dattāṁ ca te mālāṁ na paśyāmy asurādhipa

I do not see here the golden vessel with which you were anointed as king, nor your parasol or fan. Neither, O lord of the *asuras*, do I see your garland, which was presented to you by Brahmā himself.

24. *balir uvāca*
na tvaṁ paśyasi bhṛṅgāraṁ na chatraṁ vyajanaṁ na ca
brahma-dattāṁ ca me mālāṁ na tvaṁ drakṣyasi vāsava

Bali said: No, you do not see that golden vessel here, nor the parasol or fan. Neither will you see the garland that was given to me by Brahmā, O Vāsava.

25. *guhāyāṁ nihitāni tvaṁ mama ratnāni pṛcchasi*
yadā me bhavitā kālas tadā tvaṁ tāni drakṣyasi

These treasures of mine that you are asking about are now kept in a secret place, but when my time comes then you will see them.

26. *na tv etad anurūpaṁ te yaśaso vā kulasya vā*
samṛddhārtho 'samṛddhārthaṁ yan māṁ katthitum icchasi

The words you have spoken are unworthy of one of your reputation and high birth. Now that your fortunes are flourishing and my glory has vanished you wish to speak to me in this way.

27. *na hi duḥkheṣu śocanti na prahṛṣyanti carddhiṣu*
kṛta-prajñā jñāna-tṛptāḥ kṣāntāḥ santo manīṣiṇaḥ

Wise men are satisfied by knowledge alone. They are patient, righteous, and intelligent. Such persons do not lament when misfortune arises, nor do they rejoice in times of prosperity.

28. *tvaṁ tu prākṛtayā buddhyā puraṁdara vikatthase*
yadāham iva bhāvī tvaṁ tadā naivaṁ vadiṣyasi

But you boast like this because you have the mind of a common man, Puraṁdara. When you live in the manner that I am living in now, you will not speak in such a way.

Śānti-parvan, Adhyāya 217

It is in the second of the three chapters of the *Bali-vāsava-saṁvāda* that we are presented with its principal line of teaching, as Bali responds to Indra's questioning by explaining his ability to remain undisturbed by the changing fortunes of the world. As with the speech of Prahrāda in the previous passage, the main idea here is a relatively simple one: Bali insists on the absolute control of time over all events. Human endeavour is entirely ineffective as every outcome and every change of fortune is simply the result of the inevitable progression of time. Hence he will not rejoice over power, victory, or prosperity and he will never lament when circumstances turn against him, knowing as he does that this is nothing to do with his own or anyone else's endeavours; it is simply the influence of time taking effect. There should be no pride such as that displayed by Indra, but rather an attitude of absolute dispassion as he observes the movements of time.

We might consider the religious or philosophical perspective from which this passage is written but that is rather difficult to determine. The reference to persons who know the Vedas in verse 46 reveals that the author tends towards orthodoxy, but at the same time there is no suggestion of there being any Deity who might have control over time. Indeed verses 47 to 53 would appear to indicate that time is to be equated with Brahman and hence is the absolute principle. There is perhaps a hint of Sāṁkhya in verse 17 with the reference to the five elements as forming the human body, but the emphasis on the absolute supremacy of time is not typical in Sāṁkhya discourses. We must be aware, however, that there was more than one school of Sāṁkhya thought and the connection does serve to demonstrate that the emphases on *sva-bhāva* and then on *kāla* we are encountering here are not necessarily incompatible with Sāṁkhya teachings. One final feature of this chapter that may be worth noting is the number of phrases it uses in common with the *Bhagavad-gītā*. Although the subject matter here and the direction of instruction are both quite different to those of the *Gītā*, one feels that these appear too frequently for it to be mere coincidence.

1. *bhīṣma uvāca*
punar eva tu taṁ śakraḥ prahasann idam abravīt
niḥśvasantaṁ yathā nāgaṁ pravyāhārāya bhārata

Bhīṣma said: With a smile on his face, Śakra spoke again to Bali, who was hissing like a snake, with words that were even more spiteful than before, O Bhārata.

2. *yat tad yāna-sahasreṇa jñātibhiḥ parivāritaḥ*
lokān pratāpayan sarvān yāsy asmān avitarkayan

'It was you who went forth with a thousand chariots, surrounded by your kinsmen. Whilst scorching all the worlds in this way you paid us no heed at all.

3. *dṛṣṭvā sukṛpaṇāṁ cemām avasthām ātmano bale*
jñāti-mitra-parityaktaḥ śocasy āho na śocasi

Beholding the miserable state you have fallen into, Bali, deserted by kinsmen and friends, do you now lament or does it not distress you at all?

4. *prītiṁ prāpyātulāṁ pūrvaṁ lokāṁś cātma-vaśe sthitān*
vinipātam imaṁ cādya śocasy āho na śocasi

Previously the joy you felt was unequalled, for the worlds were under your control. Do you lament over the way you have fallen from power or does it not distress you at all?'

5. *balir uvāca*
anityam upalakṣyedaṁ kāla-paryāyam ātmanaḥ
tasmāc chakra na śocāmi sarvaṁ hy evedam antavat

Bali said: Time is the cause of this inversion of my fortunes. Knowing as I do, O Śakra, the temporary nature of such changes I do not lament for any of this. It will pass away.

6. *antavanta ime dehā bhūtānām amarādhipa*
tena śakra na śocāmi nāparādhād idaṁ mama

The bodies of these living beings must all pass way, O lord of the immortals. I do not lament for this, Śakra, for the position I now occupy is not the result of any offence I have committed.

7. *jīvitaṁ ca śarīraṁ ca pretya vai saha jāyate*
ubhe saha vivardhete ubhe saha vinaśyataḥ

After death, the life force and the body are again born in association with one another. They grow together and together they meet with death.

8. *tad īdṛśam idaṁ bhāvam avaśaḥ prāpya kevalam*
yady evam abhijānāmi kā vyathā me vijānataḥ

Such then is all that the existence I have gained amounts to and I have no control over these circumstances. If I understand my plight in this way, what anguish can overcome me in this state of knowledge?

9. *bhūtānāṁ nidhanaṁ niṣṭhā śrotasām iva sāgaraḥ*
naitat samyag vijānanto narā muhyanti vajra-bhṛt

For living beings, death marks the conclusion of their existence, just as for rivers the sea is their ultimate end. If they fully understand this truth then men no longer exist in a state of illusion, O bearer of the thunderbolt.

10. *ye tv evaṁ nābhijānanti rajo-moha-parāyaṇāḥ*
te kṛcchraṁ prāpya sīdanti buddhir yeṣāṁ praṇaśyati

But those under the sway of passion and illusion who do not understand this truth meet with nothing but trouble and then sink down with their intelligence destroyed.

11. *buddhi-lābhe hi puruṣaḥ sarvaṁ nudati kilbiṣaṁ*
vipāpmā labhate sattvaṁ sattva-sthaḥ saṁprasīdati

When a person develops his intelligence, he pushes aside all contamination. Freeing himself from iniquity, he reaches the quality of *sattva*; and when he exists in the realm of *sattva* his suffering is assuaged.

12. *tatas tu ye nivartante jāyante vā punaḥ punaḥ*
kṛpaṇāḥ paritapyante te 'narthaiḥ paricoditāḥ

But those who move away from the quality of *sattva*, and are reborn over and over again, are the wretched souls who endure the sufferings of this existence under the impulse of things that have no value.

13. *artha-siddhim anarthaṁ ca jīvitaṁ maraṇaṁ tathā*
sukha-duḥkha-phalaṁ caiva na dveṣmi na ca kāmaye

I neither loathe nor hanker after the acquisition of wealth, poverty, life, death, or the joy and sorrow one gains from previous actions.

14. *hataṁ hanti hato hy eva yo naro hanti kaṁcana*
ubhau tau na vijānīto yaś ca hanti hataś ca yaḥ

A killer slays his victim and so there is one man who kills. Neither of these two properly understands, neither the one who kills nor the one who is slain.

15. *hatvā jitvā ca maghavan yaḥ kaścit puruṣāyate*
akartā hy eva bhavati kartā tv eva karoti tat

None of those who pose as heroes after slaying and conquering their foes, O Maghavan, are the true performers of that action. But there is a doer who executes the deed.

16. *ko hi lokasya kurute vināśa-prabhavāv ubhau*
kṛtaṁ hi tat kṛtenaiva kartā tasyāpi cāparaḥ

Who is it then who brings about both the destruction and creation of the world? The doer performs an action by means of something that has already been created, and some other doer previously created that performer of action.

17. *pṛthivī vāyur ākāśam āpo jyotiś ca pañcamam*
etad yonīni bhūtāni tatra kā paridevanā

Earth, air, space, water, and light are the five sources of origin for these living beings. This being so what cause is there for lamentation?

18. *mahā-vidyo 'lpa-vidyaś ca balavān durbalaś ca yaḥ*
darśanīyo virūpaś ca subhago durbhagaś ca yaḥ

One who has vast learning and one who knows little, one who is strong and one who is weak, one who is delightful to behold and one who is unsightly, one who is fortunate and one bereft of good fortune:

19. *sarvaṁ kālaḥ samādatte gambhīraḥ svena tejasā*
tasmin kāla-vaśaṁ prāpte kā vyathā me vijānataḥ

By its own power the mysterious force of time carries all of them away. Understanding as I do this control of time over our existence, what is there for me to lament over?

20. *dagdham evānudahati hatam evānuhanti ca*
naśyate naṣṭam evāgre labdhavyaṁ labhate naraḥ

One burns what time has burnt already and kills a person who is already slain. When something meets with destruction it was destroyed from its very beginning. A man attains what he is destined to attain.

21. *nāsya dvīpaḥ kutaḥ pāraṁ nāvāraḥ saṁpradṛśyate*
nāntam asya prapaśyāmi vidher divyasya cintayan

There is no island in this ocean of time. Where is its further shore? Its limits can never be seen. When I contemplate the truth, I can find no end to this divine force that controls all things.

22. *yadi me paśyataḥ kālo bhūtāni na vināśayet*
syān me harṣaś ca darpaś ca krodhaś caiva śacī-pate

If it were my understanding that time is not the killer of living beings, husband of Śacī, then joy, pride, and anger would surely be present within me.

23. *tuṣa-bhakṣaṁ tu māṁ jñātvā pravivikta-jane gṛhe*
bibhrataṁ gārdabhaṁ rūpam ādiśya parigarhase

Knowing that I live by eating chaff in a house apart from other people and seeing that I bear the form of an ass, you now despise me.

24. *icchann ahaṁ vikuryāṁ hi rūpāṇi bahudhātmanaḥ*
vibhīṣaṇāni yānīkṣya palāyethās tvam eva me

But if I so desire, I can assume for myself many frightening forms, and if you were to see them you would flee from me in terror.

25. *kālaḥ sarvaṁ samādatte kālaḥ sarvaṁ prayacchati*
kālena vidhṛtaṁ sarvaṁ mā kṛthāḥ śakra pauruṣam

Time carries everything away and time brings everything forth. Everything is ordained by time, so do not make a show of your prowess, Śakra.

26. *purā sarvaṁ pravyathate mayi kruddhe puraṁdara*
avaimi tv asya lokasya dharmaṁ śakra sanātanam

It is true that in the past, Puraṁdara, everyone used to tremble with fear when I was angry. But now I understand the eternal dharma, the changeless principle that sustains this world, O Śakra.

27. *tvam apy evam apekṣasva mātmanā vismayaṁ gamaḥ*
prabhavaś ca prabhāvaś ca nātma-saṁsthaḥ kadācana

You should try to see things in this way and not be so thrilled with yourself. Neither power nor its origin are ever dependent on one's own endeavours.

28. *kaumāram eva te cittaṁ tathaivādya yathā purā*
samavekṣasva maghavan buddhiṁ vindasva naiṣṭhikīm

Your mentality is as childish now as it was in the past. Try to see things properly, Maghavan, and cultivate an understanding based on certainty.

29. *devā manuṣyāḥ pitaro gandharvoraga-rākṣasāḥ*
āsan sarve mama vaśe tat sarvaṁ vettha vāsava

All the gods, human beings, forefathers, *gandharvas*, *uragas*, and *rākṣasas* were under my control. You know all about this, Vāsava.

30. *namas tasyai diśe 'py astu yasyāṁ vairocano baliḥ*
iti māṁ abhyapadyanta buddhi-mātsarya-mohitāḥ

'I offer my respects towards whatever direction Bali the son of Virocana now occupies.' They used to come before me with such words, their intelligence deluded by envy.

31. *nāhaṁ tad anuśocāmi nātma-bhraṁśaṁ śacī-pate*
evaṁ me niścitā buddhiḥ śāstustiṣṭhāmy ahaṁ vaśe

I do not lament for the praise I received, husband of Śacī, nor for my loss of status. My understanding is now firmly resolved as I remain here under the control of the force which directs all things.

32. *dṛśyate hi kule jāto darśanīyaḥ pratāpavān*
duḥkhaṁ jīvan sahāmātyo bhavitavyaṁ hi tat tathā

It is often seen that a person born in a noble family who possesses good looks and great power still leads a miserable existence along with all his companions because this is what is ordained for him.

33. *dauṣkuleyas tathā mūḍho durjātaḥ śakra dṛśyate*
sukhaṁ jīvan sahāmātyo bhativyaṁ hi tat tathā

And it can also be seen, O Śakra, that a foolish, low-born person who comes from a worthless family may lead a joyful existence along with all his companions, for again this is what is ordained for him.

34. *kalyāṇī rūpa-saṁpannā durbhagā śakra dṛśyate*
alakṣaṇā virūpā ca subhagā śakra dṛśyate

Similarly, it is seen that a virtuous woman who possesses great beauty is unfortunate in her life, O Śakra, whilst another woman who has no auspicious qualities and is devoid of beauty may still enjoy good fortune.

35. *naitad asmat-kṛtaṁ śakra naitac chakra tvayā kṛtam*
yat tvam evaṁ-gato vajrin yad vāpy evaṁ-gatā vayam

Your present position, Śakra, is not of your own making and neither is my position the result of anything that I have done, O Vajrin.

36. *na karma tava nānyeṣāṁ kuto mama śata-krato*
ṛddhir vāpy atha vā narddhiḥ paryāya-kṛtam eva tat

No deed of yours, of mine, or of anyone else has brought us to these states of prosperity and poverty, O performer of a hundred sacrifices, for these are caused by the inevitable revolution of time.

37. *paśyāmi tvā virājantaṁ deva-rājam avasthitam*
śrīmantaṁ dyutimantaṁ ca garjantaṁ ca mamopari

I see you now in your glory, installed as the lord of the gods, endowed with wealth and splendour, calling down to me from your position on high.

38. *etac caivaṁ na cet kālo mām ākramya sthito bhavet*
pātayeyam ahaṁ tvādya savajram api muṣṭinā

But this would not be the case if time were to turn in my favour and remain there. Even though you carry a thunderbolt, I would then immediately strike you down with my fist.

39. *na tu vikrama-kālo 'yaṁ kṣamā-kālo 'yam āgataḥ*
kālaḥ sthāpayate sarvaṁ kālaḥ pacati vai tathā

But this is not my time of strength; the time for patience has come. Time allots a place for everything and time brings everything to a conclusion as well.

40. *māṁ ced abhyāgataḥ kālo dānaveśvaram ūrjitam*
garjantaṁ pratapantaṁ ca kam anyaṁ nāgamiṣyati

If time has overwhelmed even myself, the powerful master of the Dānavas who shouted aloud as he scorched the world, can there be anyone it will not fall upon?

41. *dvādaśānāṁ hi bhavatāṁ ādityānāṁ mahātmanām*
tejāṁsy ekena sarveṣāṁ deva-rāja hṛtāni me

You twelve sons of Aditi were great persons, O king of the gods, but single-handedly I took away that power from all of you.

42. *aham evodvahāmy āpo visṛjāmi ca vāsava*
tapāmi caiva trailokyaṁ vidyotāmy aham eva ca

I alone lifted up the waters and showered them down as rain, O Vāsava. And it was I alone who filled the three worlds with warmth and light.

43. *saṁrakṣāmi vilumpāmi dadāmy aham athādade*
saṁyacchāmi niyacchāmi lokeṣu prabhur īśvaraḥ

I protected and I plundered, I gave away gifts and I seized property, I governed and I controlled, for I was the lord and master of the worlds.

44. *tad adya vinivṛttaṁ me prabhutvam amarādhipa*
kāla-sainyāvagāḍhasya sarvaṁ na pratibhāti me

That dominance is now lost, O lord of the immortals, for time's army has overwhelmed me and that power no longer illuminates my life.

45. *nāhaṁ kartā na caiva tvaṁ nānyaḥ kartā śacī-pate*
paryāyeṇa hi bhujyante lokāḥ śakra yadṛcchayā

I have not brought this about, nor have you, and nor has anyone else, O husband of Śacī. These worlds are governed by the cycles of time, O Śakra, which move of their own accord.

46. *māsārdha-māsa-veśmānam aho-rātrābhisaṁvṛtam*
ṛtu-dvāraṁ varṣa-mukham āhur veda-vido janāḥ

Persons conversant with the Vedas speak of the months and fortnights as its body, with the days and nights as its clothing; the seasons are its senses, and the years are its mouth.

47. *āhuḥ sarvam idaṁ cintyaṁ janāḥ kecin manīṣayā*
asyāḥ pañcaiva cintāyāḥ paryeṣyāmi ca pañcadhā

There are some people who on the basis of their wisdom assert that this should conceived of as all this world. There are five elements that should be considered and hence it is fivefold.

48. *gambhīraṁ gahanaṁ brahma mahat toyārṇavaṁ yathā*
anādi-nidhanaṁ cāhur akṣaraṁ param eva ca

They say that Brahman is mysterious and hard to comprehend, just like the vast waters of the ocean. It has neither beginning nor end, it does not decay, and it stands above everything else.

49. *sattveṣu liṅgam āveśya na liṅgam api tat svayam*
manyante dhruvam evainaṁ ye narās tattva-darśinaḥ

Even after it has taken on attributes in its various forms of existence it still remains free of attributes in itself. Men who have seen the truth conceive of Brahman as the changeless principle.

50. *bhūtānāṁ tu viparyāsaṁ manyate gatavān iti*
na hy etāvad bhaved gamyaṁ na yasmāt prakṛteḥ paraḥ

The opposite view is held in relation to living beings, which are regarded as impermanent. This view should not be held in relation to Brahman by regarding it as not superior to *prakṛti*.

51. *gatiṁ hi sarva-bhūtānām agatvā kva gamiṣyasi*
yo dhāvatā na hātavyas tiṣṭhann api na hīyate
tam indriyāṇi sarvāṇi nānupaśyanti pañcadhā

If you do not follow this path of all beings, where is there that you can go? It is not left behind by one's running away, nor is it abandoned when one is standing still. None of the five senses can perceive it.

52. *āhuś cainaṁ kecid agniṁ kecid āhuḥ prajāpatim*
ṛtu-māsārdha-māsāṁś ca divasāṁs tu kṣaṇāṁs tathā

Some say that it is Agni, some argue that it is Prajāpati, the lord of all creatures, whilst others refer to it as the seasons, fortnights, and months, and the days and moments as well.

53. *pūrvāhṇam aparāhṇaṁ ca madhyāhnam api cāpare*
muhūrtam api caivāhur ekaṁ santam anekadhā
taṁ kālam avajānīhi yasya sarvam idaṁ vaśe

Others say that it is the morning, the afternoon, and the middle of the day, or else just an instant. Thus they speak of this one reality in various different ways. You should understand that it is time and the whole world is in its power.

54. *bahūnīndra-sahasrāṇi samatītāni vāsava*
bala-vīryopapannāni yathaiva tvaṁ śacī-pate

In the past, O Vāsava, there have been many thousands of Indras endowed with strength and valour just like yourself, O husband of Śacī.

55. *tvām apy atibalaṁ śakraṁ deva-rājaṁ balotkaṭam*
prāpte kāle mahā-vīryaḥ kālaḥ saṁśamayiṣyati

Now you are Śakra, the mighty king of the gods who possesses tremendous power, but when the moment arrives all-powerful time will end even your existence.

56. *ya idaṁ sarvam ādatte tasmāc chakra sthiro bhava*
mayā tvayā ca pūrvaiś ca na sa śakyo 'tivartitum

It is time that carries away the whole world so just show some restraint, Śakra. It is impossible for me or for you to overcome the power of time, just as it was for our predecessors.

57. *yām etāṁ prāpya jānīṣe rāja-śriyam anuttamām*
sthitā mayīti tan mithyā naiṣā hy ekatra tiṣṭhati

You consider the royal opulence you have gained to be unrivalled, and think, 'This will remain with me forever.' But this is a false notion, for wealth never stays in one place.

58. *sthitā hīndra-sahasreṣu tvad-viśiṣṭatameṣv iyam*
māṁ ca lolā parityajya tvām agād vibudhādhipa

In the past, this opulence settled upon thousands of Indras who were greater than you are. Because it moves constantly from one to another, that opulence abandoned me and moved on to you, O lord of the gods.

59. *maivaṁ śakra punaḥ kārṣīḥ śānto bhavitum arhasi*
tvām apy evaṁ-gataṁ tyaktvā kṣipram anyaṁ gamiṣyati

So do not behave like this again, Śakra. You need to steady yourself. In spite of your elevated status, this opulence will soon abandon you and move on to someone else.

Śānti-parvan, Adhyāya 218

In its third and final chapter, the *Bali-vāsava-saṁvāda* moves in a different direction with Bali withdrawing from the conversation to be replaced by the goddess Śrī who emerges from out of his body. Śrī, or Lakṣmī, is well known in later Hindu thought as the consort of Viṣṇu, often represented as being by his side and occasionally as participating in his divinity as the female counterpart of the male Deity. In the *Mahābhārata*, however, this association between Śrī and Viṣṇu is unknown and she is shown as a goddess in her own right. Here her identity is exactly as revealed by the name Śrī, prosperity or good fortune, as she shows her inconstant nature in moving constantly from one person to another.

The conversation here between the goddess and Indra adds relatively little to the ideas presented by Bali in the previous chapter. As prosperity, she is 'hard to keep' and no one can control her movements. As Bali has insisted, she is controlled by time alone, but she qualifies his absolute fatalism somewhat by stating that she is drawn towards virtue and *dharma*, indicating that human endeavour does have some power to influence good or bad fortune. Indeed, the reason that she is now abandoning Bali is that he has given up his previous good conduct due his overweening arrogance. Indra then allots four auspicious places in which Śrī can permanently reside – the earth, water, fire, and virtuous persons – and the passage as a whole concludes with Bali still insisting that one day his fortunes will be revived so that he can rise again and cast down Indra from his position of dominance.

1. *bhīṣma uvāca*
śata-kratur athāpaśyad baler dīptāṁ mahātmanaḥ
sva-rūpiṇīṁ śarīrād dhi tadā niṣkrāmatīṁ śriyam

Bhīṣma said: The performer of a hundred sacrifices then saw the effulgent form of Śrī, the Goddess of Prosperity, emerging from the body of that great person, Bali.

2. *tāṁ dīptāṁ prabhayā dṛṣṭvā bhagavān pāka-śāsanaḥ*
vismayotphulla-nayano baliṁ papraccha vāsavaḥ

Seeing that brilliant form with its bright effulgence, the exalted Vāsava, the chastiser of Pāka, questioned Bali about what he saw, his eyes open wide with amazement.

3. *bale keyam apakrāntā rocamānā śikhaṇḍinī*
tvattaḥ sthitā sakeyūrā dīpyamānā sva-tejasā

'Who is this woman, Bali, so agreeable to behold with decorations in her hair? Emerging from out of your body, she now stands with bracelets on her upper arms, shining with her own effulgence.'

4. *balir uvāca*
na hīmām āsurīṁ vedmi na daivīṁ na ca mānuṣīm
tvam evaināṁ pṛccha mā vā yatheṣṭaṁ kuru vāsava

Bali said: I do not know if this woman was born amongst the *asuras*, gods, or human beings. Ask her yourself who she is or else remain silent. Do as you wish, Vāsava.

5. *śakra uvāca*
kā tvaṁ baler apakrāntā rocamānā śikhaṇḍinī
ajānato mamācakṣva nāmadheyaṁ śuci-smite

Śakra said: Appearing from Bali's body, you are beautiful to behold with decorations in your hair. Who are you? Your smile is radiant, but you are unknown to me, so tell me your name.

6. *kā tvaṁ tiṣṭhasi māyeva dīpyamānā sva-tejasā*
hitvā daityeśvaraṁ subhru tan mamācakṣva tattvataḥ

You stand before me like the goddess Māyā, shining with your own effulgence. Who are you? Now that you have abandoned the lord of the Daityas, O you of beautiful eyebrows, give me a proper answer to my question.

7. *śrīr uvāca*
na mā virocano veda na mā vairocano baliḥ
āhur māṁ duḥsahety evaṁ vidhitseti ca māṁ viduḥ

Śrī said: Virocana knew me not, nor does Bali the son of Virocana. They refer to me as 'Hard to Stay With' and they also know me as 'Purpose for Action'.

8. *bhūtir lakṣmīti mām āhuḥ śrīr ity evaṁ ca vāsava*
tvaṁ māṁ śakra na jānīṣe sarve devā na māṁ viduḥ

O Vāsava, they also refer to me as Bhūti, Lakṣmī, and Śrī – Prosperity, Good Fortune, and Wealth. You do not know me, Śakra, nor do any of the gods comprehend me.

9. *śakra uvāca*
kim idaṁ tvaṁ mama kṛte utāho balinaḥ kṛte
duḥsahe vijahāsy enaṁ cira-saṁvāsinī satī

Śakra said: You are indeed 'Hard to Stay With' and are abandoning Bali though you have been faithful and lived with him for a long time. But is this on my account or on account of Bali himself?

10. *śrīr uvāca*
na dhātā na vidhātā māṁ vidadhāti kathaṁcana
kālas tu śakra paryāyān mainaṁ śakrāvamanyathāḥ

Śrī said: Neither the Ordainer nor the Controller has any influence over me. Time alone controls my movements, Śakra, so do not show such contempt for Bali.

11. *śakra uvāca*
kathaṁ tvayā balis tyaktaḥ kim arthaṁ vā śikhaṇḍhini
kathaṁ ca māṁ na jahyās tvaṁ tan me brūhi śuci-smite

Śakra said: Your hair is beautifully adorned and your smile is radiant. How is it that you have given up your association with Bali? What is your purpose? And how is it that you are not abandoning me in the same way? Explain this to me.

12. *śrīr uvāca*
satye sthitāsmi dāne ca vrate tapasi caiva hi
parākrame ca dharme ca parācīnas tato baliḥ

Śrī said: I am to be found in truthfulness, charity, religious vows, austerity, courage, and dharma. But now Bali has turned away from such conduct.

13. *brahmaṇyo 'yaṁ sadā bhūtvā satya-vādī jitendriyaḥ*
abhyasūyad brāhmaṇān vai ucchiṣṭaś cāspṛśad ghṛtam

He always used to be devoted to Brahmins, he spoke the truth and he controlled his senses, but then he became envious of the Brahmins and polluted the sacred offerings by touching the ghee without washing his hands after eating.

14. *yajña-śīlaḥ purā bhūtvā mām eva yajatety ayam*
provāca lokān mūḍhātmā kālenopanipīḍitaḥ

Previously he was a zealous performer of sacrifices but then, being foolish at heart, he issued this command to all the worlds, 'You must worship me alone', for he was afflicted by the force of time.

15. *apākṛtā tataḥ śakra tvayi vatsyāmi vāsava*
apramattena dhāryāsmi tapasā vikrameṇa ca

So now I am abandoning him, Śakra, and I will take up residence within you. I am to be maintained through vigilance, austerity, and courage, O Vāsava.

16. *śakra uvāca*
asti deva-manuṣyeṣu sarva-bhūteṣu vā pumān
yas tvām eko viṣahituṁ śaknuyāt kamalālaye

Śakra said: Amongst the gods, human beings, and other living entities there must be one individual who is able to bring you under control, O you who make your abode in the lotus flower.

17. *śrīr uvāca*
naiva devo na gandharvo nāsuro na ca rākṣasaḥ
yo mām eko viṣahituṁ śaktaḥ kaścit puraṁdara

Śrī said: No god, *gandharva*, *asura*, or *rākṣasa* has the power to bring me under his control, Puraṁdara.

18. *śakra uvāca*
tiṣṭhethā mayi nityaṁ tvaṁ yathā tad brūhi me śubhe
tat kariṣyāmi te vākyam ṛtaṁ tvaṁ vaktum arhasi

Śakra said: Please tell me, beautiful one, how you might dwell constantly within me. I will then act in accordance with your words. You must tell me the truth.

19. *śrīr uvāca*
sthāsyāmi nityaṁ devendra yathā tvayi nibodha tat
vidhinā veda-dṛṣṭena caturdhā vibhajasva mām

Śrī said: Now learn, O king of the gods, how I may come to remain within you constantly. You must divide me in four ways according to the regulations presented in the teachings of the Vedas.

20. *śakra uvāca*
ahaṁ vai tvā nidhāsyāmi yathā-śakti yathā-balam
na tu me 'tikramaḥ syād vai sadā lakṣmi tavāntike

Śakra said: I will certainly assign places for you according to the strength and power they possess. There will be no neglect on my part, Lakṣmī. I will always stay close to you.

21. *bhūmir eva manuṣyeṣu dhāraṇī bhūta-bhāvinī*
sā te pādaṁ titikṣeta samarthā hīti me matiḥ

Amongst men, the earth is the sustainer who provides for all living beings. In my opinion she is certainly capable of bearing one of your parts.

22. *śrīr uvāca*
eṣa me nihitaḥ pādo yo 'yaṁ bhūmau pratiṣṭhitaḥ
dvitīyaṁ śakra pādaṁ me tasmāt sunihitaṁ kuru

Śrī said: This is the part of me that is assigned to take up its place on earth. Now, Śakra, establish a proper place for my second part.

23. *śakra uvāca*
āpa eva manuṣyeṣu dravantyaḥ paricārikāḥ
tās te pādaṁ titikṣantām alam āpas titikṣitum

Śakra said: The waters flow amongst men and assist them in their lives. So let the waters bear one of your parts. They are surely able to bear it.

24. *śrīr uvāca*
eṣa me nihitaḥ pādo yo 'yam apsu pratiṣṭhitaḥ
tṛtīyaṁ śakra pādaṁ me tasmāt sunihitaṁ kuru

Śrī said: This is the part of me that is assigned to take up its place in the waters. Now, Śakra, establish a proper place for my third part.

25. *śakra uvāca*
yasmin devāś ca yajñāś ca yasmin vedāḥ pratiṣṭhitāḥ
tṛtīyaṁ pādam agnis te sudhṛtaṁ dhārayiṣyati

Śakra said: The gods, the sacrifices, and the Vedas all exist on the basis of fire. So fire will easily bear your third part.

26. *śrīr uvāca*
eṣa me nihitaḥ pādo yo 'yam agnau pratiṣṭhitaḥ
caturthaṁ śakra pādaṁ me tasmāt sunihitaṁ kuru

Śrī said: This is the part of me that is assigned to take up its place in fire. Now, Śakra, establish a proper place for my fourth part.

27. *śakra uvāca*
ye vai santo manuṣyeṣu brahmaṇyāḥ satya-vādinaḥ
te te pādaṁ titikṣantām alaṁ santas titikṣitum

Śakra said: Amongst men some are virtuous, being devoted to Brahmins and truthful in their speech. So let those righteous persons bear one of your parts. They are surely able to bear it.

28. *śrīr uvāca*
eṣa me nihitaḥ pādo yo 'yaṁ satsu pratiṣṭhitaḥ
evaṁ vinihitāṁ śakra bhūteṣu paridhatsva mām

Śrī said: This is the part of me that is assigned to take up its place amongst the righteous. Having placed me amongst various living beings, Śakra, you must now take care of me.

29. *śakra uvāca*
bhūtānām iha vai yas tvā mayā vinihitāṁ satīm
upahanyāt sa me dviṣyāt tathā śṛṇvantu me vacaḥ

Śakra said: I have allocated you various places, O virtuous woman, and now hear this proclamation of mine: If any living being causes you harm he will become my enemy.

30. *bhīṣma uvāca*
tatas tyaktaḥ śriyā rājā daityānāṁ balir abravīt
yāvat purastāt pratapet tāvad vai dakṣiṇāṁ diśam

Bhīṣma said: Having been abandoned by Śrī, Bali the king of the Daityas then spoke these words, 'The sun shines in the east and in the southerly direction as well.

31. *paścimāṁ tāvad evāpi tathodīcīṁ divākaraḥ*
tathā madhyaṁ-dine sūryo astam eti yadā tadā
punar devāsuraṁ yuddhaṁ bhāvi jetāsmi vas tadā

It shines in the west just as it does in the north. But when the sun passes beyond the western horizon at midday there will again be war between the gods and *asuras* and at that time I will triumph over all of you.

32. *sarvāḷ lokān yadāditya eka-sthas tāpayiṣyati*
tadā devāsure yuddhe jetāhaṁ tvāṁ śata-krato

When the sun remains in one place and shines down on all the worlds, I will triumph over you in a war between the gods and *asuras*, O performer of a hundred sacrifices.'

33. *śakra uvāca*
brahmaṇāsmi samādiṣṭo na hantavyo bhavān iti
tena te 'haṁ bale vajraṁ na vimuñcāmi mūrdhani

Śakra said: I have been instructed by Brahmā that you are not to be slain. It is for this reason alone, Bali, that I do not release this thunderbolt to strike your head.

34. *yatheṣṭaṁ gaccha daityendra svasti te 'stu mahāsura*
ādityo nāvatapitā kadācin madhyataḥ sthitaḥ

You may go wherever you wish, king of the Daityas, and good luck to you, mighty *asura*. The sun will never remain in the middle of the sky as the scorcher of the worlds.

35. *sthāpito hy asya samayaḥ pūrvam eva svayaṁbhuvā*
ajasraṁ pariyāty eṣa satyenāvatapan prajāḥ

The rules governing the movements of the sun were established by the self-born Brahmā at the beginning of creation. Hence the sun must perpetually follow its course, providing heat for all creatures.

36. *ayanaṁ tasya ṣaṇ-māsā uttaraṁ dakṣiṇaṁ tathā*
yena saṁyāti lokeṣu śītoṣṇe visṛjan raviḥ

It takes a northerly course for six months and then for six months it is in the south. In this way the sun journeys through the worlds creating the winter and summer seasons.

37. *bhīṣma uvāca*
evam uktas tu daityendro balir indreṇa bhārata
jagāma dakṣiṇām-āśām udīcīṁ tu puraṁdaraḥ

Bhīṣma said: Addressed in this way by Indra, Bali the king of the Daityas departed in a southerly direction, O Bhārata, whilst Puraṁdara set off for the north.

38. *ity etad balinā gītam anahaṁkāra-saṁjñitam*
vākyaṁ śrutvā sahasrākṣaḥ kham evāruruhe tadā

This discourse was presented by Bali without any sense of pride. After hearing his words, he of a thousand eyes then ascended into the sky.

The Śakra-Namuci-Saṁvāda

Śānti-parvan, Adhyāya 219

THE FINAL PASSAGE in this section is very similar to the previous two, with Indra encountering a vanquished adversary and inquiring as to why he does not lament for his loss of status. In this case the defeated foe is an *asura* named Namuci who is mentioned in both the Vedas and elsewhere in the *Mahābhārata*, though in both cases he is said to have been slain by Indra, a point that would seem to be contradicted by his presence alive and well in the present passage. The *Śalya-parvan* (Book 9) of the *Mahābhārata* contains an account Baladeva's visit to various pilgrimage sites in the course of which Vaiśaṁpāyana describes how Indra tricked Namuci, promising that he would not kill him with a weapon that was wet or dry and would not attack him in either day or night. Accepting this promise, Namuci appears from his hiding place only for Indra to strike him dead on a foggy day using a weapon forged out of foam. Because of this wicked act the severed head of Namuci pursues Indra until the latter becomes relieved of the sin by bathing in the River Sarasvati at the place visited by Baladeva.

In the present passage, however, no reference is made to this story and we have a short and quite straightforward reiteration of the ideas previously presented by Prahrāda and Bali. In reply to Indra's questioning, Namuci insists that lamentation is useless for it can do nothing to ease one's troubles. Everything that happens is destined to occur and cannot be avoided. Namuci refers to neither inherent nature nor time as the controlling force, but he does accept the existence of a *dhātṛ*, a controlling or ordaining deity, though he does not elaborate upon the concept. Essentially the idea here is exactly the same as what we have heard before. One's destiny is fixed and so the wise man neither rejoices nor laments as he observes these fluctuations in fortune. Endeavour is ineffective for one can obtain only what has been preordained by destiny. Hence Namuci does not suffer for his loss and does not lament over the inevitable transformations in fortune.

1. *bhīṣma uvāca*
atraivodāharantīmam itihāsaṁ purātanam
śata-kratoś ca saṁvādaṁ namuceś ca yudhiṣṭhira

Bhīṣma said: On this subject, Yudhiṣṭhira, they also recite this ancient account of a discussion that took place between the performer of a hundred sacrifices and Namuci.

2. *śriyā vihīnam āsīnam akṣobhyam iva sāgaram*
bhavābhava-jñaṁ bhūtānām ity uvāca puraṁdaraḥ

Although Namuci had lost all his wealth he remained undisturbed like the ocean, for he understood the birth and death of living beings. Puraṁdara addressed him as follows.

3. *baddhaḥ pāśaiś cyutaḥ sthānād dviṣatāṁ vaśam āgataḥ*
śriyā vihīno namuce śocasy āho na śocasi

'You are bound by ropes, you have fallen from your position and you are now in the power of your enemies. You have been deprived of your opulence, Namuci; do you lament over this or does it not distress you at all?'

4. *namucir uvāca*
anavāpyaṁ ca śokena śarīraṁ copatapyate
amitrāś ca prahṛṣyanti nāsti śoke sahāyatā

Namuci said: Nothing is gained through lamentation. If one laments, the body is afflicted with pain whilst one's enemies rejoice at such distress. There is no one who is a companion in grief.

5. *tasmāc chakra na śocāmi sarvaṁ hy evedam antavat*
saṁtāpād bhraśyate rūpaṁ dharmaś caiva sureśvara

Therefore, Śakra, I do not lament. Everything in this world will pass away. Because of anguish one's bodily appearance decays and one's dharma declines as well, lord of the gods.

6. *vinīya khalu tad duḥkham āgataṁ vaimanasya-jam*
dhyātavyaṁ manasā hṛdyaṁ kalyāṇaṁ saṁvijānatā

Sorrow arises from a dejected state of mind. Firmly putting such sorrow behind him, the wise man should occupy his mind with pleasant and auspicious thoughts.

7. *yathā yathā hi puruṣaḥ kalyāṇe kurute manaḥ*
tadaivāsya prasīdanti sarvārthā nātra saṁśayaḥ

By various means a person thus creates an auspicious disposition within his mind. Then all his goals are achieved; there is no doubt about this.

8. *ekaḥ śāstā na dvitīyo 'sti śāstā*
garbhe śayānaṁ puruṣaṁ śāsti śāstā
tenānuśiṣṭaḥ pravaṇād ivodakaṁ
yathā niyukto 'smi tathā vahāmi

In life there is only one controlling force and no other. Even when a person is lying down in the womb, that controlling force controls his life. I am directed by that force in the same way that water flows down a slope and so I endure whatever I am compelled to undergo.

9. *bhāvābhāvāv abhijānan garīyo*
jānāmi śreyo na tu tat karomi
āśāsu dharmyāḥ suhṛdāṁ sukurvan
yathā niyukto 'smi tathā vahāmi

I know the relative significance of both being and non-being and I understand which of them is better, but still I do not act. Performing actions in accordance with dharma, which meet the expectations of well-disposed people, I then endure whatever I am compelled to undergo.

10. *yathā yathāsya prāptavyaṁ prāpnoty eva tathā tathā*
bhavitavyaṁ yathā yac ca bhavaty eva tathā tathā

One attains whatever one is destined to attain. Only what is destined to occur can ever come to pass.

11. *yatra yatraiva saṁyuṅkte dhātā garbhaṁ punaḥ punaḥ*
tatra tatraiva vasati na yatra svayam icchati

Again and again one takes up residence in whatever womb the Ordainer bestows and not where one wishes to be born.

12. *bhāvo yo 'yam anuprāpto bhavitavyam idaṁ mama*
iti yasya sadā bhāvo na sa muhyet kadācana

'The state of existence I have now attained is that which was destined to be.' One who always sees his existence in this way is never perplexed.

13. *paryāyair hanyamānānām abhiyoktā na vidyate*
duḥkham etat tu yad dveṣṭā kartāham iti manyate

Amongst people who repeatedly meet with death, there is no one who is the cause of the results of action. There is misery for a misguided person who thinks that he is the performer of actions.

14. *ṛṣīṁś ca devāṁś ca mahāsurāṁś ca*
trai-vidya-vṛddhāṁś ca vane munīṁś ca
kān nāpado nopanamanti loke
parāvara-jñās tu na saṁbhramanti

In this world there are *rishis*, gods, mighty *asuras*, venerable sages learned in the three Vedas, and holy men who live in the forest. Are any of these untouched by calamities? But those who understand the superior and inferior natures remain undisturbed.

15. *na paṇḍitaḥ krudhyati nāpi sajjate*
na cāpi saṁsīdati na prahṛṣyati
na cārtha-kṛcchra-vyasaneṣu śocati
sthitaḥ prakṛtyā himavān ivācalaḥ

A man of true learning never becomes angry and never has any attachments for this world. He becomes neither depressed nor elated. He does not lament over the misfortunes that arise in times of difficulty. By his very nature he remains as steady as the Himalayas.

16. *yam artha-siddhiḥ paramā na harṣayet*
tathaiva kāle vyasanaṁ na mohayet
sukhaṁ ca duḥkhaṁ ca tathaiva madhyamaṁ
niṣevate yaḥ sa dhuraṁdharo naraḥ

If achieving great success does not delight him and the misfortune that follows in time does not perplex him, and if he can accept happiness and distress and any state between them, then he is a man who can endure the burdens of life.

17. *yāṁ yām avasthāṁ puruṣo 'dhigacchet*
tasyāṁ rametāparitapyamānaḥ
evaṁ pravṛddhaṁ praṇuden mano-jaṁ
saṁtāpam āyāsa-karaṁ śarīrāt

Whatever the situation a person finds himself in, he should relish that position without feeling any distress. In this way, he can put aside the ever-increasing anguish that arises in the mind due to his bodily condition and which is the true cause of his discomfort.

18. *tat sadaḥ sa pariṣat sabhā-sadaḥ*
prāpya yo na kurute sabhā-bhayam
dharma-tattvam avagāhya buddhimān
yo 'bhyupaiti sa pumān dhuraṁdharaḥ

When a member of an assembly arrives at the gathering and it does not cause him any apprehension, then that is truly a congregation of righteous persons. The wise man who absorbs himself in understanding the true nature of dharma, and thereby approaches that understanding, is a person who can endure the burdens of life.

19. *prājñasya karmāṇi duranvayāni*
na vai prājño muhyati moha-kāle
sthānāc cyutaś cen na mumoha gautamas
tāvat kṛcchrām āpadaṁ prāpya vṛddhaḥ

The ways of a wise man are difficult to follow, for the wise man is never confounded in times of perplexity. When the venerable Gautama fell from his position and experienced such excruciating difficulties, still he was not perplexed.

20. *na mantra-bala-vīryeṇa prajñayā pauruṣeṇa vā*
alabhyaṁ labhate martyas tatra kā paridevanā

Not through *mantras*, physical strength, vigour, wisdom, or courage can a mortal being ever attain what he is not destined to attain. Is this any cause for lamentation?

21. *yad evam anujātasya dhātāro vidadhuḥ purā*
tad evānubhaviṣyāmi kiṁ me mṛtyuḥ kariṣyati

I will experience only those things that even before my birth the Ordainers had already bestowed upon me. So what can death do to me?

22. *labdhavyāny eva labhate gantavyāny eva gacchati*
prāptavyāny eva prāpnoti duḥkhāni ca sukhāni ca

One attains what one is destined to attain; one goes to the places one is destined to reach; one experiences the sorrows and joys one is destined to experience.

23. *etad viditvā kārtsnyena yo na muhyati mānavaḥ*
kuśalaḥ sukha-duḥkheṣu sa vai sarva-dhaneśvaraḥ

Any man who fully understands this teaching and is no longer perplexed, maintaining a positive disposition in both happiness and distress, is certainly the lord of all opulence.

The Bali-Vāsava-Saṁvāda

Śānti-parvan, Adhyāya 220

Comprising a single long chapter, the *Bali-Vāsava-Saṁvāda* appears at first glance to do no more than restate the idea encountered throughout this section of the *Mokṣa-dharma-parvan*. The passage is introduced in the usual way with a question from Yudhiṣṭhira, followed by Bhīṣma's account of a conversation between the triumphant Indra and one of his defeated adversaries who displays an aloof forbearance in the face of defeat. Here the question raised relates to how a person should deal with adversity, and the initial response from Bhīṣma is that *dhṛti*, fortitude or forbearance, is the only thing that can bring relief from the suffering brought about by misfortune.

The *Saṁvāda* is then introduced; as in Chapters 216 to 218 it is Bali who instructs Indra (Vāsava) on how to tolerate catastrophic loss. Here we might note that this passage shows an awareness of the story of the Vāmana *avatāra*, as narrated in the Purāṇas, in which Viṣṇu appears in the form of a dwarf Brahmin and seizes control of the world from

Bali by begging three paces of land from him and then covering the whole of creation with two of these steps. This account is referred to in verses 7 and 25 of this passage, and elsewhere in the *Mahābhārata*, although the actual story is never told in full.

Perhaps the most interesting feature of this passage is the emphasis placed on *kāla*, time, as the dominant element that has all things under its control. Time is here more or less synonymous with destiny, but what is particularly noteworthy is Bali's insistence that the course of time and changes of fortune are inevitable and unavoidable, making human endeavour entirely irrelevant. One might act in a pious manner or be wholly lacking in virtue, but this will have no effect on the inevitable progression of time and the unfolding of destiny. This passage is therefore to be noted for displaying the most marked tendency towards absolute determinism to be found anywhere in the *Mahābhārata* and stands in marked contrast to the *Śrī-Vāsava-Saṁvāda*, which follows it. In the latter treatise the Goddess Śrī informs Indra that the *asuras*, of whom Bali was the king, lost their position of power and prosperity because they deviated from *dharma* and began to act in an unrighteous manner. Here, however, Bali dismisses any such notion and is adamant in his insistence that Indra should feel no sense of pride over his conquests; this came about simply as a result of the inevitable progression of time and not as a consequence of any action Indra himself performed. At the end of the passage, Bali reinforces his point by giving a list of the righteous kings of the past, all of whom were supremely virtuous and yet, like Bali, were ultimately overcome by time and cast down from their elevated positions.

1. *yudhiṣṭhira uvāca*
magnasya vyasane kṛcchre kiṁ śreyaḥ puruṣasya hi
bandhu-nāśe mahī-pāla rājya-nāśe 'pi vā punaḥ

Yudhiṣṭhira said: What will benefit a person who is submerged in a state of painful suffering when his friends or even his kingdom are lost to him, O lord of the earth.

2. *tvaṁ hi naḥ paramo vaktā loke 'smin bharatarṣabha*
etad bhavantaṁ pṛcchāmi tan me vaktum ihārhasi

O lord of the Bharata dynasty, you are the best teacher we have in this world. Therefore I am putting this question to you. Please explain this matter to me.

3. *bhīṣma uvāca*
putra-dāraiḥ sukhaiś caiva viyuktasya dhanena ca
magnasya vyasane kṛcchre dhṛtiḥ śreyas-karī nṛpa

Bhīṣma said: O king, fortitude restores the good fortunes of one who is deprived of his sons, wives, pleasures, and wealth, and is submerged in a state of painful suffering.

4. *dhairyeṇa yuktasya sataḥ śarīraṁ na viśīryate*
ārogyāc ca śarīrasya sa punar vindate śriyam

Because of his resolute attitude towards suffering, the body of a righteous person who follows this course does not waste away. And because of the healthy condition of his body he will again enjoy prosperity.

5. *yasya rājño narās tāta sāttvikīṁ vṛttim āsthitāḥ*
tasya sthairyaṁ ca dhairyaṁ ca vyavasāyaś ca karmasu

When a king rules over men who engage in righteous occupations, my child, there will be firmness, resolution, and determination in his actions.

6. *atraivodāharantīmam itihāsaṁ purātanam*
bali-vāsava-saṁvādaṁ punar eva yudhiṣṭhira

Concerning this subject, Yudhiṣṭhira, they again recite this account of a conversation between Bali and Vāsava.

7. *vṛtte devāsure yuddhe daitya-dānava-saṁkṣaye*
viṣṇu-krānteṣu lokeṣu deva-rāje śata-kratau

In the war between the gods and *asuras* many Daityas and Dānavas were slain. When it was over and Viṣṇu's steps had covered the worlds, kingship over the gods was restored to the performer of a hundred sacrifices.

8. *ijyamāneṣu deveṣu cātur-varṇye vyavasthite*
samṛdhyamāne trai-lokye prīti-yukte svayaṁbhuvi

Then sacrifices to the gods were resumed and the four divisions of human society restored. With the three worlds prospering once more, Brahmā, the self-born Deity, was contented.

9. *rudrair vasubhir ādityair aśvibhyām api carṣibhiḥ*
gandharvair bhujagendraiś ca siddhaiś cānyair vṛtaḥ prabhuḥ

The lord was surrounded by the Rudras, Vasus, and Ādityas, as well the two Aśvins, various *rishis*, *gandharvas*, kings of the snakes, *siddhas*, and other celestial beings.

10. *catur-dantaṁ su-dāntaṁ ca vāraṇendraṁ śriyā vṛtam*
āruhyairāvataṁ śakras trai-lokyam anusaṁyayau

Airāvata, the king of the elephants, had four tusks, he was well controlled and adorned with rich decorations. Mounting this carrier, Śakra then set out to tour the three worlds.

11. *sa kadācit samudrānte kasmiṁścid giri-gahvare*
baliṁ vairocaniṁ vajrī dadarśopasasarpa ca

After travelling for some time, the bearer of the thunderbolt saw Bali the son of Virocana within a mountain cave by the shore of the ocean. He then approached him.

12. *tam airāvata-mūrdha-sthaṁ prekṣya deva-gaṇair vṛtam*
surendram indraṁ daityendro na śuśoca na vivyathe

Seeing Indra, the king of the gods, seated on the head of Airāvata, surrounded by hosts of divine beings, the king of the Daityas did not grieve and neither was he agitated.

13. *dṛṣṭvā tam avikāra-sthaṁ tiṣṭhantaṁ nirbhayaṁ balim*
adhirūḍho dvipa-śreṣṭham ity uvāca śata-kratuḥ

Seeing Bali standing there unmoved and quite fearless, the performer of a hundred sacrifices spoke the following words to him, whilst remaining seated on the back of the best of elephants.

14. *daitya na vyathase śauryād atha vā vṛddha-sevayā*
tapasā bhāvitatvād vā sarvathaitat suduṣkaram

'You are not agitated, O Daitya. Is this due to courage alone or is it a result of the service you have rendered to your elders; or is it because you have purified your existence through acts of austerity? Whatever the cause, the composure you show is rarely achieved.

15. *śatrubhir vaśam ānīto hīnaḥ sthānād anuttamāt*
vairocane kim āśritya śocitavye na śocasi

You have been brought under their control by your enemies and are now bereft of the unrivalled position you occupied. What refuge have you found, son of Virocana, so that you do not grieve over your lamentable position?

16. *śraiṣṭhyaṁ prāpya sva-jātīnāṁ bhuktvā bhogān anuttamān*
hṛta-sva-bala-rājyas tvaṁ brūhi kasmān na śocasi

Although you achieved pre-eminence amongst your kinsmen and enjoyed unrivalled pleasures, you are now bereft of power and sovereignty. So tell me why it is that you do not lament.

17. *īśvaro hi purā bhūtvā pitṛ-paitāmahe pade*
tattvam adya hṛtaṁ dṛṣṭvā sapatnaiḥ kiṁ na śocasi

Previously you were the lord of your domain, holding the position occupied by your father and grandfather. Seeing yourself deprived of this status by your enemies, how is it that you do not lament?

18. *baddhaś ca vāruṇaiḥ pāśair vajreṇa ca samāhataḥ*
hṛta-dāro hṛta-dhano brūhi kasmān na śocasi

Having been bound by the ropes of Varuṇa and struck down by my thunderbolt, you are now bereft of wives and wealth. So tell me why it is that you do not lament.

19. *bhraṣṭa-śrīr vibhava-bhraṣṭo yan na śocasi duṣkaram*
trai-lokya-rājya-nāśe hi ko 'nyo jīvitum utsahet

Though stripped of wealth and majesty, you do not lament. This is difficult to achieve. Who else could bear to go on living when his sovereignty over the three worlds was destroyed?'

20. *etac cānyac ca paruṣaṁ bruvantaṁ paribhūya tam*
śrutvā sukham asaṁbhrānto balir vairocano 'bravīt

Having disregarded these and other cruel words, and having listened contentedly to what was said, Bali the son of Virocana spoke as follows without any agitation.

21. *nigṛhīte mayi bhṛśaṁ śakra kiṁ katthitena te*
vajram udyamya tiṣṭhantaṁ paśyāmi tvāṁ puraṁdara

'When I have already been afflicted so harshly what can be gained by this mockery, Śakra? I see you before me, Puraṁdara, standing with your thunderbolt raised on high.

22. *aśaktaḥ pūrvam āsīs tvaṁ kathaṁcic chaktatāṁ gataḥ*
kas tvad-anya imā vācaḥ sukrūrā vaktum arhati

Previously you were not able to act like this but now you have become powerful by your strategies. Who but yourself could speak such cruel words?

23. *yas tu śatror vaśa-sthasya śakto 'pi kurute dayām*
hasta-prāptasya vīrasya taṁ caiva puruṣaṁ viduḥ

If one has the power to punish but still shows mercy to a heroic enemy who has been captured and is in his power, they consider him to be a real man.

24. *aniścayo hi yuddheṣu dvayor vivadamānayoḥ*
ekaḥ prāpnoti vijayam ekaś caiva parābhavam

In warfare between two contending parties the outcome is uncertain. One will gain victory whilst the other will be defeated.

25. *mā ca te bhūtsva bhāvo 'yaṁ mayā daivata-puṁgava*
īśvaraḥ sarva-bhūtānāṁ vikrameṇa jito balāt

So do not maintain this attitude towards me, lord of the gods. Due to his power, I was conquered by the lord of all beings through a single great stride.

26. *naitad asmat kṛtaṁ śakra naitac chakra tvayā kṛtam*
yat tvam evaṁ-gato vajrin yad vāpy evaṁ-gatā vayam

The position you find yourself in was not gained by your actions, Śakra, nor is our position a result of our actions, bearer of the thunderbolt.

27. *aham āsaṁ yathādya tvaṁ bhavitā tvaṁ yathā vayam*
māvamaṁsthā mayā karma duṣkṛtaṁ kṛtam ity uta

I was what you are now, and you will be what we are now. So do not be contemptuous towards me, imagining that you have performed some difficult feat.

28. *sukha-duḥkhe hi puruṣaḥ paryāyeṇādhigacchati*
paryāyeṇāsi śakratvaṁ prāptaḥ śakra na karmaṇā

It is through the revolutions of time that a person meets with joy and misery. It is because of this cycle that you now possess great power, Śakra; this has not been gained through any action of yours.

29. *kālaḥ kāle nayati māṁ tvāṁ ca kālo nayaty ayam*
tenāhaṁ tvaṁ yathā nādya tvaṁ cāpi na yathā vayam

It is through its progression that time alone leads me through life and it is time that leads you through life as well. Because of time I am no longer as you are now, and you are no longer as we are now.

30. *na mātṛ-pitṛ-śuśrūṣā na ca daivata-pūjanam*
nānyo guṇa-samācāraḥ puruṣasya sukhāvahaḥ

Happiness is not bestowed upon a person as a result of obedience to his mother and father, nor is it brought about by worship of the gods, or indeed by any other good qualities in his conduct.

31. *na vidyā na tapo dānaṁ na mitrāṇi na bāndhavāḥ*
śaknuvanti paritrātuṁ naraṁ kālena pīḍitam

Knowledge, austerity, charity, friends, and relatives: none of them can deliver a man who is afflicted by time.

32. *nāgāminam anarthaṁ hi pratighāta-śatair api*
śaknuvanti prativyoḍhum ṛte buddhi-balān narāḥ

Even if they employ hundreds of defences, men cannot resist an unwanted event that is approaching; even intelligence and power are of no use.

33. *paryāyair hanyamānānāṁ paritrātā na vidyate*
idaṁ tu duḥkhaṁ yac chakra kartāham iti manyate

When people are afflicted due to the passage of time there is no one who can protect them. So if you think, 'I am the controller of events', Śakra, then there must be suffering.

34. *yadi kartā bhavet kartā na kriyeta kadācana*
yasmāt tu kriyate kartā tasmāt kartāpy anīśvaraḥ

If one is truly the performer of action, then that performer of action cannot be produced by anyone else. So because this apparent performer of action is himself a product of action he cannot be the real master of events.

35. *kālena tvāham ajayaṁ kālenāhaṁ jitas tvayā*
gantā gatimatāṁ kālaḥ kālaḥ kalayati prajāḥ

It is because of time that I defeated you and because of time that I have been conquered by you. Time is the mover of everything that proceeds onwards, and time carries all creatures forward.

36. *indra prākṛtayā buddhyā pralapan nāvabudhyase*
kecit tvāṁ bahu manyante śraiṣṭhyaṁ prāptaṁ sva-karmaṇā

You are talking with the intelligence of a common person, Indra, and you have no real understanding of the truth. Some people, however, think highly of you, believing that your pre-eminence has been achieved through your own actions.

37. *katham asmad-vidho nāma jānaḷ loka-pravṛttayaḥ*
kālenābhyāhataḥ śocen muhyed vāpy artha-saṁbhrame

Understanding the force that activates the world, how can a person as qualified as we are be in a state of confusion when afflicted by time and thus lament or be perplexed?

38. *nityaṁ kāla-parītasya mama vā mad-vidhasya vā*
buddhir vyasanam āsādya bhinnā naur iva sīdati

Will my intellect or the intellect of anyone like me who is seized by time ever become so disturbed upon encountering misfortune that it sinks into a mood of despondency, like a boat sinking beneath the waves?

39. *ahaṁ ca tvaṁ ca ye cānye bhaviṣyanti surādhipāḥ*
te sarve śakra yāsyanti mārgam indra-śatair gatam

I and you and others in the future who will be lords of the gods will all follow the path taken by hundreds of previous Indras, O Śakra.

40. *tvām apy evaṁ sudurdharṣaṁ jvalantaṁ parayā śriyā*
kāle pariṇate kālaḥ kālayiṣyati mām iva

Now you are completely unassailable, radiant with your supreme good fortune. But when the moment arrives, time will sweep you away, just as it did to me.

41. *bahūnīndra-sahasrāṇi daiteyānāṁ yuge yuge*
abhyatītāni kālena kālo hi duratikramaḥ

As one age has followed another, many thousands of the lords of the Daiteyas have passed away due to the influence time. Time indeed is insurmountable.

42. *idaṁ tu labdhvā tvaṁ sthānam ātmānaṁ bahu manyase*
sarva-bhūta-bhavaṁ devaṁ brahmāṇam iva śāśvatam

But after acquiring this position you now think so highly of yourself, imagining yourself to be like Brahmā, the eternal Deity who is the origin of all beings.

43. *na cedam acalaṁ sthānam anantaṁ vāpi kasyacit*
tvaṁ tu bāliśayā buddhyā mamedam iti manyase

There was no one for whom such a position proved unchanging or without end. But with your childish understanding you think, 'All this is mine.'

44. *aviśvāsye viśvasiṣi manyase cādhruvaṁ dhruvam*
mameyam iti mohāt tvaṁ rāja-śriyam abhīpsasi

You have faith in something that cannot be relied on and you consider what is temporary to be permanent. Because of illusion you think, 'This royal opulence is mine', and indeed you covet such opulence.

45. *neyaṁ tava na cāsmākaṁ na cānyeṣāṁ sthirā matā*
atikramya bahūn anyāṁs tvayi tāvad iyaṁ sthitā

It should not be supposed that this opulence will remain consistently with you, nor indeed with us or anyone else. It has come to rest upon you only after moving on from numerous others who formerly possessed it.

46. *kaṁcit kālam iyaṁ sthitvā tvayi vāsava cañcalā*
gaur nipānam ivotsṛjya punar anyaṁ gamiṣyati

After remaining with you for a certain time, Vāsava, this flickering opulence will again move on, just like a cow when it wanders from one watering hole to another.

47. *rāja-lokā hy atikrāntā yān na saṁkhyātum utsahe*
tvatto bahutarāś cānye bhaviṣyanti puraṁdara

I am unable to count the number of kings who have already passed away. And there will be innumerable others in the future, Puraṁdara, who will follow after yourself.

48. *sa-vṛkṣauṣadhi-ratneyaṁ sa-sarit-parvatākarā*
tān idānīṁ na paśyāmi yair bhukteyaṁ purā mahī

This earth possesses trees, herbs, jewels, rivers, mountains, and mines, but I do not see any of those kings who enjoyed the earth in the past still here today.

49. *pṛthur ailo mayo bhaumo narakaḥ śambaras tathā*
aśvagrīvaḥ pulomā ca svarbhānur amitadhvajaḥ

Pṛthu, Aila, Maya, Bhauma, Naraka, and Śambara; Aśvagrīva, Puloman, Svarbhānu, and Amitadhvaja;

50. *prahrādo namucir dakṣo vipracittir virocanaḥ*
hrīniṣedaḥ suhotraś ca bhūrihā puṣpavān vṛṣaḥ

Prahrāda, Namuci, Dakṣa, Vipracitti, and Virocana; Hrīniṣeda, Suhotra, Bhūrihan, Puṣpavat, and Vṛṣa.

51. *satyeṣur ṛṣabho rāhuḥ kapilāśvo virūpakaḥ*
bāṇaḥ kārtasvaro vahnir viśvadaṁṣṭro 'tha nairṛtaḥ

Satyeṣu, Ṛṣabha, Rāhu, Kapilāśva, and Virūpaka; Bāṇa, Kārtasvara, Vahni, Viśvadaṁṣṭra, and Nairṛta;

52. *ritthāhutthau vīra-tāmrau varāhāśvo ruciḥ prabhuḥ*
viśvajit pratiśauriś ca vṛṣāṇḍo viṣkaro madhuḥ

Rittha, Āhuttha, Vīra, Tāmra, Varāhāśva, Ruci, and Prabhu; Viśvajit, Pratiśauri, Vṛṣāṇḍa, Viṣkara, and Madhu;

53. *hiraṇyakaśipuś caiva kaiṭabhaś caiva dānavaḥ*
daityāś ca kālakhañjāś ca sarve te nairṛtaiḥ saha

Hiraṇyakaśipu and Kaiṭabha the Dānava; all of the Daityas and Kālakhañjas, along with the Nairṛtas as well.

54. *ete cānye ca bahavaḥ pūrve pūrvatarāś ca ye*
daityendrā dānavendrāś ca yāṁś cānyān anuśuśruma

These and many others lived in the past and there were some who lived even before these. We have heard the names of these kings of the Daityas and Dānavas and of others as well.

55. *bahavaḥ pūrva-daityendrāḥ saṁtyajya pṛthivīṁ gatāḥ*
kālenābhyāhatāḥ sarve kālo hi balavattaraḥ

So many previous Daitya kings have left this earth and passed away. All of them were seized by the grip of time, for time was mightier than any of them.

56. *sarvaiḥ kratu-śatair iṣṭaṁ na tvam ekaḥ śata-kratuḥ*
sarve dharma-parāś cāsan sarve satata-satriṇaḥ

All these kings performed a hundred sacrifices; you are not the only one to have made a hundred such offerings. They were all devoted to dharma and they always executed the sacrificial ceremonies.

57. *antarikṣa-carāḥ sarve sarve 'bhimukha-yodhinaḥ*
sarve saṁhananopetāḥ sarve parigha-bāhavaḥ

All of them were able to travel through the sky and they were all courageous warriors. All of them were endowed with great physical strength and their arms were as mighty as iron clubs.

58. *sarve māyā-śata-dharāḥ sarve te kāma-cāriṇaḥ*
sarve samaram āsādya na śrūyante parājitāḥ

All of them could practise a hundred magic arts and they all lived their lives exactly as they pleased. When battle was joined none of them was ever known to meet with defeat.

59. *sarve satya-vrata-parāḥ sarve kāma-vihāriṇaḥ*
sarve veda-vrata-parāḥ sarve cāsan bahu-śrutāḥ

All of them were committed to a vow of truthfulness and they all roamed this world at will. All of them followed the vows enjoined by the Vedas and they were all vastly learned.

60. *sarve saṁhatam aiśvaryam īśvarāḥ pratipedire*
na caiśvaryam adas teṣāṁ bhūta-pūrvo mahātmanām

All of them were lords of the world who possessed a great mass of treasure. No one in the past ever possessed wealth like that of these great persons.

61. *sarve yathārtha-dātāraḥ sarve vigata-matsarāḥ*
sarve sarveṣu bhūteṣu yathāvat pratipedire

They all gave charity in the proper manner for they were all free from envy. All of them behaved towards all living beings in a manner that was appropriate.

62. *sarve dākṣāyaṇī-putrāḥ prājāpatyā mahā-balāḥ*
jvalantaḥ pratapantaś ca kālena pratisaṁhṛtāḥ

All were descended from the daughters of Dakṣa, and these offspring of the Prajāpati possessed great strength. They blazed with an effulgent splendour, but all of them were subdued by time.

63. *tvaṁ caivemāṁ yadā bhuktvā pṛthivīṁ tyakṣyase punaḥ*
na śakṣyasi tadā śakra niyantuṁ śokam ātmanaḥ

And after enjoying this earth you will also give up that sovereignty. At that time, Śakra, you will be unable to hold back your own grief.

64. *muñcecchāṁ kāma-bhogeṣu muñcemaṁ śrī-bhavaṁ madam*
evaṁ sva-rājya-nāśe tvaṁ śokaṁ saṁprasahiṣyasi

So let go of your desire for the objects of pleasure and let go of the arrogance your prosperity has produced. In this way you will be able to withstand the grief that will ensue when your kingdom is lost to you.

65. *śoka-kāle śuco mā tvaṁ harṣa-kāle ca mā hṛṣaḥ*
atītānāgate hitvā pratyutpannena vartaya

You should not lament in times of sorrow, nor should you be elated in times of joy. Ignoring what has gone and what has not yet happened, you should live entirely in the present.

66. *māṁ ced abhyāgataḥ kālaḥ sadāyuktam atandritam*
kṣamasva na cirād indra tvām apy upagamiṣyati

Even though I was always properly engaged and was never indolent, still time overcame me. So start to show some composure, Indra, for very soon time will come upon you as well.

67. *trāsayann iva devendra vāgbhis takṣasi mām iha*
saṁyate mayi nūnaṁ tvam ātmānaṁ bahu manyase

It seems you want to cause me distress, lord of the gods, as you pierce me with your barbed words. Because I have been subjugated, you hold such a high opinion of yourself.

68. *kālaḥ prathamam āyān māṁ paścāt tvām anudhāvati*
tena garjasi devendra pūrvaṁ kāla-hate mayi

Time overcame me first, but now it is coming up behind you. You roared with delight when I was afflicted by time, O lord of the gods.

69. *ko hi sthātum alaṁ loke kruddhasya mama saṁyuge*
kālas tu balavān prāptas tena tiṣṭhasi vāsava

Was there anyone in this whole world who could remain standing in the presence of my anger? But now I am beset by the powerful force of time and it is for this reason that you can stand here before me now, Vāsava.

70. *yat tad varṣa-sahasrāntaṁ pūrṇaṁ bhavitum arhati*
yathā me sarva-gātrāṇi na sva-sthāni hataujasaḥ

But after a thousand years have passed this reign of yours will be complete. Then your limbs will be as weak as mine are now and your healthy vigour will be destroyed.

71. *aham aindrāc cyutaḥ sthānāt tvam indraḥ prakṛto divi*
sucitre jīva-loke 'sminn upāsyaḥ kāla-paryayāt

I have fallen from my regal position and you have become the king of heaven. Throughout this world with its varieties of living beings you are now universally revered. All this is due to the revolutions of time.

72. *kiṁ hi kṛtvā tvam indro 'dya kiṁ hi kṛtvā cyutā vayam*
kālaḥ kartā vikartā ca sarvam anyad akāraṇam

What have you done that would make you the Indra today? What have we done to make us fall from our position? Time is both the instigator and destroyer of everything. There is no other cause.

73. *nāśaṁ vināśam aiśvaryaṁ sukha-duḥkhe bhavābhavau*
vidvān prāpyaivam atyarthaṁ na prahṛṣyen na ca vyathet

When a wise man encounters extremes in terms of decay and loss, wealth, happiness and misery, birth and death, he should neither rejoice nor become agitated.

74. *tvam eva hīndra vetthāsmān vedāhaṁ tvāṁ ca vāsava*
vikatthase māṁ kiṁ baddhaṁ kālena nirapatrapa

You surely know us, Indra, and I know you as well, Vāsava. How can you mock me in this way, shameless one, bound as I am by the ropes of time.

75. *tvam eva hi purā vettha yat tadā pauruṣaṁ mama*
samareṣu ca vikrāntaṁ paryāptaṁ tan nidarśanam

In the past you certainly knew all about my courage for it was shown well enough by the valour I displayed in the battles between us.

76. *ādityāś caiva rudrāś ca sādhyāś ca vasubhiḥ saha*
mayā vinirjitāḥ sarve marutaś ca śacī-pate

The Ādityas, Rudras, and Sādhyas, along with the Vasus and the Maruts, were all completely vanquished by me, husband of Śacī.

77. *tvam eva śakra jānāsi devāsura-samāgame*
sametā vibudhā bhagnās tarasā samare mayā

You are surely aware, Śakra, of how in the encounter between the gods and *asuras* these celestial beings were together defeated by me through my strength in battle.

78. *parvatāś cāsakṛt kṣiptāḥ sa-vanāḥ sa-vanaukasaḥ*
sa-ṭaṅka-śikharā ghorāḥ samare mūrdhni te mayā

And in that battle, I repeatedly hurled at your head great mountains with terrible jagged peaks that were covered with forests and wild beasts.

79. *kiṁ nu śakyaṁ mayā kartuṁ yat kālo duratikramaḥ*
na hi tvāṁ notsahe hantuṁ sa-vajram api muṣṭinā

But what can I do now? It is impossible to escape the influence of time. I can do nothing at all. Armed as you are with that thunderbolt, I cannot now afflict you with my fist.

80. *na tu vikrama-kālo 'yaṁ kṣamā-kālo 'yam āgataḥ*
tena tvā marṣaye śakra durmarṣaṇataras tvayā

For this is not my time of strength; the time for patience has come. In this way I can endure your presence, Śakra, though I have less tolerance than you do.

81. *tvaṁ mā pariṇate kāle parītaṁ kāla-vahninā*
niyataṁ kāla-pāśena baddhaṁ śakra vikatthase

So, Śakra, do not mock a person whose time has passed, who is engulfed by the raging fire of time and is tightly bound by the ropes of time.

82. *ayaṁ sa puruṣaḥ śyāmo lokasya duratikramaḥ*
baddhvā tiṣṭhati māṁ raudraḥ paśuṁ raśanayā yathā

Here is that dark person and it is impossible for anyone in the world to resist him. Having bound me with a rope, like an animal, that ferocious individual now stands before me.

83. *lābhālābhau sukhaṁ duḥkhaṁ kāma-krodhau bhavābhavau*
vadho bandhaḥ pramokṣaś ca sarvaṁ kālena labhyate

Gain and loss, happiness and distress, desire and anger, birth and death, injury, bondage and freedom: all these are experienced due to the influence of time.

84. *nāhaṁ kartā na kartā tvaṁ kartā yas tu sadā prabhuḥ*
so 'yaṁ pacati kālo māṁ vṛkṣe phalam ivāgatam

I am not the enactor of deeds and neither are you, for whoever is the enactor will always be the master of events. It is time that has brought me to this state, just like the ripening of a fruit on a tree.

85. *yāny eva puruṣaḥ kurvan sukhaiḥ kālena yujyate*
punas tāny eva kurvāṇo duḥkhaiḥ kālena yujyate

Due to the influence of time a person gains pleasure from the performance of certain actions, but the influence of time is such that when he performs the same actions again they result in misery.

86. *na ca kālena kāla-jñaḥ spṛṣṭaḥ śocitum arhati*
tena śakra no śocāmi nāsti śoke sahāyatā

One who understands the influence of time should not lament when he is touched by time. It is for this reason, Śakra, that I do not lament. Grief brings no relief in times of sorrow.

87. *yadā hi śocatāṁ śoko vyasanaṁ nāpakarṣati*
sāmarthyaṁ śocato nāsti nādya śocāmy ahaṁ tataḥ

Because lamentation does not destroy the misfortune of those who are distressed there is no purpose in such grieving. Therefore I am not lamenting now.'

88. *evam uktaḥ sahasrākṣo bhagavān pāka-śāsanaḥ*
pratisaṁhṛtya saṁrambham ity uvāca śata-kratuḥ

When he was addressed in this way, that exalted deity who has a thousand eyes, who defeated Pāka, and who performed a hundred sacrifices, first controlled his passions and then spoke these words.

89. *sa-vajram udyataṁ bāhuṁ dṛṣṭvā pāśāṁś ca vāruṇān*
kasyeha na vyathed buddhir mṛtyor api jighāṁsataḥ

'After seeing my raised arm holding the thunderbolt and seeing the ropes of Varuṇa as well, who could keep his intellect from being disturbed, even if it were Mṛtyu himself who brings death to all beings?

90. *sā te na vyathate buddhir acalā tattva-darśinī*
bruvan na vyathase sa tvaṁ vākyaṁ satya-parākrama

But your intellect has perceived the truth and wavers not, remaining undisturbed. Whilst presenting your discourse you were not disturbed at all, for you are truly courageous.

91. *ko hi viśvāsam artheṣu śarīre vā śarīra-bhṛt*
kartum utsahate loke dṛṣṭvā samprasthitaṁ jagat

Is there any embodied being in this world who can put his faith in his possessions or in his body after recognising the transient nature of this creation?

92. *aham apy evam evainaṁ lokaṁ jānāmy aśāśvatam*
kālāgnāv āhitaṁ ghore guhye satata-ge 'kṣare

I also understand the temporary nature of this world. The terrible fire of time remains concealed but moves constantly and never diminishes. This world is the fuel placed on that fire.

93. *na cātra parihāro 'sti kāla-spṛṣṭasya kasyacit*
sūkṣmāṇāṁ mahatāṁ caiva bhūtānāṁ paripacyatām

Whether small or large in form, there is no escape for any living being when touched by time and when existence is brought to its conclusion.

94. *anīśasyāpramattasya bhūtāni pacataḥ sadā*
anivṛttasya kālasya kṣayaṁ prāpto na mucyate

Time has no master and is ever vigilant as it constantly draws living beings to their inevitable conclusion. It cannot be turned back; one who has fallen prey to the destructive force of time cannot be set free.

95. *apramattaḥ pramatteṣu kālo jāgarti dehiṣu*
prayatnenāpy atikrānto dṛṣṭa-pūrvo na kenacit

Embodied beings are careless, but time remains awake and vigilant amongst them. It has been seen in the past that even through strenuous endeavours time cannot be resisted by anyone.

96. *purāṇaḥ śāśvato dharmaḥ sarva-prāṇa-bhṛtāṁ samaḥ*
kālo na parihāryaś ca na cāsyāsti vyatikramaḥ

This is the ancient, eternal dharma that is equal for all those that bear life. Time cannot be avoided, and it can never be turned back.

97. *aho-rātrāṁś ca māsāṁś ca kṣaṇān kāṣṭhāḥ kalā lavān*
saṁpiṇḍayati naḥ kālo vṛddhiṁ vārdhuṣiko yathā

Time causes the days, nights, months, *kṣaṇas*, *kāṣṭhās*, *kalās*, and *lavas* to stack up against us, just like a moneylender accumulating interest on a loan.

98. *idam adya kariṣyāmi śvaḥ kartāsmīti vādinam*
kālo harati saṁprāpto nadī-vega ivoḍupam

A man thinks, 'I will achieve this today and something else tomorrow.' But when the moment arrives, time sweeps him away just as the current of a river carries away a boat.

99. *idānīṁ tāvad evāsau mayā dṛṣṭaḥ kathaṁ mṛtaḥ*
iti kālena hriyatāṁ pralāpaḥ śrūyate nṛṇām

'I saw him such a short while ago, how can he be dead?' This sort of talk is heard amongst men when a person is seized by time.

100. *naśyanty arthās tathā bhogāḥ sthānam aiśvaryam eva ca*
anityam adhruvaṁ sarvaṁ vyavasāyo hi duṣkaraḥ
ucchrāyā vinipātāntā bhāvo 'bhāva-stha eva ca

His possessions, his objects of pleasure, his status, and his wealth are all lost to him. Everything is temporary and unstable. It is impossible to be sure of anything. Whatever arises will fall down and any state of existence is based on a state of non-existence.

101. *sā te na vyathate buddhir acalā tattva-darśinī*
aham āsaṁ purā ceti manasāpi na budhyase

But your understanding has perceived the truth and wavers not. Hence it is not disturbed. Even in your mind you never dwell on what you were before.

102. *kālenākramya loke 'smin pacyamāne balīyasā*
ajyeṣṭham akaniṣṭhaṁ ca kṣipyamāṇo na budhyase

In this world everything is brought to its conclusion by the force of time. Having been assailed by time, you have been struck down and do not regard anything as superior or inferior.

103. *īrṣyābhimāna-lobheṣu kāma-krodha-bhayeṣu ca*
spṛhā-mohābhimāneṣu lokaḥ sakto vimuhyati

Absorbed as it is in envy, pride, greed, lust, anger, fear, hankering, illusion, and hatred, this whole world is deluded.

104. *bhavāṁs tu bhāva-tattva-jño vidvāñ jñāna-taponvitaḥ*
kālaṁ paśyati suvyaktaṁ pāṇāv āmalakaṁ yathā

But you understand the truth about this existence. Being wise and endowed with both knowledge and austerity, you perceive the presence of time as clearly as an *āmalaka* fruit held in your hand.

105. *kāla-cāritra-tattva-jñaḥ sarva-śāstra-viśāradaḥ*
vairocane kṛtātmāsi spṛhaṇīyo vijānatām

You understand the movements of time, you are learned in all the scriptures, and you are in control of your own being. Therefore, son of Virocana, you are well thought of by wise men.

106. *sarva-loko hy ayaṁ manye buddhyā parigatas tvayā*
viharan sarvato-mukto na kvacit pariṣajjase

I think you have grasped the nature of this whole world with your understanding. Wherever you wander you still remain free for there is nothing for which you have any attachment.

107. *rajaś ca hi tamaś ca tvā spṛśato na jitendriyam*
niṣprītiṁ naṣṭa-saṁtāpaṁ tvam ātmānam upāsase

Neither *rajas* nor *tamas* ever affects you for you have mastered your senses. You are devoted to the *ātman*, which does not seek pleasure and is free from pain.

108. *suhṛdaṁ sarva-bhūtānāṁ nirvairaṁ śānta-mānasam*
dṛṣṭvā tvāṁ mama saṁjātā tvayy anukrośinī matiḥ

You are a friend to all living beings, you have no sense of enmity, and your mind is at peace. After seeing you in this way, my sense of compassion towards you has been aroused.

109. *nāham etādṛśaṁ buddhaṁ hantum icchāmi bandhane*
ānṛśaṁsyaṁ paro dharmo anukrośas tathā tvayi

I have no desire to kill such an enlightened person who has been taken captive. Not harming is the highest form of dharma and hence I feel this compassion towards you.

110. *mokṣyante vāruṇāḥ pāśās taveme kāla-paryayāt*
prajānām apacāreṇa svasti te 'stu mahāsura

In due course of time these ropes of Varuṇa that bind you will release their hold as a result of other people's misconduct. So let good fortune come to you, mighty *asura*.

111. *yadā śvaśrūṁ snuṣā vṛddhāṁ paricāreṇa yokṣyate*
putraś ca pitaraṁ mohāt preṣayiṣyati karmasu

When the daughter-in-law engages her aged mother-in-law in service, and due to illusion the son forces his father to perform various labours,

112. *brāhmaṇaiḥ kārayiṣyanti vṛṣalāḥ pāda-dhāvanam*
śūdrāś ca brāhmaṇīṁ bhāryām upayāsyanti nirbhayāḥ

When men of low birth have their feet washed by Brahmins and *śūdras* fearlessly make sexual advances towards the wives of Brahmins,

113. *viyoniṣu ca bījāni mokṣyante puruṣā yadā*
saṁkaraṁ kāṁsya-bhāṇḍaiś ca baliṁ cāpi kupātrakaiḥ

When men discharge semen in forbidden wombs, when rubbish is swept into brass vessels whilst sacred offerings are kept on filthy plates,

114. *cātur-varṇyaṁ yadā kṛtsnam unmaryādaṁ bhaviṣyati*
ekaikas te tadā pāśaḥ kramaśaḥ pratimokṣyate

And when the regulations governing the four *varṇas* have completely broken down, then one by one the ropes that bind you will gradually release their grip.

115. *asmattas te bhayaṁ nāsti samayaṁ pratipālaya*
sukhī bhava nirābādhaḥ sva-stha-cetā nirāmayaḥ

You need have no fear from us, so just wait for that time to arrive. Now be content and undisturbed, with your mind at ease and your body in good health.'

116. *tam evam uktvā bhagavāñ śata-kratuḥ*
pratiprayāto gaja-rāja-vāhanaḥ
vijitya sarvān asurān surādhipo
nananda harṣeṇa babhūva caikarāṭ

After speaking in this way, the exalted lord who performed a hundred sacrifices returned home, borne thither by the king of the elephants. Having defeated all the *asuras*, the leader of the gods rejoiced with joy in his heart and took his place as the sole ruler of the world.

117. *maharṣayas tuṣṭuvur añjasā ca taṁ*
vṛṣā-kapiṁ sarva-carācareśvaram
himāpaho havyam udāvahaṁs tvaraṁs
tathāmṛtaṁ cārpitam īśvarāya ha

The great *rishis* began at once to sing their hymns, praising him as Vṛṣākapi, the lord of all moving and non-moving beings. Moving swiftly, the fire god began to carry the oblation once more and the celestial nectar was returned to the lord.

118. *dvijottamaiḥ sarva-gatair abhiṣṭuto*
vidīpta-tejā gata-manyur īśvaraḥ
praśānta-cetā muditaḥ svam ālayaṁ
tri-viṣṭapaṁ prāpya mumoda vāsavaḥ

Whilst being glorified by the highest Brahmins who travel throughout the creation, the lord shone with a brilliant effulgence and the anger he had felt was dispelled. With his mind at peace and joy in his heart, Vāsava experienced delight as he entered his own abode in heaven.

The Śrī-Vāsava-Saṁvāda

Śānti-parvan, Adhyāya 221

THE FINAL PASSAGE in this section of the *Mokṣa-dharma-parvan*, the *Śrī-Vāsava-Saṁvāda*, is rather different from those previously considered: there is no encounter with a fallen adversary and the conversation presented is between Indra and the Goddess Śrī, the embodiment of prosperity and good fortune. In later Hinduism, Śrī is more usually referred to as Lakṣmī and plays a significant role in the Pāñcarātra system of Vaiṣṇavism where she is revered and worshipped as the consort of Viṣṇu. Generally the *Mahābhārata* does not recognise this relationship between Viṣṇu and Śrī, so it is interesting to note here that the Goddess is referred to as arriving on the back of the bird carrier in the *vaiṣṇavaṁ padam*, the position of Viṣṇu. This connection between Śrī and Viṣṇu, unusual for the *Mahābhārata*, may indicate a late date for the composition of this particular treatise.

The passage itself is fairly straightforward, but it is notable for the manner in which it appears to directly contradict the ideas presented by

Bali in the previous chapter. The conversation here begins with Yudhiṣṭhira asking about the characteristic marks that indicate good or bad fortune for an individual, to which inquiry Bhīṣma replies that such indications are present in a person's mind. He then begins his narration of the encounter between Indra and Śrī from which his initial response becomes clearer; the point made is that when the mind is inclined towards *dharma* there is an indication of good fortune, but when the mind inclines in a contrary direction then misfortune and suffering are indicated.

This is in fact the sole theme of the goddess's discussion with Indra, who questions her as to why it is that she has abandoned the *asuras*, with whom she used to reside, so that their prosperity and good fortune is now lost. The answer is that in earlier times they were righteous in all their actions and adhered strictly to the principles of *dharma*. At that time Śrī was happy to dwell amongst them, with the result that their prosperity grew and they were triumphant over their adversaries. Then, however, a change occurred, and the goddess goes to some length to explain the type of wicked actions they began to indulge in. As a result, she has abandoned her previous residence amongst the *asuras* and now wishes to make her dwelling place amongst the gods. One might even suggest that the main point of this passage is to provide indications of the manner in which *dharma* is to be integrated into one's life and a revelation of the type of conduct that runs contrary to *dharma*. In this sense, we should probably best regard this as a moral treatise rather than a passage of any great philosophical import; its main point of interest would seem to lie in the brahminical view of dharmic behaviour it provides.

If there is a significant philosophical message to be derived from Śrī's words then it is one that is quite straightforward, asserting that one's good or bad fortune is not simply the inevitable result of time, as Bali insisted, but is in fact a direct consequence of a person's adherence to *dharma* or deviation from its precepts. Again we see how the *Mahābhārata* refrains from giving its readers a single, clearly stated answer. Instead it offers us a range of different and, at times, antithetical views, leaving it to each individual to arrive at his or her own conclusion.

1. *yudhiṣṭhira uvāca*
pūrva-rūpāṇi me rājan puruṣasya bhaviṣyataḥ
parābhaviṣyataś caiva tvaṁ me brūhi pitāmaha

Yudhiṣṭhira said: Explain to me, O king, the indications that reveal a person's future good fortune and also the indications that reveal the misfortunes that will befall him, grandfather.

2. *bhīṣma uvāca*
mana eva manuṣyasya pūrva-rūpāṇi śaṁsati
bhaviṣyataś ca bhadraṁ te tathaiva na-bhaviṣyataḥ

Bhīṣma said: The mind displays those indications that reveal a man's future good fortune, and also the indications that reveal the misfortunes that will befall him. May good fortune come to you.

3. *atrāpy udāharantīmam itihāsaṁ purātanam*
śriyā śakrasya saṁvādaṁ tan nibodha yudhiṣṭhira

And concerning this subject they recite this ancient account of Śakra's conversation with the goddess Śrī. Now learn about this, Yudhiṣṭhira.

4. *mahatas tapaso vyuṣṭyā paśyaḷ lokau parāvarau*
sāmānyam ṛṣibhir gatvā brahma-loka-nivāsibhiḥ

As a result of his severe austerities, Nārada was able to perceive both this world and the world to come. Having attained a position equal to that of the *rishis* who inhabit the world known as Brahma-loka,

5. *brahmaivāmita-dīptaujāḥ śānta-pāpmā mahā-tapāḥ*
vicacāra yathā-kāmaṁ triṣu lokeṣu nāradaḥ

His effulgent energy was unlimited, like that of Brahmā himself, and because of his severe acts of austerity his sins were nullified. In this way he wandered throughout the worlds according to his desire.

6. *kadācit prātar utthāya pispṛkṣuḥ salilaṁ śuci*
dhruva-dvāra-bhavāṁ gaṅgāṁ jagāmāvatatāra ca

One day after rising at daybreak, Nārada wanted to find pure running water to bathe in. He travelled to the source of the Gaṅgā, which is the gateway to the pole star, and descended into its waters.

7. *sahasra-nayanaś cāpi vajrī śambara-pāka-hā*
tasyā devarṣi-juṣṭāyās tīram abhyājagāma ha

The thousand-eyed bearer of the thunderbolt, who slew both Śambara and Pāka, then approached the same place on the bank of the river that the celestial *rishi* was visiting.

8. *tāv āplutya yatātmānau kṛta-japyau samāsatuḥ*
nadyāḥ pulinam āsādya sūkṣma-kāñcana-vālukam

After bathing, with their minds perfectly controlled and their prayers complete, they sat down together. Sitting on the fine golden sand by the side of the river,

9. *puṇya-karmabhir ākhyātā devarṣi-kathitāḥ kathāḥ*
cakratus tau kathā-śīlau śuci-saṁhṛṣṭa-mānasau
pūrva-vṛtta-vyapetāni kathayantau samāhitau

The celestial *rishi* narrated accounts of the deeds of righteous men. With their minds filled with purity and joy, they thus passed the time engaging in conversation, absorbed in narrating events that happened in the past.

10. *atha bhāskaram udyantaṁ raśmi-jāla-puraskṛtam*
pūrṇa-maṇḍalam ālokya tāv utthāyopatasthatuḥ

When they saw the sun rising in the sky, casting its rays in all directions with its disc fully visible, they stood up and turned to face in that direction.

11. *abhitas tūdayantaṁ tam arkam arkam ivāparam*
ākāśe dadṛśe jyotir udyatārciḥ-samaprabham

But there in the sky, right next to the rising sun, they saw a brilliant light that cast rays of equal splendour as if it were another sun.

12. *tayoḥ samīpaṁ samprāptaṁ pratyadṛśyata bhārata*
tat suparṇārka-caritam āsthitaṁ vaiṣṇavaṁ padam
bhābhir apratimaṁ bhāti trai-lokyam avabhāsayat

That light, Bhārata, was then seen to arrive close by where they stood. It was situated in Viṣṇu's place on the back of Garuḍa as he followed the course of the sun. Its brilliance was incomparable, and it shone with an effulgence that illuminated the three worlds.

13. *divyābhirūpa-śobhābhir apsarobhiḥ puraskṛtām*
bṛhatīm aṁśumat prakhyāṁ bṛhad-bhānor ivārciṣam

14. *nakṣatra-kalpābharaṇāṁ tārā-bhakti-sama-srajam*
śriyaṁ dadṛśatuḥ padmāṁ sākṣāt padma-tala-sthitām

In fact, they were seeing before them the goddess Śrī, Padmā herself, who is situated within a lotus flower. In front of her there were heavenly *apsarases*, all radiantly beautiful. She appeared brilliantly effulgent, emanating rays like those of the fire god; her ornaments were like the heavenly constellations and the garland she wore was like a succession of stars.

15. *sāvaruhya vimānāgrād aṅganānām anuttamā*
abhyagacchat tri-lokeśaṁ śakraṁ carṣiṁ ca nāradam

After getting down from the best amongst aerial carriers, that woman who had no equal approached Śakra, the lord of the three worlds, and the *rishi* Nārada.

16. *nāradānugataḥ sākṣān maghavāṁs tām upāgamat*
kṛtāñjali-puṭo devīṁ nivedyātmānam ātmanā

With Nārada following behind him, Maghavan then moved towards the goddess with his palms folded together, surrendering himself to her with his entire being.

17. *cakre cānupamāṁ pūjāṁ tasyāś cāpi sarva-vit*
deva-rājaḥ śriyaṁ rājan vākyaṁ cedam uvāca ha

The all-knowing king of the gods performed matchless acts of worship in honour of Śrī, and then addressed her with the following words.

18. *kā tvaṁ kena ca kāryeṇa samprāptā cāru-hāsini*
kutaś cāgamyate subhru gantavyaṁ kva ca te śubhe

'Your smile is entrancing, your brow is fair, and you are very beautiful. Who are you? What is your purpose in coming here? Where have you come from and what is your destination?'

19. *śrīr uvāca*
puṇyeṣu triṣu lokeṣu sarve sthāvara-jaṅgamāḥ
samātma-bhāvam icchanto yatante paramātmanā

Śrī said: Throughout these three auspicious worlds, all stationary and moving beings long to exist in my company and they endeavour for this with their whole being.

20. *sāhaṁ vai paṅkaje jātā sūrya-raśmi-vibodhite*
bhūty-arthaṁ sarva-bhūtānāṁ padmā śrīḥ padma-mālinī

I am the one who was born from a lotus flower, blossoming in the sun's rays, in order to bring prosperity to all living beings. I am Padmā; I am Śrī with her garland of lotus flowers.

21. *ahaṁ lakṣmīr ahaṁ bhūtiḥ śrīś cāhaṁ bala-sūdana*
ahaṁ śraddhā ca medhā ca sannatir vijitiḥ sthitiḥ

I am Lakṣmī, I am Bhūti, I am Śrī, O destroyer of Bala. I am faith, wisdom, humility, victory, and steadfastness.

22. *ahaṁ dhṛtir ahaṁ siddhir ahaṁ tviḍ bhūtir eva ca*
ahaṁ svāhā svadhā caiva saṁstutir niyatiḥ kṛtiḥ

I am patience, success, splendour, and prosperity. I am Svāhā and Svadhā. I am praise, destiny, and creativity.

23. *rājñāṁ vijayamānānāṁ senāgreṣu dhvajeṣu ca*
nivāse dharma-śīlānāṁ viṣayeṣu pureṣu ca

I am found at the head of the armies of victorious kings and on their banners as well. I reside in the houses of those who adhere to the rules of dharma and in the countries and towns they rule over.

24. *jita-kāśini śūre ca saṁgrāmeṣv anivartini*
nivasāmi manuṣyendre sadaiva bala-sūdana

I always reside with a heroic king, O destroyer of Bala, one who acts like a conqueror and never turns his back in battle.

25. *dharma-nitye mahā-buddhau brahmaṇye satya-vādini*
praśrite dāna-śīle ca sadaiva nivasāmy aham

And I always reside with that highly intelligent king who never deviates from dharma, who serves the Brahmins, speaks only the truth, is courteous in his demeanour, and is inclined to give gifts in charity.

26. *asureṣv avasaṁ pūrvaṁ satya-dharma-nibandhanā*
viparītāṁs tu tān buddhvā tvayi vāsam arocayam

Previously I made my abode amongst the *asuras*, but I am bound to truth and dharma and when I saw that they had adopted the opposite disposition, I decided to take up residence with you.

27. *śakra uvāca*
kathaṁ-vṛtteṣu daityeṣu tvam avātsīr varānane
dṛṣṭvā ca kim ihāgās tvaṁ hitvā daiteya-dānavān

Śakra said: What behaviour amongst the Daityas caused you to dwell with them, O you whose face is so fair? And what was it that you observed so that you came here instead, abandoning the Daiteyas and Dānavas?

28. *śrīr uvāca*
sva-dharmam anutiṣṭhatsu dhairyād acaliteṣu ca
svarga-mārgābhirāmeṣu sattveṣu niratā hy aham

Śrī said: I am attracted to those who have the determination to adhere to their personal dharma and who never deviate from it. Such persons exist on the path of joy that leads to heaven.

29. *dānādhyayana-yajñejyā guru-daivata-pūjanam*
viprāṇām atithīnāṁ ca teṣāṁ nityam avartata

The Daityas and Dānavas always used to give charity, study the Vedas, and execute rituals of sacrifice and worship, and they always showed reverence to teachers, gods, Brahmins, and guests.

30. *susaṁmṛṣṭa-gṛhāś cāsañ jita-strīkā hutāgnayaḥ*
guru-śuśrūṣavo dāntā brahmaṇyāḥ satya-vādinaḥ

Their homes were always thoroughly cleaned, they kept their women under control, and they made offerings into the fire. They rendered service to their teachers, they were self-controlled, they were devoted to the Brahmins, and they always spoke the truth.

31. *śraddadhānā jita-krodhā dāna-śīlānasūyakāḥ*
bhṛta-putrā bhṛtāmātyā bhṛta-dārā hy anīrṣavaḥ

They possessed faith, they controlled their anger, they gave charity, and they were never malicious. They provided support for their sons, ministers, and wives, and they were never envious of others.

32. *amarṣaṇā na cānyonyaṁ spṛhayanti kadācana*
na ca jātūpatapyante dhīrāḥ para-samṛddhibhiḥ

They never became angry or were envious of one another, and being of a calm disposition they were never pained by the good fortune of others.

33. *dātāraḥ saṁgṛhītāra āryāḥ karuṇa-vediṇaḥ*
mahā-prasādā ṛjavo dṛḍha-bhaktā jitendriyāḥ

They were generous, they enforced due control, they were properly behaved, and showed compassion. They were very merciful by nature, straightforward in their dealings, steady in their devotion, and in control of their senses.

34. *saṁtuṣṭa-bhṛtya-sacivāḥ kṛta-jñāḥ priya-vādinaḥ*
yathārtha-mānārtha-karā hrī-niṣedhā yata-vratāḥ

Their servants and companions were always content for they showed gratitude and spoke in a pleasant manner. Indeed they acted properly in relation to each person according to the honour due to them. They never made others feel shame and they were observant of their vows.

35. *nityaṁ parvasu su-snātāḥ sv-anuliptāḥ sv-alaṁkṛtāḥ*
upavāsa-tapaḥ-śīlāḥ pratītā brahma-vādinaḥ

For the festivals marking the movements of the moon, they always bathed properly and put on fragrant oils and precious ornaments. They observed fasts and austerities, they trusted others, and they used to recite the hymns of the Vedas.

36. *nainān abhyudiyāt sūryo na cāpy āsan prage-niśāḥ*
rātrau dadhi ca saṁktūṁś ca nityam eva vyavarjayan

The sun would never rise before they did, for they never carried on sleeping into the morning. At night they always avoided eating curds and whey or crushed grains.

37. *kālyaṁ ghṛtaṁ cānvavekṣan prayatā brahmacāriṇaḥ*
maṅgalān api cāpaśyan brāhmaṇāṁś cāpy apūjayan

At daybreak they would look at ghee, remaining pure and observing celibacy. They also looked at other auspicious substances and they worshipped the Brahmins.

38. *sadā hi dadatāṁ dharmaḥ sadā cāpratigṛhṇatām*
ardhaṁ ca rātryāḥ svapatāṁ divā cāsvapatāṁ tathā

They always adhered to the dharma of those who give gifts and refuse to accept them, who sleep at midnight and never sleep during the day,

39. *kṛpaṇānātha-vṛddhānāṁ durbalātura-yoṣitām*
dāyaṁ ca saṁvibhāgaṁ ca nityam evānumodatām

And who always delight in acts of kindness and in sharing their wealth with persons who are wretched and who have no protector, and with the elderly, the sick, the penniless, and with women.

40. *viṣaṇṇaṁ trastam udvignaṁ bhayārtaṁ vyādhi-pīḍitam*
hṛta-svaṁ vyasanārtaṁ ca nityam āśvāsayanti te

They always brought comfort to persons who were depressed, fearful, anxious, worried, afflicted by disease, bereft of riches, or beset by misfortune.

41. *dharmam evānvavartanta na hiṁsanti parasparam*
anukūlāś ca kāryeṣu guru-vṛddhopasevinaḥ

They adhered absolutely to the principles of dharma and they never harmed one another. They were attentive to the duties incumbent on them and they rendered service to their teachers and elders.

42. *pitṛ-devātithīṁś caiva yathāvat te 'bhyapūjayan*
avaśeṣāṇi cāśnanti nityaṁ satya-tapo-ratāḥ

They offered their respects to the ancestors, gods, and guests in the appropriate manner and always ate the remnants of the offerings made to them. They remained devoted to truth and austerity.

43. *naike 'śnanti susaṁpannaṁ na gacchanti para-striyam*
sarva-bhūteṣv avartanta yathātmani dayāṁ prati

They never ate the very best foods alone, nor did they ever approach another man's wife. They behaved with kindness towards all beings, treating them as they would their own selves.

44. *naivākāśe na paśuṣu nāyonau na ca parvasu*
indriyasya visargaṁ te 'rocayanta kadācana

They never enjoyed discharging semen into open space, into animals, in any place apart from the vagina, or during festivals marking the changes of the moon.

45. *nityaṁ dānaṁ tathā dākṣyam ārjavaṁ caiva nityadā*
utsāhaś cānahaṁkāraḥ paramaṁ sauhṛdaṁ kṣamā

At all times charity, expertise, honesty, fortitude, a lack of arrogance, the greatest goodwill to others, tolerance,

46. *satyaṁ dānaṁ tapaḥ śaucaṁ kāruṇyaṁ vāg-aniṣṭhurā*
mitreṣu cānabhidrohaḥ sarvaṁ teṣv abhavat prabho

Truthfulness, charity, austerity, cleanliness, compassion, avoidance of harsh words, and a gentle disposition towards friends, all existed within them.

47. *nidrā tandrīr asaṁprītir asūyā cānavekṣitā*
aratiś ca viṣādaś ca na spṛhā cāviśanta tān

Sloth, laziness, dissatisfaction, envy, inattention, anxiety, despondency, and desire never entered their hearts.

48. *sāham evaṁ-guṇeṣv eva dānaveṣv avasaṁ purā*
prajā-sargam upādāya naikaṁ yuga-viparyayam

From the time of the creation of the living beings, I dwelt amongst the Dānavas who possessed these excellent qualities and stayed with them as several *yugas* passed by.

49. *tataḥ kāla-viparyāse teṣāṁ guṇa-viparyayāt*
apaśyaṁ vigataṁ dharmaṁ kāma-krodha-vaśātmanām

But then as the times changed, I saw that dharma had departed from them because of a transformation in the qualities they possessed. Their very nature was now under the control of desire and anger.

50. *sabhā-sadāṁ te vṛddhānāṁ satyāḥ kathayatāṁ kathāḥ*
prāhasann abhyasūyaṁś ca sarva-vṛddhān guṇāvarāḥ

They ridiculed the elders who sat in their assemblies, even though the speeches they delivered were true. And even though they possessed inferior qualities to those of all these elders, still they responded indignantly to their words.

51. *yūnaḥ saha-samāsīnān vṛddhān abhigatān sataḥ*
nābhyutthānābhivādābhyāṁ yathā-pūrvam apūjayan

When the elders they sat with in the assembly arrived there, the younger Dānavas who were present did not show their respect as they had done previously by rising from their seats and greeting them.

52. *vartayanty eva pitari putrāḥ prabhavatā ''tmanaḥ*
amitra-bhṛtyatāṁ prāpya khyāpayanto 'napatrapāḥ

Acting on their own strength, sons directed events even in the presence of their fathers. If any of them became dependent on the goodwill of their enemies, they spoke of it openly without any sense of shame.

53. *tathā dharmād apetena karmaṇā garhitena ye*
mahataḥ prāpnuvanty arthāṁs teṣv eṣām abhavat spṛhā

There was a sense of admiration amongst them for those who gained great riches by abandoning dharma and performing wicked deeds.

54. *uccaiś cāpy avadan rātrau nīcais tatrāgnir ajvalat*
putrāḥ pitṝn abhyavadan bhāryāś cābhyavadan patīn

They talked loudly through the night whilst the light of the sacred fire dwindled. Sons spoke abusively to their fathers, addressing them by name, and wives spoke abusively to their husbands.

55. *mātaraṁ pitaraṁ vṛddham ācāryam atithiṁ gurum*
guru-van nābhyanandanta kumārān nānvapālayan

Acting as if they were teachers themselves, they showed no respect to the mother, father, elders, spiritual guide, guests, or teachers, and they did not care for their children properly.

56. *bhikṣāṁ balim adattvā ca svayam annāni bhuñjate*
aniṣṭvā saṁvibhajyātha pitṛ-devātithīn gurūn

They ate their own meals without giving anything as an offering of alms or for sacrifice and were unwilling to set aside a portion for the ancestors, gods, guests, and teachers.

57. *na śaucam anurudhyanta teṣāṁ sūda-janās tathā*
manasā karmaṇā vācā bhaktam āsīd anāvṛtam

The cooks did not maintain a state of purity in their thoughts, deeds, or words, and food was left uncovered.

58. *viprakīrṇāni dhānyāni kāka-mūṣaka-bhojanam*
apāvṛtaṁ payo 'tiṣṭhad ucchiṣṭhāś cāspṛśan ghṛtam

Grains were left scattered and became food for crows and rats. Milk remained uncovered and people touched ghee without washing their hands.

59. *kuddāla-pāṭī-paṭakaṁ prakīrṇaṁ kāṁsya-bhājanam*
dravyopakaraṇaṁ sarvaṁ nānv avaikṣat kuṭumbinī

Spoons, knives, cloths, and brass vessels lay scattered all around, for the woman of the house paid no attention to any of the objects used by the household.

60. *prākārāgāra-vidhvaṁsān na sma te pratikurvate*
nādriyante paśūn baddhvā yavasenodakena ca

They did not repair their enclosures and dwelling places when they fell into a state of decay and after tethering their cows they did not provide them with sufficient fodder or water.

61. *bālānāṁ prekṣamāṇānāṁ svayaṁ bhakṣān abhakṣayan*
tathā bhṛtya-janaṁ sarvaṁ paryaśnanti ca dānavāḥ

While their children watched them, the Dānavas ate their own meals and they treated all their dependents in the same way.

62. *payasaṁ kṛsaraṁ māṁsam apūpān atha śaṣkulīḥ*
apācayann ātmano 'rthe vṛthā-māṁsāny abhakṣayan

They prepared milk, pulses, meat, bread, and rice cakes for their own consumption and they ate meat that had not been offered in sacrifice.

63. *utsūrya-śāyinaś cāsan sarve cāsan pragenisāḥ*
avartan kalahāś cātra divā-rātraṁ gṛhe gṛhe

They all stayed in bed whilst the sun rose and slept late into the morning. In every household there were quarrels throughout the day and night.

64. *anāryāś cāryam āsīnaṁ paryupāsan na tatra ha*
āśrama-sthān vikarma-sthāḥ pradviṣanti parasparam
saṁkarāś cāpy avartanta na ca śaucam avartata

Lowborn persons would never pay their respects to a person of high birth who was seated nearby. Those whose behaviour was unregulated despised persons who dwelt in religious communities and were in turn despised by them. There were children born from parents of different *varṇas* and the standards of purity were no longer sustained.

65. *ye ca veda-vido viprā vispaṣṭam anṛcaś ca ye*
nirantar-aviśeṣās te bahumānāvamānayoḥ

Both those Brahmins who were learned in the Vedas and those who quite obviously had no knowledge of the Vedic hymns were grouped together, without any distinction being made between those who were worthy of respect and those who were not.

66. *hāvam ābharaṇaṁ veṣaṁ gatiṁ sthitim avekṣitum*
asevanta bhujiṣyā vai durjanācaritaṁ vidhim

Their serving maids followed the ways of wicked people in their gestures, jewellery, clothes, movements, posture, and the glances they gave.

67. *striyaḥ puruṣa-veṣeṇa puṁsaḥ strī-veṣa-dhāriṇaḥ*
krīḍā-rati-vihāreṣu parāṁ mudam avāpnuvan

In their pursuit of leisure and sensual enjoyment, women found pleasure by wearing male clothing and men found pleasure in wearing women's garments.

68. *prabhavadbhiḥ purā dāyān arhebhyaḥ pratipāditān*
nābhyavartanta nāstikyād vartantaḥ saṁbhaveṣv api

Previously those who were rich offered a portion of their wealth to worthy recipients. But now because of their lack of faith they never made such gifts even though they possessed the means to do so.

69. *mitreṇābhyarthitaṁ mitram arthe saṁśayite kvacit*
vāla-koṭy-agra-mātreṇa svārthenāghnata tad vasu

If ever someone was advised by a friend over a doubtful matter, then for personal gain as small as the tip of a hair that friend would act to thwart its successful outcome.

70. *para-svādāna-rucayo vipaṇya-vyavahāriṇaḥ*
adṛśyantārya-varṇeṣu śūdrāś cāpi tapo-dhanāḥ

Persons who sought to acquire other people's property by engaging in various business transactions were now seen amongst the superior *varṇas* whilst *śūdras* were seen practising religious austerities.

71. *adhīyante 'vratāḥ kecid vṛthā-vratam athāpare*
aśuśrūṣur guroḥ śiṣyaḥ kaścic chiśya-sakho guruḥ

Some of them engaged in study without following any of the rules whilst others followed rules that were pointless. The student no longer rendered service to his teacher for the teacher was like a friend to his student.

72. *pitā caiva janitrī ca śrāntau vṛttotsavāv iva*
aprabhutve sthitau vṛddhāv annaṁ prārthayataḥ sutān

Both the father and the mother were as exhausted as persons who have just celebrated a great festival. In their old age they were poverty-stricken and begged their sons for food.

73. *tatra veda-vidaḥ prājñā gāmbhīrye sāgaropamāḥ*
kṛṣy-ādiṣv abhavan saktā mūrkhāḥ śrāddhāny abhuñjata

Learned persons who had studied the Vedas and were like the ocean in the depth of their wisdom took to agriculture and other mundane professions whilst unlearned fools enjoyed the remnants of the *śrāddha* offerings.

74. *prātaḥ prātaś ca supraśnaṁ kalpanaṁ preṣaṇa-kriyāḥ*
śiṣyānuprahitās tasminn akurvan guravaś ca ha

Each day teachers would follow after their students making inquiries as to their welfare and performing service on their behalf.

75. *śvaśrū-śvaśurayor agre vadhūḥ preṣyān aśāsata*
anvaśāsac ca bhartāraṁ samāhūyābhijalpatī

Even in the presence of her parents-in-law, the daughter-in-law would exert her authority over the members of the household. Calling her husband to her, she gave him instruction and various orders.

76. *prayatnenāpi cārakṣac cittaṁ putrasya vai pitā*
vyabhajaṁś cāpi saṁrambhād duḥkha-vāsaṁ tathāvasan

The father made every effort to preserve the good nature of his son. Because of this anxiety he divided his wealth with his son and then lived in a miserable abode.

77. *agni-dāhena corair vā rājabhir vā hṛtaṁ dhanam*
dṛṣṭvā dveṣāt prāhasanta suhṛt-saṁbhāvitā hy api

After seeing someone's property carried away by a blazing fire, by thieves, or by kings, even persons who were supposed to be friends of the owner would laugh out loud because of their malevolent attitude.

78. *kṛta-ghnā nāstikāḥ pāpā guru-dārābhimarśinaḥ*
abhakṣya-bhakṣaṇa-ratā nirmaryādā hata-tviṣaḥ

They were ungrateful and faithless, wicked people who would even lay hands on the wife of their teacher. They enjoyed feasting on forbidden foods, for they observed no rules at all and had lost their previous glory.

79. *eṣv evam ādīnācārān ācaratsu viparyaye*
nāhaṁ devendra vatsyāmi dānaveṣv iti me matiḥ

Because they have changed and are now following perverse modes of conduct, O lord of the gods, I will no longer dwell amongst the Dānavas. That is my conviction.

80. *tāṁ māṁ svayam anuprāptām abhinanda śacī-pate*
tvayārcitāṁ māṁ deveśa purodhāsyanti devatāḥ

So now, husband of Śacī, you may welcome me to you, for I have been obtained through my own desire. Being worshipped by you, lord of the gods, all the gods will also show me due respect.

81. *yatrāhaṁ tatra mat-kāntā mad-viśiṣṭhā mad-arpaṇāḥ*
sapta devyo mayāṣṭamyo vāsaṁ ceṣyanti me 'ṣṭadhā

Seven other goddesses, with an eighth as well, will wish to be with me in whatever abode I adopt, together forming a group of eight. They are very dear to me for they represent my characteristic features and they are dependent upon me.

82. *āśā śraddhā dhṛtiḥ kāntir vijitiḥ sannatiḥ kṣamā*
aṣṭamī vṛttir etāsāṁ purogā pāka-śāsana

The seven are hope, faith, determination, beauty, victory, humility, and tolerance. The eighth, who is proper conduct, is the chief amongst them, chastiser of Pāka.

83. *tāś cāhaṁ cāsurāṁs tyaktvā yuṣmad viṣayam āgatā*
tri-daśeṣu nivatsyāmo dharma-niṣṭhāntarātmasu

Having abandoned the *asuras*, I and these others will enter your domain. We will now reside amongst the thirty gods who keep devotion to dharma in their hearts.

84. *bhīṣma uvāca*
ity ukta-vacanāṁ devīm atyarthaṁ tau nanandatuḥ
nāradaś ca tri-lokarṣir vṛtra-hantā ca vāsavaḥ

Bhīṣma said: As instructed by her words, both Nārada, the *rishi* who travelled throughout the three worlds, and Vāsava, the slayer of Vṛtra, then offered that goddess the warmest of greetings.

85. *tato 'nala-sakho vāyuḥ pravavau deva-veṣmasu*
iṣṭa-gandhaḥ sukha-sparśaḥ sarvendriya-sukhāvahaḥ

Then the wind god, the friend of the fire god, began to blow through the dwelling places of the gods with a breeze that was sweet smelling, pleasing to feel, and which brought happiness to all the senses.

86. *śucau cābhyarcite deśe tri-daśāḥ prāyaśaḥ sthitāḥ*
lakṣmyā sahitam āsīnaṁ maghavantaṁ didṛkṣavaḥ

The thirty gods then gathered in a pure and sacred place, desiring to see Maghavan seated alongside Lakṣmī.

87. *tato divaṁ prāpya sahasra-locanaḥ*
śriyopapannaḥ suhṛdā surarṣiṇā
rathena haryaśva-yujā surarṣabhaḥ
sadaḥ surāṇām abhisat-kṛto yayau

After returning to the heavens, that thousand-eyed lord of the gods, riding on a chariot drawn by bay horses and accompanied by Śrī and his friend the celestial *rishi*, came to the place where the gods were assembled and was received by them with reverence.

88. *atheṅgitaṁ vajra-dharasya nāradaḥ*
śriyāś ca devyā manasā vicārayan
śriyai śaśaṁsāmara-dṛṣṭa-pauruṣaḥ
śivena tatrāgamanaṁ maharddhimat

At the indication of the bearer of the thunderbolt and acting in accordance with the will of the goddess Śrī, Nārada, whose ability was well known to the gods, began to offer words of praise to Śrī, lauding her auspicious arrival there that brought with it the greatest good fortune.

89. *tato 'mṛtaṁ dyauḥ pravavarṣa bhāsvatī*
pitā-mahasyāyatane svayaṁbhuvaḥ
anāhatā dundubhayaś ca nedire
tathā prasannāś ca diśaś cakāśire

Thereupon the sky was filled with light and rained down drops of nectar on the abode of the self-born grandfather of the world. Kettledrums resounded without being struck and all directions became tranquil and beautiful to behold.

90. *yathārtu sasyeṣu vavarṣa vāsavo*
na dharma-mārgād vicacāla kaścana
aneka-ratnākara-bhūṣaṇā ca bhūḥ
sughoṣa-ghoṣā bhuvanaukasāṁ jaye

During the proper season, Vāsava poured down rain on the crops and no one deviated from the path of dharma. The earth was adorned with numerous mines filled with gems, and both heaven and earth were filled with a resounding noise because of the triumph of Vāsava.

91. *kriyābhirāmā manujā yaśasvino*
babhuḥ śubhe puṇya-kṛtāṁ pathi sthitāḥ
narāmarāḥ kiṁnara-yakṣa-rākṣasāḥ
samṛddhimantaḥ sukhino yaśasvinaḥ

Human beings were celebrated for the delight they took in their ritual duties and for remaining true to the auspicious path followed by righteous persons. Men, gods, *kiṁnaras*, *yakṣas*, and *rākṣasas* were celebrated for their good fortune and happiness.

92. *na jātv akāle kusumaṁ kutaḥ phalaṁ*
papāta vṛkṣāt pavaneritād api
rasa-pradāḥ kāma-dughāś ca dhenavo
na dāruṇā vāg vicacāra kasyacit

Even when blown by the wind, neither flowers nor fruits would fall from the tree out of season. Cows gave as much milk as one could desire, and harsh words were never used by anyone.

93. *imāṁ saparyāṁ saha sarva-kāma-daiḥ*
śriyāś ca śakra-pramukhaiś ca daivataiḥ
paṭhanti ye vipra-sadaḥ samāgame
samṛddha-kāmāḥ śriyam āpnuvanti te

This hymn of glorification is dedicated to the goddess Śrī along with the gods who have Śakra as their leader and can grant all desires. Those who recite it in an assembly of Brahmins have their desires fulfilled and gain prosperity.

94. *tvayā kurūṇāṁ vara yat pracoditaṁ*
bhavābhavasyeha paraṁ nidarśanam
tad adya sarvaṁ parikīrtitaṁ mayā
parīkṣya tattvaṁ parigantum arhasi

At your urging, O best of the Kurus, I have now explained in full the key indicators of the presence and absence of good fortune. After considering this conclusion you should act accordingly.

The Jaigīṣavyāsita-Saṁvāda

Śānti-parvan, Adhyāya 222

Following on from the series of conversations between Indra and his adversaries, we have two short passages which are to some extent related to these earlier discussions inasmuch as they deal primarily with the advocacy of emotional detachment as the ideal basis for living in this world. It may be that the redactor placed these two short passages at this point because of the descriptions of good and bad conduct in the speech of Śrī in the previous chapter, thereby establishing something of a logical sequence. The first of the two chapters takes the form of a conversation between two well known sages, Asita Devala and Jaigīṣavya, in which the latter explains how it is that he remains at peace in all circumstances. In the second, Kṛṣṇa reveals to his grandfather Ugrasena why it is that the sage Nārada is universally admired. The first treatise is primarily concerned with emotional detachment from the world, with the suggestion that all good qualities in a human being arise from this state of consciousness. Kṛṣṇa's eulogy of Nārada provides a more detailed listing of his qualities and modes of conduct but the point made is essentially the same. Nārada is honest, truthful, and free from anger or malice because he is detached from the world and has withdrawn from emotional involvement. This of course is the ideal state of consciousness for one pursuing the goal of liberation from rebirth as is recognised in Yudhiṣṭhira's initial question and Bhīṣma's response. In Jaigīṣavya's instruction to Asita Devala this ultimate goal of detachment from the world is overtly acknowledged, but in Kṛṣṇa's discourse there is no mention made of *mokṣa* as the ultimate goal of detachment or good conduct.

The chapter opens with a question from Yudhiṣṭhira about the type of conduct and disposition required for a person who is seeking to achieve *brahmaṇaḥ sthānam*, the position or the status of Brahman, which we may take as another way of expressing the concept of liberation from rebirth. In response, Bhīṣma first gives his own suggestion before referring to instructions given on the subject by Jaigīṣavya to Asita Devala. The main theme here is remaining aloof and essentially indifferent to the changing fortunes every person must experience in life. One should be humble, respectful, and free of any sense of malice; there should be no feelings of anger or envy and no desire to harm any other living being. One should be equal to all, without friends or enemies, and entirely indifferent to both praise and blame. If one can conduct oneself in this way and adopt this view of life, then it is possible to transcend the material dimension and achieve the ultimate spiritual goal, the *brahmaṇaḥ sthānam* referred to by Yudhiṣṭhira in his initial question.

1. *yudhiṣṭhira uvāca*
kiṁ-śīlaḥ kiṁ-samācāraḥ kiṁ-vidyaḥ kiṁ-parāyaṇaḥ
prāpnoti brahmaṇaḥ sthānaṁ yat paraṁ prakṛter dhruvam

Yudhiṣṭhira said: What conduct, what behaviour, what form of knowledge, and what form of dedication brings one to the position of Brahman, which is changeless and beyond *prakṛti*.

2. *bhīṣma uvāca*
mokṣa-dharmeṣu niyato laghv-āhāro jitendriyaḥ
prāpnoti brahmaṇaḥ sthānaṁ yat paraṁ prakṛter dhruvam

Bhīṣma said: Dedicating oneself to the forms of dharma that aim at liberation, eating only a small amount, and controlling the senses bring one to the position of Brahman, which is changeless and beyond *prakṛti*.

3. *atrāpy udāharantīmam itihāsaṁ purātanam*
jaigīṣavyasya saṁvādaṁ asitasya ca bhārata

And in this connection, they recite this ancient account of a conversation that took place between Jaigīṣavya and Asita, O Bhārata.

4. *jaigīṣavyaṁ mahā-prājñaṁ dharmāṇām āgatāgamam*
akrudhyantam ahṛṣyantam asito devalo 'bravīt

Jaigīṣavya was a man of great wisdom who possessed knowledge of different forms of dharma and who neither became angry nor rejoiced. Asita Devala said to him,

5. *na prīyase vandyamāno nindyamāno na kupyasi*
kā te prajñā kutaś caiṣā kiṁ caitasyāḥ parāyaṇam

'You feel no pleasure when you are praised, and you do not become angry when you are condemned. What is this wisdom you possess, from whence is it derived, and what is its ultimate goal?'

6. *iti tenānuyuktaḥ sa tam uvāca mahā-tapāḥ*
mahad vākyam asaṁdigdhaṁ puṣkalārtha-padaṁ śuci

When questioned in this way, the mighty ascetic presented him with a wonderful treatise that could be clearly understood, that possessed a very deep meaning and was completely pure.

7. *yā gatir yā parā niṣṭhā yā śāntiḥ puṇya-karmaṇām*
tāṁ te 'haṁ sampravakṣyāmi yan māṁ pṛcchasi vai dvija

'I will speak to you on the subject you have inquired about, O Brahmin, concerning the final goal, the highest position, and the peace attained by those who act righteously.

8. *nindatsu ca samo nityaṁ praśaṁsatsu ca devala*
nihnuvanti ca ye teṣāṁ samayaṁ sukṛtaṁ ca ye

These are persons, Devala, who are always equal to those who condemn them and to those who offer praise, and who conceal their religious observance and their righteous action.

9. *uktāś ca na vivakṣanti vaktāram ahite ratam*
pratihantuṁ na cecchanti hantāraṁ vai manīṣiṇaḥ

When criticised, they are never inclined to respond to the speaker in a hostile way, nor will such wise persons ever wish to strike one who attacks them.

10. *nāprāptam anuśocanti prāpta-kālāni kurvate*
na cātītāni śocanti na cainān pratijānate

They never lament for what has not yet happened and they act only in terms of the present time. Nor do they lament over what is in the past, for they never even think of such things.

11. *samprāptānāṁ ca pūjyānāṁ kāmād artheṣu devala*
yathopapattiṁ kurvanti śaktimantaḥ kṛta-vratāḥ

In relation to desirable objects and wealth, Devala, those wise ones who possess great power and are true to their vows respect whatever comes to them. They act in accordance with whatever they acquire in this way.

12. *pakva-vidyā mahā-prājñā jita-krodhā jitendriyāḥ*
manasā karmaṇā vācā nāparādhyanti kasyacit

Their understanding is mature, their wisdom is vast, and they have gained mastery over their anger and their senses. They never give offence to any living being with their thoughts, deeds, or words.

13. *anīrṣavo na cānyonyaṁ vihiṁsanti kadācana*
na ca jātūpatapyante dhīrāḥ para-samṛddhibhiḥ

They are free from envy and never at any time do they bring harm to others. Nor do such steady-minded persons ever feel distress because of the prosperity of others.

14. *nindāpraśaṁse cātyarthaṁ na vadanti parasya ye*
na ca nindāpraśaṁsābhyāṁ vikriyante kadācana

These are persons who do not speak excessive words in condemnation or praise of others. And they are never affected by the blame and praise that come their way.

15. *sarvataś ca praśāntā ye sarva-bhūta-hite ratāḥ*
na krudhyanti na hṛṣyanti nāparādhyanti kasyacit
vimucya hṛdaya-granthīṁś caṅkramyante yathā-sukham

They are persons who remain tranquil in all circumstances and dedicate themselves to the welfare of other living beings. They feel no anger, they do not rejoice, and neither do they give offence to anyone. Having slipped the knots that bind the heart, they proceed as they please.

16. *na yeṣāṁ bāndhavāh santi ye cānyeṣāṁ na bāndhavāḥ*
amitrāś ca na santy eṣāṁ ye cāmitrā na kasyacit

No one is their friend and they are not friends to anyone else. Similarly, no one is their enemy and they are not the enemies of any other person.

17. *ya evaṁ kurvate martyāḥ sukhaṁ jīvanti sarvadā*
dharmam evānuvartante dharma-jñā dvija-sattama
ye hy ato vicyutā mārgāt te hṛṣyanty udvijanti ca

Mortal beings who act in this way live joyfully at all times. Understanding the true nature of dharma, they always adhere to the dictates of dharma, O best of Brahmins. But those who have deviated from this path experience both joy and sorrow.

18. *āsthitas tam ahaṁ mārgam asūyiṣyāmi kaṁ katham*
nindyamānaḥ praśasto vā hṛṣyeyaṁ kena hetunā

Situated as I am on that path, how could I ever feel any sense of ill will? Whether I am condemned or praised, is there any reason for me to rejoice?

19. *yad yad icchanti tan mārgam abhigacchanti mānavāḥ*
na me nindā-praśaṁsābhyāṁ hrāsa-vṛddhī bhaviṣyataḥ

People follow a particular path according to the desires they nurture. For me detriment and progress will never be derived from condemnation and praise.

20. *amṛtasyeva saṁtṛpyed avamānasya tattva-vid*
viṣasyevodvijen nityaṁ saṁmānasya vicakṣaṇaḥ

One who understands the truth is satisfied by the contempt shown him, regarding it as nectar; the wise person will always recoil from honour as if it were deadly poison.

21. *avajñātaḥ sukhaṁ śete iha cāmutra cobhayoḥ*
vimuktaḥ sarva-pāpebhyo yo 'vamantā sa badhyate

Though treated with contempt, he sleeps happily both in this world and in the world to come, for he is free from all sinful deeds. But one who despises him remains bound to this world.

22. *parāṁ gatiṁ ca ye kecit prārthayanti manīṣiṇaḥ*
etad vrataṁ samāśritya sukham edhanti te janāḥ

Having adopted this mode of conduct, those wise persons who seek the highest goal will increase the joy they experience.

23. *sarvataś ca samāhṛtya kratūn sarvāñ jitendriyaḥ*
prāpnoti brahmaṇaḥ sthānaṁ yat paraṁ prakṛter dhruvam

And after properly performing all the sacrifices, one who brings his senses under control reaches the position of Brahman, which is changeless and beyond *prakṛti.*

24. *nāsya devā na gandharvā na piśācā na rākṣasāḥ*
padam anvavarohanti prāptasya paramāṁ gatim

Gods, *gandharvas*, *piśācas*, and *rākṣasas* can never rise up to the position of one who has reached that highest goal.

The Vāsudevograsena-Saṁvāda

Śānti-parvan, Adhyāya 223

THE QUESTION POSED HERE by Yudhiṣṭhira appears more contrived than usual in giving the editor the opportunity to introduce his next short treatise, the conversation between Kṛṣṇa (Vāsudeva) and his grandfather, Ugrasena. The appearance of these two within the *Mahābhārata* is of interest in itself as it represents one of the few occasions in which there is an acknowledgement of Kṛṣṇa's other life, beyond his support for the Pāṇḍava cause; as far as I am aware this is the only occasion on which his relationship with Ugrasena is referred to. The passage itself is rather similar to *Jaigīṣavyāsita-Saṁvāda*, though here the emphasis on liberation is absent and it appears that, despite the mood of renunciation he displays, Nārada, the object of the discussion, is still very much involved with the world. The discourse takes the form of Kṛṣṇa outlining the qualities Nārada possesses which make him beloved to all. These are essentially those mentioned previously by Jaigīṣavya: Nārada is gentle, kind, and generous, he harms no one and he adheres to the proper rules. He has no friends and no enemies, he is equal to all, and he is indifferent to praise or condemnation. He interacts with the world but remains indifferent to the vicissitudes of fortune, whilst seeking the welfare of all beings. It is not made clear whether or not this state of consciousness is the means by which Nārada has achieved liberation from rebirth, but it does make him an object of affection for all the people of the world.

1. *yudhiṣṭhira uvāca*
priyaḥ sarvasya lokasya sarva-sattvābhinanditā
guṇaiḥ sarvair upetaś ca ko nv asti bhuvi mānavaḥ

Yudhiṣṭhira said: Is there any person on earth who is dear to the whole world, who brings delight to all existence, and who possesses all good qualities?

2. *bhīṣma uvāca*
atra te vartayiṣyāmi pṛcchato bharatarṣabha
ugrasenasya saṁvādaṁ nārade keśavasya ca

Bhīṣma said: In relation to this topic, O lord of the Bharatas, I will reveal to you a conversation that took place when Ugrasena questioned Keśava about Nārada.

3. *ugrasena uvāca*
paśya saṁkalpate loko nāradasya prakīrtane
manye sa guṇa-saṁpanno brūhi tan mama pṛcchataḥ

Ugrasena said: Look how the world delights in its praise of Nārada. I think he possesses all good qualities. I want to ask you about this, so tell me about it.

4. *vāsudeva uvāca*
kukurādhipa yān manye śṛṇu tān me vivakṣataḥ
nāradasya guṇān sādhūn saṁkṣepeṇa narādhipa

Vāsudeva said: Listen, O king, O lord of the Kukuras, as I seek to concisely delineate the excellent qualities displayed by Nārada.

5. *na cāritra-nimitto 'syāhaṁkāro deha-pātanaḥ*
abhinna-śruta-cāritras tasmāt sarvatra pūjitaḥ

His good conduct does not give rise to that sense of pride which afflicts the body. There is no difference between his reputation and his good conduct; therefore he is universally revered.

6. *tapasvī nārado bāḍhaṁ vāci nāsya vyatikramaḥ*
kāmād vā yadi vā lobhāt tasmāt sarvatra pūjitaḥ

Nārada is a performer of religious austerity. He would never break a promise because of desire or greed; therefore he is universally revered.

7. *adhyātma-vidhi-tattva-jñaḥ kṣāntaḥ śakto jitendriyaḥ*
ṛjuś ca satya-vādī ca tasmāt sarvatra pūjitaḥ

He fully understands the precepts that lead to spiritual wisdom, he is patient, he is empowered, and he has control over his senses. He is honest and he always speaks the truth; therefore he is universally revered.

8. *tejasā yaśasā buddhyā nayena vinayena ca*
janmanā tapasā vṛddhas tasmāt sarvatra pūjitaḥ

He has attained his high status because of his potency, renown, intelligence, wisdom, gentility, birth, and austerity; therefore he is universally revered.

9. *sukha-śīlaḥ su-saṁbhogaḥ su-bhojyaḥ svādaraḥ śuciḥ*
su-vākyaś cāpy anīrṣyaś ca tasmāt sarvatra pūjitaḥ

He has a most agreeable disposition, he enjoys the proper objects of pleasure, he eats the proper foods, he is mindful of his behaviour, and he is pure. He speaks pleasing words and is free from envy; therefore he is universally revered.

10. *kalyāṇaṁ kurute bāḍhaṁ pāpam asmin na vidyate*
na prīyate parānarthais tasmāt sarvatra pūjitaḥ

He performs righteous deeds and it is certain that no wickedness exists in him. He never takes pleasure in the misfortunes of others; therefore he is universally revered.

11. *veda-śrutibhir ākhyānair arthān abhijigīṣate*
titikṣur anavajñaś ca tasmāt sarvatra pūjitaḥ

He pursues his goals in life by adhering to the injunctions contained in the Vedas and other scriptures. He shows forbearance and never despises anyone; therefore he is universally revered.

12. *samatvād dhi priyo nāsti nāpriyaś ca kathaṁcana*
manonukūla-vādī ca tasmāt sarvatra pūjitaḥ

Because of his equanimity, no person is dear to him, and he does not regard anyone as an enemy. His words are always pleasing to the mind; therefore he is universally revered.

13. *bahu-śrutaś citra-kathaḥ paṇḍito 'nalaso 'śaṭhaḥ*
adīno 'krodhano 'lubdhas tasmāt sarvatra pūjitaḥ

He has a vast knowledge of the Vedas, he is a wonderful speaker, and he is a learned scholar. He is never lazy or insincere, he is noble-minded, and he is free from anger and greed; therefore he is universally revered.

14. *nārthe na dharme kāme vā bhūta-pūrvo 'sya vigrahaḥ*
doṣāś cāsya samucchinās tasmāt sarvatra pūjitaḥ

Never in his life has he ever quarrelled over wealth, dharma, or pleasure. His faults have all been eradicated; therefore he is universally revered.

15. *dṛḍha-bhaktir anindyātmā śrutavān anṛśaṁsavān*
vīta-saṁmoha-doṣaś ca tasmāt sarvatra pūjitaḥ

He is firm in his devotion, his character is irreproachable, he possesses sacred knowledge, and there is no malice in his personality. He is free from delusion and free from fault; therefore he is universally revered.

16. *asaktaḥ sarva-saṅgeṣu saktātmeva ca lakṣyate*
adīrgha-saṁśayo vāgmī tasmāt sarvatra pūjitaḥ

He remains unattached to any of the objects of affection even though he appears to be attached at heart. His life is free from any lasting doubt and he is an eloquent speaker; therefore he is universally revered.

17. *samādhir nāsya mānārthe nātmānaṁ stauti karhicit*
anīrṣyur dṛḍha-saṁbhāṣas tasmāt sarvatra pūjitaḥ

His inner contemplation is never performed for reasons of conceit and he never sings his own praises. He is never envious, and he is resolute in keeping his word; therefore he is universally revered.

18. *lokasya vividhaṁ vṛttaṁ prakṛteś cāpy akutsayan*
saṁsarga-vidyā-kuśalas tasmāt sarvatra pūjitaḥ

Never condemning the various affairs of the world and the manifold forms of human nature, he remains fully conversant with the art of social interaction; therefore he is universally revered.

19. *nāsūyaty āgamaṁ kaṁcit svaṁ tapo nopajīvati*
avandhya-kālo vaśyātmā tasmāt sarvatra pūjitaḥ

He never criticises any religious doctrine, nor does he try to make a living from the austerity he performs. His time is never wasted, and he has full control over himself; therefore he is universally revered.

20. *kṛta-śramaḥ kṛta-prajño na ca tṛptaḥ samādhitaḥ*
niyama-stho 'pramattaś ca tasmāt sarvatra pūjitaḥ

He is a man of action and a man of wisdom, and he is never satiated by his practice of inner contemplation. He follows a controlled way of life and he is never negligent in his observances; therefore he is universally revered.

21. *sāpatrapaś ca yuktaś ca su-neyaḥ śreyase paraiḥ*
abhettā para-guhyānāṁ tasmāt sarvatra pūjitaḥ

He is both bashful and also fully engaged. He is an appropriate person for others to resort to in seeking their welfare for he never betrays other people's secrets; therefore he is universally revered.

22. *na hṛṣyaty artha-lābheṣu nālābheṣu vyathaty api*
sthira-buddhir asaktātmā tasmāt sarvatra pūjitaḥ

He does not rejoice when he achieves his aims, nor does he lament when he fails to achieve them. His intelligence remains firm and his mind is free of attachments; therefore he is universally revered.

23. *taṁ sarva-guṇa-saṁpannaṁ dakṣaṁ śucim akātaram*
kāla-jñaṁ ca naya-jñaṁ ca kaḥ priyaṁ na kariṣyati

He is blessed with all good qualities, he is proficient, pure, and never disturbed. He understands both the passage of time and proper conduct. Who is there who would not make him the object of their affection?

www.ingramcontent.com/pod-product-compliance
Lightning Source LLC
Chambersburg PA
CBHW060102170426
43198CB00010B/737